Nonprofit Law for Religious Organizations

Essential Questions & Answers

Nonprofit Law for Religious Organizations

Essential Questions & Answers

BRUCE R. HOPKINS and
DAVID O. MIDDLEBROOK

WILEY

John Wiley & Sons, Inc.

Library of Congress Cataloging-in-Publication Data:

Hopkins, Bruce R.

    Nonprofit law for religious organizations : essential questions & answers / Bruce R. Hopkins and David O. Middlebrook.

        p.   cm.

    Includes index.

    ISBN 978-0-470-11440-7 (pbk.)

    1. Religious institutions—Law and legislation—United States—Miscellanea.

    2. Nonprofit organizations—Law and legislation—United States—Miscellanea.

    I. Middlebrook, David. II. Title.

    KF4865.H67   2007

    346.73'064—dc22

                                      2007049355

10 9 8 7 6 5 4 3 2 1

About the Authors

BRUCE R. HOPKINS is licensed to practice law in Missouri and the District of Columbia; he is a senior partner with the firm Polsinelli Shalton Flanigan Suelthaus PC. He is also the author of more than 20 books on nonprofit tax and law issues, including *The Law of Tax-Exempt Organizations, 9th ed., Planning Guide for the Law of Tax-Exempt Organizations, Nonprofit Law Made Easy, Charitable Giving Law Made Easy, 650 Essential Nonprofit Law Questions Answered, The Law of Fundraising, 3rd ed., Private Foundations: Tax Law and Compliance, 2nd ed., The Tax Law of Charitable Giving, 3rd ed., The Law of Intermediate Sanctions,* and *The Law of Tax-Exempt Healthcare Organizations, 2nd ed.,* as well as the monthly newsletter, *Bruce R. Hopkins' Nonprofit Counsel,* all published by Wiley. Mr. Hopkins received the 2007 Outstanding Nonprofit Lawyer Award (Vanguard Lifetime Achievement Award), from the American Bar Association, Section of Business Law, Committee on Nonprofit Corporations. He is listed in *The Best Lawyers in America,* Nonprofit Organizations/Charities Law, 2007-2008.

DAVID O. MIDDLEBROOK is licensed to practice law in Texas, Colorado, and the District of Columbia, and his practice emphasis is focused on religious nonprofit organizations. He is a senior partner with the firm of Anthony & Middlebrook, PC and founder of the Church Law Group (ChurchLawGroup.com), a practice section within the firm whose clients include all types of charitable, religious, and educational organizations. Mr. Middlebrook has authored and published numerous articles on nonprofit topics. He is the author of *The Guardian System,* a risk management system for church organizations, for which he was awarded the national Gold Medallion book award in recognition of publishing excellence.

Preface

The U.S. Constitution, along with the Bill of Rights, introduced a radically new relationship between government and religion, by means of adoption of the First Amendment's religion clauses. Prior to 1789, when the First Amendment was first proposed, and 1791, when it was ratified, every European country maintained a close relationship between the church and the state. James Madison, a principal drafter of the First Amendment, believed that all religions would flourish when the government did not promote certain religious belief to the exclusion of others. He was correct.

On January 1, 1802, in a letter to the Danbury Baptist Association, Thomas Jefferson first used the phrase *building a wall of separation between church and state*. Jefferson's wall was designed not just to prevent the church from interfering with the state, but also to prevent the state from interfering with the church.

Because of the efforts of Madison, Jefferson, and others, practitioners of diverse religious beliefs have benefited from a unique and protected position in our nation's history. Unfortunately, the latter half of the 20th century brought unprecedented governmental scrutiny (some would say interference) with the exercise of religious beliefs. The beginning of the 21st century appears to hold in store more laws applicable to religious nonprofit organizations, as well as a new willingness of the federal, state, and local governments to intervene in day-to-day operations of religious nonprofit organizations.

Application of these laws to religious nonprofits organizations can definitely cause confusion and uncertainty, especially for the leaders of these organizations. The purpose of this book is to help its readers gain understanding of some common, yet complicated and often confusing, topics in the realm of religious nonprofits through an easy-to-read and user-friendly format.

Bruce Hopkins' additional comments. A book of this nature has been on my mind, and the mind of my editor at John Wiley & Sons, Susan McDermott, for years. I did not feel comfortable undertaking a project of this nature alone. While I can write about the corporate and tax laws in the nonprofit organizations context, I am not sufficiently experienced in the "law of religion" to write a book like this without help. When I met Dave Middlebrook a few years ago, I took an instant liking to him; his intellect, enthusiasm, and personality is engaging. This book is his idea, and I am grateful for the opportunity to work on this project with him. We both hope the readers of this book will be benefited by it; I wonder if there is anyone out there who will learn more from it than I have. Dave, thanks for your hard work on this book and your ongoing friendship, and for relieving me of the fret of wondering if I ever will be able to be involved in writing a book about the law of religious organizations.

David Middlebrook's additional comments. When I first began the practice of law, a highlight of each new year was attending the Nonprofit Corporations Institute sponsored by the University of Texas School of Law. The featured speaker was always Bruce R. Hopkins. Bruce's leadership and scholarship in the area of nonprofit law is without equal. It has been a remarkable road to travel from a young lawyer being taught at the "feet of Gamaliel" to coauthoring a book with the master himself. Bruce, for this opportunity and for your friendship, I am thankful.

Bruce R. Hopkins
David O. Middlebrook
2008

 NOTE: As a general matter, when the term religious *nonprofit organization* or *church* is used in this book, it refers generically to organized institutions that promote a particular faith without regard to which faith is being described or how it is promoted. The authors recognize the term *church* is not used by all faiths; however, in an attempt to make this publication easy to read, we use it in the generic sense as a place of regular religious worship, including, but not limited to, synagogues, temples, and mosques. In general, the use of the term *church* throughout this publication also includes conventions and associations of churches, interchurch organizations, local units of a church, as well as integrated auxiliaries of a church. Similarly, when this publication uses the term *religious nonprofit organization(s)*, it is referring to churches, integrated auxiliaries, and organizations that are not churches, including nondenominational ministries, interdenominational and ecumenical organizations, and other entities whose principal purpose is the study of or advancement of religion. Finally, as with the term *church,* the authors recognize that the term *minister* is not used by all faiths; however, in an attempt to make this publication easy to read, we use it to denote members of the clergy of all religions, denominations, and sects, including, but not limited to, priests, rabbis, imams, and similar members of the clergy.

From time to time, this publication will use the terms *church, religious organization,* and *minister of the gospel* more precisely to refer to those terms as defined in the Internal Revenue Code and other related authorities for purposes of the law of tax-exempt organizations. The definition of *church* for federal tax law purposes is particularly significant when discussing the special rules for church audits by the IRS.

List of Questions

PART I	**Creation of a Nonprofit Organization**	**1**
CHAPTER 1	**Nonprofit Organizations—Generally**	**3**
1.1	What is a *nonprofit organization*?	3
1.2	What is the difference between the terms *not-for-profit* and *nonprofit*?	4
1.3	What is an *unincorporated nonprofit association*?	4
1.4	How is an unincorporated association started?	5
1.5	What is the role of a lawyer who represents one or more nonprofit organizations?	5
1.6	Is a "nonprofit lawyer" necessary to form a nonprofit organization or religious nonprofit organization?	5
1.7	How should the lawyer representing a nonprofit organization be compensated?	6
1.8	How is a nonprofit organization started?	6
1.9	How does a nonprofit organization incorporate?	7
1.10	How does a nonprofit organization decide in which state to incorporate?	8
1.11	How does a nonprofit organization qualify to do business in another state(s)?	8
1.12	Who are the *incorporators*?	8
1.13	Who owns a nonprofit organization?	9
1.14	Who controls a nonprofit organization?	9
1.15	What is a *registered agent*?	9
1.16	Can the same individual be a director, officer, incorporator, and registered agent?	9
1.17	What are the types of nonprofit organizations?	10
1.18	How is the appropriate form of nonprofit organization selected?	10
1.19	Can the name of a nonprofit organization be protected?	11
1.20	What does the term *ultra vires act* mean?	12

CHAPTER 2   **Governance: Principles and Documents**   **13**

2.1   What is the meaning of the phrase *corporate governance principles?*   13

2.2   Are there any emerging governance principles of best practices?   14

2.3   How does a church govern itself if it is an unincorporated association and has no bylaws?   15

2.4   What are the legal standards for operation of nonprofit organizations?   16

2.5   What does the term *fiduciary* mean?   16

2.6   Who are the fiduciaries of a charitable organization?   17

2.7   What is the meaning of the term *reasonable?*   17

2.8   What is the law as to board management responsibilities?   17

2.9   What is the *duty of care?*   18

2.10   What is the *duty of loyalty?*   19

2.11   What is the *duty of obedience?*   19

2.12   How do these principles relate to a board member's personal liability?   19

2.13   How do these principles relate to non-governmental watchdog agencies' principles?   20

2.14   How will the federal tax law be affected by emerging corporate governance principles?   20

2.15   Can an organization owe a fiduciary duty to another organization?   21

2.16   What are the *articles of incorporation/articles of organization?*   21

2.17   What is a *constitution?*   22

2.18   What are *bylaws?*   22

2.19   What is a *statement of purpose?*   23

2.20   What is a *statement of faith?*   23

2.21   What is a *dissolution clause?*   24

2.22   What are the *organizational, operational,* and *primary purpose tests?*   24

CHAPTER 3   **Religious Nonprofit Organizations and Churches—Generally**   **27**

3.1   What is the definition of *religion?*   27

3.2   What are the *Establishment Clause* and the *Free Exercise Clause* (also known as the *Religion Clauses*)?   28

3.3   What is the difference between a nonprofit organization and a religious nonprofit organization?   28

3.4   What is a *church?*   28

3.5   How is it determined whether a religious nonprofit organization possesses the authority to undertake a particular action?   30

3.6   What is a *non-church religious organization?*   30

3.7   What is a *convention* or *association of churches?*   31

3.8   What is an *integrated auxiliary* of a church?   31

3.9   What is a *hierarchical church organization?*   32

3.10   What is a *congregational church organization?*   32

3.11   What is a *religious order?*   32

3.12   What is an *apostolic organization?*   33

3.13   What are the special rules limiting or restricting IRS authority to conduct an audit of a church?   33

CHAPTER 4 **Administration of a Congregational Church**   **35**

4.1   How are the rights of a church's membership determined?   35
4.2   Do members have voting rights?   35
4.3   Are members presumed to be voting?   36
4.4   Can members vote by proxy?   37
4.5   Is it possible to have more than one class of membership?   37
4.6   How are the qualifications for membership determined?   37
4.7   What is the legal authority of members?   38
4.8   What is the personal legal liability of a member?   39
4.9   What is the procedure for membership meetings?   39
4.10   What right does a church have to discipline or expel a member, and what cautions should be used in undertaking discipline proceedings?   40
4.11   Are courts willing to intervene in disputes between a church and its membership?   40

CHAPTER 5 **The Board of Directors**   **43**

5.1   What is the origin and importance of the board of directors of a religious nonprofit organization?   43
5.2   What is the function of the board of directors?   43
5.3   What is the difference between the terms *directors, elders, deacons,* and *trustees*?   44
5.4   What is the difference between the regular board of directors and the initial board of directors?   44
5.5   What are the rules concerning the composition of the board of directors?   45
5.6   How does a charitable organization know whether its board of directors is lawfully constructed?   45
5.7   Must the board of directors of a religious nonprofit organization be comprised of representatives of its congregation or membership?   45
5.8   Can the members of a religious nonprofit organization's board be related?   45
5.9   Can related directors also be the officers of the religious nonprofit organization?   46
5.10   In any instance, can the same individual be both a director and an officer?   46
5.11   What is the function of the officers?   46
5.12   Can the same individual hold more than one officer position?   47
5.13   What are the methods by which a board of directors of a religious nonprofit organization can vote?   47
5.14   Can members of a religious nonprofit organization's board of directors vote by proxy?   47
5.15   What materials should be included in the minutes of the meetings of the board of directors of a religious nonprofit organization?   48
5.16   What happens if the board of directors of a religious nonprofit organization makes a mistake?   48

5.17   How likely is it that a member of the board of directors of a religious nonprofit organization will be found personally liable for something done or not done while serving the organization?   49

5.18   How can a religious nonprofit organization provide some protection for its board against the likelihood of personal liability for the result of something they did or did not do while serving the organization?   50

5.19   Does a religious nonprofit organization really have to indemnify its officers and director and purchase liability insurance? Can't they just be certain their acts are always in good faith?   51

CHAPTER 6   **Conflicts of Interest**   **53**

6.1   What is *self-dealing*?   53
6.2   Is self-dealing the same as a *conflict of interest*?   53
6.3   What language should be contained in a conflict-of-interest policy?   54
6.4   Is a conflict-of-interest policy legally binding on the individuals covered by it and/or the nonprofit organization?   55
6.5   How does an individual know when a conflict of interest is present?   55
6.6   What are the obligations of a board member or officer when a conflict of interest is disclosed?   55
6.7   How should a nonprofit organization respond to a disclosure of a conflict of interest?   55
6.8   What are the penalties when a conflict-of-interest policy is breached?   56
6.9   Can a nonprofit organization receive contributions from an entity where a board member has a conflict of interest?   56
6.10   Can a nonprofit organization negotiate for discounted prices for goods or services to be purchased from a source where a board member or officer has disclosed a conflict of interest?   56

CHAPTER 7   **Expenditure of the Religious Nonprofit Organization's Funds**   **59**

7.1   What is expected in terms of program expenditures?   59
7.2   What are the rules pertaining to employee compensation?   60
7.3   What discretion does the management of a religious nonprofit organization have in the expenditure of funds? (Lessons from the *New York Settlement*)   61
7.4   Does this standard of fiduciary responsibility apply to every expense incurred by a religious nonprofit organization?   62
7.5   Can a board member borrow money from a religious nonprofit organization?   63
7.6   Can a religious nonprofit organization purchase or rent property from a board member?   64
7.7   In addition to expenses, what else should a religious nonprofit organization be concerned about?   64

CHAPTER 8   **Acquiring Tax-Exempt Status**   67

8.1	Are all nonprofit organizations tax-exempt organizations?	67
8.2	Are all tax-exempt organizations nonprofit organizations?	67
8.3	Concerning tax exemption, what taxes are involved?	67
8.4	How many categories of tax-exempt organizations are provided for in the federal income tax law?	68
8.5	What are the regulations accompanying the federal tax law concerning charitable organizations and the advancement of religion?	68
8.6	What is the *public policy doctrine* and its impact on religious nonprofit organizations, including racial discrimination, gender-based discrimination, and other forms of discrimination?	69
8.7	How does a nonprofit organization become a tax-exempt organization?	69
8.8	Is a nonprofit organization required to apply to the IRS for tax-exempt status?	70
8.9	What does *recognition of tax exemption* mean?	70
8.10	Are certain organizations required by law to seek recognition and exempt status from the IRS?	70
8.11	What are the advantages of obtaining recognition of exempt status from the IRS?	71
8.12	Are there charitable organizations that can be tax-exempt without having to file an application for recognition of tax exemption?	71
8.13	Should an organization that is not required to obtain recognition of tax-exempt status think about doing it anyway?	71
8.14	Are copies of exemption applications available to the public from the IRS?	72
8.15	What are the *distribution rules*?	72
8.16	What is the disclosure requirement with respect to applications for recognition of exemption?	74
8.17	Do the distribution requirements apply to applications for recognition of exemption?	74
8.18	What is an individual able to do if denied a copy of the exemption application or a copy of an annual return?	74
8.19	Are there any exceptions to the inspection requirement?	74
8.20	Are there any exceptions to the distribution requirement?	74
8.21	What does the term *widely available* mean?	74
8.22	What does the term *harassment campaign* mean?	75
8.23	What is the procedure for seeking recognition of tax-exempt status?	76
8.24	What is an *IRS determination letter*? What is an *IRS ruling*?	76
8.25	Where are these applications filed?	77
8.26	How long does it take the IRS to process an application for recognition of exemption?	77
8.27	Is there a process by which the applicant organization can request the IRS to expedite the processing of its application?	77
8.28	How long does an exemption ruling remain in effect?	78

8.29   Once the ruling is obtained, is it a recommended practice to
       periodically review the application to determine whether
       substantial change has occurred?   78
8.30   What happens if there is a substantial change in an organization's
       character, purposes, or methods of operation?   78
8.31   Is it necessary to report insubstantial changes to the IRS as part
       of the filing of the organization's annual information return?   78
8.32   Will the IRS issue a ruling to an organization in advance of its
       operations?   78
8.33   How much information must be provided to the IRS?   79
8.34   Is it necessary to treat the application as a business plan?   79
8.35   What happens if the IRS decides the application is incomplete?   80
8.36   What is a *substantially completed* application?   80
8.37   Is the application for recognition of exemption an important
       document for a nonprofit organization?   81
8.38   How long does it take to prepare an application for
       recognition of tax exemption?   82
8.39   Is there a charge for the processing of an application for
       recognition of exemption?   82
8.40   Can an application for recognition of exemption be referred
       to the National Office of the IRS?   82
8.41   Can the applicant organization seek the assistance of the
       National Office?   83
8.42   Can an application for recognition of exemption be withdrawn?   83
8.43   If an organization is denied recognition of exemption, may it
       later reapply?   83
8.44   What is the effective date of these rulings?   83
8.45   To what extent can the organization rely on its ruling?   84
8.46   How does an organization remain tax-exempt?   84
8.47   When might an organization's tax exemption be revoked?   84
8.48   If an organization loses its tax-exempt status, can it reacquire it? 84
8.49   Are tax-exempt organizations completely immune from taxation?   85
8.50   Why would a church file an application with the IRS for
       recognition of its tax-exempt status?   85
8.51   Isn't the filing of an application for recognition by a church akin
       to the federal government licensing churches, a clear violation
       of religious liberties protected by the Constitution?   86
8.52   In view of the massive amount of government regulation
       of nonprofit organizations, why don't nonprofit organizations
       forfeit tax-exempt status and be treated for tax purposes
       the same as for-profit organizations?   86
8.53   What are the contents of the application?   86
8.54   What is required in part I of Form 1023?   87
8.55   What is required in part II of Form 1023?   87
8.56   What is required in part III of Form 1023?   87
8.57   What is required in part IV of Form 1023?   87
8.58   What is required in part V of Form 1023?   88
8.59   What is required in part VI of Form 1023?   89
8.60   What is required in part VII of Form 1023?   89
8.61   What is required in part VIII of Form 1023?   89
8.62   What is required in part IX of Form 1023?   90

8.63	What is required in part X of Form 1023?	90
8.64	What is required in part XI of Form 1023?	91
8.65	What happens when the requested ruling as to tax-exempt status is not granted?	91
8.66	What is the *group exemption* procedure?	91
8.67	What are the advantages of the group exemption to a religious nonprofit organization?	92
8.68	What are the disadvantages of the group exemption to a religious nonprofit organization?	92
8.69	How is the group exemption initially established?	93
8.70	How is the group exemption maintained?	94
8.71	How are the annual information returns reporting requirements satisfied?	94
8.72	Can a central organization exclude subordinate organizations from its group return?	94
8.73	Do the central organization and the subordinate organizations have to have the same tax-exempt status?	95
8.74	Can the group exemption be terminated?	95

CHAPTER 9	**The IRS Annual Information Return**	**97**
9.1	What is an *annual information return?*	97
9.2	Generally, do tax-exempt organizations have to file an annual return with the IRS?	98
9.3	What organizations are not required to file an annual return?	98
9.4	Should an organization with gross receipts that are normally not more than $25,000 consider filing with the IRS anyway?	99
9.5	What constitutes *gross receipts?*	99
9.6	What does the term *normally* mean?	100
9.7	What happens once the $25,000 gross receipts test is exceeded?	100
9.8	What IRS form is this annual information return?	101
9.9	Is there any reason to file the simpler version of the annual information return when the organization is exempt from the filing requirement because of the amount of its gross receipts?	101
9.10	When is this annual information return due?	102
9.11	Are extensions of this filing due date available?	102
9.12	Where is the annual information return filed?	102
9.13	How does an organization amend its return?	102
9.14	Does the IRS provide copies of previously filed annual information returns?	103
9.15	What if the return is a final return?	103
9.16	What happens when an organization is engaging in an activity that was not previously disclosed to the IRS?	103
9.17	What happens when an organization changed its operating documents but did not previously report this to the IRS?	104
9.18	What are the penalties on organizations concerning annual information returns?	104
9.19	Are there penalties on individuals as well as organizations for non-filing and the like?	105

PART II	Ministers, Employees, and Volunteers	107
CHAPTER 10	**Clergy, Ministers, and Pastors**	**109**

10.1	How have organizational structures of churches affected the selection of the organization's ministers?	109
10.2	How has the nature of the relationship between ministers and the church affected how disputes between ministers and their church are resolved?	109
10.3	What are the implications of self-employment versus employee classification for ministers?	110
10.4	How have ministers been distinguished from other employees in the context of employment and other benefits?	110
10.5	What does it mean to be *ordained, commissioned,* or *licensed*?	110
10.6	From what other sources does a minister derive authority within the organization?	111
10.7	What retirement plans are available to ministers?	111
10.8	What exemptions are available to a minister?	112
10.9	What is the *duty of confidentiality* as it pertains to ministers?	112
10.10	How does the duty of confidentiality apply to the reporting of criminal activities other than suspected child abuse?	113
10.11	What is the duty to report suspected child abuse as it pertains to a minister?	114
10.12	Why do we have the clergy–penitent privilege?	114
10.13	What are the boundaries of the clergy–penitent privilege?	115
10.14	What qualifies as a privileged communication?	115
10.15	Can the privilege protecting confidential minister communications be waived?	116
10.16	What does it mean for a protected communication to be made to a *minister*?	116
10.17	What does it mean for a protected communication to be made to a minister in a professional capacity as a spiritual advisor?	116
10.18	To whom does the clergy–penitent privilege belong?	117
10.19	How does one assert the clergy–penitent privilege?	117
10.20	What liability can arise from a breach of the clergy–penitent privilege?	117
10.21	Are there exceptions to the clergy–penitent privilege?	118
10.22	What visitation privileges apply for ministers at penal institutions?	118
10.23	What are the common sources of a minister's legal liability to third parties?	118
10.24	What are the differences between libel and slander?	119
10.25	Is truth an absolute defense to defamation?	119
10.26	What is the potential liability of disclosing communications and records that are confidential?	119
10.27	How is child abuse defined?	120
10.28	Is there liability for failing to report child abuse or neglect?	120
10.29	Is there immunity for persons reporting or assisting in the investigation of a report of child abuse or neglect?	121

10.30 As an employer, are religious nonprofit organizations generally
       subject to the same legal requirements applicable to
       for-profit entities?   121
10.31 What does it mean to have an *at-will employment relationship*?   122
10.32 What requirements must employers follow for new hires?   122
10.33 How do religious nonprofit organizations conduct lawful
       background checks?   123
10.34 What should religious nonprofit organizations do in the event
       of receiving negative information about an applicant?   124
10.35 What are the sources of liability in the context of employment?   124
10.36 Should religious nonprofit organizations use employment
       contracts?   125
10.37 Should religious nonprofit organizations use
       written employee manuals?   125

CHAPTER 11   Employee Rights   127

11.1   What laws prohibit impermissible discrimination based upon
       race, color, national origin, sex, or religion?   127
11.2   Is a religious nonprofit organization automatically exempted
       from the laws contained in Title VII?   127
11.3   Are all religious nonprofit organizations automatically covered
       by the laws contained in Title VII?   128
11.4   What is the *religious organizations exception* to Title VII?   128
11.5   What is a *bona fide occupational qualification* and how does
       it modify antidiscrimination laws?   129
11.6   What is the prohibition against pregnancy discrimination?   129
11.7   What is the prohibition against unequal pay for men and
       women?   130
11.8   What is the prohibition against age discrimination?   130
11.9   What is *disability discrimination*?   131
11.10 What affirmative obligations do religious nonprofit
       organizations have as an employer to accommodate an
       employee's disability?   131
11.11 When does the organization's affirmative obligation to
       accommodate arise?   132
11.12 What rights are extended to employees or prospective
       employees who provide services to the military?   132
11.13 What is *sexual harassment*?   132
11.14 How can religious nonprofit organizations prevent sexual
       harassment in the workplace?   133
11.15 How should religious nonprofit organizations react if they
       suspect sexual harassment?   133
11.16 What should religious nonprofit organizations do if they are
       told sexual harassment is occurring?   134
11.17 What is *remedial action*?   134
11.18 What are the advisable steps to include when terminating
       an employee?   134
11.19 What special circumstances should alert the employer to
       the possibility of a termination being contested as wrongful?   135

11.20 Are employment decisions other than termination possibly
       adverse?   135
11.21 How should employers document their employment
       decision-making process to demonstrate the appropriateness
       of their actions?   136
11.22 What are the benefits of *alternative dispute resolution*?   136
11.23 What steps can religious nonprofit organizations take
       to require alternative dispute resolution in the event of a conflict? 136
11.24 What is *mediation*?   137
11.25 What is *arbitration*?   137
11.26 Can religious nonprofit organizations designate neutral
       third-party mediators and arbitrators that adhere to
       the value system of their entity?   138

PART III   **Operation of a Religious Nonprofit Organization**   **139**

CHAPTER 12   **General Operations**   **141**

12.1   How does a religious nonprofit organization that is required to
       file an informational return (Form 990) change its
       accounting period (tax year)?   141
12.2   What is the *state income tax exemption*?   141
12.3   What is the *state sales tax exemption* for religious nonprofit
       organizations, and do the exemptions vary from state to state?   142
12.4   What is the *state property tax exemption*, and do the
       exemptions vary from state to state?   142
12.5   What corporate records are required to be maintained?   142
12.6   What is the length of time required to retain records?   143
12.7   What are the different types of minutes and what should
       minutes contain?   144
12.8   Should the religious nonprofit organization's corporate
       minutes be reviewed by a lawyer?   145
12.9   What is a *personal board meeting book,* and why is every
       religious nonprofit board member well advised to maintain
       his or her own copy?   145
12.10 What right do members of a religious nonprofit organization
       have to inspect the religious nonprofit organization's
       corporate records?   146
12.11 What right does the public have to inspect the
       corporate records of a religious nonprofit organization?   146

CHAPTER 13   **Charitable Giving Rules**   **147**

13.1   Are all tax-exempt organizations eligible to receive
       tax-deductible contributions?   147
13.2   What are the rules for deductibility of contributions
       of money?   147
13.3   What are the rules for deductibility of contributions
       of property?   148
13.4   What is *planned giving*?   149

13.5	What are *income interests* and *remainder interests*?	149
13.6	How are these interests created?	150
13.7	What are the tax advantages for the charitable gift of a remainder interest?	150
13.8	What is a *charitable remainder trust*?	151
13.9	What is a *pooled income fund*?	151
13.10	What is a *charitable lead trust*?	152
13.11	What is a *charitable gift annuity*?	153
13.12	What about gifts of life insurance?	153
13.13	Are there other ways to make deductible gifts of remainder interests?	154
13.14	How does the federal government regulate fundraising for charitable purposes?	154
13.15	How do state governments regulate fundraising for charitable purposes?	154
13.16	Are there exceptions to these state laws?	155
13.17	Are these state laws constitutional?	155
13.18	What IRS audit practices are applied to fundraising charitable organizations?	155
13.19	How do the charitable giving rules apply?	156
13.20	What are the charitable gift *substantiation requirements*?	156
13.21	What does the phrase *goods or services* mean?	157
13.22	Do these rules apply with respect to benefits provided to donors after the gifts were made, where there was no prior notification of the benefit, such as a recognition dinner?	157
13.23	How do the substantiation rules apply to gifts made through charitable remainder trusts, charitable lead trusts, and pooled income funds?	158
13.24	What are the *quid pro quo contribution rules*?	158
13.25	What is a *good faith estimate*?	158
13.26	Are there any exceptions to the quid pro quo contribution rules?	159
13.27	How does a charitable organization value the involvement of a celebrity for purpose of the quid pro quo contribution rules?	159
13.28	What are the *appraisal requirements*?	160
13.29	What does the IRS look for with respect to new charitable organizations?	160
13.30	What reporting rules apply?	160
13.31	Do the *unrelated business income* rules apply in the fundraising setting?	161
13.32	Are there limitations on the use of the *royalty exception* in the fundraising setting?	162
13.33	Are there fundraising disclosure requirements for noncharitable organizations?	162
13.34	Are there any other federal law requirements as to fundraising?	163
13.35	What constitutes a *charitable gift*?	164
13.36	Can a family member be a designated beneficiary of a charitable gift?	164
13.37	What is the nature of an *unrestricted charitable gift*?	165
13.38	What are some examples of unrestricted charitable gifts?	165
13.39	What is the nature of a *donor-restricted charitable gift*?	165

13.40	What is the nature of *endowment fund*?	165
13.41	What is the nature of *donor-restricted use funds*?	166
13.42	How are donor-restricted use funds created?	166
13.43	What is the nature of *restricted charitable trust property*?	166
13.44	How are restricted charitable trust properties created?	167
13.45	What happens when property subject to a restricted charitable trust is transferred?	167
13.46	What is the failure of a donor restriction?	167
13.47	What is the failure of a restricted charitable trust?	168
13.48	When have courts modified restricted charitable gifts to prevent the failure of the gift and give effect to the donor's intent?	168
13.49	What duties are associated with donor-restricted charitable gifts?	168
13.50	What are the legal consequences of failing to comply with donor restrictions?	169
13.51	Are contributions by an individual directly to a foreign entity or organization not created or organized in the United States deductible?	169
13.52	Can contributions by an individual directly to a binational charitable foundation organized under the laws of both the U.S. and a foreign country qualify as a charitable contribution and be deducted for U.S. income tax purposes?	170
13.53	Can deductible contributions to a U.S. charity be channeled abroad through a foreign branch office or subsidiary?	170
13.54	Can a U.S. public charity be formed exclusively to support a foreign charity or charities?	170
13.55	What are the procedures that must be followed when U.S. charities make grants to foreign charities?	171
13.56	Are there any special restrictions that apply to corporate contributions?	172
13.57	What needs to be added to the bylaws of religious nonprofit organizations when they make grants to non-U.S. organizations?	173
13.58	How has September 11, 2001 complicated the making of grants for charitable uses abroad?	173
13.59	Do treaty exceptions override the general statutory limitations on the deductions for contributions by U.S. citizens and residents to foreign charities?	173
13.60	What are the *U.S.–Canada Tax Treaty*, the *U.S.–Mexico Tax Treaty*, and the *U.S.–Israel Tax Treaty*, and what are their effects?	174
13.61	What is the future of U.S. treaty policy?	174
CHAPTER 14	**Combinations of Entities**	**175**
14.1	What is *a subsidiary* in the nonprofit law context?	175
14.2	Why would a tax-exempt organization establish a subsidiary?	175
14.3	How does a nonprofit organization control a subsidiary?	175
14.4	What body can act as the incorporator to establish a subsidiary?	176
14.5	Is there a minimum number of board members required for a subsidiary?	177

14.6 What legal requirements should be followed in maintaining the parent–subsidiary relationship? 177

14.7 What are the powers and oversight requirements of the parent organization? 177

14.8 How is revenue from a for-profit subsidiary taxed? 178

14.9 What are the tax consequences of liquidation of a subsidiary into its parent organization? 179

14.10 What are the federal tax reporting requirements with respect to subsidiaries? 179

14.11 What are the state law reporting requirements with respect to subsidiaries? 180

14.12 Why would a tax-exempt organization establish a tax-exempt subsidiary? 180

14.13 What are some of the common uses of tax-exempt subsidiaries? 181

14.14 Is it necessary for a tax-exempt subsidiary to obtain separate recognition of tax-exempt status? 182

14.15 Should the tax-exempt status of the subsidiary be as a charitable entity or as a supporting organization? 182

14.16 What are the reporting requirements between the parent and subsidiary organization? 182

14.17 If a tax-exempt subsidiary can raise money in its own name, what disclosure requirement should it observe with respect to the parent organization? 183

14.18 What formal action is required to transfer funds between a tax-exempt parent and a tax-exempt subsidiary? 183

14.19 Can a tax-exempt subsidiary raise funds for an endowment and hold those funds separate from the parent? 183

14.20 Why would a tax-exempt organization establish a for-profit subsidiary? 184

14.21 What are some of the common uses of for-profit subsidiaries? 184

14.22 Are there limits on the use of tax-exempt assets to capitalize a for-profit subsidiary? 186

14.23 Are there any rules concerning accumulations of income and other assets in a for-profit subsidiary? 186

14.24 Can a supporting organization have a for-profit subsidiary? 187

14.25 What is the legal definition of a *partnership*? 187

14.26 What is a *general partnership*? 188

14.27 What is a *limited partnership*? 188

14.28 Why is the partnership vehicle used? 188

14.29 What is the legal definition of a *joint venture*? 189

14.30 Why is the joint venture vehicle used? 190

14.31 How are joint ventures taxed? 190

14.32 What is a *limited liability company*? 190

14.33 Can a tax-exempt organization be involved in a general partnership? 191

14.34 Can a tax-exempt organization be involved in a limited partnership? 191

14.35 Can a tax-exempt organization be involved in a limited partnership as a limited partner? 191

14.36 Can a tax-exempt organization be involved in a limited partnership as a general partner? 191

14.37	What are IRS concerns about public charities as general partners and limited partnerships?	192
14.38	Why has the controversy lasted so long?	192
14.39	What was the original IRS hard-line position?	192
14.40	What became of the per se rule of the IRS?	193
14.41	When can a tax-exempt organization be involved in a limited partnership as a general partner and still be tax exempt?	194
14.42	Are there any other aspects of this matter?	195
14.43	How do the unrelated business income rules apply in the partnership context?	196
14.44	How does an exempt organization know what income and the like to report from a partnership?	196
14.45	Can a tax-exempt organization be involved in a joint venture?	197
14.46	Why would a tax-exempt organization want to participate in a joint venture?	197
14.47	What does a tax-exempt organization in a joint venture have to do to retain its tax-exempt status?	197
14.48	How can a tax-exempt organization be involved in a joint venture against its will?	198
14.49	How do the unrelated business income rules apply in a joint venture context?	198

CHAPTER 15   Liability of Religious Organizations   199

15.1	What is *vicarious liability*?	199
15.2	Can an organization be liable for the acts of volunteers?	199
15.3	Can an organization be directly liable for the negligent hiring of an individual?	200
15.4	Does negligent hiring apply to volunteers?	201
15.5	Can an organization be liable for the negligent retention of an agent?	201
15.6	Can an organization be liable for hazardous activities?	201
15.7	Can an organization be liable based on inadequate or negligent supervision?	202
15.8	Should an organization implement a child abuse prevention policy?	202
15.9	Are *waiver of liability forms* useful?	202
15.10	What is *premises liability*?	203
15.11	Does an organization have a duty to protect against attractive nuisances to children?	204
15.12	Does an organization have a duty to inspect its premises?	204
15.13	Can an organization be held liable for injuries sustained while their premises are being used by outside groups?	205
15.14	What is the purpose of *charitable immunity statutes*?	205
15.15	What are the parameters for immunity from civil liability for the charitable organization?	205
15.16	What are the parameters for immunity from civil liability for employees?	206
15.17	What are the parameters for immunity from civil liability for volunteers?	206

CHAPTER 16   **Insurance Coverage Considerations**   **207**

16.1   Should a religious nonprofit organization consider obtaining insurance coverage?   207

16.2   What is *general liability insurance*?   207

16.3   What is *umbrella liability coverage*?   208

16.4   What is *directors and officers* and *errors and omissions liability coverage*?   208

16.5   What is *minister's professional and personal liability coverage*?   208

16.6   What is *employee and volunteer dishonesty liability coverage*?   208

16.7   What is *employment practices liability coverage*?   208

16.8   What is *educator's legal liability coverage*?   208

16.9   What is *sexual misconduct liability coverage*?   209

16.10   What is *automobile liability coverage*?   209

16.11   What is *travel accident insurance*?   209

16.12   What is *foreign travel liability*?   209

16.13   What is *property insurance*?   209

16.14   What is *builder's risk insurance*?   210

16.15   What is a *bond*?   210

16.16   What is *group medical insurance*?   210

16.17   What is *disability and long-term care coverage*?   210

16.18   What are optional provisions for the medical benefit plans?   210

16.19   What is *workers' compensation insurance*?   211

16.20   What is *life insurance*?   211

16.21   What is a *403(b) retirement savings plan*?   211

CHAPTER 17   **Real Property and the Religious Nonprofit**   **213**

17.1   What is a *reversionary clause*?   213

17.2   Where can reversionary clauses be found?   213

17.3   Can a religious nonprofit organization add reversionary clauses to property it is selling?   213

17.4   Are reversionary clauses enforceable against religious nonprofit organizations?   213

17.5   What is a *zoning law*?   214

17.6   What are *building codes*?   214

17.7   Where does a religious nonprofit organization find building codes that are applicable to it?   214

17.8   Are building codes enforceable against religious nonprofit organizations?   214

17.9   Can a religious nonprofit organization or a church be excluded from a residential area?   215

17.10   Can activities of a religious nonprofit organization or a church located within a residential district be legally regulated?   215

17.11   What is a *nuisance*?   215

17.12   Can the religious activities of a religious nonprofit organization or a church be deemed a nuisance?   215

17.13   What types of activities are defined as a nuisance?   215

17.14   What is *eminent domain*?   215

17.15   Can government legally enforce eminent domain rights against a church?   216

17.16   Can a municipality prevent a religious nonprofit organization, including a church, from making changes to its property by enforcing *landmark laws*?   216

17.17   In a hierarchical church structure, who owns the church property and the right to make decisions about it when there is a dispute as to the property?   216

17.18   In a congregational church structure, who owns the church property and the right to make decisions about it when there is a dispute as to the property?   216

17.19   Is church property public or private?   217

17.20   Does the church have the right to remove a disruptive person from a service? What if the disruptive person is a member of the church?   217

CHAPTER 18   Competition and Commerciality   219

18.1   Just what is this matter of a nonprofit/for-profit competition all about?   219

18.2   What is the problem with nonprofit/for-profit competition?   220

18.3   How common is this form of competition?   220

18.4   Has Congress responded to these complaints about unfair competition?   221

18.5   What are some of the contemporary illustrations of issues in this area of competition?   222

18.6   What is the *convenience doctrine* and what is its effect on this area of competition?   224

18.7   How does a religious nonprofit organization determine if an enterprise is an unrelated trade or business that is subject to taxation?   225

18.8   How does this matter of competition relate to commerciality?   226

18.9   What is the *commerciality doctrine*?   227

18.10   What factors are looked at in determining commerciality?   228

18.11   What is to be made of the commerciality doctrine?   229

18.12   Are there other factors that are taken into account in determining commerciality?   230

18.13   What is the future of the commerciality doctrine?   231

18.14   What should tax-exempt organizations be doing in this regard in the interim?   232

CHAPTER 19   Intellectual Property   233

19.1   What is *intellectual property*?   233

19.2   Do religious nonprofit organizations own intellectual property?   233

19.3   What is the *works-made-for-hire doctrine*?   233

19.4   If I report my taxes as a self-employed contractor for a religious nonprofit organization, can I still be considered as an "employee" for purposes of the works-made-for-hire doctrine?   234

19.5   When is a creative work made in the *scope of an employee's employment*?   234

19.6   How can a religious nonprofit organization eliminate any disagreement about whether a creative work was made as a work for hire?   234

19.7   What is a *copyright*?   234

19.8   Why would a religious nonprofit organization want to register its copyrights?   235

19.9   What is the *fair use exception* to the copyright law?   235

19.10   What is the *religious services exception* to the copyright law?   235

19.11   What is the *nonprofit performance exception* to the copyright law?   235

19.12   What damages are available if someone is found to be responsible for infringing on a copyright?   236

19.13   What is a *trademark*?   236

19.14   What is a *service mark*?   236

19.15   How does someone obtain protection of a trademark or service mark?   236

19.16   What duties do I have to protect my trademarks and service marks?   236

19.17   Is there a fair use exception to the trademark restrictions?   237

19.18   What is a *patent*?   237

19.19   What is a *trade secret*?   237

19.20   What is the *face-to-face teaching activities exception* to copyright law?   237

19.21   Can a church make and distribute recordings of worship services in which copyrighted music is performed?   237

CHAPTER 20   Lobbying and Political Activities   239

20.1   What is *lobbying*?   239

20.2   What is *legislation*?   240

20.3   Is lobbying a necessary or appropriate activity for a nonprofit organization?   240

20.4   What are the most current federal tax rules concerning lobbying that are unique to tax-exempt organizations?   240

20.5   How do charitable organizations measure substantiality?   241

20.6   Is there more than one form of lobbying?   241

20.7   What are the various ways by which lobbying can be accomplished?   241

20.8   Are there laws concerning lobbying by nonprofit organizations other than the federal tax rules?   242

20.9   What are *political activities*?   242

20.10   What are the rules, for tax-exempt organizations, concerning political activities?   242

20.11   What do *participation* and *intervention* mean?   243

20.12   Can a charitable organization educate the public about candidates and issues in the setting of a political campaign?   244

20.13   Does the law differentiate between the political positions of organizations and those of individuals associated with them?   245

20.14   When is an individual a *candidate*?   245

20.15   When does a *campaign* begin?   245

20.16   What is a *public office*?   246

20.17	Is there a substantiality test for charitable organizations concerning political activities?	246
20.18	What happens when a public charity engages in a political campaign activity?	246
20.19	Do these rules apply to churches and other religious organizations?	247
20.20	Are these rules enforced against religious organizations?	247
20.21	Is the prohibition against political campaigning by religious organizations constitutional?	248

CHAPTER 21   **Employee Compensation**   **249**

21.1	What is the definition of *compensation*?	249
21.2	How does *executive* compensation differ from *regular or non-executive* employee compensation?	249
21.3	What are the other components unique to religious nonprofit organizations that would be included in calculating executive compensation?	250
21.4	What is the income exclusion available for *ministers of the gospel* by use of a parsonage or housing allowance?	250
21.5	What is *deferred compensation*?	251
21.6	What is a *qualified retirement plan*?	251
21.7	What is a *403(b) plan*?	251
21.8	What is a *nonqualified retirement plan*?	251
21.9	What is a *Rabbi trust*?	252
21.10	What is *excessive compensation*?	252
21.11	How does the IRS measure whether compensation is excessive?	252
21.12	Who determines *reasonableness*?	254
21.13	What is the rebuttable presumption of reasonableness as it relates to compensation?	254
21.14	Can a bonus system be utilized?	255
21.15	How should a bonus compensation program for employees be defined?	255
21.16	What role should the board of directors play in the annual review and approval of bonus awards to employees?	256
21.17	How is a bonus compensation program reported to the IRS and disclosed to the public if the filing of an annual information return is required?	256
21.18	Can a portion of compensation be based on performance of the nonprofit entity or results achieved?	257
21.19	What happens if performance exceeds even the bonus goals?	257
21.20	What happens if the executive or the religious nonprofit organization underperforms as it relates to bonus goals?	257
21.21	What if board members include the executive or disqualified persons?	257
21.22	What is an *independent compensation committee*?	257
21.23	Why have an independent compensation committee?	258
21.24	What is a *compensation study*?	258
21.25	Who performs them?	258
21.26	Why use a professional?	259
21.27	How should the religious nonprofit organization go about selecting a compensation study expert?	259

21.28 Can compensation studies be performed from within
       the religious nonprofit organization, perhaps by the
       CFO or bookkeeper?   259
21.29 What data should be used for a compensation study?   260
21.30 Which employees or executives of religious nonprofit
       organizations should have a compensation study performed
       for their compensation?   260
21.31 What time period should compensation studies cover?   260
21.32 What does *past undercompensation* mean?   261
21.33 Why is the IRS so concerned about executive compensation
       in the nonprofit world and what are their "hot button" issues
       in this regard?   261
21.34 What is the IRS looking for?   261
21.35 What is *private inurement*?   262
21.36 When is a person an insider?   263
21.37 What types of tax-exempt organizations are expressly subject
       to the private inurement rule?   263
21.38 What is *private benefit*?   263
21.39 What is the difference between private inurement and
       private benefit?   263
21.40 What happens when a nonprofit organization engages
       in either practice?   264
21.41 What are the principal types of transactions that constitute
       private inurement?   264
21.42 When is *compensation* private inurement?   264
21.43 Are the seven factors mentioned above the only elements
       to take into account in determining the reasonableness
       of compensation?   266
21.44 How do the *intermediate sanctions rules* interrelate?   266
21.45 When is a *loan* private inurement?   268
21.46 When is a *rental arrangement* private inurement?   268
21.47 Are there other forms of private inurement?   269
21.48 What is the tax treatment of communal groups?   270
21.49 How is *private benefit* determined in actual practice?   270
21.50 What is *primary* private benefit?   270
21.51 What is *secondary* private benefit?   271
21.52 What is the current status of the private benefit doctrine? 271
21.53 Is it possible for a donor, when making a gift to
       a religious nonprofit organization, to realize a private
       benefit from the gift?   271
21.54 How is incidental private benefit measured?   272

CHAPTER 22   **Intermediate Sanctions**   **273**

22.1   What does the term *intermediate sanctions* mean?   273
22.2   What is the effective date of the intermediate sanctions rules? 273
22.3   When were these rules enacted?   273
22.4   What is the legislative history of this legislation?   274
22.5   Have the Treasury Department and the IRS issued
       guidance as to these rules?   274
22.6   What types of tax-exempt organizations are involved
       in these rules?   274

22.7	Are there any exceptions to these rules?	274
22.8	To what types of transactions do these rules apply?	275
22.9	How is *value* measured?	275
22.10	Can an economic benefit be treated as part of the recipient's compensation?	275
22.11	What happens if an economic benefit cannot be regarded as part of the recipient's compensation?	276
22.12	What does the phrase *directly or indirectly* mean?	276
22.13	What does the phrase *for the use of* mean?	276
22.14	Is there any other definition of the term *excess benefit transaction*?	276
22.15	Are any economic benefits disregarded for these purposes?	277
22.16	In the context of compensation, how does one determine whether it is *excessive*?	277
22.17	What are the tax law standards used in determining the reasonableness of compensation?	278
22.18	What items are included in determining the value of compensation?	279
22.19	Do these rules apply to rental transactions?	279
22.20	Do these rules apply to lending transactions?	279
22.21	Do these rules apply to sales transactions?	280
22.22	Who has the burden of proof in a dispute with the IRS as to whether a transaction involves an excess benefit?	280
22.23	What does the phrase *conflict of interest* mean?	282
22.24	What does the term *disqualified person* mean?	282
22.25	What is the scope of the *substantial influence rule*?	283
22.26	What does the term *organization manager* mean?	284
22.27	What does the term *member of the family* mean?	284
22.28	What is the definition of a *controlled entity*?	285
22.29	What are the sanctions?	285
22.30	What does the term *correction* mean?	286
22.31	What does the term *participation* mean?	286
22.32	What does the term *knowing* mean?	286
22.33	What does the term *willful* mean?	287
22.34	What does the term *reasonable cause* mean?	287
22.35	Can there be joint liability for these taxes?	288
22.36	If the executive of a religious nonprofit organization is receiving compensation that he or she believes to be unreasonable, should the executive voluntarily reduce the compensation or wait to see whether the IRS raises the issue?	288
22.37	If the IRS raises questions about an executive compensation, should the executive voluntarily reduce his or her compensation in order to minimize the risk of imposition of the sanctions?	288
22.38	If the board of directors approves an employment contract with an executive and later determines that the compensation provided in the contract is excessive, what steps, if any, should the board take prior to expiration of the contract?	289

22.39	Is there any relief from this tax? Is there any basis for being excused from these penalties?	289
22.40	How are these taxes reported and paid?	290
22.41	Can an organization reimburse a disqualified person for these taxes?	290
22.42	Can an organization purchase insurance for a disqualified person to provide coverage for these taxes?	290
22.43	Does the payment of an intermediate sanctions tax have any direct impact on a tax-exempt organization?	291
22.44	Is there a limitations period after which these taxes cannot be imposed?	291
22.45	Do intermediate sanctions take precedence over other sanctions used by the IRS?	291
22.46	Does the private inurement doctrine have an impact on definitions of excess benefit transactions?	292
22.47	Won't private foundation rules as to self-dealing have a similar impact?	292
22.48	Won't determinations as to what is an excess benefit shape the law of private inurement and self-dealing?	292

CHAPTER 23   Unrelated Business Activities   293

23.1	A religious nonprofit organization often needs more money than it can generate. Management of the organization is thinking about raising money by charging fees for certain activities, products, or services, but is concerned about taxation. Where does it begin?	293
23.2	How does an organization measure what is primary?	293
23.3	How does a religious nonprofit organization know whether an activity is a related one or an unrelated one?	294
23.4	What is the rationale underlying the *unrelated income rules*?	295
23.5	Are these claims of unfair competition leading to anything, such as law changes?	295
23.6	What is the *trade or business* requirement?	296
23.7	Does this mean that the law considers the programs of exempt organizations as businesses?	296
23.8	When the federal tax law regards an exempt organization as a composite of businesses, isn't that different from how nonprofit organizations see themselves?	297
23.9	Why would a tax-exempt organization object to the additional element of the definition concerning profit motive? Wouldn't that rule always favor exempt organizations, causing some activities to not be businesses in the first instance?	297
23.10	What are some of the other elements being grafted onto this definition?	298
23.11	What is a *commercial activity*?	298
23.12	What are these statutory and regulatory references to the commerciality doctrine?	298
23.13	What are the rules as to whether a business activity is regularly carried on?	299
23.14	How is *regularity* measured?	299

23.15	Are there any other aspects of this level of analysis?	299
23.16	What are the other two aspects of regularity?	299
23.17	Do some operations get converted into regular ones by using that approach?	300
23.18	What about the third level of analysis concerning the substantially related requirement?	300
23.19	How is *relatedness* determined?	301
23.20	What are some examples of these judgments?	301
23.21	Are there any other aspects of the substantially related test?	302
23.22	How is the unrelated business income tax calculated?	303
23.23	What types of activities are exempt from unrelated income taxation?	303
23.24	What types of income are exempt from unrelated income taxation?	304
23.25	How can the royalty exclusion be effectively utilized?	305
23.26	Are there any exceptions to the rule stating these exclusions?	306
23.27	Are there any exceptions to these exceptions?	306
23.28	What are the contemporary unrelated business issues for religious nonprofit organizations?	306
23.29	How do the unrelated business rules apply in the context of charitable fundraising?	310
23.30	How is the unrelated income tax reported?	311

CHAPTER 24   IRS Audits of Religious Nonprofit Organizations   313

24.1	Should a religious nonprofit organization be concerned about accumulating a large amount of net assets or large fund balance?	313
24.2	Are there special rules pertaining to the IRS's audits of religious nonprofit organizations?	313
24.3	How is the IRS organized from the standpoint of its audit function?	314
24.4	What is the IRS Whistleblower Office?	315
24.5	From where does the IRS derive its audit authority?	315
24.6	What issues are addressed in a religious nonexempt organizations audit?	315
24.7	Why is an IRS audit initiated?	315
24.8	How is an IRS audit initiated?	316
24.9	What items of a tax-exempt organization will the IRS review on audit?	316
24.10	Are there different types of IRS audits?	317
24.11	How does an exempt organization cope with IRS personnel during an audit?	318
24.12	What does the IRS do after the audit has been completed?	318
24.13	What is the likelihood that a tax-exempt organization will be audited by the IRS?	318
24.14	Can IRS prevent abuse by tax-exempt organizations by means other than examination and revocation of exempt status?	319
24.15	Are there special rules pertaining to the IRS's audit of a church?	319
24.16	What are the restrictions on church tax inquiries and examinations?	320

24.17	What is a *church tax inquiry*?	320
24.18	What is a *church tax examination*?	321
24.19	What is the *conference of right* and what is its purpose?	321
24.20	What *church records* may be examined by the IRS during an audit?	321
24.21	Can the IRS examine the religious content and activities of a church during its tax inquiry and/or audit?	322
24.22	What is the deadline for completing any church tax inquiry or examination?	322
24.23	What is the remedy should the IRS violate any of the church audit provisions?	323

PART IV — The Constitution, Religious Freedom, and Interaction with the Government — **325**

CHAPTER 25 — Protection of Religious Liberties — **327**

25.1	What is the source of constitutional protection of religious liberties?	327
25.2	What is the primary test(s) that all law or government action must pass so as not to violate the Establishment Clause?	327
25.3	What is the test(s) applied by the Supreme Court toward an individual's right to freely exercise religious beliefs?	328
25.4	What rights did Congress intend to confer on individuals in passing the *Religious Freedom Restoration Act* (RFRA)?	329
25.5	Our country's Constitution prohibits the government from establishing *it* and, at the same time, protects the rights of its citizenry to engage in *its* free exercise; federal, state, and local laws protect against discrimination based on *it*, while giving organizations that promote *it* preferential tax treatment. *Religion*, what is its definition?	329
25.6	To qualify as a religious organization, must the organization propagate a belief in God or the existence a Supreme Being?	330
25.7	Is the display of the Ten Commandments and other religious symbols on public property constitutional?	330
25.8	Is it constitutional for the government to place the words "In God We Trust" on its currency and on public buildings, and "Under God" in the classrooms of public schools via the pledge of allegiance?	330
25.9	Can the government display a nativity scene or Chanukah menorah during the holiday season without violating the Establishment Clause?	331
25.10	Can the government refuse to rent or prohibit the use of public facilities to religious nonprofit organizations solely because the meetings conducted by the organization promote a particular religious tenet or belief?	331
25.11	Is prayer in public schools constitutional?	331
25.12	Is prayer at public school sporting events, such as football games, constitutional?	332

25.13   Is prayer at public schools' graduation ceremonies constitutional?   332

CHAPTER 26   Guidance on Partnering with the Federal Government   333

26.1   Are religious nonprofit organizations permitted to apply for and receive funds from the government to provide charitable services to the public?   333

26.2   What kinds of grants are available from the federal government?   334

26.3   How can a religious nonprofit organization find out about federal grants?   334

26.4   How does a religious nonprofit organization go about applying for a federal grant?   335

26.5   What if a religious nonprofit organization is a small one and can't afford to hire a grant writer to help it seek a federal grant. Is there any help available for the organization?   335

26.6   What are *Charitable Choice* laws?   336

26.7   Do the Charitable Choice laws mean that religious nonprofit organizations can apply for funds only from these four federal programs?   336

26.8   Do the Charitable Choice laws mean that religious nonprofit organizations get "special treatment" by the government?   337

26.9   What if a religious nonprofit applies for a federal grant, but its request is denied?   337

26.10   What happens if the organization is successful in applying for a grant?   337

26.11   What can an organization do to ensure it correctly follows the federal and state regulations that apply to the grant?   337

26.12   Which guidance documents and regulations apply to a grant project?   338

26.13   What are some of the legal obligations that accompany a federal grant?   338

26.14   What are some of the common problems found by auditors?   339

26.15   After a grant project has ended, may an organization keep items it purchased with grant funds?   340

26.16   What are *indirect costs*?   340

26.17   What are the rules on funding religious activity with federal money?   341

26.18   How does the religious nonprofit organization separate its religious activities from the federally funded social service program?   342

26.19   Can people who receive federally funded services from the organization also participate in its religious activities?   342

26.20   What about religious activities that a religious nonprofit organization has with its staff and volunteers in the presence of those whom it is helping?   342

26.21   Can federal funds be used to purchase religious materials or materials that are faith-filled?   343

26.22   Can federal funds be used to pay the salary of a member
         of a religious nonprofit organization's staff?   343

26.23   What if the staff member working for the government-sponsored
         program works only part-time?   343

26.24   Will the way in which the religious nonprofit organization
         hires employees change if it receives federal funding?   343

26.25   If a religious nonprofit organization receives federal
         funds, can it choose not to provide services to some people?   344

26.26   What will happen if the religious nonprofit organization
         violates any of these rules?   344

26.27   Does a religious organization have to form a special nonprofit
         organization in order to receive federal funding?   344

26.28   Can a religious nonprofit organization use facility space
         on its church property to provide a federal service, and if
         so, does it have to take down any religious symbols inside?   344

26.29   If a religious nonprofit organization has a religious name
         and its chartering documents contain religious references,
         is it still eligible to receive federal funding?   345

26.30   If a religious nonprofit organization has a requirement that
         the members of its governing board be members of its faith,
         is it still eligible to receive federal funding?   345

Index   **347**

Creation of a Nonprofit Organization

CHAPTER 1

Nonprofit
Organizations—Generally

1.1 What is a *nonprofit organization*?

The term *nonprofit organization* is a misleading term; regrettably, the English language lacks a better one. It does not mean that the organization cannot earn a profit. Many nonprofit organizations are enjoying profits. An entity of any type cannot long exist without revenues that at least equal expenses.

The easiest way to define a nonprofit organization is to first define its counterpart, the *for-profit organization*. A for-profit organization exists to operate a business and to generate profits (revenue in excess of expenses) from that business for those who own the enterprise. As an example, the owners of a for-profit corporation are stockholders, who take their profits in the form of dividends. Thus, when the term *for-profit* is used, it refers to profits acquired by the owners of the business, not by the business itself. The law, therefore, differentiates between profits at the entity level and profits at the ownership level.

Both for-profit and nonprofit organizations are allowed by the law to earn profit at the entity level. But only for-profit organizations are permitted profits at the ownership level. Nonprofit organizations rarely have owners; these organizations are not permitted to pass along profits (net earnings) to those who control them.

Profits permitted to for-profit entities but not nonprofit entities are forms of private inurement. That is, *private inurement* refers to ways of transferring an organization's net earnings to persons (insiders) in their private capacity. The purpose of a for-profit organization is to engage in private inurement. By contrast, nonprofit organizations may not engage in acts of private inurement. (Economists call this fundamental standard the *nondistribution constraint*.) Nonprofit organizations are required to use their profits for their program activities. In the case of tax-exempt nonprofit organizations, these activities are termed their *exempt functions.*

> **NOTE:** The prohibition on private inurement does not mean that a nonprofit organization cannot pay compensation to its employees and others. The law requires, however, that these payments be reasonable.

Consequently, the doctrine of private inurement is the essential dividing line, in the law, between nonprofit and for-profit organizations.

1.2 What is the difference between the terms *not-for-profit* and *nonprofit*?

Although the term *not-for-profit* organization is sometimes used instead of *nonprofit* organization, as a matter of law, the terms are not synonymous. People use the two terms interchangeably in good faith, but the proper legal term is *nonprofit organization.*

The law uses the term *not-for-profit* to apply to an activity rather than to an entity. For example, the federal tax law denies business expense deductions for expenditures that are for a not-for-profit activity. Basically, this type of activity is not engaged in with a business or commercial motive; a not-for-profit activity is essentially a hobby.

The term *not-for-profit* is often applied in the nonprofit context by those who do not understand or appreciate the difference between profit at the entity level and profit at the ownership level.

1.3 What is an *unincorporated nonprofit association*?

An *unincorporated nonprofit association* is defined as an organization consisting of members joined by mutual consent for a common, nonprofit purpose. Historically, people have formed associations in order to share interests or further common goals. Small religious organizations, for example, may not feel they have the financial or human resources to obtain and maintain corporate status.

Just because an association takes a less formal approach to its formation does not mean that it should grow haphazardly. Members of unincorporated associations should be aware that without some formal planning, associations risk running afoul of the law, which is the most important shortcoming of this form of self-government. Historically, an unincorporated association was not liable for actions of its members because it was not a legal entity subject to suit. However, the trend in the law is to allow even unincorporated associations to sue and be sued. Furthermore, individual members may be liable for acts of other members under the traditional law of agency.

The Internal Revenue Code restricts tax-exempt status to corporations, community chests, funds, and foundations organized and operated exclusively for religious and other charitable purposes, but the IRS construes the term *corporations* to include unincorporated associations. Internal Revenue Code Section 7701(a)(3) defines *corporation* to include associations. As such, the exemption available to charitable nonprofit corporations and religious nonprofit corporations is available to unincorporated associations that meet the other conditions required by the federal tax law for exempt status. A church, for example, that is not incorporated is, by definition, an unincorporated association.

1.4 How is an unincorporated association started?

Being incorporated becomes particularly useful once an association starts to grow in membership and resources. Some states do not have laws that govern unincorporated associations in general, although they may have statutes concerning specific types of associations. Even if there are no state statutes dealing with unincorporated associations, some legal principles may be applicable to such groups. Every association should have a constitution (also referred to as the *charter* or the *articles of association*; what name it is called is of no legal significance). The constitution is the document containing a statement of the association's purpose and an outline of the procedures it will follow.

Some states require an unincorporated association to file its constitution with the secretary of state, the county clerk, or another state or local agency. The constitution should be tailored to the particular organization, but most constitutions contain the following:

* Organizational purpose
* Organizational structure
* Qualifications for membership
* Methods for appointing leaders
* Internal governance guidelines, such as frequency of meetings and authority for handling finances
* Tax status

1.5 What is the role of a lawyer who represents one or more nonprofit organizations?

Overall, the role of a lawyer for a nonprofit organization—sometimes termed a *nonprofit lawyer*—is no different from that of a lawyer for any other type of client. The requisite skills are to know the law, represent the client in legal matters to the fullest extent of one's capabilities and energy, and otherwise zealously perform legal services without violating the law or breaching professional ethics.

1.6 Is a "nonprofit lawyer" necessary to form a nonprofit organization or religious nonprofit organization?

No. But, use of a nonprofit lawyer is helpful. The typical lawyer today is a specialist; the nonprofit lawyer is no exception. Nonprofit law is unique and complex; the lawyer who dabbles in it does so at his or her peril. A lawyer may be the best of experts on family law or real estate law, and know nothing about nonprofit law. The reverse is, of course, also true: the nonprofit lawyer is likely to know nothing about personal injury or labor law.

The first task of a lawyer is to "know the law." That is literally impossible: No lawyer can know all of the law. The nonprofit lawyer, like any other lawyer, needs to be just as aware of what he or she does *not* know as of what is known. The nonprofit lawyer may be called in as a specialist to assist another lawyer, or, occasionally, a nonprofit lawyer may turn to a specialist in other fields that can pertain to nonprofit entities, such as construction law or bankruptcy law.

Some lawyers represent nonprofit organizations that have a significant involvement in a field that entails a considerable amount of federal and/or state regulation. These lawyers may know much about the regulatory law in a particular field, yet know little about the law pertaining to nonprofit organizations as such.

1.7 How should the lawyer representing a nonprofit organization be compensated?

There is nothing unique about the compensation arrangements for lawyers representing nonprofit organizations (other than the fact that the compensation may be comparatively lower). Most lawyers representing nonprofit organizations will determine their fee solely on an hourly rate for the time expended. In these circumstances, the client is entitled to a statement (usually monthly) that clearly reflects the time that was expended, who expended it (including paralegals), and the hourly rates. These statements usually itemize expenses to be reimbursed.

It is a good practice to provide the nonprofit organization client, at the outset of the relationship, with a letter that spells out the billing practices.

Some lawyer–client relationships in the nonprofit realm are based on a retainer fee arrangement. The client pays the lawyer a fixed fee for a stated period, irrespective of the volume of services provided. The retainer arrangement gives the nonprofit organization a budgeting advantage: It knows what its legal fee exposure will be for the period. A lawyer gains an advantage of cash flow. Both parties should monitor the arrangement on an ongoing basis—the lawyer to ward off undercompensation and the nonprofit organization to avoid overcompensation.

The fee arrangement may blend a retainer with additional hourly rate fees for specified services.

Other fee relationships include bonuses and contingencies. A nonprofit organization should always be mindful of the private inurement constraint—the rule that compensation, including legal fees, must always be reasonable.

1.8 How is a nonprofit organization started?

Nearly every nonprofit organization is a creature of state law (or District of Columbia law). Thus, a nonprofit organization is started by creating it under the law of a state.

There are only four types of nonprofit organizations: corporations, unincorporated associations, trusts, and limited liability companies. The document by which a nonprofit organization is formed is generally known as its *articles of organization*. For a corporation, the articles are commonly called *articles of incorporation* or *certificate of formation*. For an unincorporated association, the articles are in the form of a *constitution*. The articles of a trust are called a *trust agreement* or *declaration of trust*.

Most nonprofit organizations also have a set of *bylaws*—the rules by which they are operated. Some organizations have additional rules: codes of ethics, manuals of operation, employee handbooks, and the like.

A nonprofit organization formed as a corporation commences its existence by filing articles of incorporation with the appropriate state. Some states require the filing of trust documents. It is rare for a state to require the filing of a constitution or a set of bylaws as part of the process of forming the organization. (Bylaws and similar documents may have to be filed under other state laws, however.)

 NOTE: These observations pertain to the filing of the document as part of the process of creating the nonprofit organization. A nonprofit that is soliciting contributions is likely to have to file its articles of organization and bylaws in every state in which it is fundraising, as part of the solicitation registration requirements. A religious nonprofit organization, however, may be exempted from solicitation registration requirements based on constitutional, first amendment, and free exercise of religion grounds.

Following the creation (and, if necessary, the filing) of the articles of organization, the newly formed entity should have an organizational meeting of the initial board of directors. At that meeting, the directors will adopt a set of bylaws, elect the officers, pass a resolution to open a bank account, and attend to whatever other initial business there may be.

1.9 How does a nonprofit organization incorporate?

The state usually has a form set of articles of incorporation. A lawyer who knows something about nonprofit organizations can prepare this document or the incorporators can do it themselves. They need to agree on the organization's name, state the corporate purposes, list the names and addresses of the directors, name a registered agent, and include the names and addresses of the incorporators. The incorporators are the individuals who signed the articles.

This is not entirely a matter of state law. What is or is not in a set of articles of incorporation can be determinative of whether the organization is able to become tax-exempt under federal law. The two most important elements are the statement of the organization's purposes and, in the case of charitable entities, the inclusion of a clause preserving income and assets for charitable purposes.

1.10 How does a nonprofit organization decide in which state to incorporate?

Generally, a nonprofit organization is formed in the state in which it is to be headquartered. Most frequently, this is the state in which those who are forming the entity and who will be operating it are residents and/or maintain their offices. An organization can be formed in only one state at a time.

A nonprofit organization (particularly a nonprofit corporation) must be qualified to do business in every state in which it has an operational presence. In some states, for purposes of this qualification, the solicitation of gifts (irrespective of the means) is considered doing business.

Any entity that is formed in one state (the domestic state) and is doing business in another state (a foreign state) is regarded, by the latter state, as a foreign corporation.

1.11 How does a nonprofit organization qualify to do business in another state(s)?

A nonprofit organization qualifies to do business in another state by filing a *certificate of authority* to do business in the state. The process of obtaining this certificate is much like incorporating in a state. Also, the entity is required to have a *registered agent* in each state in which it is certified to do business (as well as in the domestic state).

The law of each state should be checked to see what persons qualify to be registered agents. An organization that is doing business in several states may find it more efficient to retain the services of a commercial firm licensed to function as a registered agent in all of the states.

1.12 Who are the *incorporators*?

Under the typical legal requirement around the country, anyone who is 18 years of age and a U.S. citizen can incorporate a nonprofit corporation. Each state's law should be confirmed on that point, however. The initial board members can be the incorporators. Many states require three incorporators.

Some groups are very sensitive to the matter of who is listed as an incorporator. They see the articles of incorporation as being of great historical significance to the organization—a document to be preserved and treasured for posterity. Others prefer to let the lawyers working on the case be the incorporators. No particular legal significance is attached to service as an incorporator.

Generally, directors and officers of the organization can also be incorporators. However, the law of the appropriate state should be reviewed.

1.13 Who owns a nonprofit organization?

For the most part, a nonprofit organization does not have owners who would be comparable to stockholders of a for-profit corporation or general partners in a partnership.

There are some very limited exceptions: A few states allow nonprofit corporations to be established with the authority to issue stock. This type of stock is not paid dividends, because that would contravene the prohibition on private inurement. The stock can be transferred to others, however, by sale, gift, or otherwise.

1.14 Who controls a nonprofit organization?

It depends on the nature of the organization. Usually, control of the nonprofit organization is vested in its governing body, frequently termed a *board of directors* or *board of trustees*. Actual control may lie elsewhere, with the officers or key employees, for example. It is unlikely that control of a large-membership organization would be with the membership, because that element of power is too dissipated. In a small-membership entity, control may well be with the membership.

1.15 What is a *registered agent*?

Typically, the registered agent must be either an individual who is a resident of the state or a company that is licensed by the state to be a commercial registered agent.

The registered agent functions as the corporation's point of communication to the outside world. Any formal communication for the corporation as a whole is sent to the registered agent. Thus, if the state's authorities want to communicate with the corporation, they do so by contacting its registered agent. If someone wants to sue the corporation, the agent is served with the papers.

The registered agent as such is not a director or officer of the corporation. Thus, the agent has no exposure to liability for the corporation's activities. The agent would be held liable for his or her own offenses, such as breach of contract.

1.16 Can the same individual be a director, officer, incorporator, and registered agent?

Yes, unless state law expressly forbids such a multi-role status, which is unlikely. The registered agent, if an individual, must be a resident of the state in which the entity is functioning, but the requirement of residency is not applicable to the other roles.

1.17   **What are the types of nonprofit organizations?**

Just as the corporation became the preeminent mode for conducting business in the United States, the nonprofit corporation is the most widely chosen platform from which to advance nonprofit activities. With the inherent flexibility to embrace any number of activities and the benefits and familiarity of the corporate modality, the nonprofit corporation can readily underpin such charitable entities as churches, charities, schools, and orphanages, to name but a few examples. Every endeavor should consider early on the legal form the nonprofit organization will take. This is, as noted, basically a matter of state law. (Again, this assumes that the organization is not formed by statute or ordinance.)

Tax-exempt, nonprofit organizations generally are of three types:

1. Corporation
2. Unincorporated association
3. Trust

There are other forms of tax-exempt organizations, such as a limited liability company or a professional corporation. These forms are, however, rare in the nonprofit world.

1.18   **How is the appropriate form of nonprofit organization selected?**

Several factors need to be considered in deciding which form a nonprofit organization should select, particularly if tax-exempt status is desired. Generally, the pivotal factor concerns the personal liability of the organization's trustees, directors, and officers. The corporate form has the advantage of shielding board members and officers (and perhaps key employees) from most types of personal liability. With the corporation, liability, if any, is generally confined to the corporation; that is, it does not normally extend to those who manage it, regardless of the organization's chosen purposes and activities.

Another factor is the state law that would be applicable to the entity under consideration. The law of a state usually provides answers to many of the questions that inevitably arise when forming and operating a nonprofit organization. These answers are most likely found in the state's nonprofit corporation act. The specific degree of regulation, the limitations imposed on operating the entity, and the public perception the entity desires factor into both the form and location of the entity chosen.

A third factor is privacy. In exchange for the grant of corporate status, the state usually expects certain forms of compliance by the organization, such as adherence to rules of operations, an initial filing fee, annual reports, and public disclosure requirements. There rarely are comparable filing requirements for trusts and unincorporated associations. Although articles of incorporation are public documents, trust documents and unincorporated association constitutions often are not.

In most cases, federal tax law is silent as to the form of tax-exempt organizations, expressing no preference or limitation with respect to the three types. In a few instances, however, a specific form of organization is required to qualify under federal law as a tax-exempt organization.

1.19 Can the name of a nonprofit organization be protected?

A nonprofit organization has the same set of rights available to protect its name as any other enterprise. Certain limited protection arises simply by selecting the name to incorporate under and using the name, while more extensive protection may be sought through formal applications for trademark and service mark protection.

Churches, for example, often have similar names derived from prevalent principles or themes contained in the Bible or other sacred texts. The preferred and most extensive protection for the name of a church, religious organization, or other nonprofit organization is protection under federal trademark law. A trademark is defined by the Federal Trademark Act as "any work, symbol, or device, or any combination thereof adopted and used by a manufacturer and sold by others." Trademark protection is thus available when an organization has put a symbol, mark, name, or the like, to use in commerce, such as publishing literature with the mark affixed to such literature, thereby identifying the source of the goods and services. Obviously, the same principle holds equally true for any number of nonprofit entities such as counseling centers, correspondence schools, private elementary or secondary schools, nursing homes, radio or television stations, publishers, or the like.

U.S. and state common law protects the names of existing enterprises against unauthorized use of confusingly similar names by other organizations. Most states prohibit new corporations from using names that are identical or confusingly similar to those of existing organizations registered in that state. The names of nonprofit organizations have been protected as well on the basis of one or more of the following theories: the applicable nonprofit corporation statute protecting preexisting registered names, application of the name protection provided by business corporation statutes to nonprofit corporations when the state nonprofit law does not specifically provide such protection, the common law of unfair competition, as well as trademark protection.

Some states have a statute protecting the names of religious corporations, such that a church's name will be protected against later use of the same or a confusingly similar name in either of two ways: The state official (typically the secretary of state) charged with the duty of reviewing applications for incorporation rejects the application of an organization whose name is either identical or deceptively similar to the name of an existing corporation, or if the state recognizes the corporate status of an organization whose name is either identical or confusingly similar to an existing entity's, the offended corporation may seek legal recourse to stop further use of the name.

1.20 **What does the term *ultra vires act* mean?**

Ultra vires is a Latin phrase that literally means "beyond the power." Ultra vires describes acts attempted by a corporation that are beyond the scope of powers granted by the corporation's governance documents, the laws authorizing its formation, or similar founding documents. Acts attempted by a corporation that are beyond the scope of its charter are void or voidable. Even though dicta supporting the view that ultra vires acts were totally void appeared in many cases, most courts actually adopted the view that such acts were voidable rather than void.

The concept of *ultra vires* can arise in the following kinds of activities in some states:

* Loans to officers or directors
* Charitable or political contributions
* Pensions, bonuses, stock option plans, job severance payments, and other fringe benefits
* Guaranty of indebtedness of another

CHAPTER 2

Governance: Principles and Documents

2.1 **What is the meaning of the phrase** *corporate governance principles?*

Traditionally, the law as to governance of a nonprofit organization—corporation or otherwise—has been largely confined to state rules. These principles, however, are now quickly becoming part of the federal tax law. It is apparent that much new federal law on the subject is imminent, through legislation, regulations, and IRS forms and instructions, for example.

The essence of the emerging corporate governance principles is that a charitable organization (and perhaps other types of tax-exempt entities) must be *managed* by its board of directors or board of trustees. The authors perceive a trend toward more expansive expectations on the role of directors, and with broader responsibility, more oversight may follow as an expectation or requirement. Societal sensitivity toward organizational misfeasance has unquestionably increased in recent years, and increasing accountability appears to be the policy being promoted, while greater board involvement is among the structural means to advance such policy. This is especially true in the case of tax-exempt organizations where the federal government has an established right to regulate the safeguarding of assets, in exchange for having forgone the treatment of those assets as taxable.

It is becoming unacceptable for a board of directors to meet infrequently and be merely the recipient of reports from an organization's officers and staff. The developing law is requiring the board of the nonprofit organization to become directly involved, to be knowledgeable about the organization's programs and finances, to understand the climate in which the entity operates, to avoid conflicts of interest, to place the objectives of the organization above personal desires, and to govern.

These emerging principles are also forcing structural changes in the operations of nonprofit organizations. No longer are the operative documents only articles of organization and bylaws. The law is beginning to demand organizational and management policies and procedures, conflict-of-interest policies, codes of ethics for senior officers, whistleblower policies, document retention policies, investment policies, and written program objectives and performance measures. Independent audit committees are becoming common. Lawyers, accountants, and other consultants must be hired directly by the board, not the executive staff. Compensation arrangements for top positions have to be approved at the board level. Independent auditors may have to be rotated periodically, such as every five years. Corporate executives may have to certify financial statements and perhaps annual information returns.

Federal tax or other law may contain rules on topics that previously have been the sole province of state law, such as the composition of the board, the compensation of the board, a requirement of some independent board members, and prohibition of board service by certain individuals. The IRS may be accorded the authority to require the removal of board members, officers, or employees in instances of law violations. The agency may also be given the ability to prohibit certain types of individuals from sitting on the boards of nonprofit organizations, particularly charitable ones.

2.2 Are there any emerging governance principles of best practices?

The basics as to corporate principles of best practices are beginning to yield specific direction. On February 2, 2007, the IRS released its draft of "Good Governance Practices for 501(c)(3) Organizations." This document attempts to address best practices for nonprofit organizations related to board composition, mission statement, due diligence, duty of loyalty, transparency, fundraising policy, financial audits, compensation practices, document retention policies, and codes of ethics. Although these best practices are not law, but merely suggestions, as the IRS does not have authority to directly regulate the governance of nonprofits, it is a window into the thought processes of the IRS as it pertains to nonprofit governance and, as such, warrants careful contemplation. Moreover, Congress, the IRS, or other entities may enact these or other variations of these best practices into law for nonprofit organizations.

Much of what is inventoried next is not law, yet law (federal and state) on these points seems to be in the immediate offing. Here are the concepts that appear to be emerging:

- Governing boards that are very large or very small may be problematic. (The *Goldilocks rule* applies: A governing board should not be too big, or too small, but just right.)
- The board must establish basic organizational and management policies and procedures for the nonprofit organization, and review any proposed deviations.

- The board must establish, review, and approve program objectives and performance measures.
- The board must review and approve the organization's budget and financial objectives.
- The board must review and approve significant transactions, investments, and joint ventures.
- The board must oversee the conduct of the organization's programs and evaluate whether the programs are being properly managed.
- The board must review and approve the auditing and accounting principles and practices used in preparing the organization's financial statements (and, as noted previously, must retain and replace the organization's independent auditor).
- The board must establish and oversee a compliance program to address regulatory and liability concerns.
- The board must establish procedures to address complaints and prevent retaliation against whistleblowers.
- The board may be required to adopt a policy forbidding loans by nonprofit organizations to their directors and/or officers.
- The board may be required to adopt a policy pursuant to which a nonprofit organization's lawyers are required to report breaches of fiduciary responsibility to the chief executive.

If the organization is required to file an annual information return (Form 990), many of these precepts will be reflected in this return in the form of questions as to whether the organization has prepared certain documents and developed certain policies and procedures. That is, the foregoing and/or other requirements may have to be confirmed on the organization's annual return. Penalties for breach of board members' duties may be introduced into federal law.

 NOTE: The board of directors should avoid situations where the "independent auditor" also acts as the personal accountant and tax preparer for the chief executive and/or directors such that the potential for conflicts of interest arising out of the various roles can be avoided.

2.3 How does a church govern itself if it is an unincorporated association and has no bylaws?

Although it is preferable for members of an unincorporated association to adopt bylaws pertaining to governance of the association, including election of members, election of leadership, and rules pertaining to the calling of meetings, and so forth, the members of the association are not required to do so by state law or otherwise.

2.4   What are the legal standards for operation of nonprofit organizations?

It depends on the type of organization. If the nonprofit organization is not tax-exempt, the standard is nearly the same as that for a for-profit entity. If the nonprofit organization is tax-exempt, but is not a charitable organization, the standard is higher. The legal standard is highest for any tax-exempt charitable organization. In general, the standard is easy to articulate, but often difficult to implement.

The legal standard by which all aspects of operations of the organization should be tested is that of *reasonableness* and *prudence*. Everything the organization does should be undertaken in a reasonable manner and to a reasonable end. Also, those working for or otherwise serving the charitable organization should act in a way that is prudent.

The federal tax exemption granted to charitable and other forms of tax-exempt organizations can be revoked if the organization makes expenditures or engages in some other activity that is deemed to be not reasonable. The same is likely true at the state level: Alleged or actual unreasonable behavior may cause an attorney general to investigate the organization.

The principles underlying the laws concerning charitable organizations, both federal and state, are taken from English common law, principally those elements pertaining to trusts and property. The standards formulated by English law hundreds of years ago for the administration of charitable trusts were very sound and very effective, and they underpin the laws today. The heart of the standards is the *fiduciary* relationship.

2.5   What does the term *fiduciary* mean?

A *fiduciary* is a person who has special responsibilities in connection with the administration, investment, and distribution of property, where the property belongs to someone else. This range of duties is termed *fiduciary responsibility*. For example, guardians, executors, and receivers are fiduciaries. Today, a director or officer of a charitable organization is a fiduciary. Indeed, the law can make anyone a fiduciary. As an illustration of the broad reach of this term, in a few states, professional fundraisers are deemed, by statute, fiduciaries of the charitable gifts raised during the campaigns in which they are involved. The importance of the term in this context is that it implies a duty to act with *prudence* in all matters involving income and property. Prudence in turn means no less care than one would use to administer one's own affairs, but with an objective component that would not excuse a careless person from discharging her director's duties in the same way she might her own.

The rationale for this standard is, in a word, *prudence*. A fiduciary is expected to act, with respect to the income and assets involved, in a way that is *prudent*. This standard of behavior is known as the *prudent person rule*. This rule means that fiduciaries are charged with acting with the same degree of judgment in administering the affairs of the organization as they would in their personal affairs. Originally devised to apply in the context of investments, this rule today applies to all categories of behavior, both commissions and omissions, undertaken in relation to the organization being served.

2.6 Who are the fiduciaries of a charitable organization?

The principal fiduciaries of a charitable organization are the directors. The officers are also fiduciaries. Other fiduciaries may include an employee who has responsibilities similar to those of an officer, such as a chief executive officer or a chief financial officer who is not officially a director or officer. Outsiders, such as those hired to administer charitable funds on behalf of the organization, are fiduciaries with respect to the organization. Each of these individuals has what is known as *fiduciary responsibility*.

2.7 What is the meaning of the term *reasonable*?

The word *reasonable* is much more difficult to define than *prudence*. A judge, attorney general, IRS agent, and the like will say that the word is applied on a case-by-case basis. In other words, the term describes one of those things that one "knows when one sees it," much like obscenity.

The term *reasonable* is basically synonymous with *rational*. A faculty of the mind enables individuals to distinguish truth from falsehood and good from evil by deducing inference from facts. (Other words that can be substituted for reasonable are *appropriate, proper, suitable, equitable,* and *moderate.*) Whichever term is used, an individual in this setting is expected to use this faculty, and act in an appropriate and rational manner.

2.8 What is the law as to board management responsibilities?

One of the bedrock principles in the law is that trustees of charitable trusts are deemed to have the same obligation (duty of care) toward the assets of the trust as they do their personal resources. Their responsibility is to act *prudently* in their handling of the nonprofit organization's income and assets. The trustees are *fiduciaries;* the law (for now, largely state law) imposes on them standards of conduct and management that together comprise principles of *fiduciary responsibility*. Most state law, whether statutory or court opinions, imposes the standards of fiduciary responsibility on directors of nonprofit organizations, whether or not the organizations are trusts and whether or not they are charitable.

The contemporaneous general standard is that a member of the board of a nonprofit organization is required to perform his or her duties in good faith, with the care an ordinary prudent person in a like position would exercise under similar circumstances, and in a manner the director reasonably believes to be in the best interests of the mission, goals, and purposes of the organization.

Thus, one of the main responsibilities of nonprofit board members is to maintain financial accountability and effective oversight of the organizations they serve. Fiduciary duty requires board members to remain objective, unselfish, responsible, honest, and trustworthy in relation to the organization. Board members are stewards of the entity, and are expected to act for the good of the organization rather than for their personal aggrandizement. They need to exercise reasonable care in all decision making, without placing the nonprofit organization at unnecessary risk.

NOTE: The duties of board members of nonprofit organizations can be encapsulated into *three D's:* duty of care, duty of loyalty, and duty of obedience. These are the legal standards against which all actions taken by directors are tested. They are collective duties adhering to the entire board and require the active participation of all board members. Accountability can be demonstrated by a showing of the effective discharge of these duties.

2.9 What is the *duty of care*?

The *duty of care* requires that directors of a nonprofit organization be reasonably informed about the organization's activities, participate in the making of decisions, and do so in good faith and with the care of an ordinarily prudent person in similar circumstances. Obviously, such a definition subjects a director to the notions of what an ordinarily prudent person is, in the minds of a member, judge, jury, or regulatory authority, and thus prudence suggests a director be familiar with the historical and regional practices of directors, in his or her context, and in his or her geographical proximity. This duty, therefore, requires the individual board members to pay attention to the entity's activities and operations.

The duty of care is carried out by the following acts:

- Attendance at meetings of the board and committees on which the board member is serving
- Preparation for board meetings, such as by reviewing the agenda and reports
- Obtaining information, before voting, to make appropriate decisions
- Use of independent judgment
- Periodic examination of the credentials and performance of those who serve the organization
- Frequent review of the organization's finances and financial policies
- Oversight of compliance with important filing requirements, such as federal annual information returns

2.10   What is the *duty of loyalty*?

The *duty of loyalty* requires board members to exercise their power in the interest of the organization and not in their own interest or the interest of another entity, particularly one in which they have a formal relationship. When acting on behalf of the organization, board members must place the interests of the entity before their personal and professional interest.

The duty of loyalty is carried out by these acts:

* Disclosure of any conflicts of interest
* Adherence to the organization's conflict-of-interest policy
* Avoidance of the use of corporate opportunities for the individual's personal gain or benefit
* Nondisclosure of confidential information about the organization

NOTE: Although conflicts of interest are not inherently illegal—in fact, they can be quite lawful—and because board members are often affiliated with different entities, how the board reviews and evaluates them is important. Conflict-of-interest policies can help protect the organization and board members by establishing a process for disclosure and voting when situations arise in which board members may actually or potentially derive personal or professional benefit from the organization's activities.

2.11   What is the *duty of obedience*?

The *duty of obedience* requires that directors of a nonprofit organization comply with applicable federal, state, and local laws, adhere to the entity's articles of organization and bylaws, and remain guardians of the organization's mission.

The duty of obedience is carried out by the following acts:

* Examination and understanding of all documents governing the organization and its operation, such as the bylaws
* Making decisions that fall within the scope of the organization's mission and governing documents
* Compliance with all regulatory and reporting requirements, such as overseeing filing of federal annual information returns and payment of employment taxes

2.12   How do these principles relate to a board member's personal liability?

Generally, if a director carries out his or her duties faithfully and in adherence to the three above duties (the duty of care, loyalty, and obedience), the director will not be found personally liable for a commission or omission. Personal liability can result, however, when a trustee or director—and an officer or key employee—of a nonprofit organization breaches standards of fiduciary responsibility.

2.13 How do these principles relate to non-governmental watchdog agencies' principles?

From a compliance perspective, nonprofit organizations are principally concerned with operating in conformity with the law or rules of the accounting profession. There is, however, another consideration with which some organizations must also cope: the role and influence of the *watchdog agencies* that monitor and publicize endeavors of nonprofit entities, principally those that solicit contributions from the public. These agencies have and enforce rules that sometimes are inconsistent with or attempt to supersede legal requirements. For example, those standards may include requirements about board compensation and frequency of board meetings.

A charity watchdog agency basically has three functions:

* It writes standards to which charitable organizations are expected to adhere.
* It enforces the standards, in part by rating organizations in relation to the standards and by making the ratings public.
* It prepares and publicly circulates reports about charitable organizations.

2.14 How will the federal tax law be affected by emerging corporate governance principles?

In addition to the IRS's recent release of its draft of good governance practices for 501(c)(3) organizations, it appears that the corporate governance movement will be reflected in the federal tax law; it is unclear as to how this will be manifested. The application for recognition of exemption filed by organizations that wish classification as charitable organizations (Form 1023) is replete with questions that attempt to push (using the technique of shaming) applicant organizations into compliance with a variety of corporate governance principles. Moreover, the annual information return (Form 990) is being revised to include many questions that relate to these principles.

Congress provided somewhat of a signal as to where it may be headed in this regard when it updated the charter of the American National Red Cross (by enactment of the American National Red Cross Governance Modernization Act of 2007). In this legislation, Congress authored the following responsibilities of a "governance and strategic oversight" board:

* Review and approve the organization's mission statement.
* Approve and oversee the organization's strategic plan and maintain strategic oversight of operational matters.
* Select, evaluate, and determine the level of compensation of the organization's chief executive officer.
* Evaluate the performance and establish the compensation of the senior leadership team and provide for management succession.

* Oversee the financial reporting and audit process, internal controls, and compliance with the law.
* Hold management accountable for performance.
* Provide oversight of the financial stability of the organization.
* Ensure the inclusiveness and diversity of the organization.
* Provide oversight of the protection of the brand of the organization.
* Assist with fundraising on behalf of the organization.

2.15 Can an organization owe a fiduciary duty to another organization?

Yes, in limited circumstances. There can be a formal fiduciary relationship, such as a financial institution serving as a trustee of an entity, an organization serving as the general partner in a limited partnership, an arrangement between a principal and agent, and entities in a joint venture. An informal fiduciary relationship can arise from a moral or personal relationship of trust and confidence; this relationship can be established by a long relationship of working together for a mutual goal, such as a joint acquisition and development of property. Informal fiduciary relationships are, however, infrequently recognized, because a fiduciary duty is an extraordinary one and is not lightly created.

2.16 What are the *articles of incorporation/articles of organization*?

Generically, the document by which a tax-exempt organization is created is known, in the parlance of the federal tax law, as *articles of organization*. There usually is a separate document containing rules by which the organization conducts its affairs; this document is most often termed *bylaws*. The organization may develop other documents governing its operations, such as an employee handbook, a conflict-of- interest policy (although that may be part of the bylaws), code of ethics, code of conduct, an investment policy, a document retention policy, a whistleblower policy, and/or various other policies and procedures.

There are several types of articles of organization for each of the principal types of tax-exempt, nonprofit organizations:

* Corporation: articles of incorporation (or certificate of formation)
* Unincorporated association: constitution
* Trust: declaration of trust or trust agreement

The contents of a set of articles of organization should include the following:

* The name of the organization
* A statement of its purpose
* The name(s) and address(es) of its initial directors or trustees
* The name and address of the registered agent (if a corporation)
* The name(s) and address(es) of its incorporator(s) (if a corporation)

* A statement as to whether the entity has members
* A statement as to whether the entity can issue stock (if a corporation)
* Provisions reflecting any other state law requirements
* A dissolution clause

The *articles of incorporation* is in fact a single document, filed with the state in which incorporation is sought, that formally begins an entity's existence as a corporation and sets forth such matters as would be included in *articles of organization*, including but not limited to the organization's name, corporate purposes, the identity of its directors, the identity of its registered agent, and the identity of its incorporators.

2.17 **What is a *constitution*?**

An unincorporated association, like a corporation or trust, also has articles of organization, which are referred to as a *constitution* in the context of an unincorporated association. The form and contents of such a document are not prescribed by law and are rarely filed with the state, and often an informal organization may set forth its basic guiding principles and manner of operation in a constitution before the decision to incorporate has been made. Thus, the same entity at different times may have and refer to both documents. The constitution will likely be the only document that memorializes the consent to promote a common objective shared by the group of persons comprising the unincorporated association.

2.18 **What are *bylaws*?**

Bylaws contain the rules of internal governance an entity has chosen to adopt, or in some cases, is required to follow by statute. It is contemplated by state law governing corporations in most states that bylaws will be adopted, though unlike articles of incorporation, bylaws are rarely filed with the state. The bylaws of a nonprofit organization will usually include provisions with respect to the following:

* The organization's purposes
* The origins (e.g., election) and duties of its directors
* The origins and duties of its officers
* The role of its members (if any)
* Meetings of members and directors, including dates, notice, quorum, and voting
* The role of executive and other committees
* The role of its chapters (if any)
* The organization's fiscal year
* A conflict-of-interest policy (if not separately stated)
* Reference to (any) affiliated entities
* Restatement of the federal tax law requirements

2.19 **What is a *statement of purpose*?**

One of the fundamental first steps a nonprofit organization must necessarily take is recitation of its purposes. This is not just dictated by the law; an organization simply, as a practical matter, must state its purpose or purposes for existence in writing. An organization's purposes are different from the organization's activities. Activities are undertaken to effectuate purposes (mission).

An organization's statement of purpose must first be written to comport with the applicable state's nonprofit law. This usually is not too difficult to achieve, as long as the statement does not empower the organization to engage in substantial commercial activities.

Second, the statement of purpose needs to be prepared properly to enable the organization to qualify for tax-exempt status (assuming that classification is available and desired). This statement must be in the organization's *articles of organization,* which is, as noted, the document creating the entity. The contents of this aspect of the statement are dependent on the type of tax-exempt organization the nonprofit entity intends to be.

The types of tax-exempt organizations are, generally, the following:

* Charitable (religious, educational, or scientific) organization
* Social welfare (e.g., advocacy) organization
* Labor organization
* Business league (association)
* Social club
* Employee benefit fund
* Fraternal society
* Political society
* Political organization

The wording of the statement of purpose, even independent of the actual purposes pursued, is reviewed and becomes important when tax exemption is sought. The organization's statement of purpose needs to be written so as to bring the entity into conformity with the appropriate category of exempt organization; thus, it should expressly make reference to the specific Internal Revenue Code section that is or will be the basis for the exemption where the statement of purpose is confined to those purposes that are inherently exempt. Otherwise, the statement of purpose must state that the organization will not engage in any activities outside the scope of the selected category of exemption.

2.20 **What is a *statement of faith*?**

Religious nonprofit organizations, in order to be eligible to receive tax-deductible contributions, must qualify for exemption from federal taxation under IRC § 501(c)(3). One of the requirements (covered in greater detail throughout this publication) is that the religious nonprofit organization must be organized and operated exclusively for religious, educational, or other charitable purposes. The *statement of faith* is usually contained within the initial provisions of the bylaws, and summarizes key beliefs of the organization in the areas of religious doctrine and creed and their authority, the religious purpose of the organization, its ordinances, religious education philosophy, interaction with society, religious liberty, and the like.

2.21 What is a *dissolution clause*?

A *dissolution clause* is a provision in the organizing document that dictates where the organization's net income and assets (if any) will be distributed should the organization liquidate or otherwise dissolve. The "organizational test" for charitable organizations (discussed below), in addition to requiring a suitable statement of purposes, mandates a *dissolution clause.*

Permissible recipients are one or more other charitable organizations or governmental agencies. Apart from charitable organizations, no other type of tax-exempt organization is required by federal law to have a particular dissolution clause in its articles of organization.

2.22 What are the *organizational, operational,* and *primary purpose tests*?

Organizational test: The *organizational test* is among the criteria imposed by the IRS in the process of tax exemption determination. Pursuant to the federal tax regulations, an organization must meet three requirements. First, its articles of organization must (a) limit its purposes to one or more exempt purposes and (b) not expressly permit substantial activities that do not further those exempt purposes. Second, the articles must not permit (a) devoting more than an insubstantial part of its activities to lobbying, (b) any participation or intervention in the campaign of a candidate for public office, and (c) objectives and activities that would characterize it as an "action" organization. Third, the organization's assets must be dedicated to exempt purposes. The IRS determines compliance with the organizational test solely by reference to an organization's articles of organization.

Organizations usually should expressly make reference to the specific Internal Revenue Code section that is the basis for the exemption where the statement of purpose is confined to those purposes that are inherently exempt. Otherwise, the statement of purpose must state that the organization will not engage in any activities outside the scope of the selected category of exemption.

Operational test: Tax-exempt, charitable organizations must also comply with an *operational test.* This concerns whether the organization is in fact operated for exempt purposes. Generally, defects in an entity's articles of organization cannot be cured by complete adherence to the operational test. To satisfy the operational test, an organization must be operated "exclusively" for an exempt purpose;

however, "exclusively" in this context does not mean "solely." Nevertheless, the presence of a substantial nonexempt purpose will cause an organization to fail the operational test. The presence of a single nonexempt purpose, if substantial in nature, will destroy the exemption regardless of the number or importance of qualifying exempt purposes.

Primary purpose test: There are a number of categories of tax exemption and the primary purpose rule is designed to determine which, if any, of the types applies to an organization. The organization's statement of purpose needs to be written so as to bring the entity into conformity with the appropriate category of exempt organization. The purposes of an organization may partake of more than one of these categories. Tax-exempt status will be dependent on which of the types of purposes is primary—this is the primary purpose rule.

CHAPTER 3

Religious Nonprofit Organizations and Churches—Generally

3.1   What is the definition of *religion*?

It is difficult to define what *religion* is, and what it is not. The federal income tax law provides for tax exemption for religious organizations, yet there is no statutory or regulatory definition of the terms *religious* or *religion* for this purpose. Indeed, by reason of the religion clauses of the First Amendment, it would be unconstitutional for the federal government to adopt and apply a strict definition of these terms.

This definitional challenge is not limited to the courts, Congress, and the IRS; academia wrestles with defining religion as well. The *Encyclopedia of Religion* defines *religion* this way:

> In summary, it may be said that almost every known culture involves the religious in the above sense of a depth dimension in cultural experiences at all levels—a push, whether ill-defined or conscious, toward some sort of ultimacy and transcendence that will provide norms and power for the rest of life. When more or less distinct patterns of behaviour are built around this depth dimension in a culture, this structure constitutes religion in its historically recognizable form. Religion is the organization of life around the depth dimensions of experience—varied in form, completeness, and clarity in accordance with the environing culture. [*Religion* (First Edition). Winston King. *Encyclopedia of Religion*, ed. Lindsay Jones, vol. 11, 2nd ed. Detroit: Macmillan Reference USA, 2005, pp. 7692–7701.]

The Supreme Court interprets the term *religion* broadly, and does not include as a requirement the belief in the existence of God or a Supreme Being and that "religions" need not be based on a belief in the existence of God. In 1961, the Court stated that "neither [the federal nor state government] can constitutionally pass laws or impose requirements which aid all religions as against nonbelievers, and neither can aid those religions based on a belief in the existence of God as against those religions founded on different beliefs." The Court noted that "among religions in this country which do not teach what would generally be considered as a belief in the existence of God are Buddhism, Taoism, Ethical Culture, Secular Humanism and others."

3.2 What are the *Establishment Clause* and the *Free Exercise Clause* (also known as the *Religion Clauses*)?

The *Free Exercise Clause* of the U.S. Constitution, taken with the *Establishment Clause of the First Amendment*, makes up the Religion Clauses.

The Religion Clauses read in full:

Congress shall make no law respecting an establishment of religion, or prohibiting the free exercise thereof.

The Free Exercise Clause has often been interpreted to include two freedoms: the freedom to believe and the freedom to act. The former liberty is absolute, while the latter often faces state restriction. In 1879, the Supreme Court was first called to interpret this clause and stated: "Laws are made for the government of actions, and while they cannot interfere with mere religious beliefs and opinions, they may with practices."

3.3 What is the difference between a nonprofit organization and a religious nonprofit organization?

Congress has enacted special tax laws applicable to churches and religious organizations in recognition of their unique status in American society and of their rights guaranteed by the First Amendment of the Constitution. Churches and religious organizations are generally exempt from income tax and receive other favorable treatment under the tax law; however, certain income of a church or religious organization may be subject to tax, such as income from an unrelated business. Religious nonprofit organizations are churches, conventions, and associations of churches, integrated auxiliaries of churches, and religious organizations that are not churches, including nondenominational ministries, interdenominational and ecumenical organizations, and other entities whose principal purpose is the study or advancement of religion.

3.4 What is a *church*?

A bona fide church (including institutions such as synagogues, temples, and mosques) is, of course, a religious entity. Yet, just as in the case with respect to the term *religious*, there is no definition in the Internal Revenue Code or any currently applicable tax regulation of the term *church*. In a vague and somewhat redundant definition, Section 7611 of the Internal Revenue Code provides that the term "church" includes any organization claiming to be a church and any convention or association of churches. Again, a rigid regulatory definition would undoubtedly be found unconstitutional.

The IRS has formulated the criteria that it uses to ascertain whether an organization qualifies as a church. The IRS position is that, to be a church for tax purposes, an organization must satisfy at least some of the following criteria.

The characteristics of a church, often referred to as the "Fourteen Factors Test," include:

* Distinct legal existence
* Recognized creed and form of worship
* Definite and distinct ecclesiastical government
* Formal code of doctrine and discipline
* Distinct religious history
* Membership not associated with any other church or denomination
* Organization of ordained ministers
* Ordained ministers selected after completing prescribed courses of study
* Literature of its own
* Established places of worship
* Regular congregations
* Regular religious services
* Sunday schools for the religious instruction of the young
* Schools for the preparation of its ministers

The Commissioner of Internal Revenue, Jerome Kurtz, first made these criteria public in 1977. He observed that "few, if any, religious organizations—conventional or unconventional—could satisfy all these criteria" and that the IRS does "not give controlling weight to any single factor." Further, the Commissioner asserted that "[t]his is obviously the place in the decisional process requiring the most sensitive and discriminating judgment." He concluded by noting that the IRS has "been criticized for the scope and breadth of the criteria we use and it has been implied that the Service has been trying in recent years to discourage new religions and new churches"; he offered the assurance "that this is not the case with the IRS."

The courts and the IRS use a combination of these fourteen criteria, together with other facts and circumstances, to determine whether an organization is considered a church for federal tax purposes. In making this decision, there should be no attempt on the part of the IRS (or the courts) to evaluate the content of whatever doctrine the organization claims is religious, provided the particular beliefs of the organization are truly and sincerely held by those professing them and the practice and rites associated with the organization's belief or creed are not illegal or contrary to clearly defined public policy.

The IRS, in recent private letter rulings, is taking a hard line in application of these criteria. An organization can meet several of these criteria, only to have the IRS dismiss that fact on the ground that they are not "distinctive characteristics" of a church but are "common to both churches and non-church religious organizations." The IRS is demanding that, to be a church, an organization must have a "regular congregation," engage in "regular worship services," and have an "established place of worship." Also, the IRS has added a fifteenth criterion, which is that the organization must "hold itself out" as a church, such as being listed as a church in telephone book yellow pages.

Thus, just as the law cannot formulate a tax definition of the term *religion*, it seems unable to formulate a formal definition of the term *church*. This is not surprising, in that the religion clauses preclude the strict application of definitions of this nature.

3.5   How is it determined whether a religious nonprofit organization possesses the authority to undertake a particular action?

To determine the extent of a religious nonprofit corporation's powers:

- Review the governance documents articles of incorporation (constitution) and bylaws.
- Review the minutes of the religious nonprofit organization.
- Review the state statute by which the religious nonprofit organization was incorporated.
- If the powers are not expressly enumerated therein, determine if the powers are implied as necessary for the fulfillment of the religious nonprofit organization's exempt purpose.
- If the religious nonprofit organization is a part of a denomination or other religious hierarchy, determine if its power is restricted by a higher religious or ecclesiastical authority.

 NOTE: Actions that violate the law or public policy are never authorized.

3.6   What is a *non-church religious organization*?

Although all churches are religious organizations, not all religious organizations are churches. An organization performing one or several facets (but not a preponderance) of traditional church activities is generally classified as a *non-church religious organization* or ministry. A non-church religious organization is an organization carrying out particular religious functions (e.g., irregularly scheduled religious meetings, "crusade events," religious literature distribution, and missions activities).

Organizations engaged in the advancement of religion will qualify for tax exempt status if they comply with certain requirements. The advancement of religion can be promoted, for example, by any of the following:

* A church
* A non-church religious organization (or ministry)
* A religious order
* A church auxiliary
* A mission
* Missionary activities
* Evangelism
* Religious publishing activities
* A religious bookstore

3.7 What is a *convention* or *association of churches*?

The IRS recognizes that the phrase *convention or association of churches* has a historical meaning generally referring to a cooperative undertaking by churches of the same denomination. The IRS ruled that the term also applies to cooperative undertakings by churches of different denominations, assuming that the convention or association otherwise qualifies as a religious organization. The IRS distinguishes somewhat the definitions of associations or conventions of churches by stating that an association of churches is more likely a statewide or regional organization and a convention is national in scope.

3.8 What is an *integrated auxiliary* of a church?

The term *integrated auxiliary of a church* refers to a class of organizations that are related to a church or convention or association of churches, but are not such organizations themselves. In general, the IRS will treat an organization that meets the following three requirements as an integrated auxiliary of a church.
The organization must:

1. Be described both as an IRC § 501(c)(3) charitable organization and as a public charity under IRC § 509(a)(1), (2), or (3).
2. Be affiliated with a church or convention or association of churches.
3. Receive financial support primarily from internal church sources as opposed to public or governmental sources.

An organization is internally supported, for these purposes, unless it both offers admissions, goods, services, or facilities for sale, other than on an incidental basis, to the public and normally receives more than 50 percent of its support from a combination of government sources, public solicitation of contributions, and receipts from the sale of admissions, goods, performance of services, or furnishing of facilities in activities that are not in related trade or business.

Men's and women's organizations, seminaries, mission societies, and youth groups that satisfy the first two requirements above are considered integrated auxiliaries whether or not they meet the internal support requirements.

The same rules that apply to a church apply to the integrated auxiliary of a church, with the exception of those rules that apply to the audit of a church.

3.9 What is a *hierarchical church organization*?

A *hierarchical church organization* is, generally, a church organization structured, by way of its organizational documents, in such a way that every entity in the organization, except one, is *subordinate* to a single other entity. This is sometimes referred to as a pyramidal power structure; those nearest the top have more power than those nearest the bottom, and there are fewer people at the top than at the bottom. This is the dominant mode of organization among the largest organized Christian denominations such as the Roman Catholic and Eastern Orthodox. In these organizations, the *Pope* or *Patriarch* is the highest visible part of the hierarchy, with God as the top of the hierarchy.

3.10 What is a *congregational church organization*?

A *congregational church organization* is, generally, a church organization structured by way of its organizational documents in such a manner that each entity is independent and autonomous from any other entity or organization, and retains full autonomy to manage its own affairs. This is sometimes referred to as a *horizontal power structure*; each member of the church congregation, in accordance with its governance documents, has a voice in the government of the church.

3.11 What is a *religious order*?

Another type of religious organization is the *religious order*, a term that is not defined in the Internal Revenue Code or the tax regulations. The IRS promulgated guidelines for determining whether an organization qualifies as a religious order, utilizing a variety of characteristics drawn from the case law.

These characteristics are as follows:

* The organization is a charitable one.
* The members of the organization have vowed to live under a strict set of rules requiring moral and spiritual self-sacrifice and dedication to the goals of the organization at the expense of their material well-being.
* The members of the organization, after successful completion of the organization's training program and probationary period, make a long-term commitment to the organization (normally more than two years).

- The organization is, directly or indirectly, under the control and supervision of a church or convention or association of churches, or is significantly funded by a church or convention or association of churches.
- The members of the organization normally live together as part of a community and are held to a significantly stricter level of moral and religious discipline than that required by lay church members.
- The members of the organization work or serve full time on behalf of the religious, educational, or charitable goals of the organization.
- The members of the organization participate regularly in activities such as public or private prayer, religious study, teaching, care of the aging, missionary work, or church reform or renewal.

In determining whether an organization is a religious order, all of the facts and circumstances must be considered. Generally, the presence of all of these characteristics is determinative that the organization is a religious order; however, the absence of the first of these characteristics, whether or not the organization is a charitable one, is determinative that the organization is not a religious order.

3.12 What is an *apostolic organization*?

Certain *religious or apostolic organizations* are exempt from federal income taxation, even though they are not embraced by the general reference to religious organizations. According to IRC § 501(d), these are "religious or apostolic associations or corporations, if such associations or corporations have a common treasury or community treasury, even if such associations or corporations engage in business for the common benefit of the members, but only if the members thereof include (at the time of filing their returns) in their gross income their entire pro rata shares, whether distributed or not, of the taxable income of the association or corporation for such year."

Organizations contemplated by these rules are those that are supported by internally operated businesses in which all the members have an individual interest. It is the position of the IRS (general counsel) that failure to qualify as an apostolic organization under these rules does not preclude the possibility that an organization may qualify as a communal religious organization. In other words, the IRS does not believe that Congress occupied the field with respect to tax exemption of all communal religious organizations in enacting these rules for apostolic organizations.

3.13 What are the special rules limiting or restricting IRS authority to conduct an audit of a church?

Congress has limposed special limitations, found in the Church Tax Inquiries and Examinations Rules of IRC § 7611 on how and when the IRS may conduct civil tax inquiries and examinations of churches. The IRS may only initiate a church tax inquiry if the Director, Exempt Organizations, Examinations, reasonably believes, based on a written statement of the facts and circumstances, that the organization:

* May not qualify for the exemption, or
* May not be paying tax on an unrelated business or other taxable activity.

Restrictions on church inquiries and examinations apply only to churches (including organizations claiming to be churches if such status has not been recognized by the IRS) and conventions or associations of churches. They do not apply to related persons or organizations. Thus, for example, the rules do not apply to schools that, although operated by a church, are organized as separate legal entities. Similarly, the rules do not apply to an integrated auxiliary of a church.

Restrictions on church inquiries and examinations do not apply to all church inquiries by the IRS. The most common exception relates to routine requests for information. For example, IRS requests for information from churches about filing of returns, compliance with income, or Social Security and Medicare tax withholding requirements, supplemental information needed to process returns or applications, and other similar inquiries are not covered by IRC § 7611 audit rules.

Restrictions on church inquiries and examinations do not apply to criminal investigations or to investigations of the tax liability of any person connected with the church (e.g., a church contributor or minister).

The procedures of IRC § 7611 are used in initiating and conducting any inquiry or examination into whether an excess benefit transaction has occurred between a church and an insider.

CHAPTER 4

Administration of a Congregational Church

4.1 How are the rights of a church's membership determined?

The essence of the legal relationship between members of an organization, such as a church or religious nonprofit organization, consists of an understanding or agreement between the parties. In the case of a church, this might be through a profession of faith, adherence to the doctrines of the church, and submission to its government. The qualifications for membership to a church are typically determined and defined legally in its articles of incorporation and bylaws, and according to any applicable state corporation law.

 NOTE: A church may be organized in such a way that the corporate documents state that there are no "members" as such. The existence of a membership is, however, one of the fourteen factors the IRS considers in determining whether an organization is a church for tax purposes. A church might consider having two classes of membership—voting and non-voting. Voting members might be those members who serve on the board of directors. Non-voting members would be members of the congregation at large.

4.2 Do members have voting rights?

It is optional for a nonprofit corporation, such as a church or religious nonprofit organization, to have or not to have members with voting rights. The existence of a membership is, however, one of the fourteen factors the IRS considers in determining whether an organization is a church for tax purposes. If a church establishes a voting membership structure in its articles of incorporation, then voting members of the corporation will be granted fundamental rights to participate in the affairs and governance of the entity.

Depending on the organizational documents of the church, there may be members who do not have the right to vote. Interested people who attend church services, volunteer for and give money to a church, but who are not voting members because the church's governance documents do not provide for voting membership, are often called "congregants," "tithing members," "supporters," "partners," or "members." The rights, if any, such persons have in the governance of the church are determined by the church's governing documents, not the designation or term used to identify them.

The inclusion of a voting membership, which generally implies that at least some level of decision-making authority has been conferred by a governing instrument, arises from the desire to promote inclusion between the affected class of individuals and the actions undertaken by the organization.

4.3 Are members presumed to be voting?

Again, membership implies participatory privileges, but the extent of those privileges is to be established by the organization. As a general rule, except as limited by charter, bylaw, statute, or custom, every member is presumed to be entitled to vote at a membership meeting, and a majority of those members present at a duly called meeting, at which a quorum is present, may act. Members' participation may be limited to a role that is advisory only or they may be advisory with the ability to elect board members, similar to citizens electing their representatives, who alone hold decision-making power.

Many states have adopted a version of the following:

* The right of the members to vote may be limited, enlarged, or denied to the extent specified in the articles of incorporation or the bylaws. Unless so limited, enlarged, or denied, each member shall be entitled to one vote on each matter submitted to a vote of the members.

* The articles of organization, bylaws, customs, and applicable state nonprofit corporation laws occasionally impose limitations on the right to vote. An organization can require that financial support from members be current as a condition of participation. A member's right to vote may be waived or lost by noncompliance with rules or withdrawal from the organization, actual or deemed. A smaller membership will, of course, reduce the burden of determining the pool of eligible voting members and thereby increase the certainty that an organization's meetings, voting, and action are valid and unassailable.

* Members have the right to contest irregularity and validity of particular voting, actions, and elections, and are expected to object to the irregularity at the meeting, thus creating the possibility that meetings will become procedurally controversial and protracted in length.

NOTE: Nevertheless, as in judicial proceedings, some courts have held that objections to procedures must be made by members when a vote is being taken, not months later after the events have been forgotten and the matters that were voted on have been completed.

4.4 Can members vote by proxy?

Yes, absent a provision to the contrary in its governing documents. *Proxy voting* means a substitute is permitted to vote on behalf of a member.

Section 7.24(a) of the Revised Model Nonprofit Corporation Act states, "Unless the articles or bylaws prohibit or limit proxy voting, a member may appoint a proxy to vote or otherwise act for the member by signing an appointment form either personally or by an attorney-in-fact."

Churches that are incorporated and do not want proxy voting should review their governing documents to ensure they contain a provision prohibiting it.

4.5 Is it possible to have more than one class of membership?

Yes. Beyond the typical broadening of those members recognized as able to participate in decision making, membership can also be used to draw a distinction in governance between the founding members and a more expanded member board. In the event that the founders desire a permanent, secured role in the organization, not subject to the removal or discretion of other individuals, membership may be of assistance in two ways.

Two classes of membership can be defined by the governing documents, one class of membership that is comprised of the founding members and another class that is composed of other individuals. The governing documents can specify that certain decisions can be made only by the majority vote of both classes.

Moreover, the founders could be the only members, as set forth in the governing documents, and with certain decisions allocated to the members, and not the board of directors. Similarly, founding members could control the composition of the board of directors, by way of the governing documents.

4.6 How are the qualifications for membership determined?

The qualification for membership in an organization is typically defined in its articles of incorporation and bylaws, and according to any applicable state law. Qualifications for membership are within the sound discretion of the organization. It is well-established that the right to determine the qualifications for membership belongs to the entity.

In the case of a church, the determination as to who are members "in good standing" and who are not is an ecclesiastical question relating to the government and discipline of a church. A church's decision about either matter is recognized by the courts as being within the unilateral discretion of the church, as opposed to either the courts or members of the public. The Supreme Court has held to the general rule of judicial nonintervention in the ecclesiastical affairs of churches, including determinations regarding membership.

For most religious nonprofit organizations, freedom to determine the selection criteria and manner of membership recognition are afforded the entity with very limited, if any, constraints. Some courts might review the selection and removal decisions of members in cases where civil, contract, or property rights were violated, as well as cases alleging fraud and collusion, or perhaps the unusual case where statutes protecting fundamental rights might be contradicted by the organization's practices.

An organization may delegate membership decisions to a committee, may vest the decisions in the board of directors, or may specify that the existing members approve new members by their vote.

Members are typically expected to have fulfilled predetermined criteria for membership and to maintain their membership in good standing by conforming to a set of continuing requirements. The criteria for ongoing membership are designed so that the member necessarily advances the purposes of the organization, and is eventually dropped from the membership if circumstances and compliance change in that regard after membership status has been conferred.

4.7 What is the legal authority of members?

This is defined by the governing documents and state law. Members can generally expect that their authority, as granted by the governing documents, will be enforced by the courts. Looking again at the example of churches, the membership in churches with a congregational form of government actually have quite significant authority when the majority has spoken, and has acted consistent with church rules, customs, and practices, at a meeting duly called. The generally accepted principle is that a majority of the members represent the church and have the right to manage its affairs and to control its property for the use and benefit of the church, and if challenged, the courts will protect such authority at least as it relates to civil, contract, or property rights.

Members may have rights defined by state law; the Model Nonprofit Corporation Act, which has been adopted in whole or in part in a majority of states, specifies that all books and records of a corporation may be inspected by any member, or his agent or attorney, for any proper purpose at any reasonable time.

At least one court has opined that when the authority of the membership is described in bylaws but not clearly delineated, the membership may have all authority that is not strictly granted elsewhere to the directors, officers, committees, and staff. Some courts have indicated that the majority rule of the membership may be sustained even if it constitutes a deviation from beliefs and customs of the entity, though not where a majority would act in violation of a state or federal law, especially where the property or liberty rights of others are concerned.

Membership, considered for some purposes to be the entity, may have authority over the property affairs of an organization, although individual members do not have a personal interest in the same.

4.8 What is the personal legal liability of a member?

Liability depends on the type of organization to which the member belongs. It is the established policy of jurisprudence to promote accountability through organizational formalization, with incorporation being the prime example. Through the process of incorporation, the members can, in most cases, avoid personal liability.

Corporations have powers and rights associated with individuals, and logically such liabilities as well, including, for example, the right to sue and be sued, to enter contracts, to incur tax liability, and where a corporation has had the power to act, the corporation itself should be made to answer. The corporation generally should be liable for its valid acts, rather than the members of a non-profit corporation, though exceptions to the generalization may be found under state law.

4.9 What is the procedure for membership meetings?

Membership meetings generally follow a prescribed list of matters that have been circulated on an agenda, and which are discussed and acted on according to some prescribed and agreed-on procedural rules of order. Such rules in turn tend to reflect the rules legislative bodies have found effective through decades of refinement. Members may exercise the authority conferred on them only when acting at a meeting convened according to procedural requirements defined in the organization's articles or bylaws, or applicable state law. Actions taken at improperly called meetings may be considered invalid unless subsequently ratified or affirmed at a duly convened meeting. Bylaws commonly call for annual general meetings of the organization's membership and for such special meetings as the members or board of directors consider appropriate.

Although an organization may determine the order of business to be placed on the agenda at general or special meetings, this order is commonly followed:

- Reading and approval of minutes
- Reports of officers, boards, and standing committees
- Reports of special committees
- Special orders
- Unfinished business and general orders
- New business

Members, within limitations, may express their views at meetings, as the major purpose of such meetings is to arrive at decisions by consensus through a free and open exchange of ideas. To ensure the validity of action taken, most rules of order suggest the moderator of the meeting call for discussion on both subject matters and motions made thereunder.

4.10 What right does a church have to discipline or expel a member, and what cautions should be used in undertaking discipline proceedings?

In accordance with the Free Exercise Clause of the Constitution, a church has the protected right to expel or discipline its members. A church member who concludes that he or she has been improperly disciplined or expelled from membership in a church has several potential claims or causes of action against the church available.

The remedies, claims, and causes of action include the following:

- If the church is located in a jurisdiction that permits review of church membership disputes, the member can seek to obtain a judicial review of the discipline or expulsion process. If, following a judicial review, a court determines that the discipline or expulsion was improper, the court can rule that the discipline and/or expulsion was defective and declare the action of the church null and void, and, thereby, reinstate the member.
- A member can seek injunctive relief against the church, thereby barring the church from any actions of discipline or expulsion.
- A member can seek a declaratory judgment from the court clarifying and setting forth the member's rights, powers, and privileges.
- A member can sue the church, its board of directors, and other members under tort law seeking monetary damages. Possible causes of action include invasion of privacy, defamation, and negligent and intentional infliction of emotional distress.

When undertaking discipline or expulsion of a member, a church should take care to follow the rules that it has set forth in its organizational documents or internal policies and to document the measures taken to follow that process.

4.11 Are courts willing to intervene in disputes between a church and its membership?

An organization, especially one the purpose of which is the advancement of religion, generally has the final word in deciding the criteria for removal of members, if not the final word in whether it followed its own criteria. As noted above, the choice over the factors an organization applies to the selection and removal of members is theoretically within the discretion of an organization.

Inconsistent treatment and recognition of an individual's rights in some circumstances have modified the inherent autonomy of the organization. The Constitutional guarantee of free exercise of religion is a powerful motivator behind courts' general policy of nonintervention. Tending to avoid entertaining the reversal of an arbitrary decision, some courts have reviewed church membership expulsions for compliance with the bylaws or articles of organization. If the removal resulted from the decision of the specified body, which body duly passed on the decision, then for the purposes of determining whether members' expulsion is actionable, many courts have expressed a lack of jurisdiction over the decision, deferring to the ecclesiastical authority that made the decision.

One court, in agreeing to review a church's expulsion of certain members, commented:

> If a decision is reached by somebody not having ecclesiastical jurisdiction over the matter, then the civil court would not be bound by that decision. . . . Once [a] determination is made that the proper ecclesiastical authority has acted in its duly constituted manner, no civil review of the substantive ecclesiastical matter may take place as this would be prohibited by Amendments I and XIV of the Federal Constitution.

Secular entities can expect far less deference, especially to the extent that bad faith, arbitrariness, fraud, or collusion motivates a removal that appears inconsistent with established organization customs and practices. For that matter, even religious entities, when not specifically deciding a matter that encroaches on religion, may place their decision under review of the courts, if the member sues.

Rules to assist in protecting an organization's removal decisions include:

- Formalize the procedure that will be followed.
- Adhere to the formalized procedure.
- Document the reasons that action is being taken.
- Compare the action being taken in the case at hand to the organization's treatment of members in similar circumstances.
- Consider why alternative options would not be as feasible as the action being taken.
- Try to eliminate from the process anyone who cannot deliberate in good faith.
- Treat the individual throughout the process just as you would if you expected that he or she might again become a member.

CHAPTER 5

The Board of Directors

5.1 What is the origin and importance of the board of directors of a religious nonprofit organization?

There are many ways for the board of directors of a religious nonprofit organization to originate. Often, in the context of a church, these individuals are elected by the church's membership. For a religious nonprofit organization, the board of directors is (or should be) the critical body that determines the entity's programs and investments and provides management guidance. The role of the officers and employees is important, but the board of directors has the responsibility to frame the organization's overall policy directions and objectives. The governing board has the ultimate responsibility for the organization's activities—and can be a prime target when matters of liability arise.

The members of the board are fiduciaries; they are charged with treating the organization's assets and other resources with the same degree of care and sustenance that they would their own. When there is wrongdoing or misguided practices, the abuse is all too frequently traceable to an inattentive or passive board of directors. More frequently than before, government regulators are emphasizing more extensive duties and responsibilities on the board of directors, in the hope of averting misdeeds.

5.2 What is the function of the board of directors?

There is considerable disagreement on this point, specifically among churches and other religious nonprofit organizations. Setting aside issues of religious polity, the ideal standard is: setting of policy, objectives, and general direction for the nonprofit organization. The board is there to direct, but only in an overarching, big-picture sense. That body should not micromanage the entity.

In practice, a board's degree of involvement has every sort of gradation. The size of the board and the frequency of its meetings are likely to be determining factors.

Particularly in the case of charitable organizations, the members of the board are *fiduciaries*. Because of this standard, the individuals are required to act with the same degree of judgment—*prudence*—in administering the affairs of the organization as they would in their personal affairs.

The officers and key employees should administer the organization on a day-to-day basis, not the board of directors. However, in actuality, board members often inject themselves into the details of administration. The law basically is powerless to draw lines here; the degree of management involvement by an individual board member is a function of the tolerance of the other board members, the energy and personality of the board member, the amount of time he or she has available for the pursuit, and the reaction and tolerance of the officers and key employees.

5.3 What is the difference between the terms *directors, elders, deacons,* and *trustees*?

It depends. Churches and other religious nonprofit organizations must conduct their business affairs through individuals. The meaning of the terms *director, elder, deacon,* or *trustee,* or the like, is determined by inspecting the organization's governing documents. If the terminology contained within the governing documents is not clear regarding who is charged with oversight of the organization and its temporal affairs, then the governing documents should be revised.

The governing board of a nonprofit organization, religious or otherwise, may be termed a board of directors, board of trustees, board of governors, board of elders, board of deacons, or some other title. The name itself rarely has any legal significance. If, however, use of a title other than director is interfering with recruitment of members to serve on the board, or it is confusing or misleading, then it is best to abandon the usage of the term and adopt the generally accepted term of *director.*

Nearly all state laws use the term *director*. The words *director* and *trustee,* however, are essentially synonymous. If an organization wants to be certain of avoiding adverse technicalities, it need only reference the word *director* once in its bylaws and then note what is the term to be used thereafter.

5.4 What is the difference between the regular board of directors and the initial board of directors?

An initial board of directors is the group of individuals who formed the organization, perhaps selected by the incorporator. Once the corporation is formed, the incorporator's legal role is complete. Then, the initial board of directors will adopt the corporation's bylaws, which sets forth the rules of governance, including how to elect the corporation's president, secretary, treasurer, and board of directors.

5.5 What are the rules concerning the composition of the board of directors?

For the most part, the law does not contain rules of this nature. The IRS suggests that "governing boards should be composed of persons who are informed and active in overseeing the charities' operations and finances." The IRS further suggests that "governing boards should include individuals not only knowledgeable and passionate about the organization's programs, but also those with expertise in critical areas involving accounting, finance, compensation, and ethics." These are, however, merely suggestions from the IRS and the unique circumstances of different organizations may merit different approaches to board composition. For the most part, the federal tax law is silent on the composition of a board of directors of a nonprofit organization.

5.6 How does a charitable organization know whether its board of directors is lawfully constructed?

The subject of board composition is essentially a matter of state law. The IRS does not have the authority to regulate nonprofit governance directly, although several of the tax rules (e. g., private inurement, private benefit, and excess benefit rules), however, reinforce certain concepts that parallel state law fiduciary duties, such as the duties of loyalty and care.

5.7 Must the board of directors of a religious nonprofit organization be comprised of representatives of its congregation or membership?

No. As discussed above, neither federal nor state law dictates the characteristics of a religious nonprofit organization's board. Furthermore, to do so would likely violate constitutional law protections.

5.8 Can the members of a religious nonprofit organization's board be related?

Yes. It is common for a nonprofit organization—charitable, religious, or otherwise—to be founded by one or two individuals. In the beginning, these individuals may comprise or dominate the board of directors and also be the officers of the organization. This type of organization is the nonprofit equivalent of what is known in the for-profit world as a *closely held corporation.* Close governance in the nonprofit sector is completely in conformity with the law.

In most jurisdictions, as few as three directors are required for a nonprofit corporation. (The minimum number of directors for a nonprofit corporation varies from state to state. Some states require only one.) If an entity is to be a corporation and it has the requisite number of directors, this approach is fully lawful.

Despite the fact that a close board is wholly legal, it likely will subject the organization to a greater degree of scrutiny by government officials, particularly when they are concerned about private inurement or private benefit. The IRS occasionally will balk at a close board when considering recognition of tax-exempt status, although technically the IRS has no general authority to preclude one.

5.9 Can related directors also be the officers of the religious nonprofit organization?

Yes. The law in most states requires a president, a treasurer, and a secretary. Board members can also be officers. One individual can hold officer positions, except that the same individual cannot be both president and secretary, as frequently an organization's documents must be signed by the president and attested to by the secretary. The law does not recognize an attestation of one's own signature as effective.

5.10 In any instance, can the same individual be both a director and an officer?

Yes. There is no legal prohibition against the dual role. In fact, in both nonprofit and for-profit organizations, some or all of the officers are quite commonly also members of the board.

5.11 What is the function of the officers?

The law is rather vague on this point. An officer usually is expected to provide more "hands-on" management than a director but not as much as a key employee. These distinctions often become muddled, particularly when the same individual plays two or more of these roles. Further, the degree of involvement by an officer is likely to be determined by whether he or she is a volunteer or is an employee.

The function of the *president* is to serve as the chief executive officer of the organization. It is common to state in the entity's bylaws that, subject to the overall supervision of the board of directors, the president shall perform all duties customary to that office.

The function of the *treasurer* is to have custody of and be responsible for all funds and assets of the organization. He or she keeps, or causes to be kept, complete and accurate accounts of receipts and disbursements of the organization. The treasurer is responsible for the deposit of money in such banks or other depositories as the board of directors may designate. He or she is to periodically render a statement of accounts to the board. It is common to state in the entity's bylaws that, subject to the overall supervision of the board of directors, the treasurer shall perform all duties customary to the office.

NOTE: Proper management practice is to obtain a security bond to protect the organization should the treasurer abuse that position for personal gain.

The functions of the secretary are to keep an accurate record of the proceedings of all meetings of the board of directors, and to provide notice of meetings and other events as the law or the bylaws may require. It is common to state in the entity's bylaws that, subject to the overall supervision of the board of directors, the secretary shall perform all duties customary to that office.

5.12 Can the same individual hold more than one officer position?

It depends on the positions. For example, it is common for the same individual to be the secretary and treasurer. By contrast, it is not a good idea to have the same individual be the president and secretary. The law often requires the signatures of both of these officers on legal documents and contemplates two individuals. The laws of some states prohibit an individual from being both president and secretary of a nonprofit corporation as the law does not recognize attestation of one's own signature as effective.

5.13 What are the methods by which a board of directors of a religious nonprofit organization can vote?

The methods by which a board of directors of a religious nonprofit organization can vote are a subject of state law; nearly every state's nonprofit corporation act addresses the subject. Obviously, the board members can meet and cast votes while they are together (assuming the presence of a quorum). Most states allow these boards to act by written consent in lieu of a meeting, although the members must be unanimous on any decision so made. If state law approves (and, in some instances, if provided for in the bylaws), the board members can hold a meeting by conference call, as long as all of them can hear each other. Thus, for example, unless state law expressly permits the practice, members of the board of directors of a nonprofit organization cannot vote by regular mail or e-mail ballot.

5.14 Can members of a religious nonprofit organization's board of directors vote by proxy?

A meeting of the board of directors is legal only if a quorum is present. A quorum for the transaction of business by the board means the number or percentage of the total authorized number of directors that must be present in order for the board to transact business. Some states permit directors to be present by proxy and vote; however, directors who are present by proxy generally are not counted toward a quorum.

The bylaws typically set forth the requirements for a quorum. Generally, religious nonprofit organizations do not permit directors to be present by proxy. In the absence of a bylaw provision, however, the number of directors constituting a quorum ordinarily will be determined by the nonprofit corporation law of the state where incorporation occurred.

A majority of the number of directors fixed by the bylaws constitutes a quorum, or in the absence of such a provision, a majority of the number of directors stated in the articles of incorporation, or a majority of the board, will constitute a quorum in the absence of a statutory provision to the contrary. Some state nonprofit corporation laws specify that a quorum shall not consist of less than three directors. Some state nonprofit statutes permit the board to meet for the purpose of filling vacancies, if vacancies on the board reduce the number of directors to less than a quorum.

5.15   What materials should be included in the minutes of the meetings of the board of directors of a religious nonprofit organization?

There is no rule of law that applies to the contents of minutes of directors' meetings. The minutes should be complete, in that they reflect all material subjects discussed at the meeting, and accurate. Statements that are defamatory, willful misrepresentations of fact, or incriminating should be avoided.

The minutes should tell the substantive story of what transpired at the meeting; they should not be verbatim transcripts of the dialog or otherwise be in exhaustive detail. They should enable someone looking at them years later to glean the essence of the meeting and the decisions made in it. Those looking at the minutes may not be confined to subsequent boards; other readers can be representatives of the government or the media. Thus, the matters recorded can be as important as what is said. In one instance, a public charity described a series of apparent private inurement transactions in a set of board minutes, which the IRS reviewed on audit; the contents of the minutes were cited by the IRS as a factor in revoking the organization's tax-exempt status. Alternatively, it is a question of judgment as to what goes in and what stays out of minutes; there is no bright line of distinction as to what is suitable for inclusion in the document. This is a judgment that can be easily questioned with the benefit of hindsight.

5.16   What happens if the board of directors of a religious nonprofit organization makes a mistake?

The answer depends on the nature of the "mistake."

- Was the mistake an "honest" one, or did it involve the kind of behavior that the board knew or should have known was inappropriate or insufficient? The action or decision should be tested against the principles of *fiduciary responsibility*. Whose interests were being pursued, the organization's or those of one or more individuals? Did the mistake entail a violation

of a law? Is it a civil or criminal violation? Did the board seek the advice of a lawyer or other appropriate professional before undertaking the transaction? In essence, the question always is: Did the board members act *reasonably?* In this context, that means: Did they act in *good faith?*
* Did the mistake damage the organization or any other person?
* How easily can the mistake be undone?
* What protections were in place to shield the organization and the directors from liability?

For example, in 1994 the board of an organization in New York was charged with the mistake of condoning lavish and extravagant expenditures. Their "mistake" damaged the organization, but corrective action could be and was taken: In settlement of the case, the New York attorney general mandated that each member of the board was to pay the organization $10,000 as restitution for his or her misconduct. A few other states will surcharge the directors for similar behavior.

When an action by a board of directors of a nonprofit organization causes damage, either to the organization or to someone else, most consequences do not include personal liability on the part of the directors. Instead, the offensive activity is considered by the law to be a responsibility of the organization itself. Thus, the likelihood that the members of the board of directors of a nonprofit organization will be punished in some way because they did something they should not have done (a commission) or they failed to do something they should have done (an omission) is remote.

But suppose that (1) a board approves a significant investment that was speculative, (2) the organization incurs a substantial economic loss as a result, and (3) it is subsequently shown that the board should have known that the investment was inappropriate. In these circumstances, there could be adverse consequences. An attorney general may pursue a surcharge of the board and/or proceedings to remove and replace one or more board members.

Still, it is unusual for members of the board of a nonprofit organization, particularly a religious nonprofit, to be found personally liable for something done or not done involving the organization. Yet, it can happen. In one case, some members of the board of a charitable organization were found to have conspired to discharge an employee on the basis of racial discrimination. Their acts violated civil rights laws and the individuals were found personally liable. Personal liability can also arise in the area of defamation, removal of members, and tort law, generally.

5.17 **How likely is it that a member of the board of directors of a religious nonprofit organization will be found personally liable for something done or not done while serving the organization?**

As discussed previously, the likelihood is not great because the law first regards the action or nonaction as that of the organization. Even if there is liability, the liability almost always is that of the organization. This is particularly true where the organization is a corporation.

Still, a member of the board of directors (or an officer) who is held personally liable will not find solace in knowing that he or she stands with a select few. Personal liability may attach where the conduct is wrongful and willful, continuous, and not due to reasonable cause.

5.18   How can a religious nonprofit organization provide some protection for its board against the likelihood of personal liability for the result of something they did or did not do while serving the organization?

Basically, there are four means of protection. One of them is to *incorporate* the organization. The law recognizes corporations as separate legal entities, and the corporate form usually serves as a shield against personal liability. For corporations, liability is generally confined to the organization and does not extend to those who manage it. In those extreme cases that are the exception to this rule, the jargon is that the "corporate shield has been pierced."

Today, when a nonprofit organization is formed, the resulting entity is usually a corporation. Most lawyers advise their individual clients not to sit on the board of directors of a nonprofit organization that is not incorporated.

The second form of protection is *indemnification.* A nonprofit organization should provide in its articles or bylaws that it will pay the judgments and related expenses (including legal fees) incurred by the directors and officers (and perhaps others), when those expenses are the result of a commission or omission by those persons while acting in the service of the organization. The indemnification cannot extend to criminal acts and may not cover certain willful acts that violate a civil law. The right to indemnification is a matter of applicable state law. As such, state law should be considered when drafting indemnification provisions.

 NOTE: Because the resources of the organization are involved, the true value of an indemnification depends on the economic viability of the organization. In times of financial difficulties for a nonprofit organization, an indemnification of its directors and officers can be a classic "hollow promise."

Indemnification is often confused with *insurance,* the third form of protection. Instead of shifting the risk of liability from individuals to the organization, however, insurance shifts the risk of liability to an independent third party—an insurance company. The resources of the insurer, rather than those of the insured, are then used to resolve the dispute. Some risks, such as those arising from violation of a criminal law, cannot be shifted to an insurer.

There is one caution here: An officers' and directors' liability insurance contract is likely to contain an extensive list of civil law transgressions that are *excluded* from coverage. These exclusions may include offenses such as libel and slander, employee discrimination, and antitrust activities—the most prevalent types of liability in the nonprofit context. Thus, when reviewing a prospective insurance contract that seems to offer the necessary coverage, the exclusions paragraphs should be carefully reviewed by the nonprofit and its legal counsel.

This type of insurance can be costly. Premiums can be easily thousands of dollars annually, even with a sizable deductible. Although the costs of these premiums have dropped in recent years, many nonprofit organizations still cannot afford them.

 NOTE: Because of the inadequate coverage and high cost of currently available insurance, in some states, nonprofit organizations are being created for the purpose of facilitating smaller nonprofit organizations' access to various types of insurance: These organizations—because they have this insurance-related function—cannot qualify for tax-exempt status.

Unfortunately, due to litigiousness in our society, the risks of liability usually are too great for any organization that functions without this protection. The premium for this type of insurance should be regarded as a "cost of doing business."

It is critical that the organization purchase officers' and directors' liability insurance. A lawyer will likely recommend to any individual that he or she not serve on the board of a nonprofit organization that does not have adequate insurance of this nature.

The fourth of these protections is the newest of them: *immunity*. This form of protection is available when the applicable state law provides that a class of individuals, under certain circumstances, is not liable for a particular act or set of acts or for failure to undertake a particular act or set of acts. Several states have enacted immunity laws for officers and directors of nonprofit organizations, protecting them in case of asserted civil law violations, particularly where these individuals are serving as volunteers. In 1997, the federal government enacted the Volunteer Protection Act, which provides immunity for volunteers serving nonprofit organizations from harm caused by the volunteers' acts or omissions.

5.19 Does a religious nonprofit organization really have to indemnify its officers and director and purchase liability insurance? Can't they just be certain their acts are always in good faith?

Unfortunately, reliance on assumptions of good faith can prove traumatic and expensive. A lawyer will recommend both an indemnification clause and officers' and directors' liability insurance.

There is no question, however, that the most important protection against legal liability is to act in ways that ward off liability. There are several ways to avoid personal liability while fulfilling the spirit and the rules of fiduciary responsibility. They are:

1. Learn about the legal form of the organization and its structure. For example, if the organization is a corporation, obtain copies of its articles of incorporation and bylaws—and read them. Compare the organization's operating methods with the structure and procedures that are reflected in these documents.

2. Learn how and why the organization operates—the purposes of its programs, their number, possible overlap of efforts, and the nature of its membership and/or other support.

3. Committees, subsidiaries, directors' "pet projects," members' personal interests or contacts, or community needs may have introduced activities (and corresponding budget outlays) that were not authorized in the normal way. Some may deserve more recognition and support, while others may be (albeit innocently) endangering the organization's tax-exempt status. Find out exactly what the organization is *doing*.

4. Directors should never be afraid to ask about any arrangements or information that is unclear to them. Individuals with fiduciary responsibilities should not fret about asking what may seem to them to be "dumb questions" in the presence of the other directors; many of them are likely to have the same questions on their minds.

5. Magazine articles and books describing the proper role for directors and officers of nonprofit organizations will help to update the individual's knowledge as to permissible and innovative practices. Officers and directors should periodically attend a seminar or conference to further their understanding of and effectiveness in their roles.

6. This is both the easiest and hardest rule to follow: The director or officer should, at all times, engage in behavior that prevents (or at least significantly minimizes) the possibility of personal liability even if the organization itself is found liable. The individual, being a fiduciary, has a duty to act in a prudent manner. Constant awareness of that duty offers no small measure of self-protection.

CHAPTER 6

Conflicts of Interest

6.1 What is *self-dealing*?

Self-dealing occurs when a person is engaged in a transaction with a nonprofit organization while at the same time having a significant relationship with the organization. The person is on both sides of the deal, hence the term. For example, self-dealing occurs where a nonprofit organization purchases an item of property from a business that is controlled by an individual who is on the board of directors of the nonprofit organization.

The person self-dealing in the realm of public charities is known as an *insider*. For charities, an insider is likely to be about the same as a fiduciary.

6.2 Is self-dealing the same as a *conflict of interest*?

No. The concept of a conflict of interest is broader than the concept of self-dealing. One common characteristic that these terms have, however, is that both are derogatory. Neither practice is necessarily illegal. (If an insider with respect to a public charity engages in an act of self-dealing, he or she may become subject to one or more federal excise taxes imposed as penalties.)

A *conflict of interest* presents itself when a person who has a significant relationship with a nonprofit organization also is deriving, or may be in a position to derive, a benefit from something the nonprofit organization is doing or may be doing. The person may be able to obtain some personal benefit from these circumstances; because of the duality of interests, the person is conflicted. An act of self-dealing between a nonprofit organization and an insider with respect to it also is an instance of a conflict of interest. A conflict of interest can be present, however, without a specific transaction or arrangement having yet arisen. Also, insiders are not always directly involved in a conflict-of-interest situation. For example, a religious nonprofit organization may be contemplating making a grant to a food-relief organization; a board member of the grantor entity has a conflict of interest if his or her brother or sister is the executive director at the grantee organization.

A conflict-of-interest transaction is a transaction with the nonprofit organization, or any of its affiliates, in which an individual connected with the organization (usually its directors and officers) has a direct or indirect interest.

NOTE: A conflict of interest can often be resolved by disclosure of the conflict to the board of directors of the nonprofit organization. Indeed, some nonprofit organizations have formal policies to this end. Problems associated with self-dealing, however, usually cannot be remedied merely by disclosure.

NOTE: Some nonprofit watchdog agencies require the adoption of a conflict-of-interest policy as a condition of their approval of a charitable organization.

6.3 What language should be contained in a conflict-of-interest policy?

A conflict-of-interest policy should annually elicit from each individual covered by it the disclosure of any organization that does business with or is in competition with the organization, where the individual (and/or any of his or her immediate family members) serves as a director or officer of that other entity. Similar disclosure should be made with respect to an individual's participation in partnerships, consulting arrangements, and other circumstances where the individual has significant influence over management decisions.

Moreover, the same type of disclosure should be made where the individuals receive compensation from another entity over a certain threshold (such as $10,000) or where there is an equity or debt relationship over a certain threshold (such as 10 percent).

The conflict-of-interest policy should obligate the director, officer, or any other individual to disclose a conflict of interest to the board of directors of the organization. It should require that the disclosure be reflected in the minutes of the board meeting, along with the potential adverse consequences to the organization.

The board of directors of the organization should be required to determine whether the disclosure was made adequately and forthrightly (which may require some questioning and other discussion at the board meeting), and whether the organization should proceed with the transaction involving the conflict (if that is the case). A conflict-of-interest transaction should be subject to approval by the board by a process more stringent than would otherwise be the case (such as by a two-thirds vote when normally only a majority vote would be required). The interested director or officer should not be counted in ascertaining the presence of a quorum for the meeting or in the vote itself. It is preferable that this individual not be present at the time of the voting.

6.4 Is a conflict-of-interest policy legally binding on the individuals covered by it and/or the nonprofit organization?

It should be. If the policy is adopted by the organization's board of directors in conformance with the requirements of state law and the organization's bylaws, usually pursuant to board resolution, the policy is legally binding. It is in the nature of a contract between the directors and officers of the organization and the organization itself, and between and among these individuals.

6.5 How does an individual know when a conflict of interest is present?

For the most part, the conflict-of-interest policy most likely stated on the conflict-of-interest disclosure form that is annually prepared by the covered individuals will spell out what the conflicts are. Still, some judgment may be required in determining whether there is a conflict. The initial determination may rest with the covered individual. The most prudent practice is: When in doubt, disclose the matter to the board of directors.

6.6 What are the obligations of a board member or officer when a conflict of interest is disclosed?

The principal obligation is met when the disclosure is made. The other obligations should be subject to questions by the board as to the conflict (actual, potential, or perceived), to answer those questions, to disclose to the organization any adverse consequences resulting from the conflict of which the individual is aware, and to refrain from voting on the transaction involved (if any), from being included in the quorum for the meeting, and from being present during that voting (even if the policy may not specifically require absence).

6.7 How should a nonprofit organization respond to a disclosure of a conflict of interest?

The disclosure should be made only to the board of directors. As soon as is reasonably possible following the disclosure, the board of directors should discuss the matter at a board meeting. If a particular transaction is involved, the board should vote on the conflict before considering the transaction. It is the responsibility of a board of directors to determine whether there is a conflict of interest and, if so, whether to proceed with the transaction or to use other means to reconcile the conflict.

6.8 What are the penalties when a conflict-of-interest policy is breached?

The penalties, whatever they may be, would be levied by the board of directors on the individual who breached the conflict-of-interest policy. The range of these penalties is likely to be determined by state law and the organization's bylaws. The options include a gentle rebuke, a serious rebuke, a censure, and/or removal from office.

NOTE: Some organizations state in their conflict-of-interest policy that a transaction may be void or voidable if not approved by the board of directors in accordance with the conflict-of-interest policy. This practice is quite suitable when the only parties to the transaction are the nonprofit organization and one or more individuals covered by the policy (e.g., a lease between the organization and a company wholly owned by a board member). Where the transaction involves other parties who are not covered by the conflict-of-interest policy, however, a voiding of the transaction pursuant to the policy could be an illegal breach of contract that would subject the organization (and perhaps one or more board members) to a lawsuit.

6.9 Can a nonprofit organization receive contributions from an entity where a board member has a conflict of interest?

In general, yes. It is unlikely that these contributions would be inappropriate as a matter of law. For the most part, gifts from this source would not contravene the conflict-of-interest policy of the organization because money is flowing to it, rather than from it. There is always a possibility, however, that the recipient organization could find itself in an awkward or embarrassing position as a consequence of these gifts. Prudence is always in order in this context.

6.10 Can a nonprofit organization negotiate for discounted prices for goods or services to be purchased from a source where a board member or officer has disclosed a conflict of interest?

Absolutely. The essence of the requirements in this area is disclosure, not a prohibition. The transaction may proceed if the conflict of interest is fully disclosed and considered by the board of directors, and the board decides that (1) the transaction would be reasonable with respect to the organization and (2) the presence of the conflict did not significantly influence the action of the board with respect to the conflict. These determinations should be reflected in the minutes of the relevant board meeting.

 NOTE: A conflict of interest does not automatically mean that private inurement or private benefit has occurred. The potential for difficulties of that nature is greater, however, and the parties should act with caution. When properly handled with due caution and deliberation, transactions that are technically a conflict of interest often result in a "good deal" for the organization.

CHAPTER 7

Expenditure of the Religious Nonprofit Organization's Funds

7.1 What is expected in terms of program expenditures?

The board of directors of a religious nonprofit organization, as part of its overall role in setting policy and direction, should establish a budget that governs the basic parameters of the expenditures of the organization's funds. This pertains to outlays for program, management, and fundraising.

The primary purpose of a nonprofit organization is to carry out its program function—termed the *exempt function* in the case of tax-exempt organizations. Thus, the law expects that the primary expenditures of a nonprofit organization will be for its program activities.

There are, however, no mechanical tests for measuring what is *primary* or, as is often the term, *substantial*. A tax-exempt organization can have some unrelated business activity but there is no precise standard as to how much; unrelated business obviously cannot dominate the organization's affairs. The blend of the three types of outlays will vary according to the type of organization and the particular circumstances it is in.

From time to time, the IRS will apply what it terms the *commensurate test* to the activities of a charitable organization. This involves an analysis as to whether the organization is engaging in adequate exempt functions, in relation to the resources that it has. For example, an application of this test (which the IRS subsequently abandoned) was to assert that an organization that allegedly devoted too much of its income to fundraising should lose its tax exemption because of transgression of the commensurate test.

7.2 What are the rules pertaining to employee compensation?

The subject of key employee compensation is under intense scrutiny at the IRS, at the Department of the Treasury, and on Capitol Hill. This interest in employee compensation by tax-exempt organizations was a major force in enactment of the *intermediate sanctions* rules. These rules impose excise taxes on amounts of excess compensation paid to insiders and require the employee to repay the employer organization the amount of compensation that is considered unreasonable. The rules are termed *intermediate* because, in most instances, they are applied instead of revocation of the organization's tax-exempt status.

The rules as to employee compensation are vague and complicated, and are discussed in greater detail later in this handbook. They are built on the concept of *reasonableness*. A charitable organization's ongoing tax-exempt status (federal and state) is predicated on the assumption that the compensation of all employees is reasonable. The current focus is primarily on executive compensation. For an employee who is an *insider* with respect to the organization, excessive compensation is a form of *private inurement* and can be a basis for revocation of exempt status. If the employee is not an insider and the amount of excess compensation is more than incidental, the result is *private benefit*, which also is a ground for loss of exempt status.

Whether an individual's compensation is reasonable is a question of fact, not law. Lawyers usually cannot credibly opine on that subject. There are, however, compensation experts who can legitimately advise on the appropriateness of amounts of compensation. In many instances, prudence leads an organization to procure a formal opinion from one of these experts as to the reasonableness of the compensation of one or more employees.

What lawyers can do is evaluate an individual's compensation using the various criteria that the law has devised for assessing reasonableness.

The lawyer's lot in these situations can be illustrated by the following example. A client religious nonprofit organization was hiring a new executive director, and the lawyer was asked to review the proposed contract and advise the organization accordingly. Nothing in the contract was separately inappropriate, but it was the lawyer's judgment that the overall package of salary and benefits was much too generous, to the point of being excessive. This was completely a judgment call, the use of intuition. Three aspects of the proposed arrangement were particularly troubling:

1. The incoming executive's compensation package was twice that of the outgoing executive director.
2. The salary alone was one-eighth of the organization's annual budget.
3. The individual being hired was a member of the board of directors of the organization.

To further worsen the situation, the new executive director was given express authority to consult (for fees) and to earn other forms of outside income.

The lawyer was obligated to advise the client that there was a substantial likelihood that the compensation package would be considered excessive by federal or state government authorities, and that the organization's tax exemption may be endangered. The lawyer could not point to anything specific; the client was provided with a judgment, based on an understanding of the case law. The client (specifically, the chairman of the board of directors) was very unhappy with the lawyer's position. The board went ahead and hired the individual as planned; the lawyer's days of representing that particular organization were over.

7.3 What discretion does the management of a religious nonprofit organization have in the expenditure of funds? (Lessons from the *New York Settlement*)

For example, the management wants to redecorate the offices of the organization and purchase new furniture. A precise monetary amount cannot be provided for this sort of thing. There is no mechanical standard for determining the extent of these types of expenditures. Those involved as *fiduciaries* can lawfully use the organization's income and assets for office decoration, furniture, and so forth, as long as they stay within the bounds of what *is reasonable* and *prudent*. To use other words that are easy to articulate, but often difficult to apply, they should avoid outlays that are *lavish* or *extravagant*.

An example may help clarify this matter. In 1994, the State of New York concluded an examination of a charitable organization that culminated in a settlement. This three-year investigation led to a document concerning what the attorney general referred to as the "financial administration and spending practices" of the organization. The state concluded that the board of trustees of this organization "failed to exercise appropriate cost controls in its management" of the entity. This finding specifically referred to the construction and furnishing of the entity's headquarters.

The New York attorney general found that the organization incurred "excessive" costs in furnishing the offices. The *New York Settlement* required the trustees of this charity to, in the future, "exercise cost consciousness at all times" when making spending decisions. An expense policy document observed that, "[a]s it is not always possible to apply hard-and-fast rules to every situation, all trustees and employees are expected to use common sense in the disbursement of" the organization's funds. This "standard" is nothing more than another iteration of the doctrines of *reasonableness* and *prudence*. The standard used in the settlement was that of *cost consciousness*.

 NOTE: This *New York Settlement* with the attorney general in New York required each of the organization's 14 trustees to pay $10,000 to the organization as restitution for the excessive costs incurred in constructing and furnishing the headquarters. This settlement agreement is not *law*. It applies only to the parties and involves only the State of New York. (The document specifically states that there was no admission of any wrongdoing.) It is being emphasized only because of the pertinence of its provisions and the lack of such specific guidance elsewhere.

Equally useful is *the front-page-of-the-newspaper test*. Envision how a director of a religious nonprofit would feel if a story about the organization's fiscal practices appeared on the front page of the community's newspaper. A classic example of the disasters that can be created when the front-page test is failed is the series of experiences suffered by the United Way of America because of the doings of its then president.

These guidelines are useful in testing the wisdom of decisions by the leadership of charitable organizations.

7.4 Does this standard of fiduciary responsibility apply to every expense incurred by a religious nonprofit organization?

Yes. For example, the *New York Settlement* described above also pertained to travel, hotel accommodations, location of board meetings, and use of consultants.

Travel by officers, directors, executives, and key employees: The *New York Settlement* agreement is useful as a guideline. The standard to be used is *cost consciousness*. When the directors of the organization are prudent, they authorize spending of the organization's money as if it were their own. For example, if a director travels via a commercial airline at his or her own personal expense, does he or she fly first class? If not, it is hard to justify first-class travel at the expense of the organization.

 NOTE: First-class air travel while pursuing a charity's affairs is not illegal or otherwise inherently impermissible. Only justification of the practice is involved.

Thus, the attorney general, in the *New York Settlement*, required the charitable organization to use the "most economic available" airfares. The organization was largely prohibited from paying or reimbursing for first-class airfares and using chartered airplanes. Generally, the use of limousines was also prohibited unless "international officials or other dignitaries" are involved.

Spousal travel: This is a very difficult and sensitive subject. Again, the *New York Settlement* is useful as a guideline. It generally prohibited the organization from paying or reimbursing travel expenses for spouses or other close family members. The only exception is when the individual provides a "specific contribution for the program for which the travel is incurred through an active participation in a scheduled program." Moreover, where the spouse or family member is that of an employee, prior approval of the chief executive officer is required; where a trustee is involved, prior approval of the chairperson of the audit committee is required.

Also, federal tax law relates to this subject. There is no income tax deduction for amounts paid or incurred with respect to a spouse (or dependent or other individual) accompanying an individual (or an officer or employee of the business) on business travel, unless the accompanying individual is an employee of the taxpayer, the travel of the accompanying individual is for a bona fide business purpose, and the travel expenses would otherwise be deductible by the accompanying individual. The business expense deduction, however, is available where the payment is treated as compensation to the employee. A tax-exempt organization is not concerned with these rules as to tax deductions. Where an exempt organization pays for the travel expenses of a spouse, that payment is additional income to the employee of the organization, unless the purpose of the presence of the spouse is the performance of programmatic, administrative, or other services that further the organization's exempt purposes.

Hotels: A tax-exempt organization can pay for the use of hotels for conferences, board meetings, and so forth. As always, the standard to follow is *reasonableness*. The *New York Settlement* guidelines, with their emphasis on *cost consciousness*, generally require the use of "available corporate and discount rates," and prohibit the payment of "deluxe or luxury" hotel rates and the use of hotel suites. These guidelines pertain only to the use of hotels by directors and employees; they do not specifically apply to the use of hotels for conferences and other programmatic purposes. The only exception is when a suite is used for business purposes; even then, the use requires the prior approval of the chief executive officer. The guidelines expect avoidance of locations where a sports competition or other special event is taking place, or where a particular hotel is hosting a major convention or similar event.

Meals: As a general proposition, a charitable organization can pay for meals for the board, employees, and the like, where done in a business context. The standards are *reasonableness* and *cost consciousness*. There should not be payment or reimbursement for meals that are lavish or extravagant. There should be appropriate documentation of the amounts incurred and the business purpose for them.

7.5 Can a board member borrow money from a religious nonprofit organization?

In general, the answer is yes. There are, however, several aspects to keep in mind. One is the matter of perception. A form of behavior may be legally permissible, yet still look bad. This type of transaction also has the negative connotation of *self-dealing*. Nearly all charitable organizations can lawfully engage in forms of self-dealing, but they must be prepared to withstand charges of potential wrongdoing.

Once again, the standard of *reasonableness* applies. There will not be private inurement in a loan to a board member if the features of the transaction are reasonable. The factors governing reasonableness in this situation are the reason for the loan, the likelihood of repayment, the amount of the loan, whether it is memorialized in a note, the rate of interest, the extent and amount of security, the arrangements for repayment, and the length of the borrowing term. From the standpoint of the organization, the borrowing is an investment, but those same dollars could be invested in a more conventional and secure manner. The state attorney general is likely to look closely at this type of borrowing, particularly where the loan is not being paid according to the terms of the note.

7.6 Can a religious nonprofit organization purchase or rent property from a board member?

The simple answer is yes. These circumstances have to be tested against the same considerations as those involving a loan to a board member. The standard is one of reasonableness and the transaction would be a form of self-dealing.

The factors governing reasonableness in these situations are the specific reasons for rental of that particular property, the amount of the rent, whether the arrangement is memorialized in a lease, and the length of the lease term.

7.7 In addition to expenses, what else should a religious nonprofit organization be concerned about?

The tests of what is *reasonable* and *prudent* are overarching; they apply to all expenditures, including legal and fundraising fees.

There are two other areas of some sensitivity: (1) the location of board meetings and (2) competitive bidding.

Expenses for board meetings are the subject of the *New York Settlement*, discussed above. The guidelines there are quite useful in setting general parameters. The settlement document states that the primary factors to be considered in selecting locations for board meetings (including meetings of committees) are the programs, purposes, and costs of the meetings. The charitable organization is to take into account the programmatic benefits of the location, whether it has existing facilities already available, the cost of travel and hotel accommodations, seasonal factors, the feasibility of having only a delegation of the board attending the meeting instead of the full board, the feasibility of paying for program participants to travel to the organization rather than having the board travel to their location, and the scheduling of committee or board meetings on consecutive days. The board must approve in advance the location of all of its meetings.

 NOTE: This matter of the full board attending meetings or educational functions can be problematic, particularly where the surroundings are objectively luxurious.

Where a committee meeting is held at a time other than a full meeting of the board, the committee must approve the site and date of the meeting in advance. The meeting minutes must specify the purpose of any meeting held and the reason for the site selected, if the meeting is not held at a facility of the organization.

Concerning competitive bidding, there are no legal requirements other than the very general one of *prudent behavior*. The *New York Settlement* documents require that all contracts, including leases and contracts for professional services, be procured via competitive procedures to the maximum extent feasible. Moreover, the awards are to go to firms whose "experience and capabilities are most advantageous" to the organization.

The *New York Settlement* requires that these contracts be in writing and state the fees or rates to be charged, the time for completion, and the estimated total cost. All contracts in excess of $50,000 must be the subject of written proposals or competitive bids. When the organization evaluates proposals from qualified vendors, the primary consideration is to be cost. Other factors to be taken into account are prior experience, reputation, location, and minority participation.

CHAPTER 8

Acquiring Tax-Exempt Status

8.1 Are all nonprofit organizations tax-exempt organizations?

No. The concept of the *nonprofit organization* is different from that of the *tax-exempt organization*. The term *tax-exempt organization* usually is used to mean an organization that is exempt, in whole or in part, from the federal income tax.

To be tax-exempt, it is not sufficient that an organization be structured as a nonprofit organization. The organization must meet specific statutory and other regulatory criteria to qualify for the tax-exempt status.

Some nonprofit organizations cannot qualify as certain types of tax-exempt organizations under the federal tax law. For example, a nonprofit organization that engages in a substantial amount of lobbying cannot be a tax-exempt charitable organization. Some nonprofit organizations are ineligible for any category of tax exemption. For example, an organization that provides a substantial amount of commercial-type insurance cannot be a tax-exempt charitable or social welfare organization, and may not fit within any other classification of exempt entities.

8.2 Are all tax-exempt organizations nonprofit organizations?

No. In almost all cases, however, a tax-exempt organization is a nonprofit entity. An example of an exception is an instrumentality of the U.S. government, which is likely to have been created by statute rather than as a nonprofit organization. Another illustration is the limited liability company, which can qualify for exemption despite not being a *nonprofit* entity in the conventional sense of the term.

8.3 Concerning tax exemption, what taxes are involved?

The term *tax-exempt organization* usually is used to mean an organization that is exempt, in whole or in part, from the federal income tax. There are other federal taxes for which there may be an exemption, such as certain excise and Social Security taxes.

State laws have several bases enabling an organization to qualify for a tax exemption. Taxes may be levied, at the state level, on income, franchise, sales, use, tangible property, intangible property, and real property. The law varies dramatically from state to state as to the categories of exemptions that are available.

Frequently, the law providing exemption for nonprofit organizations from state income tax tracks the rules for exemption from federal income tax. Therefore, the federal rules are usually the place to start.

8.4 How many categories of tax-exempt organizations are provided for in the federal income tax law?

Most tax-exempt organizations under the federal tax law are those that are described in Section 501(c)(1)–(27) of the Code. Other Code provisions that provide for income tax exemption are Sections 521 and 526–529. Depending on how these provisions are parsed and the breadth of the term *tax-exempt organization* used, there are at least 72 categories of tax-exempt organizations provided for in the federal income tax law.

The most frequently utilized categories of tax-exempt organizations are contained in Section 501(c)(1)–(7) of the Internal Revenue Code:

- ("501(c)(1)")—corporations organized under Acts of Congress such as Federal Credit Unions (26 U.S.C. § 501(c)(1))
- ("501(c)(2)")—title-holding corporations for exempt organizations (26 U.S.C. § 501(c)(2))
- ("501(c)(3)")—charitable, nonprofit, religious, and educational organizations (26 U.S.C. § 501(c)(3))
- ("501(c)(4)")—social welfare organizations (26 U.S.C. § 501(c)(4))
- ("501(c)(5)")—labor organizations (26 U.S.C. § 501(c)(5))
- ("501(c)(6)")—business leagues and chambers of commerce (26 U.S.C. § 501(c)(6))
- ("501(c)(7)")—social clubs (26 U.S.C. § 501(c)(7))

8.5 What are the regulations accompanying the federal tax law concerning charitable organizations and the advancement of religion?

The advancement of religion has long been considered a charitable purpose, although the scope of this category of charitable endeavors is imprecise because of the separate enumeration in the federal tax law of religious activities as being in furtherance of exempt purposes. The concept of advancement of religion includes construction or maintenance of a church building, monument, memorial window, or burial ground, and collateral services such as the provision of music, payment of salaries to employees of religious organizations, dissemination of religious doctrines, maintenance of missions, and distribution of religious literature.

This category of tax exemption includes organizations the works of which extend to the advancement of particular religions, religious sects, or religious doctrines, as well as religion in general.

8.6 What is the *public policy doctrine* and its impact on religious nonprofit organizations, including racial discrimination, gender-based discrimination, and other forms of discrimination?

Bob Jones University, a private, protestant-fundamentalist, liberal arts university located in Greenville, South Carolina, because of its interpretation of Biblical principles, denied "admission to applicants engaged in an interracial marriage or known to advocate interracial marriage or dating." The University had received a ruling letter in 1942, confirming its tax-exempt status.

A case involving the University was decided by the Supreme Court May 24, 1983. The Court in an 8–1 decision, speaking through Chief Justice Burger, ruled that tax exemption for charitable organizations may be granted only where organizations are operating in conformity with public policy, and that discrimination on the basis of race in private schools (including religious ones) is contrary to public policy; the Court cited Congress's refusal to intervene as proof that it approved of the IRS's construction of the statute.

Although the reach of this Supreme Court decision has not been extensive, certainly the public policy doctrine will be applied far beyond the scope of racial discrimination and private schools. In one case, the government contended that an organization was ineligible for tax exemption because it engaged in violent and illegal activities. It is clear that the IRS will continue to apply the rule that an organization must satisfy the public policy test to qualify under IRC § 501(c)(3). For example, in determining whether activities such as demonstrations, economic boycotts, strikes, and picketing are permissible means of furthering charitable ends, the IRS adheres to the public policy doctrine.

8.7 How does a nonprofit organization become a tax-exempt organization?

To be tax-exempt, an organization must meet the specific statutory and other regulatory criteria for the exempt status it is seeking. This is true for both federal and state tax exemptions.

The process for acquiring one or more state tax exemptions varies from state to state. Usually the procedure entails filing a form, accompanied by an explanation of the organization's programs, so the tax authorities can assess the suitability of the organization for the exemption(s) being sought. The criteria for a tax exemption, however, are basically established by a statute.

The federal income tax exemption is available to organizations that satisfy the appropriate criteria stated in applicable provisions of the Internal Revenue Code.

Thus, Congress ultimately grants the federal income tax (and other federal tax) exemption. The IRS does not grant tax-exempt status; the agency grants *recognition* of tax-exempt status.

Consequently, whether an organization is entitled to tax exemption, on either an initial or an ongoing basis, is a matter of statutory law. It is Congress that, by statute, defines the categories of organization that are eligible for tax exemption, and it is Congress that determines whether a type of tax exemption should be continued.

 NOTE: It should come as no surprise that this matter of eligibility for tax exemption has been litigated. The government, however, frequently wins these cases—the courts repeatedly have held that Congress has great discretion in this area.

8.8 Is a nonprofit organization required to apply to the IRS for tax-exempt status?

There are two aspects of this answer. A very literal answer to the question is no. This is because, as noted, the IRS does not grant tax-exempt status; that is a tax feature of an organization that is available to it by operation of law.

What the IRS does is grant *recognition* of tax-exempt status. This role of the IRS in recognizing the exempt status of organizations is part of its overall practice of evaluating the tax status of organizations.

8.9 What does *recognition of tax exemption* mean?

Eligibility for tax-exempt status is different from *recognition* of that status. When the IRS *recognizes* the exempt status of an organization, it makes a written determination that the entity constitutes a tax-exempt organization. When exercising this function, the IRS reviews, analyzes, and interprets the law, and agrees with the organization that it is exempt. The process is almost always begun by the organization's filing an application for recognition of tax-exempt status with the IRS.

8.10 Are certain organizations required by law to seek recognition and exempt status from the IRS?

Yes. As a general rule, an organization desiring tax-exempt status pursuant to the federal tax law is not *required* to secure recognition of tax exemption from the IRS. Nonetheless, an organization *may*, on its own volition, seek recognition of tax-exempt status.

There are, however, two categories of organizations that are required by law to seek recognition of tax-exempt status from the IRS. Most charitable organizations (with the exception of churches) must seek this recognition. Likewise, certain employee benefit organizations must seek exemption recognition. Moreover, an organization that wishes to be a central organization providing tax exemption on a group basis for subordinate organizations must first obtain recognition of its own tax-exempt status.

For this purpose, a *charitable organization* is an entity that is organized and operated primarily for purposes such as charitable, educational, scientific, and religious. (This category also includes organizations that foster national or international amateur sports competition, prevent cruelty to children or animals, and test for public safety, as well as cooperative hospital service organizations and cooperative service organizations of operating educational organizations.) These entities are collectively referenced in Section 501(c)(3) of the Internal Revenue Code.

8.11 What are the advantages of obtaining recognition of exempt status from the IRS?

The advantages to be gained by obtaining recognition of exempt status include the comfort of knowing that the IRS agrees that the organization qualifies for exempt status, the classification (in the case of charitable organizations) is assurance to donors that their contributions are deductible as charitable gifts, the status is a pathway to state tax exemption(s), and the eligibility for various nonprofit mailing privileges.

8.12 Are there charitable organizations that can be tax-exempt without having to file an application for recognition of tax exemption?

Yes. The following *charitable* organizations can be tax-exempt without having to file an application for recognition of tax exemption: (1) churches (including synagogues and mosques), interchurch organizations, local units of a church, conventions and associations of churches, and integrated auxiliaries of churches, and (2) organizations (other than private foundations and supporting organizations) that have gross receipts that normally are not in excess of $5,000 annually. However, a religious organization that wishes to be a central organization providing tax exemption on a group basis for subordinate organizations must first obtain recognition of its own tax-exempt status.

8.13 Should an organization that is not required to obtain recognition of tax-exempt status think about doing it anyway?

Yes. An organization that is not required to obtain recognition of tax-exempt status should think about doing it anyway. For the most part, the considerations are the same as those underlying the potential for any other ruling request. That is, the organization may simply want the comfort of having the IRS on record as agreeing with its qualification for tax exemption.

8.14 Are copies of exemption applications available to the public from the IRS?

Yes. The application for recognition of tax exemption and any supporting documents filed by most tax-exempt organizations must be made accessible to the public by the IRS where a favorable determination letter is issued to an organization.

An organization for which application for recognition of exemption is open to public inspection may request in writing that information relating to a trade secret, patent, process, style of work, or apparatus be withheld. The information will be withheld from public inspection if the IRS determines that its disclosure would adversely affect the organization.

An application and related materials may be inspected at the appropriate field office of the IRS. Inspection may also occur at the National Office of the IRS; a request for inspection may be directed to the Assistant to the Commissioner (Public Affairs), 1111 Constitution Avenue, N.W., Washington, DC 20224.

Once an organization's exemption application and related and supporting documents become open to public inspection, the determination letter issued by the IRS becomes publicly available. Also open to inspection are any technical advice memoranda issued with respect to any favorable ruling.

8.15 What are the *distribution rules*?

In 1996, Congress enacted distribution rules in this context. These rules are amplified by tax regulations, which were issued in the final form in 1999 (for tax-exempt organizations generally) and 2000 (for private foundations).

NOTE: The distribution rules apply to organizations that are required to file information returns annually. Churches, as a general rule, are not required to file an annual information return.

Generally, under these rules, anyone who requests a copy of one or more of the three most recent annual returns, in person or in writing, must be provided these copies. The individual requesting them may retain these copies.

If a request for copies is made in person, the organization may provide them immediately. Response to a request in writing must be made within 30 days. The only charge that can be imposed for these copies is a reasonable fee for photocopying and mailing costs.

This annual return distribution requirement extends to all schedules and attachments filed with the IRS. For charitable organizations, this includes Schedule A. An organization (other than a private foundation) is not required, however, to disclose the parts of the return that identify names and addresses of contributors to the organization. Moreover, a tax-exempt organization is required to disclose its unrelated business income tax return (Form 990-T).

There are rules concerning the documents that must be made available by an organization that is recognized as tax-exempt under a group exemption.

A tax-exempt organization must make the specified documents available for public inspection at its principal, regional, and district offices. The documents generally have to be available for inspection on the day of the request during the organization's normal business hours. An office of an organization is considered a regional or district office only if it has three or more paid full-time employees (or paid employees, whether part-time or full-time, whose aggregate number of paid hours per week is at least 120).

Certain sites where the organization's employees perform solely exempt function activities are excluded from consideration as a regional or district office. The rules prescribe how an organization that does not maintain a permanent office or whose office has very limited hours during certain times of the year can comply with the public inspection requirements.

A tax-exempt organization must accept requests for copies made in person at the same place and time that the information must be available for public inspection. An organization is generally required to provide the copies on the day of the request. In unusual circumstances, an organization is permitted to provide the requested copies on the next business day.

Where a request is made in writing, an exempt organization must furnish the copies within 30 days from the date the request is received. If an organization requires advance payment of a reasonable fee for copying and mailing, it may provide the copies within 30 days from the date it receives payment (rather than from the date of the request).

There are rules that provide guidance as to what constitutes a *request*, when a request is considered *received*, and when copies are considered *provided*. Instead of requesting a copy of an entire annual return, individuals may request a specific portion of the document. A principal, regional, or district office of an organization may use an agent to process requests for copies.

The reasonable fee a tax-exempt organization is permitted to charge for copies may be no more than the fees charged by the IRS for copies of exempt organization returns and related documents. This is $1.00 for the first page and $.15 for each subsequent page. In addition, actual postage costs can be charged. An organization is permitted to collect payment in advance of providing the requested copies.

If an organization receives a written request for copies with payment not enclosed, and the organization requires payment in advance, the organization must request payment within seven days from the date it receives the request. Payment is deemed to occur on the day an organization receives the money, check (provided the check subsequently clears), or money order. An organization is required to accept payment made in the form of money or money order and, when the request is made in writing, to accept payment by personal check. An organization is permitted, though not required, to accept other forms of payment. To protect requesters from unexpected fees where an exempt organization does not require prepayment and where a requester does not enclose prepayment with a request, an organization must receive consent from a requester before providing copies for which the fee charged for copying and postage is in excess of $20.

8.16 What is the disclosure requirement with respect to applications for recognition of exemption?

The inspection requirement described earlier is likewise applicable with respect to applications for recognition of exemption. Again, certain information can be withheld from public inspection, such as trade secrets and patents.

8.17 Do the distribution requirements apply to applications for recognition of exemption?

Yes. All of the rules as to distribution of documents, and the exceptions to them, are applicable with respect to applications for recognition of exemption.

8.18 What is an individual able to do if denied a copy of the exemption application or a copy of an annual return?

The tax regulations provide guidance for an individual denied inspection, or a copy, of an annual return. Basically, the individual must provide the IRS with a statement that describes the reason that the individual believes the denial was in violation of legal requirements.

8.19 Are there any exceptions to the inspection requirement?

Not really. No excuses are allowed. As noted, certain donor information need not be provided. Otherwise, as long as the request is made during regular business hours, copies of the returns must be made available for inspection.

8.20 Are there any exceptions to the distribution requirement?

Yes, under two circumstances an exempt organization is relieved of the obligation to provide copies of the returns. An exception is available where the organization has made the documents *widely available*. The other exception obtains where the IRS determines, following application by the organization, that the organization is subject to a *harassment campaign* and that a waiver of the disclosure obligation is in the public interest.

8.21 What does the term *widely available* mean?

A tax-exempt organization is not required to comply with requests for copies of its annual returns if the organization has made them widely available. An organization can make its annual information return *widely available* by posting the document on its web page on the Internet or by having the applicable document posted on another organization's web page as part of a database of similar materials.

For this exception to be available, however, six criteria must be followed:

1. The entity maintaining the web page must have procedures for ensuring the reliability and accuracy of the application or return that is posted.
2. This entity must take reasonable precautions to prevent alteration, destruction, or accidental loss of the posted document.
3. The application or return must be posted in the same format used by the IRS to post forms and publications on the web page of the IRS.
4. The web page that is used must clearly inform readers that the document is available and provide instructions for downloading it.
5. When downloaded and printed in hard copy, the document must be in substantially the same form as the original application or return and contain the same information as provided in the original document filed with the IRS (other than information that can be lawfully withheld).
6. A person can access and download the document without payment of a fee to the organization maintaining the web page.

The IRS is authorized to prescribe, by revenue procedure or other guidance, other methods that an organization can use to make its annual return widely available.

An organization that makes its return widely available must inform individuals who request copies how and where to obtain the requested document.

8.22 What does the term *harassment campaign* mean?

Generally, a *harassment campaign* exists where an organization receives a group of requests, and the relevant facts and circumstances show that the purpose of the group of requests is to disrupt the operations of the exempt organization rather than to collect information.

These facts and circumstances include a sudden increase in the number of requests, an extraordinary number of requests made through form letters or similarly worded correspondence, evidence of a purpose to significantly deter the organization's employees or volunteers from pursuing the organization's exempt purpose, requests that contain language hostile to the organization, direct evidence of bad faith by organizers of the purported harassment campaign, evidence that the organization has already provided the requested documents to a member of the purported harassing group, and a demonstration by the exempt organization that it routinely provides copies of its documents upon request.

The regulations contain examples that evaluate whether particular situations constitute a harassment campaign and whether an organization has a reasonable basis for believing that a request is part of this type of campaign.

An organization can disregard requests in excess of two per 30-day period or four per year from the same individual or from the same address. There are

NOTE: Organizations may not suspend compliance with a request for copies from a representative of the news media even though the organization believes or knows that the request is part of a harassment campaign.

procedures for requesting a determination that an organization is subject to a harassment campaign and the treatment of requests for copies while a request for a determination is pending.

NOTE: These two exceptions are exceptions only from the rules concerning *distribution* of returns. They are not exceptions from the *inspection* requirements.

8.23 What is the procedure for seeking recognition of tax-exempt status?

The IRS has promulgated detailed rules by which a ruling as to recognition of exemption is to be sought.

In almost all instances, the process is begun by the filing of an application for recognition of tax-exempt status. These applications are available as IRS forms. An organization seeking recognition of exemption as a charitable organization should file Form 1023. (Nearly all other applicant organizations file Form 1024, although farmers, fruit growers, and like associations file Form 1028.) For a few categories of exempt organizations, there is no application form by which to seek recognition of tax exemption; in that case, the request is made by letter.

The Form 1023 application, discussed in detail below, includes a description of the purposes and activities of the organization, its fundraising plans, the composition of its board of directors, its compensation practices, and financial information. The organization's articles of organization and bylaws and perhaps other documents must be attached.

For charitable organizations, this procedure also involves classification as charitable entities for purposes of the charitable giving rules and categorization as public charities or private foundations.

8.24 What is an *IRS determination letter*? What is an *IRS ruling*?

Recognition of exemption by the IRS from an office outside Washington, DC, is termed a *determination letter*. This type of recognition from the National Office of the IRS in Washington, DC, is termed a *ruling*. In practice, both of these types of determinations are often generically referred to as *rulings*—and that will frequently be the case in this discussion.

8.25 **Where are these applications filed?**

Historically, applications for recognition of exemption were filed with the appropriate IRS key district director's office, determined in relation to the district in which the principal place of business of the organization was located. As part of the reorganization of the IRS, however, applications for recognition of exemption are filed with the IRS Service Center in Cincinnati, Ohio. Infrequently, there will be occasion to file the application with the National Office of the IRS.

8.26 **How long does it take the IRS to process an application for recognition of exemption?**

It is difficult to generalize as to the length of time required by the IRS to process an application for recognition of tax exemption. Three of the critical factors are the complexity and/or sensitivity of the case, the completeness of the application (and related documents), and the workload of the IRS representative who will be reviewing the file and preparing the ruling.

For rather straightforward filings, the organization should plan on an IRS processing period of about three to six months. The IRS is likely to have questions; this can lengthen the period. Once in a while, a case is referred to the IRS's National Office, and that development can have a bearing on the overall time period. The IRS, however, has developed a fast-track system, whereby applications that are in pristine condition can zip through the agency in a mere four or five weeks.

It is difficult to predict how long it will take for a ruling (a favorable one) to be issued in individual filings. An application virtually brimming with hearty exempt organization issues can sail through the process, without any IRS inquiries, and result in a ruling in a few months. Yet a simple case, one lacking in any issues of substance, can be worried over by an IRS exempt organizations specialist for an agonizingly long period of time.

8.27 **Is there a process by which the applicant organization can request the IRS to expedite the processing of its application?**

Yes. There is a process by which the applicant organization can request the IRS to expedite the processing of the application. For this to work, the organization must convince the IRS that there is a substantive reason as to why its application should be considered out of order (such as a large gift or grant that will be lost if recognition is not quickly extended). Understandably, out of overall fairness, the IRS is reluctant to grant expedited consideration of these applications, so the case for a quick processing must be a persuasive one.

The IRS has, however, been known to formally decline to expedite consideration of an exemption application (for the record)—and then process it speedily anyway.

8.28 How long does an exemption ruling remain in effect?

These rulings are not accompanied by an expiration date. Generally, an organization the tax-exempt status of which has been recognized by the IRS can rely on that determination as long as there are no substantial changes in its character, purposes, or methods of operation. Of course, a change in the law can void a ruling or cause a reevaluation of it.

8.29 Once the ruling is obtained, is it a recommended practice to periodically review the application to determine whether substantial change has occurred?

Yes. Once the ruling is obtained, it is a recommended practice to periodically review the application, to see whether it reflects current programs and other practices. A ruling from the IRS is only as valid as the facts on which it is based—and a substantial change in purposes and the like could void or at least threaten the validity of the ruling.

8.30 What happens if there is a substantial change in an organization's character, purposes, or methods of operation?

First, determining whether one of these changes is *substantial* is not always easy and can be a matter of considerable judgment. An applicant organization should endeavor to disclose as much information as is reasonably possible, to preclude a later contention that some material fact was omitted.

In practice, however, this rule is rarely followed. As the years go by, organizations can evolve into and out of varying programs and purposes, and/or change management and methods of operation, and never give a thought to what was said in the exemption application (or, for that matter, in the articles of organization or bylaws). This is not a good practice; a periodic review in this regard is recommended. There are organizations in operation today that have strayed so far from their original purposes and operations, and into nonexempt activities, that they would have their exempt status revoked were the IRS to learn the facts.

8.31 Is it necessary to report insubstantial changes to the IRS as part of the filing of the organization's annual information return?

Yes. Even if these changes are not substantial, they are to be reported to the IRS as part of the filing of the annual information return.

8.32 Will the IRS issue a ruling to an organization in advance of its operations?

In general, yes. The basic rule is this: A determination letter or ruling will be issued by the IRS to an organization where its application for recognition of exemption and supporting documents establish that it meets the requirements of the category of exemption that it claimed. Tax-exempt status for an organization will be recognized by the IRS in advance of operations where the entity's proposed activities are described in sufficient detail to permit a conclusion that the organization will clearly meet the pertinent statutory requirements.

The organization should not merely restate its purposes or state only that its proposed activities will be in furtherance of the organization's purposes. This approach does not satisfy the requirements and serves only to put the IRS on notice that the application has been prepared by those who lack experience with the rules.

The applicant organization is expected to fully describe the activities in which it expects to engage, including the standards, criteria, procedures, or other means adopted or planned for carrying out the activities, the anticipated sources of receipts, and the nature of contemplated expenditures.

Where an organization cannot demonstrate, to the satisfaction of the IRS, that its proposed activities will qualify it for recognition of exemption, a record of actual operations may be required before a ruling is issued.

8.33 How much information must be provided to the IRS?

There is no precise standard in this regard. As noted, the IRS expects "sufficient details" and "full descriptions." Thus, an organization that took this issue to court lost its bid to acquire recognition of exemption because it "failed to supply such information as would enable a conclusion that when operational, if ever . . . [the organization] will conduct all of its activities in a manner which will accomplish its exempt purposes." The entity was chided by the court for offering only "vague generalizations" about its ostensibly planned activities.

Likewise, this court concluded that an organization could not be exempt, because it did not provide a "meaningful explanation" of its activities to the IRS. In another instance, a court found that an organization's failure to respond "completely or candidly" to many of the inquiries of the IRS precluded it from receiving a determination as to its tax-exempt status.

An organization is considered to have made the required "threshold showing," however, where it describes its activities in "sufficient detail" to permit a conclusion that the entity will meet the pertinent requirements, particularly where it answered all of the questions propounded by the IRS.

8.34 Is it necessary to treat the application as a business plan?

The following statements by two courts summarize what this aspect of the process comes down to: The law "requires that the organization establish measurable standards and criteria for its operation as an exempt organization"; yet this standard does not necessitate "some sort of metaphysical proof of future events."

This is not the time to hold back information; it is foolish for an organization to fail to be recognized as an exempt organization on the ground that it refused to submit suitable information. The organization should be willing to tell its story fully, treating the application as a business plan. This document is, after all, a public one, and its proper preparation should be regarded as a first step in presenting the organization's justification for existence and tax-exempt status.

This application process is, in essence, a burden-of-proof issue—with the burden on the would-be exempt organization. Moreover, there is a negative presumption: When the representatives of an organization fail to submit the appropriate factual information to the IRS, an inference arises that the facts involved would denigrate the organization's cause.

8.35 What happens if the IRS decides the application is incomplete?

If an application for recognition of tax exemption does not contain the requisite information, IRS procedures authorize it to return the application to the applicant organization without considering it on its merits.

As noted, the application will be returned to the organization—not to anyone on a power of attorney (Form 2848) (such as a lawyer or accountant), with obvious implications. A competent representative of the nonprofit organization in this regard should have no experience with this rule.

The application for recognition of tax exemption as submitted by a would-be exempt organization will not be processed by the IRS until the application is at least *substantially completed*.

8.36 What is a *substantially completed* application?

An application for recognition of exemption is a substantially completed one when it:

1. Is signed by an authorized individual.
2. Includes an employer identification number.
3. Includes information regarding any previously filed federal income tax and/or exempt organization information returns.
4. Includes a statement of receipts and expenditures and a balance sheet for the current year and the three preceding years (or the years the organization has been in existence, if less than four years), although if the organization has not yet commenced operations, or has not completed one full accounting period, a proposed budget for two full accounting periods and a current statement of assets and liabilities is acceptable.
5. Includes a narrative statement of proposed activities and a narrative description of anticipated receipts and contemplated expenditures.
6. Includes a copy of the document by which the organization was established, signed by a principal officer, or is accompanied by a written declaration signed by an authorized individual certifying that the document is a complete and accurate copy of the original or otherwise meets the requirement that it be a conformed copy.

7. If the organizing document is a set of articles of incorporation, includes evidence that it was filed with and approved by an appropriate state official (such as a copy of the certificate of incorporation), or includes a copy of the articles of incorporation accompanied by a written declaration signed by an authorized individual that the copy is a complete and accurate copy of the original document that was filed with and approved by the state, and stating the date of filing with the state.
8. If the organization has adopted bylaws, and includes a current copy of that document, certified as being current by an authorized individual.
9. Is accompanied by the correct user fee.

The application for recognition of exemption submitted by charitable organizations requests information concerning the composition of the entity's governing body, any relationship with other *organizations*, the nature of its fundraising program, and a variety of other matters.

8.37 Is the application for recognition of exemption an important document for a nonprofit organization?

Yes, this application is a significant legal document for an exempt organization, and it should be prepared and retained accordingly. Yet, an unduly high proportion of exempt organizations cannot locate a copy of their application for recognition of tax exemption.

The proper preparation of an application for recognition of tax exemption involves far more than merely responding to the questions on a government form. It is a process not unlike the preparation of a prospectus for a business in conformity with the securities law requirements. Every statement made in the application should be carefully considered. Some of the questions may force the applicant organization to focus on matters that solid management practices should cause it to consider, even in the absence of the application requirements. The application is a nicely constructed and factually sweeping document, and it should be approached and prepared with care and respect.

The prime objectives in this regard must be accuracy and completeness; it is essential that all material facts be correctly and fully stated. Of course, the determination as to which facts are material and the marshaling of these facts requires judgment. Moreover, the manner in which the answers are phrased can be extremely significant; this exercise can be more one of art than of science.

The preparer or reviewer of the application should be able to anticipate the concerns the contents of the application may cause the IRS and to see that the application is properly prepared, while simultaneously minimizing the likelihood of conflict with the IRS. Organizations that are entitled to tax-exempt status have been denied recognition of exemption by the IRS, or have caused the process of gaining recognition to be more protracted, because of unartful phraseologies in the application that motivated the IRS to muster a case that the organization does not qualify for exemption.

Therefore, the application for recognition of tax exemption should be regarded as an important legal document and prepared accordingly. The fact that the application is available for public inspection only underscores the need for thoughtful preparation.

8.38 How long does it take to prepare an application for recognition of tax exemption?

It is impossible to generalize on this point. The pertinent factors include, as noted, the complexity of the organization, the extent to which the factual information and supporting documents are readily available, and the skill and expertise of those who prepare and review the document.

Nonetheless, apparently there is a way to produce some averages of time expenditures in this regard. Thus, in conjunction with the Form 1023, it is the view of the IRS that the estimated average time required to keep records so as to be able to prepare the application (not including any schedules) is 89 hours and 25 minutes. If every schedule had to be prepared (Schedules A–H), another 87 hours would be required. (The complexity of the current form is illustrated by the fact that the previous one required about 55 hours of recordkeeping.) The agency estimates that learning about the law or the form requires 5 hours and 10 minutes, and preparation of the form entails 9 hours and 39 minutes.

8.39 Is there a charge for the processing of an application for recognition of exemption?

Yes, the IRS levies a user fee for processing an organization's application for recognition of exemption. This fee must be paid at the time of the filing of the application.

Under the current schedule, the fee for the processing of one of these applications is $750, where the applicant has gross receipts that annually exceed $10,000 over a four-year period. For smaller organizations, the fee is $300. A group exemption letter fee is $900.

8.40 Can an application for recognition of exemption be referred to the National Office of the IRS?

Yes. The IRS representative considering the application must refer to the National Office of the IRS an application for recognition of tax exemption that (1) presents questions the answers to which are not specifically covered by the Internal Revenue Code, Department of Treasury regulations, an IRS revenue ruling, or court decision published in the IRS's *Internal Revenue Bulletin*, or (2) has been specifically reserved by an IRS revenue procedure and/or *Internal Revenue Manual* instructions for handling by the National Office for purposes of establishing uniformity or centralized control of designated categories of cases. In these instances, the National Office is to consider the application, issue a ruling directly to the organization, and send a copy of the ruling to the appropriate IRS office.

NOTE: One of the purposes of the centralization efforts by the IRS in this context is to centralize the processing of exemption applications so as to consolidate expertise and increase the efficiency of the process.

8.41 Can the applicant organization seek the assistance of the National Office?

Yes. If, during the course of consideration of an application for recognition of tax exemption, an applicant organization believes that its case involves an issue as to which there is no published precedent, the organization may ask the IRS to request technical advice from the National Office of the IRS.

8.42 Can an application for recognition of exemption be withdrawn?

Yes. An application for recognition of tax exemption filed with the IRS may be withdrawn, upon the written request of an authorized representative of the organization, at any time prior to the issuance of an initial adverse ruling. When an application is withdrawn, it and all supporting documents are retained by the IRS.

8.43 If an organization is denied recognition of exemption, may it later reapply?

Absolutely—the key is correction of the problem or problems that caused the denial in the first instance.

An organization may reapply for recognition of tax exemption if it was previously denied recognition, where the facts involved are materially changed so that the organization has come into compliance with the applicable requirements. For example, a charitable organization that was refused recognition of exemption because of excessive lobbying activities, by reason of the expenditure test, may subsequently reapply for recognition of exemption for any tax year following the first tax year as to which the recognition was denied. Essentially, the reapplication form must include information demonstrating that the organization was in compliance with the law during the full tax year immediately preceding the date of reapplication and that the organization will not knowingly operate in a manner that would disqualify it from exemption.

8.44 What is the effective date of these rulings?

A determination letter or ruling recognizing tax exemption usually is effective as of the date of formation of the organization, where its purposes and activities during the period prior to the date of the determination letter or ruling were consistent with the requirements for tax exemption.

If the organization is required to alter its activities or to make substantive amendments to its enabling instrument, the determination letter or ruling recognizing its tax-exempt status is effective as of the date specified in the determination letter or ruling. If a nonsubstantive amendment is made, tax exemption ordinarily is recognized as of the date the entity was formed.

8.45 To what extent can the organization rely on its ruling?

In general, an organization can rely on a determination letter or ruling from the IRS recognizing its tax exemption. Reliance is not available, however, if there is a material change, inconsistent with tax exemption, in the character, purpose, or method of operation of the organization.

8.46 How does an organization remain tax-exempt?

The simple answer is that an organization remains tax-exempt by staying in compliance with the rules governing the particular category of tax exemption. These rules are the most pronounced for charitable organizations.

Thus, for a charitable organization to remain tax-exempt, it must meet a variety of tests on an ongoing basis, including the organizational requirements, the private inurement and private benefit limitations, the lobbying restrictions, the political campaign activities prohibition, and avoidance of too many unrelated business activities.

8.47 When might an organization's tax exemption be revoked?

In general, an organization's tax exemption is revoked when the IRS determines that the organization is materially out of compliance with one or more of the requirements underlying its tax-exempt status. For example, in the case of a charitable organization, the IRS may have concluded that it engaged in a private inurement transaction or a political campaign activity.

The IRS learns of bases for revocation of tax exemption in a variety of ways. The information may come to it as the result of an audit. Someone may have provided the IRS information involving some actual or perceived wrongdoing. Often the IRS obtains information leading to a revocation from the media.

8.48 If an organization loses its tax-exempt status, can it reacquire it?

Generally, yes. An organization qualifies for tax-exempt status if it meets the statutory criteria for the particular category of exempt organization involved. If it fails to satisfy the criteria, it no longer qualifies for exemption. If it resumes qualification, then its tax-exempt status must be restored. These analyses are made on a year-by-year basis.

For tax-exempt organizations that must seek recognition of tax-exempt status, such as (non-church) charitable organizations, the process is more complex. When these exempt organizations lose their tax exemption, they can reacquire it, but they must reapply for recognition of exemption.

8.49 Are tax-exempt organizations completely immune from taxation?

No. Despite the term, a tax-exempt organization is not completely free from the prospect of taxation. Thus, nearly all exempt organizations are subject to tax on their unrelated business taxable income. Many types of tax-exempt organizations are subject to a tax if they engage in certain types of political activities. Public charities can be taxable if they undertake a substantial amount of lobbying activities or if they participate in a political campaign. Private foundations must pay an excise tax on their net investment income and are susceptible to a host of other excise taxes. Organizations such as social clubs, political organizations, and homeowners' organizations are taxable on their net investment income. State law also can impose taxes on entities otherwise classified as tax-exempt organizations.

8.50 Why would a church file an application with the IRS for recognition of its tax-exempt status?

Churches, unlike most other religious nonprofit organizations, are not required to obtain IRS recognition of their tax-exempt status. However, many churches apply for such recognition (by filing Form 1023) for numerous reasons.

The major consideration regarding obtaining tax-exempt status is that the IRS issues a *determination letter* on approval of the application. This determination letter can, for example, serve as official proof to a potential donor that a contemplated donation is tax-deductible. Additionally, in absence of the determination letter, the burden may shift to the donor if he or she is questioned by the IRS regarding the donation. A church would likely never want to place this burden upon the donor when doing so could cause the loss of future donations by the donor and possible negative publicity for the church.

The following is a list of additional benefits for a church that secures a determination letter from the IRS:

1. For a minister who wishes to elect out of the Social Security system, the determination letter provides proof the organization that ordained him or her is recognized as a church by the IRS. This can be particularly helpful to the minister.
2. The determination letter may serve as proof to state sales tax authorities that the organization is indeed tax-exempt and not subject to sales tax.
3. The determination letter may serve as proof to state and local tax authorities that the organization is tax-exempt and perhaps not subject to state and local income, property, franchise, and ad valorem taxes.

4. The determination letter is one of the documents usually used by the state when determining the organization's liability or exemption for state unemployment tax.

5. Many times, postmasters will accept the determination letter as proof of the organization's tax-exempt status and expeditiously grant special postage rates available for certain tax-exempt organizations.

8.51 Isn't the filing of an application for recognition by a church akin to the federal government licensing churches, a clear violation of religious liberties protected by the Constitution?

No. Churches, unlike other religious organizations, are not required to obtain IRS recognition of their tax-exempt status. Contrary to what some believe, however, the filing of the application (Form 1023) is not a licensing of the church by the federal government, but instead results in government recognition of the church's tax-exempt status and concurrence that the organization is, in fact, a church.

8.52 In view of the massive amount of government regulation of nonprofit organizations, why don't nonprofit organizations forfeit tax-exempt status and be treated for tax purposes the same as for-profit organizations?

For some nonprofit organizations, this course of action could be taken, looked at purely from a tax standpoint. This is because, for most of these entities, their expenses equal or *exceed* their income, so that there would not be any net taxable income in any event. Nonetheless, these organizations are not legally functioning on a *for-profit* basis. At the same time, an organization can be nonprofit and yet taxable.

Charitable organizations including religious nonprofits that are eligible to receive tax-deductible contributions would forfeit this tax feature if they were to convert to for-profit status.

8.53 What are the contents of the application?

NOTE: The reader may wish to have a copy of Form 1023 (June 2006) at hand while reviewing this portion of the chapter. The application is part of a packet that includes general instructions as to its preparation and both are available from the IRS and various commercial services and on the Internet.

This substantially revamped application, consisting of eleven parts, is designed to streamline the application process for charitable organizations, increase the amount of information provided to the IRS, and enable the agency to spot potentially abusive charities.

8.54   What is required in part I of Form 1023?

Part I of the Form 1023 requests basic information about the applicant organization and its representatives. Here the organization supplies its name, address, employer identification number, date of formation, web site address, and accounting period. If the organization is formed under the laws of a foreign country, the country must be identified.

The name and telephone number of the applicant organization's primary contact person must be provided. If the organization is represented by an *authorized representative* (such as a lawyer or accountant), the representative's name, and the name and address of the representative's firm, must be provided. A power of attorney (Form 2848) must be included if the organization wants the IRS to communicate with the representative.

If a person—who is not a trustee, director, officer, employee, or authorized representative of the organization—is paid, or promised payment, to help plan, manage, or advise the organization about its structure, activities, or its financial and tax matters, the person's name, the name and address of the person's firm, the amounts paid or promised to be paid, and a description of the person's role must be provided.

8.55   What is required in part II of Form 1023?

Part II of the Form 1023 requests information about the applicant organization's structure. The organization must be a corporation, a limited liability company, an unincorporated association, or a trust. A copy of the organization's articles of organization (articles of incorporation, articles of organization, constitution, trust agreement, or similar document) must be attached, including any amendments. If the organization has adopted bylaws, a copy of that document must also be provided.

8.56   What is required in part III of Form 1023?

Part III of the Form 1023 is designed to ensure that the applicant organization's organizing document contains the required provisions. This portion of the form focuses on the need for a correctly framed statement of purposes and a provision that states that net assets will be distributed for charitable purposes should the organization dissolve.

8.57   What is required in part IV of Form 1023?

Part IV of the Form 1023 requires an attachment describing the applicant organization's past, present, and planned activities. The organization is invited to attach representative copies of newsletters, brochures, and similar documents for supporting details. Because the application is accessible by the public, the organization is reminded that this statement of activities should be "thorough and accurate."

8.58 What is required in part V of Form 1023?

Part V of the Form 1023 requires information about the compensation of and other financial arrangements with the applicant organization's trustees, directors, officers, employees, and independent contractors.

The organization is required to list the names, titles, and mailing addresses of its trustees, directors, and officers. Their total annual compensation or proposed compensation for all services to the organization must be stated.

The organization must also list the names, titles, mailing addresses, and compensation amounts of each of its five highest compensated employees who receive or will receive compensation of more than $50,000 annually. Likewise, the organization must provide the names, names of businesses, mailing addresses, and compensation amounts of its five highest compensated independent contractors that receive or will receive compensation of more than $50,000 annually.

The organization must provide information as to whether any of its trustees, directors, or officers are related to each other through family or business relationships. It must describe any business relationship with any of its trustees, directors, or officers other than through their position as such. There must be an explanation if any of the trustees, directors, or officers are related to the organization's highest-compensated employees or highest-compensated independent contractors through family or business relationships.

For each of the trustees, directors, officers, highest-compensated employees, and highest-compensated independent contractors, the organization must provide their name, qualification, average hours worked, and duties. There must be an explanation if any of its trustees, directors, officers, highest-compensated employees, and highest-compensated independent contractors receive compensation from any other organization (tax-exempt or taxable) that is related to the organization through common control.

The organization is required to identify the practices it uses in establishing the compensation of its trustees, directors, officers, highest-compensated employees, and highest-compensated independent contractors. There are six recommended practices, including adherence to a conflict-of-interest policy, documentation of compensation arrangements, and/or use of compensation surveys or written offers from similarly situated organizations. If any of these practices are not followed, the organization is required to describe how it sets compensation for these persons.

The organization must explain whether it has adopted a conflict-of-interest policy. If such a policy has not been adopted, the organization must explain the procedures it follows to ensure that persons who have a conflict of interest will not have influence over the organization when setting their compensation and/or regarding business deals with themselves.

The organization is required to describe any compensation arrangements involving nonfixed payments (such as bonuses and revenue-based payments) with any of its trustees, directors, officers, highest-compensated employees, or highest-compensated independent contractors. If these arrangements exist, the organization must provide information such as how the amounts are determined, who is eligible for the payments, whether a limitation is placed on total compensation, and how reasonableness of compensation is determined. Information must be provided in connection with any other employees that receive annual nonfixed payments in excess of $50,000.

Information must be provided concerning any purchases or sales of goods, services, or assets from or to any trustees, directors, officers, highest-compensated employees, or highest-compensated independent contractors. Likewise, information must be provided as to any leases, other contracts, loans, or other arrangements with these persons or with organizations in which these persons have an interest (more than 35 percent) or serve as directors or officers, along with how the terms of such arrangements are or will be negotiated at arm's length and at no more than fair market value.

8.59 What is required in part VI of Form 1023?

Part VI of the Form 1023 requires the applicant organization to (1) describe any program involving the provision of goods, services, or funds to individuals or organizations; (2) explain whether, and if so how, any program limits the provision of goods, services, or funds to a specific individual or group of specific individuals; and (3) explain whether, and if so how, any individuals who receive goods, services, or funds through the organization's programs have a family or business relationship with any trustee, director, officer, highest-compensated employee, or highest-compensated independent contractor. The answers should pertain to past, present, and planned activities.

8.60 What is required in part VII of Form 1023?

Part VII of the Form 1023 relates to the history of the applicant organization. The organization must explain whether it has taken or will take over the activities of another organization, took over at least 25 percent of the fair market value of the net assets of another organization, or was established as the result of a conversion of an organization from for-profit to nonprofit status. The existence of any of these circumstances requires a filing of Schedule G.

If the organization is submitting the application more than 27 months after the end of the month in which it was legally formed, filing of Schedule E is required.

8.61 What is required in part VIII of Form 1023?

The applicant organization is required to submit information concerning many types of past, present, and planned activities, including:

* Support of or opposition to candidates in political campaigns;
* Attempts to influence legislation;
* Operation of bingo or other gaming activities;

- Fundraising, including mail solicitations; vehicle, boat, airplane, or similar contributions; foundation or government grant solicitations; and web site donations;
- Utilization of donor-advised funds;
- Affiliation with a governmental unit;
- Engagement in economic development;
- Development of the organization's facilities;
- Management of the organization's activities or facilities;
- Involvement in any joint ventures;
- Choosing exemption as a childcare organization under Section 501(k);
- Publishing, ownership of, or rights in intellectual property;
- Acceptance of contributions of property such as real estate, conservation easements, intellectual property;
- Operation in one or more foreign countries;
- Making of grants, loans, or other distributions to organizations, including foreign entities;
- Close connection with any organization;
- Operation as a school (Schedule B required);
- Operation as a hospital or other medical care facility (Schedule C required);
- Provision of housing for low-income individuals, the elderly, or the handicapped (Schedule F required);
- Provision of scholarships, fellowships, educational loans, and the like (Schedule H required).

8.62 What is required in part IX of Form 1023?

Part IX of the Form 1023 concerns financial data (including a statement of revenue and expenses) of the applicant organization. If the organization has been in existence for four or more years, the required information is that for the most recent four years. If the organization has been in existence for more than one year and less than four years, the information is that for each year of existence and a good-faith estimate of finances for the other years (up to three). If the organization has been in existence for less than one year, it must provide good-faith projections of its finances for the current year and the two subsequent years. A balance sheet for the most recently completed year is also required. If there have been any substantial changes in the assets or liabilities since the end of the periods inquired about above, the applicant is required to explain the changes.

8.63 What is required in part X of Form 1023?

Part X of the Form 1023 pertains to the organization's public charity status. The organization must identify the type of public charity status it is requesting or answer questions if it is a standard private foundation or private operating foundation. The organization, in this part, if it is to be publicly supported, requests an advance ruling or a definitive ruling. One way an organization can qualify as a public charity is to be a church.

8.64 What is required in part XI of Form 1023?

Part XI of the Form 1023 concerns the user fee payment. (This section of the application replaced the prior user fee form, Form 8718.) If the organization's average annual gross receipts have exceeded or will exceed $10,000 annually over a four-year period, the user fee is $750. Otherwise, the required user fee payment is $300.

8.65 What happens when the requested ruling as to tax-exempt status is not granted?

The IRS has developed an extensive set of procedural rules to follow, should the requested ruling be adverse to the organization. These procedures are in many ways akin to the IRS practices and procedures in any instance in which there is a tax controversy beyond the level of the initial determination.

Thus, these procedures include the right of protest and appeal, conferences, the pursuit of technical advice from the National Office of the IRS, and occasionally consideration of the case by the National Office. Beyond that, there is access to the courts. An organization can take its case to the U.S. Tax Court (without a lawyer, if it chooses) or to a U.S. District Court or the U.S. Court of Federal Claims. Appeals can be taken to the appropriate U.S. Circuit Court of Appeals; on rare occasions, an exempt organization's case will be heard by the Supreme Court. For charitable organizations, there is a declaratory judgment procedure by which issues as to tax-exempt status, private foundation/public charity status, and/or charitable donee status may be litigated.

8.66 What is the *group exemption* procedure?

The group exemption procedure was devised by the IRS to eliminate the administrative burdens that would be caused by the pursuit of rulings by identical organizations, where there are many of them (perhaps hundreds) and they are related. This procedure is designed for entities such as churches, chapters, ministerial associations, posts, or units that are affiliated with and subject to the general supervision or control of an organization, which is usually a national, regional, or state entity.

The supervisory organization is known as the *central organization*; the organizations that are affiliated with the central organization are *subordinate organizations*.

In the opinion of the authors, this is an unfortunate choice of terminology, in that many organizations and those who manage them do not care to be regarded as subordinates. A preferable term would be *affiliates*. Aside from the psychology of the terminology, there are political aspects as well: The term *central organization* to some at the affiliate level stimulates fears of too much authority and control.

Tax exemption for subordinate organizations is recognized by the IRS by reason of their relationship with the central organization. This is known as tax exemption on a group basis.

These procedures contemplate a functioning of the central organization as an agent of the IRS, requiring that the organization responsibly and independently evaluate the qualification for tax-exempt status of the subordinate organizations from the standpoint of the organizational and operational tests applicable to them.

Interestingly, the term *affiliation* is not defined in this context. Usually the requisite affiliation is found in the governance structure of the organizations involved, such as a ministerial association with members or a church denomination with many individual churches. Sometimes the affiliation is inherent in a relationship involving finances, such as dues-sharing. In general, the IRS will accept any reasonable interpretation of the word *affiliation* in this setting. This state of affairs is understandable, in that the group exemption is saving the IRS the task of processing thousands of applications for recognition of tax exemption.

8.67 What are the advantages of the group exemption to a religious nonprofit organization?

From the standpoint of the IRS, the group exemption procedure is advantageous because it relieves the agency of the processing of thousands of applications for recognition of tax exemption.

The group exemption generally is favorable for clusters of religious nonprofit organizations that are affiliated. This approach to tax exemption obviates the need for each member entity in the group to file a separate application for recognition of exemption; and this can result in savings of time, effort, and money. It is, then, a streamlined approach to the establishment of tax-exempt status for related organizations.

8.68 What are the disadvantages of the group exemption to a religious nonprofit organization?

There are several. One concerns the fact that the members of the group do not individually possess determination letters as to their tax exemption. In regard to religious nonprofit organizations, this can pose difficulties for donors and grantors. That is, a contributor of a major gift may want the security of a determination letter so as to have the requisite basis for relying on the organization's representation that it is a charitable entity.

Another disadvantage pertains to charitable subordinate organizations. By definition, the group exemption process does not entail any IRS review of these entities' public charity status. Sophisticated donors and grantors know this and thus know that they usually cannot assume that a particular subordinate entity is a public charity—which is the assurance they need. This dilemma is compounded by the practice of the IRS to automatically accord to the subordinate entities the same public charity status as that recognized for the central organization—and to do so on the basis of definitive rulings.

A third disadvantage pertains to state tax exemptions. Often the state authorities will not recognize a state tax exemption unless the organization can produce a copy of a federal determination as to exemption under a comparable status. Obviously, with the group exemption, a subordinate organization does not have that evidence to produce, which often makes the process of securing one or more state tax exemptions more difficult.

8.69 **How is the group exemption initially established?**

First, the entity intending to be a central organization must obtain recognition from the IRS of its own tax-exempt status. Then the organization applies to the IRS for classification as a central organization.

This application (oddly, there is no IRS form for it) must establish that all of the subordinate organizations to be included in the group exemption letter are properly affiliated with the central organization, are subject to its general supervision or control, have the identical tax-exempt status, are not private foundations, are not foreign organizations, have the same accounting period as the central organization if they are not to be included in group returns, and, in the case of charitable entities, are formed within the 15-month period prior to the date of submission of the group exemption application.

A central organization must submit to the IRS this information on behalf of the subordinate entities:

* Information verifying the facts evidencing the aforementioned relationships and other requirements;
* A description of the principal purposes and activities of the subordinates, including financial information;
* A sample copy of a uniform or representative governing instrument adopted by the subordinates;
* An affirmation by a principal officer of the central organization that the subordinates are operating in accordance with their stated purposes;
* A statement that each subordinate has furnished the requisite written authorization;
* A list of subordinates to which the IRS has issued a determination letter or ruling recognizing exempt status;
* If relevant, an affirmation that no subordinate organization is a private foundation;
* A list of the names, addresses, and employer identification numbers of the subordinates to be included in the group (or a satisfactory directory of them).

Certain additional information is required of a subordinate organization if it is claiming tax-exempt status as a school.

There is only one court case involving the group exemption procedures. There, the IRS procedures were upheld, with an organization found to not be eligible for classification as a central organization because the requisite information was not provided.

8.70 How is the group exemption maintained?

The group exemption is basically maintained by the central organization making an annual filing with the IRS. Certain information must be annually submitted to the IRS by the central organization (at least 90 days before the close of its annual accounting period) to sustain the group status.

This information consists of:

* Information regarding any changes in the purposes, character, or method of operation of the subordinate organization;
* A list of subordinates that have changed their names or addresses during the year;
* A list of subordinates that are no longer part of the group;
* A list of organizations that were added to the group during the year;
* The information summarized previously concerning the subordinates that joined the group during the year.

8.71 How are the annual information returns reporting requirements satisfied?

A central organization must, as a general rule, file an annual information return. So, too, must each subordinate organization. Many subordinate organizations are small, however, and thus may be able to take advantage of the exception for organizations with annual gross receipts that normally do not exceed $25,000. The law, beginning in 2008, requires organizations with less than $25,000 in receipts to file Form 990-N, also called the e-postcard. There are exceptions from this requirement for various small organizations, including those included in a group return, churches and their integrated auxiliaries, and conventions or associations of churches.

A subordinate organization has a choice in this regard. It can file its own annual information return (assuming no basis for an exception), or it can file with the central organization as part of a group annual return.

8.72 Can a central organization exclude subordinate organizations from its group return?

Yes. A central organization may exclude from its group return those subordinates the annual gross receipts of which are normally not in excess of $25,000 per year.

8.73 Do the central organization and the subordinate organizations have to have the same tax-exempt status?

No. These entities can have different tax-exempt organization classifications. For example, the central organization can be exempt as a charitable organization and the subordinates can be exempt as social welfare organizations.

8.74 Can the group exemption be terminated?

Yes. There are several instances when a group exemption may be terminated. One is when the central organization dissolves or otherwise ceases to exist. Other instances in which the group status can collapse are when the central organization ceases to qualify for tax-exempt status, fails to submit the requisite information, or fails to comply with the reporting requirements.

The loss of tax exemption by some of the subordinate organizations in a group does not, however, adversely affect the group exemption ruling for the other members of the group.

CHAPTER 9

The IRS Annual Information Return

9.1 What is an *annual information return?*

The document involved is not an *annual report* (such as may be required under state law); it is not a *tax return.* As to the latter, these documents are generally not publicly accessible. The document that must be filed is an *information return,* which means, among other things, it is a return that contains much more than financial information and it must be made available to the public.

On December 20, 2007, the IRS released a major revision of the Form 990 beginning with tax year 2008. The new return entails significant changes in the ways in which public charities and other exempt organizations will report information on finances, fundraising activities, governance, executive and board compensation, and program services. The new Form 990 provides summary information about an organization's mission, finances and fundraising expenses, and includes sections with new questions on governance, compensation, and expenses.

The new form also includes certain questions that trigger requests of organizations to complete more detailed schedules. The new Form 990 has many familiar questions or attachments from the old Form 990. Some items on the new form have been moved and arranged while others are brand new.

There are sixteen schedules included with the new form. Most charitable organizations complete Schedule A, which now includes more detailed questions about how the filing organization qualifies as a public charity. Schedule B still covers contributors. The other schedules are: political campaign and lobbying activities (Schedule C); supplemental financial statements previously disclosed through attachments (Schedule D); private schools (Schedule E); activities outside of the United States (Schedule F); fundraising and gaming activities (Schedule G); hospitals (Schedule H);

grants and other assistance (Schedule I); supplemental compensation information (Schedule J); tax-exempt bonds (Schedule K); transactions with interested persons (Schedule L); noncash contributions (Schedule M); information on liquidation, termination, dissolution, or significant disposition of assets (Schedule N); supplemental information (Schedule O); and related organizations and unrelated partnerships (Schedule R).

Thus, a new Form 990 is in place for the 2009 filing season.

9.2 Generally, do tax-exempt organizations have to file an annual return with the IRS?

In most all instances, yes. The federal tax law requires the filing of an annual information return by just about every type of tax-exempt organization. This includes charitable organizations, associations and other business leagues, social welfare organizations, social clubs, fraternal organizations, labor unions, and veterans' organizations.

There are, however, some organizations that are excused from the filing obligation. Most importantly for the purposes of this publication, generally, churches and certain church-related organizations are not required to file Form 990 returns reporting their annual activity. Churches and church-related organizations are not excused, nonetheless, from filing tax returns reporting unrelated business income (Form 990-T).

9.3 What organizations are not required to file an annual return?

Some tax-exempt organizations do not have to file because of their exemption classification. These are:

- Churches, interchurch organizations of local units of a church, conventions or associations of churches, and integrated auxiliaries of a church
- Church-affiliated organizations that are exclusively engaged in managing funds or maintaining retirement programs
- A school below college level affiliated with a church or operated by a religious order
- A mission society sponsored by or affiliated with one or more churches or church denominations, if more than one-half of the society's activities are conducted in, or directed at persons in, foreign countries
- An exclusively religious activity of a religious order
- Instrumentalities of the United States
- State institutions the gross income of which is excluded from income taxation
- Other governmental units and tax-exempt organizations that are affiliated with them

Other tax-exempt organizations are excused from filing an annual return because of the size of their gross receipts. There are two categories in this regard: organizations normally receiving $25,000 or less in gross receipts annually and foreign organizations the annual gross receipts of which from sources within the United States are normally $25,000 or less.

NOTE: Supporting organizations and private foundations are required to file annual information returns irrespective of the amount of their gross receipts.

9.4 Should an organization with gross receipts that are normally not more than $25,000 consider filing with the IRS anyway?

Yes. This is done by completing the top portion of the return (name, address, and the like) and checking the box on line K. The purpose of this is to be certain that the IRS has the organization's correct address and realizes that the organization is not filing because it is not required to, rather than because it is unaware of or is ignoring the requirement. The IRS also requests that, when an organization of this type receives a Form 990 package in the mail, the top portion of the return be filed using the mailing label.

An organization that has been filing annual information returns and then becomes no longer required to file them, because of qualification under an exemption, should notify the IRS of the change in filing status. Failure to do this is likely to result in inquiries from the IRS as to why returns are not being filed; a large expenditure of time and effort may then be required in resolving the matter.

NOTE: An organization that voluntarily files an annual information return under these circumstances is not relieved of the obligation to file the e-postcard (Form 990-N).

9.5 What constitutes *gross receipts?*

A distinction must be made between the term *gross receipts* and the term *gross revenue.*

NOTE: The reader may wish to have a copy of Form 990 at hand while reviewing the rest of this chapter. The discussion is based on the Form 990 for 2006.

On Form 990, for example, *gross revenue* means all revenue referenced in Part I, lines 1 to 12. This includes contributions, grants, exempt function revenue, investment income, and unrelated business income.

NOTE: For the most part, *gross* revenue must be taken into account in determining total revenue (i.e., expenses are irrelevant). However, there are exceptions, where only net (gross less expenses) income is taken into account for this purpose, such as rental income (or loss) (Form 990, Part VIII, lines 6a to d), and gain from sale of assets (or loss) (lines 7a to d).

Consistency is important when reporting these numbers. In this instance, these revenue items must be reported again in the context of the summary of revenue (Form 990, Part I, line 12).

In contrast, gross receipts are the total amount the organization received from all sources during its annual accounting period, without subtraction of any costs or expenses.

NOTE: Thus, these exceptions noted earlier are irrelevant in computing gross receipts. Consequently, on Form 990, gross receipts include the sum of Part VIII, lines 6a, 7a, 8a, 9a, and 10a. Gross receipts can also be calculated by adding back the amounts subtracted in ascertaining gross revenue.

9.6 What does the term *normally* mean?

The term *normally* in this context generally means an average of the most recent three tax years of the organization (including the year relating to the return). Thus, to be entitled to this reporting exception, it is not necessary that the organization be below the $25,000 threshold each year. Specifically, an organization is considered to meet the $25,000 gross receipts test if one of these three tests applies:

1. The organization has been in existence for one year and has received, or donors have pledged to give, $37,500 or less during its first year.
2. The organization has been in existence between one and three years and averaged $30,000 or less in gross receipts during each of its first two years.
3. The organization has been in existence three or more years and averaged $25,000 or less in gross receipts for the immediately preceding three years (including the year for which the return would be filed).

9.7 What happens once the $25,000 gross receipts test is exceeded?

Once it is determined that the organization's gross receipts for the measuring period are such that it has exceeded the $25,000 threshold, it has 90 days within which to file the appropriate annual return (unless another exception is available).

9.8 What IRS form is this annual information return?

For most organizations, it is Form 990. Small organizations—those with gross receipts of less than $100,000 and total assets of less than $250,000—are allowed to file a simpler (two-page) version of the return, which is Form 990-EZ. An organization that is eligible to file Form 990-EZ may nonetheless file Form 990 if it wishes (perhaps to provide more specific information) or if necessary (such as to meet state law reporting requirements).

There are other tax-exempt organizations that are not required to file this annual information return but are nonetheless required to file either another information return or a tax return. Apostolic organizations, for example, file Form 1065.

9.9 Is there any reason to file the simpler version of the annual information return when the organization is exempt from the filing requirement because of the amount of its gross receipts?

As noted, an organization with gross receipts that do not normally exceed $25,000 annually is excused from filing an annual information return. Certain organizations with gross receipts of less than $100,000 can file a simpler version of the annual return—Form 990-EZ. The question thus is whether an organization with less than $25,000 in annual gross receipts should nonetheless file Form 990-EZ.

One reason for the filing of Form 990-EZ in this situation—or at least preparing it—is so that the organization can have the benefit of understanding what its items of income, expense, assets, and liabilities are.

From a legal standpoint, however, there is a very good reason for filing Form 990-EZ even though it is not required as a matter of law. This pertains to the running of the statute of limitations on the assessment and collection of taxes. The general rule is that income taxes must be assessed within the three-year period following the filing of the return. If a return is not filed, the statute of limitations does not start to run and the tax may be assessed at any time.

As noted, the annual information return is not a tax return. The original position of the IRS was that the filing of an information return did not trigger the running of the statute of limitations for purposes of assessment of the unrelated business income tax—which is to be calculated and reported on a tax return, Form 990-T. The Tax Court held, however, that the statute of limitations does begin to run in this circumstance where the information in the annual information return clearly revealed the possibilities of unrelated business income. Thereafter, the IRS relented, announcing that it would adhere to the Tax Court's approach where adequate facts as to the presence of unrelated business income are disclosed in the annual information return and it was filed in good faith.

Of course, a small organization may not have any unrelated business income, or it may have a small amount that it shielded from tax by the $1,000 specific deduction. In many instances, however, comfort can be gained by filing an annual information return despite the fact it is not required.

Although its utility is remote, there is another reason for filing an annual information return. The statute of limitations begins to run when an organization, believing in good faith that it is a tax-exempt entity, files an annual information return and is subsequently held to be a taxable organization. This can be the outcome even where the organization has not yet been recognized as an exempt entity. Thus, there may be a measure of protection to be obtained in this connection.

 NOTE: Beginning in 2010, this filing threshold amount will be increased to $50,000.

9.10 When is this annual information return due?

The annual information return is required to be filed with the IRS by the fifteenth day of the fifth month following the close of its accounting period. Thus, for exempt organizations using the calendar year as the accounting period, the return is due by May 15. An organization with a fiscal year ending June 30 is expected to file by November 15. An organization with a fiscal year ending October 31 must file by March 15.

If the regular due date falls on a Saturday, Sunday, or legal holiday, the due date is the next business day.

If the organization is liquidated, dissolved, or terminated, the return should be filed by the fifteenth day of the fifth month after the liquidation, dissolution, or termination.

9.11 Are extensions of this filing due date available?

Yes. It is common for exempt organizations to obtain an extension of the annual information return due date. The proper way to request this extension is the filing of Form 2758.

Generally, the IRS will not grant an extension of time to file the annual information return for more than 90 days, unless sufficient need for an extended period is clearly shown. The IRS will not, in any event, grant an extension of more than six months to any domestic organization.

9.12 Where is the annual information return filed?

All annual information returns filed by tax-exempt organizations are required to be filed with the Internal Revenue Service Center in Ogden, Utah 84201–0027.

9.13 How does an organization amend its return?

To change its return for a year, the organization must file a new return, including any required attachments. It should use the version of the annual information return applicable to the year involved. The amended return must provide all of the information called for by the return and its instructions, not just the new or corrected information. The organization should check the "Amended Return" box in the heading of the return.

The organization may file an amended return at any time to change or add to the information reported on a previously filed return for the same year. It must make the amended return available for public inspection for three years from the date the original return was due.

The organization must also send a copy of the amended return to any state with which it filed a copy of the return originally to meet that state's filing requirement.

9.14 Does the IRS provide copies of previously filed annual information returns?

Yes. A tax-exempt organization may request a copy of an annual information return it has previously filed by filing Form 4506-A with the IRS.

9.15 What if the return is a final return?

In the case of a complete liquidation of a corporation, the "Final Return" box in the heading of the annual information return should be checked. An explanatory statement should be attached to the return.

This statement should indicate whether the assets have been distributed and the date of the distribution. A certified copy of any resolution, or plan of liquidation or termination, should be attached, along with all amendments or supplements not already filed. In addition, a schedule should be attached listing the names and addresses of all persons who received the assets distributed in liquidation or termination, the kinds of assets distributed to each one, and each asset's fair market value.

9.16 What happens when an organization is engaging in an activity that was not previously disclosed to the IRS?

If a tax-exempt organization has a determination letter or ruling from the IRS recognizing its tax exemption, the organization as part of that process presumably apprised the IRS of all of its programs or other activities at that time.

It is possible, of course, that an organization did not disclose all of its activities to the IRS as part of the application process. If that is the case, it could have an adverse impact on the organization's exempt status. A ruling of this nature is only as valid as the material facts on which it is based; if material facts were omitted, the IRS may have occasion to revoke the ruling, either prospectively or retroactively.

An organization may have previously reported one or more activities to the IRS on a prior annual information return or during an audit. Indeed, the law requires that an exempt organization provide the IRS with contemporaneous notice of any *material* change in the facts concerning it. This is required, of course, to accord the IRS the opportunity to review these facts, so as to determine whether the organization is no longer primarily engaged in exempt functions. It is intended to be part of the IRS's ongoing enforcement of the *operational test*.

Thus, there can be several occasions when the IRS was informed of an organization's activities. If, however, there is an activity engaged in by the organization that it did not previously report to the IRS, the entity is required to check a "Yes" box and disclose it as part of the return (Form 990, Part VI, line 76). A detailed description of each activity of this nature must be attached to the return. Otherwise, the question is answered "No."

9.17 What happens when an organization changed its operating documents but did not previously report this to the IRS?

Any changes made in the organizing or governing documents not reported to the IRS are to be disclosed as part of the return (Part VI, line 77). The organization is required to check a "Yes" box and a conformed copy of the amendments must be attached to the return. Otherwise, the question is answered "No."

The same problem can arise here as in respect to activities. A change in one of these documents can be a *material* change; an illustration is a substantial modification of the organization's statement of purposes. If this entailed a material change, the organization is obligated to communicate the change to the IRS contemporaneously. Again, this is required to accord the IRS the opportunity to review these facts, so as to determine whether the organization is no longer primarily engaged in exempt functions. It is intended to be part of the IRS's ongoing enforcement of the organizational test.

9.18 What are the penalties on organizations concerning annual information returns?

Penalties can be imposed for failure to file the return, for a late filing, an incorrect filing, or an incomplete filing.

The basic penalty is $20 per day, not to exceed the smaller of $10,000 or 5 percent of the gross receipts of the organization for the year. A penalty will not be imposed in an instance of reasonable cause for the violation.

An organization with annual gross receipts in excess of $1 million is, however, subject to a penalty of $100 for each day the failure continues. The maximum penalty per return is $50,000. These penalties begin on the due date for filing the annual return.

One way to avoid penalties is to complete all applicable line items. Each question on the return should be answered "Yes," "No," or "N/A" (not applicable). An entry should be made on all total lines (including a zero when appropriate). "None" or "N/A" should be entered if an entire part does not apply.

9.19 Are there penalties on individuals as well as organizations for non-filing and the like?

Yes. There is a separate penalty that may be imposed on *responsible persons*. This penalty is $20 per day, not to exceed $10,000. This penalty will not be levied in an instance of reasonable cause.

If an organization does not file a complete return or does not furnish correct information, it is the practice of the IRS to send the organization a letter that includes a fixed time to fulfill these requirements. After that period expires, the person failing to comply will be charged the penalty.

If more than one person is responsible, they are jointly and individually liable for the penalty.

There are other penalties, in the form of fines and imprisonment, for willfully not filing returns when they are required and for filing fraudulent returns and statements with the IRS.

PART II

Ministers, Employees, and Volunteers

CHAPTER 10

Clergy, Ministers, and Pastors

10.1 How have organizational structures of churches affected the selection of the organization's ministers?

The Supreme Court characterized *congregational* organizations as groups of individuals who have organized themselves to be independent from the control of other religious associations, while retaining the ability to choose affiliations with like-minded churches and other religious organizations. *Hierarchical* organizations function in a defined structure where the local church is subject to the control of a higher authority or tribunal that may create rules and direct the actions of its member organizations. The appointment, and removal, of a congregational organization's spiritual head is a matter decided solely by the organization's governance documents, or if not specified in any governance documents, then by the practices the organization has established. In a hierarchical church, the selection of a minister may be left to the discretion of the local church.

10.2 How has the nature of the relationship between ministers and the church affected how disputes between ministers and their church are resolved?

As a result of the deference given to the free exercise of religion in this country, the courts have traditionally been reluctant to address disputes involving ministers and their churches, particularly because these disputes tend to be ecclesiastical in nature. The roles of ministers as the selected spiritual heads of their churches are usually inextricable from their congregants' rights to practice their religion free from interference, and the courts believe that a review of any disputes between the two would involve impermissible inquiries into religious doctrine. If, however, the organization and its ministers have entered into a written contract governing their relationship, or the procedural steps they will follow for the resolution of a dispute, then the courts may be more inclined to address the issues. This is particularly true when the allegations are regarding the failure of one of the parties to follow a specific procedural step or abide by a contractual provision, and the court is not required to address or consider any religious doctrine.

10.3 What are the implications of self-employment versus employee classification for ministers?

The IRS assumes that ministers of religion are employees of the churches they serve. Self-employment, when demonstrated, involves different tax treatment for compensation and benefits. To determine whether an individual is an employee or self-employed, situation-specific factors about the performance of the duties are considered according to various tests the IRS and courts have developed. A minister must determine whether he or she wants to be considered an employee or self-employed. If he or she chooses to be self-employed, then he or she must be able to demonstrate that his or her employment relationship with the church is closer to a self-employment, contractual relationship than that of an employee.

10.4 How have ministers been distinguished from other employees in the context of employment and other benefits?

Laws referencing pastors, clergy, and ministers are designed to preserve the dignity, sensitivities, and unique responsibilities of the profession. Ministers typically are invested by society and the law with greater authority of civil association, such as to counsel and attend to the infirm, to counsel and comfort the dying and their loved ones, to solemnize marriages, and to maintain the confidences shared with them by adherents seeking spiritual guidance and counsel. These are functions where both religion and the law have well-established interests. There is an evidentiary privilege regarding communications made to clergy under certain specific circumstances. This privilege is the source of the commonly held belief that confessions to a priest will be held in strict confidence and cannot be repeated. Another example is the ability of ministers of the gospel to receive a portion of their salaries as housing allowance, which is not designated as taxable income. The election of federal tax treatment and structures for the provision of housing allowance recognizes that the traditional accumulation of wealth is forgone by choice.

10.5 What does it mean to be *ordained, commissioned,* or *licensed*?

The meanings of *ordained, commissioned,* or *licensed* are generally synonymous and usually understood as formal recognition of minister status from a higher religious organizational level, but they are not defined in the Internal Revenue Code for purposes of federal tax law. It has been noted by courts that the Code and regulations do not attempt to define a *minister* by specific credentials, but rather by his or her activities. The clear case of an *ordained, commissioned,* or *licensed* minister, pastor, or clergyperson is one where the individual has been certified and recognized by a church or denomination, and has joined a distinct class of those vested with authority to perform some or all of the rites and practices of that church or denomination.

Various laws refer to only one, or some specific aspect of, each of these terms. For example, the Military Selective Service Act specifies that "regular or duly ordained ministers of religion" may be exempted from military training and exercises. Ecclesiastically, religious entities may confer whatever privileges they wish upon commissioning clergy. The distinction between an *ordained, commissioned,* or *licensed* minister from a lay minister becomes important in the context of Social Security, housing allowances, and other areas. The phrase "ordained, commissioned, or licensed" typically amounts to recognition, appointment, or conference of a minister status, where an individual has accomplished certain customary requirements. However, in a case where an individual is operating as the functional equivalent, even if no outside authority has certified or recognized the individual, then the individual will arguably be considered to be either ordained or commissioned or licensed to be a minister for tax purposes if this status is materially more than self-appointment and not merely a label to garner a tax benefit.

10.6 From what other sources does a minister derive authority within the organization?

Religious organizations follow their own constitutions, doctrines, tenets of faith, organizational documents, and governing documents conferring principal authority on leadership. Congregational action, decisional practice, and the roles of officers and board members, interplay with affiliated or related entities, and contractual sources of rights of authority round out the balance of sources of power.

10.7 What retirement plans are available to ministers?

A variety of retirement plans are available to ministers and other religious employees, although this can be an involved subject that could require detailed practical application. These plans are tax-favored, as contributions to the plans made by or on behalf of an employee are partially or fully deductible from income for tax purposes in the year of contribution, and the income or appreciation earned by the plan ordinarily is not taxable until distributed. Some specific retirement plans are available to persons who report their federal income taxes as employees. The most common such plan is a tax-sheltered annuity, sometimes called a *403(b) plan.* Generally, only employees may participate in such plans, although ministers of religion may participate regardless of the election to be self-employed for income tax reporting purposes (though non-minister employees who are self-employed are not eligible). Other retirement plans are available only to persons who report their federal income taxes as self-employed. The common example of this type of plan is called a *Keogh plan*. Further still, many retirement plans are available to both employees and self-employed workers, including IRAs, simplified employee pensions, and rabbi trusts.

10.8 What exemptions are available to a minister?

Ministers may be exempt or excused from military training and service. In fact, the Military Service Act exempts *regular or duly ordained ministers of religion* from military training and service. However, ministers are *not* exempted from the registration requirements.

This Act attempts to distinguish bona fide vocational ministers and self-appointed ministers and lay ministers. It defines the term *duly ordained minister of religion* as a person who has been ordained, in accordance with the ceremonial, ritual, or discipline of a church, religious sect, or organization established on the basis of a community of faith and belief, doctrines, and practices of a religious character, to preach and to teach the doctrine of such church, sect, or organization, and to administer the rites and ceremonies thereof in public worship, and who as his or her regular and customary vocation preaches and teaches the principles of religion and administers the ordinances of public worship as embodied in the creed or principles of such church, sect, or organization. The Act defines the term *regular minister of religion* as one who, as his or her customary vocation, preaches and teaches the principles of religion of a church, a religious sect, or organization of which he or she is a member, without having been formally ordained as a minister of a religion, and who is recognized by such church, sect, or organization as a regular minister. But the term *regular or duly ordained minister of religion* does not include a person who irregularly or incidentally preaches and teaches the principles of a religion of a church, religious sect, or organization; or a person who has been duly ordained as a minister in accordance with the ceremonial rite or discipline or a church, religious sect, or organization, but who does not regularly, as a bona fide vocation, teach and preach the principles of a religion and administer the ordinances of public worship, as embodied in the creed or principles of his church, sect, or organization. Ministers seeking exemption must apply for exemption under the "4-D" classification contained in the Act.

In addition to the military exemptions, some states excuse or exempt members of the clergy from jury duty on the premise that a minister's availability to the community is more important than the interruption of such duties to provide jury service. This rationale is not applied by extension to other professions, and evidences the unique treatment of the minister or clergyperson by the law.

10.9 What is the *duty of confidentiality* as it pertains to ministers?

The concepts of privilege and confidentiality are closely related. Privilege prevents compelled disclosure of communications, while the duty of confidentiality addresses voluntary disclosure of communications. The *duty of confidentiality* refers to a general expectation and duty not to disclose to others the substance of communications shared in confidence. If a member of the clergy revealed confidential communication, the member's allegation would be that the minister was negligent and did not comport with the standard of care, as in the nature of malpractice. The negligence arises from an implied agreement between the parties, based on their relationship, that this information would not be shared. It would be further argued that the role of minister carries with it a professional duty to keep such communications confidential. Until recently, the duty of ministers to preserve confidences was considered to be moral rather than legal in nature, though in recent years some ministers have been sued for divulging confidences. The clear trend now is recognition that if there is no enforceable expectation of confidentiality, few would venture to accept their church's invitation (which was traditionally a requirement) to reveal sensitive and sometimes embarrassing personal facts in seeking guidance and counseling.

On the other hand, a 2007 decision by the Texas Supreme Court illustrates the tension in the law arising out of the disclosure of confidential information by a minister. The confidential information in that case was imparted by a church member to her clergy, who was also her counselor. The former member sued the minister, his church, and the church's elders alleging causes of action for defamation, professional negligence, breach of fiduciary duty, and intentional infliction of emotional distress after the minister directed his congregation to "shun" the parishioner for engaging in a "biblically inappropriate" relationship. The discipline meted out by the minister was required by and in accordance with the ecclesiastical disciplinary process outlined in the church's governance documents. The minister, who was also a licensed professional counselor, learned of the disclosed information from the former parishioner in the course of a secular counseling session. Recognizing the importance of the duty of confidentiality while acknowledging the general prohibition on adjudication of religious questions (also known as the *judicial abstention doctrine*), the Texas Supreme Court concluded that considering the various issues, including parsing the dual roles of the minister—professional counselor and religious minister—would unconstitutionally entangle the court in matters of church governance and impinge on the core religious function of the church. Accordingly, the court dismissed the case against the minister.

10.10 How does the duty of confidentiality apply to the reporting of criminal activities other than suspected child abuse?

In cases other than child abuse, where there are frequently statutory reporting requirements, the duty of confidentiality, at least in terms of secular law, does not prevent a member of the clergy, especially anonymously, from disclosing communications regarding criminal activities to law enforcement. Public policy dictates that the duty of confidentiality is not absolute, is not the only duty existing, competes with the duty to warn, and ends where information shared is of a demonstrable jeopardy to an individual or the public. Disclosures to law enforcement can sometimes be limited to tips, and by the rule of evidentiary privilege, a minister would be not be compelled to disclose any privileged communications in court.

Though in flux, 33 of the 50 states have adopted privilege provisions that include "spiritual advice." Twenty of these states, many following the federal rules of evidence, provide only for a privilege covering spiritual advice. Thirteen of the 33 jurisdictions expressly provide in a single statutory section for a privilege for both "confessions" and communications relating to "spiritual advice." Seven states may be treated separately or may be included in the spiritual-advice category that do not actually use the words "spiritual advice" or the equivalent, but rather generally cover confidential communications to a member of the ministry in his or her professional capacity.

10.11 What is the duty to report suspected child abuse as it pertains to a minister?

The trend is that states are favoring mandatory reporting of child abuse without exceptions, and the public is adopting this expectation widely. Though all states address reporting, they range in degree of exceptions to required reporting and, until verified, an organization is safer to assume mandatory reporting is required. Though many state laws require without exception the mandatory reporting of child abuse and neglect cases, a number of states have specifically exempted ministers from the *mandatory* duty to report child abuse if the information was received during a confidential communication. Reporting child abuse is nevertheless a proper election that *can* be made where not required, especially where abuse will not be otherwise reported by anyone else and continue. Other states have not specifically excluded ministers from the duty to report but have provided that information received in confidence and protected by the clergy–penitent privilege is not admissible in court in a proceeding regarding the alleged abuse. The various statutory measures taken by states are an attempt to resolve the competing interests that ministers sometimes find themselves facing—the moral or legal requirement to report wrongdoing and the ecclesiastical duty to maintain the confidentiality of privileged communications.

10.12 Why do we have the clergy–penitent privilege?

Throughout history, society has recognized the importance of allowing persons to be able to speak to their clergy in private. Today, every domestic jurisdiction and many foreign jurisdictions recognize the privilege. Courts and legislatures have said that society is benefited when people have a place to go to obtain spiritual counseling, advice, and direction. The value of that spiritual communication would be greatly diminished if the person making the communication had to worry that its contents would be disclosed to others. Without a strong privilege, people would not be as open and forthcoming about their worries and problems, clergy would not be as free to dispense advice, and the value of the spiritual counseling would be damaged. So, most courts will not require either the person who received spiritual counseling, or the clergy who provided it, to disclose what was discussed, except in limited circumstances. This privilege applies even if the information sought might otherwise be relevant and admissible in a court proceeding.

10.13 What are the boundaries of the clergy–penitent privilege?

Each jurisdiction will have varying interpretations of the limitations on the clergy–penitent privilege, but the initial questions as to whether a communication will be considered privileged are whether (1) it was given in a confessional setting, and (2) it dealt with spiritual matters or concerns. Courts have not recognized certain communications as being privileged if they were made in a setting where the person did not appear to be seeking spiritual guidance or was discussing things that did not relate to spiritual counseling. No particular or formal requirements exist to create the privilege, and the person's intent in speaking to the clergy will have great impact.

Unlike other types of privileges, such as the attorney–client privilege, many jurisdictions will allow non-clergy persons to be present during a confessional meeting with clergy. However, the safer practice is to allow only members of the clergy to be present so as to avoid any questions. The privilege will not be protected if it has been waived, meaning the person or the clergy has disclosed the same information to others. It will not apply in many jurisdictions if the communication involves child abuse or neglect, or the active or future commission of a crime. The best practice for clergy is to advise communicants before they begin if child abuse or active crimes must be reported.

10.14 What qualifies as a privileged communication?

Privileged communications may be verbal or nonverbal. Not all communications between an individual and a minister are eligible to invoke the privilege. Fairly uniform rules of evidence and state legislatures have defined a protected communication generally as a communication confidentially made to a minister acting in his or her professional capacity as a spiritual advisor.

The law of clergy–penitent privilege varies from state to state. Generally, statutes provide that the communicant must have possessed a reasonable belief at the time of the communication that he or she was speaking with an actual member of the clergy, that the clergy was acting in confidence in his or her professional capacity, and that the communication was *penitential* in nature (i.e., the communication must be akin to a confession), and/or the communication must be pursuant to a religious duty set forth by the doctrine of the church.

 NOTE: Since there are varying state statutes, members of the clergy and religious nonprofit organizations should carefully review the applicable state statutes to determine what qualifies as a protected communication in their state.

10.15 Can the privilege protecting confidential minister communications be waived?

Yes. If the same information is told to third parties, then it might no longer be considered privileged. The person who made the communication may voluntarily waive the privilege, but in most jurisdictions, the privilege cannot legally be waived by the clergy without the consent of the person who made the communication.

10.16 What does it mean for a protected communication to be made to a *minister*?

Members of the clergy, priests, and ministers are the usual recipients of protected communications. Where statutes allow room for interpretation, some courts have extended the privilege to lay religious counselors whose services are needed within a religious organization due to the sheer volume of people requiring counseling, and elsewhere to counselors in nonprofit organizations that are not otherwise religious or affiliated with a religious organization. Nonetheless, the privilege has also been found not to apply in certain jurisdictions and in other circumstances, such as with communications to nuns, deacons, and elders in the church, lay religious counselors, or non-ordained self-proclaimed ministers.

10.17 What does it mean for a protected communication to be made to a minister in a professional capacity as a spiritual advisor?

Just because a person is a spiritual advisor in a religious organization does not mean that all communications received by him or her are privileged, in the same way that a doctor or lawyer is not at all times involved in privileged communications. Most clergy–penitent privilege laws require that the protected communication be made to a member of the clergy, priest, or minister while they are acting in their capacity as a spiritual advisor. It must be made in confidence and at a time when one would expect confidentiality and there is some semblance that the clergy, priest, or minister of the religious organization is operating in his or her capacity as such. A minister should make certain the objective of the conversation in order to determine whether a communication is privileged. For example, this can be accomplished by simply asking the counselee if he or she intends for the conversations in a counseling session to be held confidential and privileged. This can be extended to any conversation no matter when and where they may be had. A conversation taking place between mere friends would not invoke the privilege even if one happened to be a minister, priest, or clergy; however, if a minister believes that the person confiding in him or her intends for the conversation to be confidential and privileged, then the minister should ask their intention and the answer should confirm whether the clergy–penitent privilege applies.

10.18 To whom does the clergy–penitent privilege belong?

It can be stated two ways: (1) that the clergy–penitent privilege belongs to a party or (2) that a party has the right to claim the privilege. Either way it is stated, in most states, the person who made the penitential communication (counselee) and the clergy, priest, or rabbi to whom the communication was made (counselor) can claim the privilege. However, the counselor cannot independently assert the privilege if the counselee chooses not to do so, and the privilege can only be claimed by the counselor on behalf of the counselee. If the counselee waives the privilege and agrees to testify, the counselor cannot assert the privilege. In other states, however, only the counselee can assert the privilege, not the counselor to whom the communication was made. Still, in other states, the counselor can assert the privilege independently of the counselee. Thus, since there are varying statutes adopted by states, a religious organization is advised to review the applicable statute to determine if, when, and how the privilege can be asserted.

10.19 How does one assert the clergy–penitent privilege?

First, it should be clarified as to when one should assert the privilege. The privilege should be asserted in court or during a deposition when one is asked to disclose communications that are protected by the privilege. In the context of criminal investigations and prosecutions, the privilege could be used to attack the basis of the charges if it had been nullified before it could be invoked and was relied upon by the state. One way it is invoked is when an attorney objects to the questions asked of the counselee or the counselor when the answer would disclose a privileged communication. Second, if an objection is not made, the counselor can merely state that he would prefer not to answer the question because his or her answer would contain privileged information.

10.20 What liability can arise from a breach of the clergy–penitent privilege?

The clergy–penitent privilege creates a situation where a minister cannot be compelled to testify in court proceedings or in a deposition under oath regarding communications had in confidence while acting as a spiritual advisor. Aside from the privilege, there is the closely related theory of confidentiality. It is universally understood that confidences should not be breached on a moral level; however, there are recent cases allowing clergy to be sued for divulging confidences. Therefore, it is essential that clergy refrain from divulging any information received during religious counseling. If confidences are breached, the minister and the religious organization can face liability based on assertions of invasion of privacy, clergy malpractice, breach of fiduciary duty, and even infliction of emotional distress.

As discussed previously, a 2007 decision by the Texas Supreme Court illustrates the tension in the law arising out of the disclosure of confidential information by a minister. The confidential information in that case was imparted by a church member to her clergy, who was also her counselor. The former member sued the minister, his church, and the church's elders alleging causes of action for defamation, professional negligence, breach of fiduciary duty, and intentional infliction of emotional distress after the minister directed his congregation to "shun" the parishioner for engaging in a "biblically inappropriate" relationship.

For the purposes of the court's review, it presumed the counseling at issue was purely secular in nature; on the other hand, it could not ignore the fact that the counselor was a member of the clergy. The court acknowledged that the minister owed conflicting duties—as a licensed counselor he owed the church member the duty of confidentiality and as her pastor he owed her and the church duties as a member of the clergy. The court concluded that, parsing the roles for purposes of determining civil liability, where health or safety are not at issue, would unconstitutionally entangle the court in matters of church governance and impinge on the core religious function of church discipline. Accordingly, the case was dismissed.

10.21 Are there exceptions to the clergy–penitent privilege?

No. Because of the nature of the privilege, there are no exceptions; there are merely windows of application. The privilege provides that ministers cannot be compelled to disclose in court or in a deposition under oath the content of confidential communications shared with them while acting in their capacity as spiritual advisor. This privilege does not prevent or excuse a minister from reporting criminal activity including child abuse and/or neglect to authorities. When a minister, priest, or clergy reports a crime or an alleged abuse, he or she is merely providing information to authorities that will later need to be confirmed by law enforcement, and that cannot be relied upon to provide evidence in a court proceeding based on its nature and the privilege connected to it.

10.22 What visitation privileges apply for ministers at penal institutions?

Often, ministers, clergy, and priests are allowed to visit penal institutions for the purpose of religious counseling and instruction. State laws allow for this; however, the penal institutions are given broad discretion in deciding when, whether, and under what conditions the visits will be allowed. Due to the First Amendment's "non-establishment of religion" clause, prisoners cannot be forced to participate in religious activities.

10.23 What are the common sources of a minister's legal liability to third parties?

Members of the clergy, like members of the public, are legally liable for torts or civil wrongs they commit, direct, or participate in, even if the religious organization they serve is also liable. Generally, however, directors and officers of a religious organization do not incur personal liability for the corporation's torts just because of their capacity. The most common basis for legal liability for ministers is negligence. *Negligence* can be either a specific act or a failure to act and is not usually intentional. In fact, negligence is often associated with carelessness and defined as conduct that creates an unreasonable and foreseeable risk of harm to another person, and that does in fact result in injury. Other examples of torts that can be the source of liability if the minister personally commits, participates in, or directs them include defamation, fraud, and wrongful termination of employees.

10.24 What are the differences between libel and slander?

Defamation, as a tort, consists of oral statements (*slander*) or written statements (*libel*) made about a person that are false, published or communicated to another person, and result in injury to the subject person's reputation. The resulting injury must be to the person's reputation and not merely to their feelings.

10.25 Is truth an absolute defense to defamation?

One cannot be held liable for defamation, under the common law, for statements made that are, in fact, true. The principle is that one should not be punished for the propagation of truthful information. Truth is not, however, always a defense to other forms of legal liability, such as claims for invasion of privacy.

10.26 What is the potential liability of disclosing communications and records that are confidential?

Invasion of privacy is recognized in many states as a basis for liability. One form of invasion of privacy is the public disclosure of private facts. The elements of this type of invasion of privacy are:

- Publicity, defined as a communication to the public or to so many people that the information is certain to become public information (communications to a church's congregation would constitute publicity),
- of a highly objectionable kind, meaning that a reasonable person would feel justified in feeling seriously aggrieved by the dissemination of the information, and
- the facts publicly disclosed were private.

Matters of public record are not private, so reference to such facts is not an invasion of privacy. Public disclosure of private facts and the liability it carries is pertinent to ministers since they are usually privy to many private facts, especially about the members of their congregation. Thus, members of the clergy should be extremely vigilant of the information they disclose.

10.27   How is child abuse defined?

A *child* is ordinarily defined by state law as a person under the age of 18. *Child abuse* is defined by statute and usually includes physical abuse, emotional abuse, neglect, and sexual molestation. Limitations on who is responsible for and what constitutes the infliction of abuse vary by state. These various state law definitions of abuse affect when and how a person has to report a condition reasonably believed to be abusive to a child.

 NOTE: Since there are varying state statutes, a religious nonprofit organization should carefully review the applicable statutes to determine how child abuse is defined in its state's statutes and what the abuse reporting requirements are.

10.28   Is there liability for failing to report child abuse or neglect?

Child abuse reporting statutes are in place in all 50 states. These statutes make it a crime to not report abuse or neglect. In the course of ministry, it is common for a minister to learn that a minor is being abused. This can occur in a number of ways. The person responsible for the abuse could seek spiritual advice on the matter or could actually confess the acts of abuse to the clergy, priest, or rabbi. Or a friend of the abused or alleged abuser could report the abuse to the minister. Finally, the minister could witness the abuse without having had it reported to him or her. When any of these situations occur, a religious nonprofit organization and its employees should not internalize the situation and attempt to resolve it privately without contacting authorities. Failure to report child abuse or neglect could have very serious consequences to the person charged with reporting it.

If a state's child abuse reporting statute defines a member of the clergy as a mandatory reporter, then failing to report would subject the person to criminal prosecution for failing to comply with his or her state's reporting laws. Many statutes define mandatory reporters as any person having a reasonable belief that child abuse has occurred. Other statutes give a list of occupations that are mandatory reporters. Some of these statutes include members of the clergy specifically, while others do not; however, a minister, clergy, or priest could fall in another category listed, such as counselor or teacher, based on the relationship had with either the abused or the alleged perpetrator. Thus, one should never assume that he or she is not under a duty to report suspected abuse or neglect. Even if the abuse is determined after a communication that would fall under the clergy–penitent privilege, it should not be assumed that the privilege keeps an individual from reporting the abuse. As discussed previously, the privilege arises in court proceedings and depositions. Merely informing the authorities of a suspected abuse would not result in a breach of the privilege and it should not be assumed that the privilege would be a defense to a failure to report.

Aside from the criminal liability for failure to report, some states have enacted laws permitting child abuse victims to sue ministers for failing to report child abuse. In the states with these statutes, only the victims of child abuse are allowed to sue mandatory reporters who fail to report the abuse. There is no such civil liability for people who are not mandatory reporters. These lawsuits may be brought many years after the suspected incident of abuse and there is nothing stipulating that such suits could not be brought even in jurisdictions without laws granting victims that right to bring such a suit. Aside from legislative efforts on this matter, some courts have also created civil liability for failing to report abuse.

10.29 Is there immunity for persons reporting or assisting in the investigation of a report of child abuse or neglect?

Every state grants legal immunity to reporters of child abuse in order to encourage child abuse reporting. No one can be sued for simply reporting suspected child abuse; however, many states require that the report be based on reasonable cause to believe that the abuse has occurred. With this immunity comes the possibility that false reports will be filed. Many states have laws that subject people to both civil liability, and in some states, criminal liability, for maliciously transmitting a false report of abuse.

10.30 As an employer, are religious nonprofit organizations generally subject to the same legal requirements applicable to for-profit entities?

Yes. A religious nonprofit organization must observe most employee rights recognized by law, with several important exceptions. The prohibition against discrimination on the basis of religion does not apply to religious organizations. A religious organization may discriminate on the basis of religion in all employment placement decisions, pursuant to Section 702 of Title VII, the Civil Rights Act of 1964. This Act protects Americans from employment discrimination based on race, color, religion, sex, national origin, age, and disability. But it also recognizes the fundamental rights of religious organizations to hire employees who share their religious beliefs. The United States Supreme Court unanimously upheld this special protection for faith-based groups in 1987, and it has been the law since then. Thus, a Jewish organization can decide to hire only Jewish employees, a Catholic organization can decide to hire only Catholics, and so on, without running into problems with the Civil Rights Act.

In general, a religious organization retains this exemption even if it receives federal, state, or local financial assistance. However, certain federal laws and regulations, as well as state and local laws, may place conditions on the receipt of government funds. For example, some employment laws may prohibit discrimination on the basis of religion. A state or local law may prohibit discrimination on the basis of sexual orientation or require certain organizations to provide benefits to employees' unmarried domestic partners. Some of these laws may exempt religious organizations, while others may not. An organization with further questions about this issue may wish to consult an attorney to determine the specific requirements that apply to it and any rights it may have under the Constitution or federal laws.

NOTE: Religion cannot be used as a pretext for other action. For example, terminating only female employees for adultery or unwed pregnancy, and not male employees, amounts to gender and possibly pregnancy discrimination. Certain terms of employment, such as pay, benefits, and working conditions, are not to be determined on the basis of religion, while the decision to hire or promote a person into a particular position can be. Certain state laws prohibiting sexual orientation discrimination exempt religious organizations from coverage to varying degrees. The requirement for unemployment insurance and workers' compensation coverage may vary for religious organizations from state to state.

10.31   What does it mean to have an *at-will employment relationship*?

The *at-will employment relationship* means that either party (the employee or the employer) can choose to end the employment relationship at any time without notice and for any reason, so long as the reason is not an illegal reason. Unlawful employment discrimination or retaliation would constitute an illegal reason. Nearly every state recognizes the doctrine of employment at will. Employment for a specific term by contract or employment until and unless there is just cause for termination stand in distinction to employment at will.

10.32   What requirements must employers follow for new hires?

Before and after hiring an employee an organization must do the following: Obtain a Federal Employer Identification Number; register with its state labor or employer division; obtain Worker's Compensation Insurance (if required); post an "Employee Poster" as required by federal and most state governments; and complete, for every new employee, a federal W-4 Form, federal I-9 Form, and any state new-hire reporting form, all of which should be kept by the employer in the "employee" files for at least four years.

It is further *recommended* and advisable to follow prudent steps for hiring that include keeping the organization's job opening records and job advertisement and recruitment records writing and use of job descriptions, screening and interviewing qualified applicants with proper employment applications, ensuring that managers are adequately trained to conduct effective and lawful interviews, and ensuring that interviews comply with the Americans with Disabilities Act and are conducted in physically accessible locations for applicants with mobility impairments with reasonable accommodations being made.

With respect to references and background checks, a prospective employer may contact former employers expecting that some will not give references apart from confirming dates of employment and job titles. Employers are generally hesitant to reveal more than the employees' date of hire, date of termination, and job title; they may consider all else prohibited confidential information. If the applicant signs a waiver and hold-harmless agreement as a condition for applying for employment, the past employer may feel more comfortable discussing additional information specified by the agreement. The organization should document responses of former employers and contact former supervisors, if possible, but limit discussion to past job performance and avoid areas such as a prospective employee's history of workers' compensation injuries and prior employment discrimination activities.

Job descriptions and employment application responses *should* advance the hiring process. A religious nonprofit organization should use its application form to give applicants notice of certain terms and conditions of employment, such as the right to consider religion and the obligation of employees to adhere to certain standards of conduct. The application should avoid unlawful preemployment inquiries, as should the interviewer, and should be reviewed by legal counsel for use in each state in which employees are hired. An organization should not make assumptions about the right to access arrest and conviction records that are public information, or the right to use such information for hiring decisions, as it varies from state to state. Certain states allow employers to discriminate based on criminal convictions, but not arrests, while other states apply considerably varying rules depending on the position being applied for.

10.33 How do religious nonprofit organizations conduct lawful background checks?

Laws regulating background checks vary among jurisdictions and can be summarized as focusing on consent and disclosure. Generally, state background check laws limit the amount and type of information employers may disclose about employees, and require employers to obtain employees' written permission before disclosing or investigating certain information. Many state background check laws also limit the degree to which employers may make employment decisions based on such information. An organization should consider utilizing a specialized investigative agency familiar with requirements for conducting background, criminal, or credit checks with a form that has properly secured the applicant's permission and disclosed the applicant's rights, considering among other elements the provisions of the Federal Fair Credit Reporting Act and Federal Bankruptcy Act pertaining to privacy, accuracy, use of, and other standards for background checks.

Some states have enacted background check laws or immunities that allow employers to speak candidly about former employees within parameters. Several states protect employers from defamation suits for disclosing truthful information specifically about job performance or reasons for discharge. State background check laws may require employers to write "service letters" for former employees to prevent inconsistent recitals of relevant information.

Religious organizations, in using criminal records information, must be aware of restrictions and prohibitions pertaining to the use, inquiry, and dissemination of criminal convictions, arrests without convictions, and impositions on the direct relationship to the job in question. State attorneys general offices and legal counsel can advise on the extent to which employers may consider criminal records in employment decisions, under each state's background check laws.

10.34 What should religious nonprofit organizations do in the event of receiving negative information about an applicant?

Assuming that an organization has properly obtained information, which it is permitted to consider in the context of employment, it may face a difficult decision in balancing negative information against making an offer of employment. As a general proposition, negative information that could impact the welfare of minors should be treated with even higher scrutiny than that which would affect adults. Information that could impact the welfare of adults is in turn more critical than that which would tend to affect resources or facilities. In the area of children, irresponsibility in the past presents a very high hurdle, while an intentional misdeed toward a minor should virtually always, if not always, preclude a position with children. For example, a past lapse in care for an employer's equipment is less critical than a taking of property for personal use, which is, relatively speaking, a less serious harm than a prior wrongful act toward an individual.

An employer is held to the standard of reasonable care in selecting and hiring employees. Therefore, great consideration should be given to condoning the employment of those with negative information in their backgrounds. Decision making depends on such factors as the type of information in question, mitigating circumstances, prevalence of occurrences, time since the occurrence(s), structural supervision of the would-be employee, duties of the would-be employee, the co-workers the would-be employee would have, and the community's standards and expectations in the area of the organization.

When the negative information is an inconsistent statement, omission, or inflation or exaggeration of a fact, the organization must assess the credibility of the would-be employee. A misunderstanding is a common guise for dishonesty, particularly where the correct information would have produced an unfavorable result for the employee. It should indeed be the very exceptional circumstance where an employee who is currently deemed to be untrustworthy is nevertheless hired or retained. Again, by common law, if an employee's actions injured someone, the employer may be liable. An inexplicably poor hiring decision can lead to financial and reputational disaster for the religious nonprofit organization.

10.35 What are the sources of liability in the context of employment?

Employers may be held liable for taking action against employees in violation of their protected rights. Generally, the action taken must be material and adverse before courts will intervene. Termination of employment is just one example of an adverse employment action. Various statutory protections are discussed below. Employers may also be liable to their employees for a breach of contract, if one exists between them, as well as for harassment and other actions by third parties that come in contact with employees. Employers may be liable to their employees for the acts of other employees, as well as for injuries caused to employees through the negligence of the employer. Employers may also be liable to third parties for the acts of their employees as well as for representations and commitments made by their employees.

10.36   Should religious nonprofit organizations use employment contracts?

Generally, yes. It is not a contradiction to use an employment contract while maintaining the employment at-will relationship. An employment contract may be useful to a religious nonprofit organization for many purposes, apart from the basic and traditional specification of duties, terms of compensation, and period of employment. Although most employers opt for employment at-will without a term of employment for most employees, a contract can memorialize that understanding and state that no oral agreements may modify that relationship. Further, contracts may contain important mandatory alternative dispute resolution provisions and include provisions for the confidentiality of private information during and after employment. Key personnel are often secured only by an employment contract, as they may place value on the certainty of a minimum employment term as well as benefits that have been offered or negotiated for. Employment contracts may also be used to identify particular performance requirements and expectations, reiterate grounds for termination of the employment relationship, and allocate the ownership interests of creative works (intellectual property) created during the employment relationship.

10.37   Should religious nonprofit organizations use written employee manuals?

Yes; so long as employee manuals are not relied on to the exclusion of having a working understanding of legal responsibilities owed to employees, employment manuals are a useful tool in the administration of human resources. Manuals are properly utilized when drafted and considered by the organization to provide general guidance, rather than an all-encompassing formula capable of generating the answer to every issue. That said, manuals should be utilized to reinforce the organization's right to discriminate in its employment decisions based on religious considerations. While the majority of policies adopted may be wholly discretionary, denying the benefits or protections of policies to classes of individuals, or selective enforcement, may have the effect of relegating an employee manual to "pretext" status. Organizations should consider written employee manuals for their discretionary policies only after discerning that what best promotes their principles and purposes has worked in practice. The manual should state clearly that its terms are not contractual but are only statements of policies and procedures.

CHAPTER 11

Employee Rights

11.1 What laws prohibit impermissible discrimination based upon race, color, national origin, sex, or religion?

Title VII of the Civil Rights of 1964 and each state through its statutes prevent employment discrimination on the basis of age, race, color, sex, religion, and national origin (protected classes). These statutes typically do not apply to the smallest private employers as defined by employee count. A plaintiff can establish a case of race discrimination by establishing that (1) he or she belongs to a protected class; (2) he or she was qualified for a job for which the employer was seeking applicants; (3) he or she was rejected for the position despite his or her qualifications; (4) the position remained open after his or her rejection; and (5) the employer continued to seek applications from other people with similar qualifications to the plaintiff. A similar analysis applies to plaintiffs' claims of discrimination for other adverse employment actions, essentially comparing the treatment of employees who are not in a protected class with the ones who are. When there is direct evidence of discrimination, for example, a comment to the effect that a female employee will be replaced by a male for her supervisor's role, the discrimination is not inferential and need not be supported by the comparative treatment of other employees.

11.2 Is a religious nonprofit organization automatically exempted from the laws contained in Title VII?

No. Religious organizations are not automatically exempt from antidiscrimination laws. An individual's religion can be taken into consideration during the decision of placement of a certain employee in a position; however, other terms of employment, such as pay and benefits, cannot differ based on the religion of the individual. Aside from the limited exception of religious discrimination, all other grounds for discrimination are equally applicable to religious nonprofit organizations.

11.3 Are all religious nonprofit organizations automatically covered by the laws contained in Title VII?

No. An employer, religious or otherwise, is covered under Title VII if it has 15 or more employees for each working day in each of 20 or more calendar weeks in the same calendar year as, or in the calendar year prior to, when the alleged discrimination occurred. Add to that figure any other individuals who have an employment relationship with the employer, such as temporary or other staffing firm workers. It is possible for affiliated religious entities, which control an employee, to be added to meet the numerical requirement in certain circumstances; for example, if an employer does not have the minimum number of employees to meet the statutory requirement, it is still covered if it is part of an integrated enterprise that meets the requirement. An *integrated enterprise* is one in which the operations of two or more employers are considered so intertwined that they can be considered the single employer of the charging party. The separate entities that form an integrated enterprise are treated as a single employer for purposes of both coverage and liability under Title VII.

NOTE: The factors a court would consider in determining whether two or more organizations are an integrated enterprise include the following: sharing of management services such as check-writing; preparation of mutual policy manuals, contract negotiations, and completion of business licenses; sharing of payroll and insurance programs; sharing of services of managers and personnel; sharing use of office space, equipment, and storage; and operating the entities as a single unit.

11.4 What is the *religious organizations exception* to Title VII?

Title VII's exception for *religious organizations* states that the law will not apply to "a religious corporation, association, educational institution, or society with respect to the employment of individuals of a particular religion to perform work connected with the carrying on by such corporation, association, educational institution, or society of its activities." 42 U.S.C. § 2000e-1(a). A similar exemption exists for certain religiously affiliated schools if they are, in whole or in part, owned, supported, controlled, or managed by a particular religion or religious group, or if the curriculum is directed toward the propagation of a particular religion. 42 U.S.C. § 2000e-2(e)(2).

The *religious organization exception* applies only to those institutions the "purpose and character [of which] are primarily religious." Although no one factor is dispositive, significant factors include whether its articles of incorporation state a religious purpose, whether its day-to-day operations are religious, and whether it is for profit or nonprofit. That determination must be based on "[a]ll significant religious and secular characteristics." The determination of whether a particular employer falls within the *religious organization exception* permitting religious preference in hiring is made on a case-by-case basis.

If an organization or school is exempt from Title VII's religious discrimination provisions, it can likely ask applicants about religious background, beliefs, and practices, and make employment decisions based on the answers to those questions without violating Title VII. The *religious organization exception*, however, is limited to discrimination based on religion, so even religious organizations are not permitted to discriminate on other protected bases, such as race, national origin, or sex.

11.5 What is a *bona fide occupational qualification* and how does it modify antidiscrimination laws?

In general, an employer would not be expected to have a legitimate (nondiscriminatory) need to take into consideration an employee's or applicant's race, color, sex, religion, and national origin. The law recognizes limited circumstances where the job at issue reasonably necessitates making such distinctions in order to sustain a profitable business. The standard is known as the *business necessity rule*. The law provides an employer with *some* leeway to accommodate the reasonable preferences of its supporting customer base, at least where the courts agree the customers have a strong and inoffensive interest. Race is not contemplated by the courts as being a protected class subject to this exception.

11.6 What is the prohibition against pregnancy discrimination?

Pregnancy discrimination is closely related to gender discrimination and is often accompanied by other acts of gender discrimination when it occurs. The Pregnancy Discrimination Act is an amendment to Title VII of the Civil Rights Act of 1964; it is investigated by the Equal Employment Opportunity Commission. As with gender discrimination, discrimination based on pregnancy, childbirth, or related medical conditions constitutes unlawful sex discrimination under Title VII. Women affected by pregnancy or related conditions must be treated by employers in the same manner as other applicants or employees with similar abilities or limitations. An employer must stop discrimination by other employees. An employer cannot refuse to hire a woman because of her pregnancy-related condition if she is able to perform the major functions of her job. An employer cannot refuse to hire her because of any bias against pregnancy or the prejudices of co-workers, clients, or customers. An employer may not single out pregnancy-related conditions for special procedures to determine an employee's ability to work. An employer may, however, use its generally applied procedures to screen all employees' ability to work, such as submission of a doctor's statement concerning their inability to work before granting leave or paying sick benefits. The same is required when an employee is temporarily unable to perform her job due to pregnancy; the employer must provide the same modified tasks, alternative assignments, disability leave, or leave without pay as would be offered others. An employer may not restrict an employee from returning to work for a predetermined length of time after childbirth and must hold open a job for a pregnancy-related absence the same length of time that jobs are held open for employees on sick or disability leave.

NOTE: In the case of an employee's pregnancy that occurred outside of the marriage relationship, this often violates the religious nonprofit organization's tenets of faith, scripture, and moral teachings. In that case, the organization may consider dismissing the employee for violation of its moral teachings. Because of the religious organization exception to Title VII (described above), such an action would likely be exempted from federal, state, and local civil rights laws. Before undertaking such an action, the organization should, however, carefully consider whether the organization has previously placed the employee on notice (through its employment application, employment agreements, employee handbook, and bylaws) that violations of the organization's moral standards can result in discipline, up to and including termination. Further, the organization is well-advised to mete out discipline for violation of its moral standards, including pregnancy outside of marriage, evenhandedly and equally to both men and women.

11.7 What is the prohibition against unequal pay for men and women?

Because gender discrimination in all its forms is prohibited under Title VII of the Civil Rights Act of 1964, paying female employees less than males constitutes gender discrimination. There is also a second federal law specifically regarding equal pay—the Equal Pay Act of 1963 (EPA). The EPA prohibits discrimination on the basis of sex in the payment of wages or benefits, where men and women perform work of similar skill, effort, and responsibility for the same employer under similar working conditions. Under this second Act, employers may not reduce wages of either sex to equalize pay between men and women. A violation of the EPA may occur where a different wage was or is paid to an individual who worked in the same job before or after an employee of the opposite sex and a violation may also occur where a third party such as a labor union causes the employer to violate the law. This Act is well defined by regulations that set out the rules as to who is covered, the constitution of wages, how to compare wages, and when pay differentials are permitted.

11.8 What is the prohibition against age discrimination?

The Age Discrimination in Employment Act of 1967 (ADEA) was intended to protect workers over 40 years of age; it applies to employers with 20 or more employees. The ADEA presumes that employers favor younger workers as a result of stereotyping; it prohibits statements or specifications in job notices or advertisements of age preference and limitations. An age limit may be specified only in the rare circumstance where age has been proven to be a *bona fide* occupational qualification. Further, denial of benefits to older employees is prohibited; an employer may reduce benefits based on age only if the cost of providing the reduced benefits to older workers is the same as the cost of providing benefits to younger workers. Under the ADEA, it is unlawful to discriminate against an individual because of his or her age with respect to any term, condition, or privilege of employment. This includes hiring, firing, promotion, layoff, compensation, benefits, job assignments, and training. It is also unlawful to retaliate against an individual for opposing employment practices that discriminate based on age, or for filing an age discrimination charge, testifying, or participating in any way in an investigation, proceeding, or litigation under the ADEA.

11.9 What is *disability discrimination*?

Religious employers are not exempted from federal disability discrimination law, which prohibits adverse treatment because of a disability, as well as requires affirmative action in the form of reasonable accommodation by employers toward those with covered disabilities. Title I of the Americans with Disabilities Act of 1990 (ADA) prohibits private employers from discriminating against qualified individuals with disabilities in job application procedures, hiring, firing, advancement, compensation, job training, and other terms, conditions, and privileges of employment. The ADA covers employers with 15 or more employees. An individual with a disability is a person who (1) has a physical or mental impairment that substantially limits one or more major life activities; (2) has a record of such impairment; or (3) is regarded as having such impairment. Covered employers are required to make reasonable accommodations to the known disabilities of employees if doing so would not impose an "undue hardship" on the operation of the employer. Employers may not allow retaliation against those employees who have resisted discrimination on their own or on behalf of others. While an organization may verify ability to perform job functions, employers may not ask job applicants about the existence, nature, or severity of a disability.

11.10 What affirmative obligations do religious nonprofit organizations have as an employer to accommodate an employee's disability?

Allowing a discriminatory motivation toward a disabled employee or applicant to result in adverse action is certainly a violation of the ADA. Retaining only individuals who need no accommodations because they are objectively less expensive to the organization is not a legally valid rationale in the context of the ADA. A qualified employee or applicant with a disability is an individual who, with or without reasonable accommodation, can perform the essential functions of the job in question. Such *reasonable accommodation* may include making existing facilities used by employees readily accessible to and usable by persons with disabilities, job restructuring, modifying work schedules, reassignment to a vacant position, acquiring or modifying equipment or devices, adjusting or modifying examinations, training materials, or policies, and providing qualified readers or interpreters. However, these are merely examples; reasonable accommodation varies under each unique circumstance.

11.11 When does the organization's affirmative obligation to accommodate arise?

Generally, it is the responsibility of the employee to inform the employer that an accommodation is needed in order to participate in the application process or to perform essential job functions, after which point affirmative obligations arise. Affirmative obligations likely arise without specific notice if the employer is already aware of the need. To be protected under the ADA, the employee must have a record of, or be regarded as having, a substantial impairment. A *substantial impairment* is one that significantly limits or restricts a major life activity, such as hearing, seeing, speaking, walking, breathing, performing manual tasks, caring for oneself, learning, or working. Further, if one has a disability, he or she must also be qualified to perform the essential functions or duties of the job, with or without reasonable accommodation, in order to be protected from job discrimination by the ADA. This means two things: (1) One must satisfy the employer's requirements for the job, such as education, employment experience, skills, or licenses; and (2) one must be able to perform the essential functions of the job with or without reasonable accommodation. *Essential functions* are the fundamental job duties that one must be able to perform at a minimum with the help of a reasonable accommodation.

11.12 What rights are extended to employees or prospective employees who provide services to the military?

The Uniformed Services Employment and Reemployment Rights Act (USERRA) protects employees serving in the armed forces, national guard, or commissioned corps of the Public Health Services for taking a military leave of absence from work. USERRA's protections include prohibiting discrimination by employers; requiring companies to reemploy or return someone to a similar position on returning from armed service with seniority; and maintenance of benefits and health plans during the service. The Act also prevents discrimination in hiring, promotion, reemployment, or any other benefit of employment. USERRA also prohibits retaliation against anyone who seeks to enforce their rights under USERRA or assists another in enforcing those rights. Employment at will is suspended under USERRA in that an employee returning from a military leave of absence of more than 30 days cannot be fired without cause within the first 180 days of returning to work. If the military leave was for more than 180 days, USERRA prohibits firing the employee without cause for a year after returning to work.

11.13 What is *sexual harassment*?

Sexual harassment is a form of discrimination that consists of unwelcome sexual advances and conduct. The atmosphere can range anywhere from mild transgressions and annoyances to serious abuses, and can even involve forced sexual activity.

Sexual harassment differs from other forms of discrimination because the offender does not have to hold any animosity toward the victim. Sexual harassment can be "quid pro quo," which is essentially a threat that the victim's job status is tied to sexual cooperation. It can also be "offensive atmosphere," where the victim is subjected to an intimidating, hostile, or offensive work environment, such as allowing co-workers to make sexual remarks or jokes, displaying sexual content on a computer or calendar, or similar conduct. It can also take the form of "preferential treatment based upon sexual favoritism," where a supervisor grants an employee preferential treatment because that employee is involved in a consensual sexual relationship with the supervisor. Any form of sexual harassment can subject a religious organization to a legal claim.

11.14 How can religious nonprofit organizations prevent sexual harassment in the workplace?

Religious nonprofit organizations have several advantages in preventing sexual harassment compared to their secular counterparts. Most adopt a code of conduct that comports with their organization's doctrinal beliefs and tenets of faith that require a respectful and dignified relationship between employees and strictly reserve the pursuit of sexual relationships to marriage.

Generally, to prevent claims of sexual harassment in the religious nonprofit workplace, employers should make sure that they define prohibited conduct, educate the staff, adopt written policies and obtain acknowledgments of receipt, enforce policies, maintain an open-door policy free of intimidation and the possibility of retaliation, promptly investigate complaints, and, when necessary, take appropriate prompt remedial action.

11.15 How should religious nonprofit organizations react if they suspect sexual harassment?

All employers have a legal obligation to promptly investigate complaints and take appropriate remedial action. Employees have a duty to report sexual harassment and cooperate fully with investigations. Employers should treat complaints as valid and worthy of consideration, while remaining impartial during the investigation. Part of the process of treating harassment complaints as valid while investigating the facts is taking steps necessary to ensure that any harassment stops or is prevented and ensuring that no retaliation can occur during the investigation itself. Separation between affected employees, modification of chain of command, and increased supervision can usually prevent misconduct. Complaining parties must not be discouraged from coming forward because of the belief they will be retaliated against, that the investigation will not be handled appropriately and discreetly, or that nothing will be done to remedy the inappropriate behavior.

11.16 What should religious nonprofit organizations do if they are told sexual harassment is occurring?

If the initial complaint comes from a witness, a religious organization should assure the witness that no retaliation will occur and then proceed to gather facts from the witness. Remedial measures should be implemented to stop the harassment, correct its effects on the employee, and ensure that the harassment does not reoccur. These remedial measures need not be those that the complainant-employee requests or prefers, as long as they are effective. In determining disciplinary measures, management should keep in mind that the employer could be found liable if the harassment does not stop; at the same time, management should also keep in mind that overly punitive measures may possibly subject the employer to claims such as wrongful discharge. To balance the competing concerns, disciplinary measures should be proportional to the seriousness of the offense. If the harassment was minor, counseling and a verbal warning might be all that is necessary. Conversely, if the harassment was severe or persistent, then suspension or discharge may be appropriate.

11.17 What is *remedial action*?

Remedial action is the action of the organization designed to stop the harassment, correct its effects on the employee, and ensure that the harassment does not recur. Examples of remedial action include warnings and reprimands, demotion, suspension, discharge, training, and counseling. Other remedial actions may be designed to correct the effects of harassment, including apologies from the harasser.

11.18 What are the advisable steps to include when terminating an employee?

Generally, once a decision to terminate an employee has been made for a legitimate nondiscriminatory reason, and as long as any prior disciplinary or improvement measures taken were consistent with practices and policy, the organization is well advised to schedule a meeting that includes the employee, the employee's supervisor, and either a human resources manager or the supervisor's manager (and an attorney, if necessary, because of egregious circumstances). Once the meeting begins, the employer should explain to the employee the reason for the employment termination in a concise way that preserves the employee's dignity. Often, there will be an extensive list of cumulative problems leading up to the termination. While it is not necessary to expound on each item in such a discussion, it is important to accurately generalize the issues. That way, if the employee contests the termination, he or she does not assert that certain reasons are responsible for the termination that were never, in fact, expressed. It is important during the process that the employer not be drawn into an argument.

If the organization utilizes separation agreements, where an amount of severance is paid in exchange for the execution of a full release, that subject needs to be discussed with the employee during the meeting. In such cases, the employee is usually deemed to have resigned instead of terminated. Where there is no animosity between the parties, employers sometimes allow employees to opt to resign, which may be of assistance to the employee when seeking subsequent employment. This meeting is also the time to collect all passwords and property, or determine the location of these items, and to allow the employee a choice about when to remove personal belongings from the work area. Finally, the organization must address the following issues: (1) unused benefits, such as accrued time off; (2) expense reimbursements or advances to the employee; (3) whether the employee desires to give written permission for reference checking; and (4) the provision of a letter from the human resources department that outlines the status of his or her benefits on termination, including life insurance, health coverage, retirement and expense account plans, and the continuation thereof under COBRA.

11.19 What special circumstances should alert the employer to the possibility of a termination being contested as wrongful?

The expression by an employee of the perception of inconsistent treatment and/ or standards that are not evenhandedly applied should alert an employer to the possibility that a termination will be deemed wrongful by the employee. If the employee has complained about objectionable treatment or assisted another in doing so, the employee is likely to view subsequent decisions adverse to the employee as retaliatory. If an employee has not been made aware of prior dissatisfaction with his or her performance or conduct and is then confronted with that reason and simultaneously replaced with an employee who is, for example, significantly younger, the employer may anticipate a challenge to its rationale. With respect to retaliation claims, the closer in time the decision is to protected activity, the stronger the presumption will be that the motive was retaliatory. Employers should be alert to the possibility that adverse actions taken against employees that are proximate in time to their entering a protected class may appear discriminatory or retaliatory.

11.20 Are employment decisions other than termination possibly adverse?

Yes, other employment decisions apart from termination may be considered adverse employment actions. These employment decisions could include verbal or written warnings or reprimands that constitute a significant change in employment status, such as preclusion from promotion, transfer, or reassignment with significantly different responsibilities, demotion, reduction of wages, or possibly suspension.

11.21 How should employers document their employment decision-making process to demonstrate the appropriateness of their actions?

The employer should begin documentation before the employee is ever hired by developing employment policies, job descriptions, and written policies for termination. Guidelines for termination should include definitions of performance, misconduct, descriptions of the review procedures that will lead to termination, and policies regarding severance, future employment references, and the return of property. When the decision at issue is termination, the employer should document the reasons over time, as they occur, and in the most quantifiable terms possible. Legal counsel should be consulted if the circumstances warrant special consideration.

11.22 What are the benefits of *alternative dispute resolution*?

Alternative Dispute Resolution (ADR) is a venue other than the judicial system in which to resolve disputes. It commonly involves progressive reconciliation efforts to attempt to bring resolution to a matter while avoiding a judicial hearing on the merits. The primary benefit to ADR is expediency in bringing the dispute to resolution. Rather than spending up to several years preparing a case for trial and waiting for a turn on the court's docket, resolution may be accomplished in a few weeks to a few months. Also, rather than spending tens of thousands of dollars to prepare for trial, the parties may spend a small fraction of that amount to resolve their contested issues. Moreover, proceedings in the judicial system are public record, while confidentiality can be maintained in ADR proceedings. Finally, the outcome of ADR proceedings can be determined by knowledgeable specialists in the area or field of the dispute, while traditional jury trials leave the outcome to a panel of laypersons who may have no prior experience with any of the issues at trial.

11.23 What steps can religious nonprofit organizations take to require alternative dispute resolution in the event of a conflict?

Alternative Dispute Resolution can be required of employees of a religious organization. Employees can be made to agree to mandatory ADR as a condition of their employment with the organization. It is necessary for an employer to demonstrate an employee's agreement to ADR before a proceeding can commence. For this reason, it is highly advisable to have all employees sign a properly drawn and enforceable written ADR agreement if mandatory alternative dispute resolution is the employer's desire. Under certain circumstances, even without a signed agreement, ADR may still be required, but there is no reason to attempt to rely on an oral policy, practice, or handbook provision alone when a signed ADR agreement can be easily procured from all employees.

11.24 What is *mediation*?

Mediation is a form of alternative dispute resolution that is confidential and voluntary. It aims, with the help of neutral mediators, to assist two or more parties in reaching an agreement over a disputed matter. The mediator is not a judge or decision maker. Instead, the mediator is a skilled facilitator who explores as many options as possible with the parties to come to a win-win solution. The benefit of mediation is that the parties retain control over the outcome of their dispute, rather than relinquishing that power to a judge or arbitrator. The disputes themselves may involve organizations, communities, individuals, or other representatives with a vested interest in the outcome of the dispute.

Mediators use appropriate techniques and/or skills to open and/or improve dialogue between the parties, aiming to help the parties reach an agreement (with concrete effects) on the disputed matter. Normally, all parties must view the mediator as impartial.

Mediation can apply in a variety of disputes. These include commercial, legal, workplace, community, and divorce or other family matters.

11.25 What is *arbitration*?

Arbitration is a process much like a court trial. In arbitration, the disputing parties submit their case to a trained, neutral third party, for fact finding and judgment. There are two types of arbitration:

1. *Binding arbitration* results in a decision by the arbitrator that is binding on the parties and is enforceable by the courts as a final judgment.
2. *Advisory (or nonbinding) arbitration* results in a decision that is neither binding nor enforceable by court. The purpose of advisory arbitration is to facilitate settlement by giving the parties an indication of the likely outcome of the case, should it proceed to trial or in binding arbitration.

Arbitration differs from judicial system litigation in that an arbitration proceeding need not adhere to the formal rules of evidence and civil procedure required at trial, which tend to be costly to comply with and are perceived as difficult to understand. In a judicial proceeding, a judge typically controls how the case will be presented and what the jury will hear, and the jury will decide what happened based on what it is told it can consider. An arbitrator decides what weight to give each piece of evidence, but does not exclude evidence from presentation, as courts typically are compelled to do by rules of evidence. An arbitrator is more likely to directly ask questions of the witnesses and openly indicate to the parties what type of evidence would be considered important to support the points in contention.

11.26 Can religious nonprofit organizations designate neutral third-party mediators and arbitrators that adhere to the value system of their entity?

Yes, most jurisdictions will recognize that the parties to a dispute should have some control over the identity of the individual(s) selected to decide the outcome of the case. Parties can have a prior agreement that the panel of candidates will come from a same-faith-based arbitration service provider. Secular arbitrators are often specialized in particular types of cases, such as employment cases, commercial contracts, and business disputes. An employer should designate in the written arbitration agreement any specific preference of arbitration provider or describe the credentials of or type of arbitrator that will be selected.

PART III

Operation of a Religious Nonprofit Organization

CHAPTER 12

General Operations

12.1 How does a religious nonprofit organization that is required to file an informational return (Form 990) change its accounting period (tax year)?

If the organization is required to file an annual information return (Form 990), then it can change its accounting period whenever it wishes, without permission from the IRS or any other government agency. When this is done, however, it must file an annual information return for the short period resulting from the change. It is helpful to write "Change of Accounting Period" at the top of the short-period return. If an organization changes its accounting period within the 10-calendar-year period that includes the beginning of one of the short periods, and it had an informational return filing requirement at any time during the 10-year period, it must prepare and attach an IRS form (Form 1128) to the short-period return.

12.2 What is the *state income tax exemption*?

IRC § 501(c)(3) nonprofit organizations are eligible for state exemptions from payment of corporate income tax, as well as other tax exemptions and benefits. All but five states have corporate income taxes, and most also have sales and other taxes. For-profit corporations are taxed by most states on their gross income.

Religious nonprofit organizations, however, receive most if not all of their income in the form of gifts that are excluded from the organization's income. Most states expressly exempt religious organizations from the tax on corporate income.

12.3 What is the *state sales tax exemption* for religious nonprofit organizations, and do the exemptions vary from state to state?

Generally, states impose a sales tax on the sale of tangible personal property or the provision of various services. Religious nonprofit organizations are exempt from some, if not all, sales tax in the vast majority of states. The extent, manner, and means of exemption vary, however, from state to state.

12.4 What is the *state property tax exemption,* and do the exemptions vary from state to state?

Each of the 50 states recognizes some type of property tax exemption for religious nonprofit organizations. The extent, manner, and means of exemption vary from state to state and an organization should consult the statutes in its state to determine how and when to file for a state property tax exemption.

12.5 What corporate records are required to be maintained?

All tax-exempt organizations, including churches and religious nonprofit organizations (regardless of whether tax-exempt status has been recognized by the IRS), are required to maintain books of account and other records necessary to justify their claim for exemption in the event of an audit. Tax-exempt organizations are also required to maintain books and records that are necessary to accurately file any federal tax and information returns that may be required.

There is no specific format for keeping records. However, the types of required records generally include articles of organization (charter, constitution, articles of incorporation), bylaws, minute books, property records, general ledgers, receipts and disbursements journals, payroll records, banking records, and invoices. The extent of the records necessary to be maintained generally varies according to the type, size, and complexity of the organization's activities.

The Revised Model Nonprofit Corporation Act is a comprehensive set of statutes that are available for adoption by states to regulate the establishment and operation of nonprofit corporations within their jurisdictions and is instructive regarding proper corporate recordkeeping.

Regarding corporate records, the Model Act states:

- A corporation shall keep as permanent records minutes of all meetings of its members and board of directors.
- A corporation shall keep a record of all actions taken by the members or directors without a meeting.
- A corporation shall keep a record of all actions taken by committees of the board of directors.
- A corporation shall maintain appropriate accounting records.
- A corporation or its agent shall maintain a record of its members in a form that permits preparation of a list of the names and addresses of all members,

in alphabetical order by class, showing the number of votes each member is entitled to cast.

* A corporation shall maintain its records in written form or in another form capable of conversion into written form within a reasonable time.

The Model Act further states a corporation shall keep a copy of the following records at its principal office:

* Its articles or restated articles of incorporation and all amendments to them currently in effect
* Its bylaws or restated bylaws and all amendments to them currently in effect
* Resolutions adopted by its board of directors relating to the characteristics, qualifications, rights, limitations, and obligations of members or any class or category of members
* The minutes of all meetings of members and records of all actions approved by the members for the past three years
* All written communications to members generally within the past three years, including the financial statements furnished for the past three years
* A list of the names and business or home addresses of its current directors and officers

NOTE: Not all states' nonprofit corporation statutes were derived from the Revised Model Nonprofit Corporation Act and those states that did adopt the Model Act have, to varying extents, altered it. Accordingly, each state's statutes must be examined to determine the law in that state regarding corporate recordkeeping requirements. Further, in those states that have adopted all or portions of the Model Act, those provisions apply unless the organization's articles and/or bylaws provide otherwise. As such, the organization's own governance documents must be examined to determine what governance provisions apply.

12.6 What is the length of time required to retain records?

The law does not specify a length of time that records must be retained. The length of time that is advisable for retaining varies depending upon the record in question. Certain records including, but not limited to, organizational documents, meetings of minutes, and deed records should be maintained throughout the lifetime of the organization. The IRS has published the following guidelines to be applied in the event that the records may be material to the administration of any federal tax law. Specifically, the IRS has recommended that records of revenue and expense, including payroll records, should be maintained for at least four years after filing the return to which they relate. The IRS similarly recommends that financial documents related to the purchase or sale of real or personal property be maintained for at least four years after filing the return to which they relate. The general requirement placed upon nonprofit organizations is that they maintain complete and accurate records. Many states allow members to view the records of a nonprofit organization upon request. Those statutes may aid in providing additional guidance as to which records to retain and the length of time they should be retained.

Aside from the IRS's published guidelines, the organization will also want to keep certain records permanently, including real estate documents, amendments to bylaws, corporate minutes, and other documents that would always retain relevance or legal significance.

12.7   What are the different types of minutes and what should minutes contain?

The proceedings of most religious nonprofit organizations are (and should be) reflected in minutes. Essentially, there are four types of minutes: organizational minutes, board-of-director minutes, committee minutes, and membership minutes.

- *Organizational minutes:* A document—in addition to articles, organization and bylaws—that is important when forming a tax-exempt organization is the organizational minutes. The organization's initial board of directors adopt these minutes. Generally, these minutes can reflect actions taken by means of an in-person meeting, a meeting by conference call, or a written unanimous consent document. At a minimum, this document should reflect:
  - Ratification of the articles of organization
  - Adoption of the bylaws
  - Election of any other directors
  - Election of the officers (if appropriate)
  - Passage of the requisite resolution(s) for establishment of a bank account (or accounts) or any other accounts at financial institutions
  - Passage of a resolution selecting legal counsel
  - Passage of a resolution selecting an accountant
  - Authorization (or ratification) of certain actions, such as preparation and filing with the IRS of an application for recognition of tax-exempt status
  - Authorization of reimbursement of expenses incurred in establishing the entity
  - Other actions of the board, such as discussion of program activities, development of one or more components of the fundraising program, or selection of management or fundraising consultants
- *Board minutes, committee minutes, and membership meeting minutes:* Complete and current minutes are one of the most important of the "corporate" formalities to observe. Each meeting of the board, committees, and the

membership of a religious nonprofit organization should be the subject of a set of minutes. Careful consideration should be given to meeting minutes. The minutes should be prepared with a heavy dose of common sense and perspective. The minutes should not be veritable transcripts of the proceedings but should memorialize material developments and decisions formally taken (as in resolutions).

It is difficult to generalize about the length and content of meeting minutes. Usually, whether something should have been in the minutes and is not, or whether something should not have been stated in the minutes and is, is determined in hindsight. The best practice is to be certain the date of the meeting is recorded, that all material voting decisions and other actions are reflected, and that a purpose statement for each action is in the document. A current and complete minute book, reflecting explanation of important decisions in transactions, can go a long way in resolving disputes, and shortening (or even forestalling) an IRS audit. Minutes should be kept in a minute book, along with other important documents, such as the articles of organization, bylaws, and IRS determination letter (if any). The point is to initiate and maintain a substantive history of the organization's decisions and progress toward achieving its exempt purposes.

NOTE: A person entitled to vote at a board, committee, and/or a membership meeting who opposes a majority action on a matter, and is sufficiently concerned about the seriousness of the issue, should be certain that this opposition is reflected in the minutes, perhaps coupled with an explanation of the member's position.

12.8 Should the religious nonprofit organization's corporate minutes be reviewed by a lawyer?

Yes. It is a good practice to have board, committee, and membership minutes drafted, and then reviewed by a lawyer before they are finalized. Experienced lawyers review and revise corporate minutes with the view that each document will someday be an exhibit in a trial.

12.9 What is a *personal board meeting book,* and why is every religious nonprofit board member well advised to maintain his or her own copy?

Each board member of a religious nonprofit organization is well advised to maintain his or her own personal board meeting book. Copies of minutes of meetings long since held can be discarded from time to time, but the thoughtful board member should bring this book to each meeting with copies of recent minutes readily available if needed.

12.10 What right do members of a religious nonprofit organization have to inspect the religious nonprofit organization's corporate records?

The right of inspection by members of a religious nonprofit organization's records is, absent provisions in the nonprofit's governance documents, governed by the laws of the state in which the organization is incorporated. Section 16 of the Revised Model Nonprofit Corporation Act is instructive. The Model Act gives a member of a nonprofit corporation (or the member's attorney) expansive rights to copy and inspect a nonprofit's corporate records for any "proper purpose" at any "reasonable time." Regarding religious nonprofit organizations, the Model Act states that the "articles or bylaws of a *religious corporation* may limit or abolish the right of a member under this section to inspect and copy any corporate record." As such, the organization's own governance documents must first be examined to determine what provisions apply, if any, regarding inspection of records by its membership.

12.11 What right does the public have to inspect the corporate records of a religious nonprofit organization?

None. The right of inspection, if any, applies only to an organization's members. The public has no right under state nonprofit corporation law to inspect the records of a religious nonprofit organization.

CHAPTER 13

Charitable Giving Rules

13.1 Are all tax-exempt organizations eligible to receive tax-deductible contributions?

No. The list of organizations that are eligible for exemption from the federal income tax is considerably longer than the list of organizations that are eligible to receive contributions that are deductible under federal tax law as charitable gifts. Five categories of nonprofit organizations are charitable donees for this purpose:

1. Charitable (including educational, religious, and scientific) organizations
2. A state, a possession of the federal government, a political subdivision of either, the federal government itself, and the District of Columbia, as long as the gift is made for a public purpose
3. An organization of war veterans, and the auxiliary unit of a foundation for a veterans' organization
4. Many fraternal societies that operate under the lodge system, as long as the gift is to be used for charitable purposes
5. Membership cemetery companies and corporations chartered for burial purposes as cemetery corporations

Generally, contributions to other types of tax-exempt organizations are not deductible.

13.2 What are the rules for deductibility of contributions of money?

A charitable contribution is often made with money. While this type of gift is usually deductible, there are limitations on the extent of deductibility in any one tax year. For a contribution of money to be deductible by an individual under the federal income tax law, he or she must itemize deductions.

For individuals, where a charitable gift is made with money and the charitable donee is a public charity, the extent of the charitable deduction under the federal income tax law cannot exceed 50 percent of the donor's adjusted gross income. In that instance, the excess portion can be carried forward and deducted over a period of up to five subsequent years. For example, if an individual had adjusted gross income of $100,000 for a particular year and made gifts of money to a religious nonprofit in that year totaling $40,000, the gifts would be fully deductible (unless other limitations apply) for that year. If the gifts totaled $60,000, the deduction for the year would be $50,000 and the excess $10,000 would be carried forward to later years. The charitable contribution deduction for individuals is subject to the 3 percent limitation on overall itemized deductions. A planned gift can be made in whole or in part with money.

A for-profit corporation may make a charitable gift of money. That contribution may not exceed, in any tax year, 10 percent of the corporation's taxable income.

13.3 What are the rules for deductibility of contributions of property?

The rules pertaining to charitable contributions of property are more complex than those involving gifts of money. This type of gift is usually deductible, but there are several limitations on the extent of deductibility in any tax year. For a contribution of property to be deductible by an individual under the federal income tax law, he or she must itemize deductions.

One set of these limitations states percentage maximums, applied in the same fashion as with gifts of money. For individuals, where a charitable gift consists of property and the charitable donee is a public charity, the extent of the charitable deduction under the federal income tax law cannot exceed 30 percent of the donor's adjusted gross income. The limitation for other charitable gifts generally is 20 percent. For example, if an individual had adjusted gross income for a year in the amount of $100,000 and made gifts of property to a religious nonprofit organization in that year totaling $25,000, the gifts would be fully deductible (unless other limitations apply) for that year. By reason of the percentage limitation, gifts of property in that year totaling $35,000 would yield, for a gift year, a charitable deduction of $30,000 and a carryforward of $5,000.

One of the appealing features of the federal income tax law in this context is that a charitable contribution of property that has appreciated in value often is deductible based on the full fair market of the property. The capital gain inherent in the appreciated property, which would be taxable had the property been sold, goes untaxed.

A gift of property may have to be substantiated, may be a quid pro quo contribution, and/or may be subjected to appraisal requirements. A planned gift can be made in whole or in part with property. A for-profit corporation may make a charitable gift of property. That contribution may not exceed, in any tax year,

10 percent of the corporation's taxable income. For corporations, there are special rules limiting the deductibility of gifts of inventory (somewhat enhanced when the property is to be used for the care of the ill, the needy, or infants) and gifts of scientific property for purposes of research. In most cases involving these two circumstances the allowable charitable contribution is an amount equal to as much as twice the corporation's basis in the property.

13.4   What is *planned giving*?

The phrase *planned giving* addresses techniques of charitable giving where the contributions (usually of property) are large in amount and are normally integrated carefully with the donor's financial and estate plans. This giving is termed *planned* giving, because of the time and planning devoted to designing the gift transition by both the donor and charitable donee.

The relationship of this type of gift to a donor's financial needs is a critical factor. The donor often structures the gift so that he, she, or it receives income as the result of the transaction. Usually this benefit is technically accomplished by creating, in the donated property (or money), *income* and *remainder interests*. Planned gifts may be of two types: (1) the gift made during the donor's lifetime by means of a trust or other agreement or (2) a planned gift made by will, so that the contribution is made from the decedent's estate (a bequest or devise).

Contributions of property to charity are often made as outright gifts of the property in its entirety. That is, the donor transfers all of his, her, or its title and interest in the property to the charitable donee. By contrast, the donor of a planned gift generally contributes something less than the donor's complete interest in the property. In the law, this is known as a contribution of a partial-interest. These partial-interests are either income interests or remainder interests.

For a charitable contribution deduction to be available, the gift must be to (or for the use of) a charitable organization. The planned gift vehicles are not themselves charities; they are conduits to charities. Nonetheless, it is common to say that a charitable deduction arises when a gift is made to, for example, a charitable remainder trust or deduction is for the remainder interest contributed to the charity; the giving vehicle is merely the intermediary that facilitates this type of gift.

13.5   What are *income interests* and *remainder interests*?

These interests are legal fictions; they are concepts of ownership rights inherent in any item of property. An *income interest* in a property is a function of the income generated by the property. A person may be entitled to all of the income from a property for a period of time or to some portion of the income. This person is said to have an *income interest* in the property. Two or more persons (such as husband and wife) may have income interests in the same property (or share an income interest in the same property). The *remainder interest* in an item of property is reflective of the projected value of the property at some future date.

These interests are principally measured by the value of the donated property, the age of the donor(s), the period of time that the income interests will exist, and the frequency of the income payout. The actual computation is made by means of actuarial tables, usually those promulgated by the Department of the Treasury.

For the most part, a planned gift is a gift of an income interest or a remainder interest in a property. Commonly, the contribution is of the remainder interest. By creating an income interest (or, more accurately, retaining the income interest), the donor forms the basis for receiving a flow of income as the result of the contribution. This is known as *partial-interest giving.*

When a gift of a remainder interest in property is made to a charitable organization, the charity cannot acquire the property represented by that interest until the income interests have expired. When a gift is made during lifetime, the contributor receives the charitable deduction for the tax year in which the recipient charity's remainder interest in the property is created. A gift of an income interest in property to a charity enables the donee to receive the income at the outset and to continue to do so as long as the income interest(s) are in existence.

13.6 How are these interests created?

Income and remainder interests in property are usually created by means of a trust. This is the vehicle used to conceptually divide the property into the two component interests. The law terms these trusts *split-interest trusts.* Usually a qualified split-interest trust is required if a charitable contribution deduction is to be available. Split-interest trusts are charitable remainder trusts, pooled income funds, and charitable lead trusts. There are several exceptions to these general requirements of a split-interest trust in planned giving. The principal exception is the charitable gift annuity, which utilizes a contract rather than a trust. Other approaches can also generate a charitable contribution deduction.

13.7 What are the tax advantages for the charitable gift of a remainder interest?

For a lifetime gift of a remainder interest in property to a charitable organization, the federal income tax advantages are manifold. The donor creates an income flow as the result of the gift; this income may be preferentially taxed. The donor receives a charitable contribution deduction for the gift of the remainder interest, which will reduce or perhaps eliminate the tax on the income from the property. The property that is the subject of the gift may have appreciated in value in the hands of the donor. Because the trust is generally tax-exempt, the capital gain from such a transaction is not taxed, nor is the income earned by the trust.

Moreover, the donor can become the beneficiary of professional fund management. All of these benefits can be available while, simultaneously, the donor is satisfying his or her charitable desires—and doing so at a level that, absent these tax incentives, would likely not be possible.

13.8 What is a *charitable remainder trust*?

A *charitable remainder trust* is one of the types of split-interest trusts. As the name indicates, it is a trust that has been used to create a remainder interest, which is destined for charity. Each charitable remainder is written specifically for the particular circumstances of the donor(s). The remainder interest in the gift property is designated for one or more charitable organizations. The donor (or donors) receives a charitable contribution deduction for the transfer of the remainder interest.

A qualified charitable remainder trust must provide for a specified distribution of income, at least annually, to one or more beneficiaries, at least one of which is *not* a charity. The flow of income must be for a life or lives, or for a term not to exceed 20 years. An irrevocable remainder interest must be held for the benefit of the charity or paid over to it. The noncharitable beneficiaries are the holders of the income interest, and the charitable organization has the remainder interest. Generally, nearly every type of property can be contributed to a charitable remainder trust.

Conventionally, once the income interest expires, the assets in a charitable remainder trust are distributed to, or for the use of, the charitable organization that is the remainder interest beneficiary. In some instances, the property comprising the remainder interest may be retained by the trust for charitable purposes.

Usually a bank or similar financial institution serves as the trustee of a charitable remainder trust. The financial institution should have the capacity to administer the trust, make appropriate investments, and timely adhere to all income distribution and reporting requirements. The charitable organization that is the remainder interest beneficiary, however, often acts as the trustee.

Usually a bank or similar financial institution serves as the trustee of a charitable remainder trust. The financial institution should have the capacity to administer the trust, make appropriate investments, and timely adhere to all income distribution and reporting requirements. The charitable organization that is the remainder interest beneficiary, however, often acts as the trustee.

13.9 What is a *pooled income fund*?

A *pooled income fund* is a type of split-interest trust. It is a trust (fund) that has been used to create a remainder interest destined for a charity. A donor to a qualified pooled income fund receives a charitable deduction for contributing the remainder interest in the donated property to charity. This use of the fund creates income interests in noncharitable beneficiaries; the remainder interest in the gift property is designated for the charitable organization that maintains the fund.

The pooled income fund's basic instrument (a trust agreement or declaration of trust) is written to facilitate gifts from an unlimited number of donors, so the essential terms of the transaction must be established in advance for all participants. This is an important distinction in relation to the charitable remainder trust. Each remainder trust is designed for the circumstances of the particular donor(s). This ability to tailor the gift can be a factor in deciding which planned gift vehicle to use. The pooled income fund is, literally, a pooling of gifts. It is sometimes characterized as functioning in the nature of a mutual fund for charities. Although there is some truth to this, the funding of a pooled income fund is motivated by charitable intent.

Each donor to a pooled income fund contributes an irrevocable remainder interest in the gift property to or for the use of an eligible charity. The donor creates an income flow for the life of one or more beneficiaries, who must be living at the time of the transfer. The properties transferred by the donors must be commingled in the fund.

Contributions to pooled income funds are generally confined to cash and readily marketable securities.

Each income interest beneficiary must receive income at least once a year. The pool amount is generally determined by the rate of return earned by the fund for the year. Income beneficiaries receive their proportionate share of the fund's income. The dollar amount of the income share is based on the number of units owned by the beneficiary; each unit must be based on the fair market value of the assets when transferred.

A pooled income fund must be maintained by one or more public charitable organizations. The charity must exercise control over the fund; it does not have to be the trustee of the fund, but it must have the power to remove and replace the trustee.

Whether a charitable organization can be the trustee of a pooled income fund is a matter of state law. A donor or an income beneficiary of the fund may not be a trustee of the fund. A donor may be a trustee or officer of the charitable organization that maintains the fund, however, as long as he or she does not have the general responsibilities with respect to the fund that are ordinarily exercised by a trustee.

13.10 What is a *charitable lead trust*?

In essence, a *charitable lead trust* is the reverse of a charitable remainder trust: The income interest is contributed to charity and the remainder interest goes to noncharitable beneficiaries. Thus, the charitable lead trust is a split-interest trust. Under these arrangements, an income interest in property is contributed to a charitable organization for a term of years or for the life of one or more individuals. The remainder interest in the property is reserved to return, at the expiration of the income interest (the *lead period),* to the donor or other income beneficiary or beneficiaries. Often, the property passes from one generation to another.

The charitable lead trust can be used to accelerate into one year a series of charitable contributions that would otherwise be made annually. In some circumstances, a charitable deduction is available for the transfer of an income interest in property to a charitable organization. There are stringent limitations, however, on the deductible amount of charitable deduction. The donor's principal motive for establishing this type of trust is estate planning.

13.11 What is a *charitable gift annuity*?

Unlike most other forms of planned giving, which are based on a type of split-interest trust, the *charitable gift annuity* is arranged as an agreement between the donor and donee. The donor agrees to make a payment and the donee agrees, in return, to provide the donor (and/or someone else) with an annuity.

With one payment, the donor actually is engaging in two transactions: (1) the *purchase* of an annuity and (2) the making of a charitable *gift*. The gift component gives rise to the charitable contribution deduction. One sum is transferred; the money in excess of the amount necessary to purchase the annuity is the charitable gift portion. As a result of the dual nature of the transaction, the charitable gift annuity transfer constitutes a bargain sale.

The annuity resulting from the creation of a charitable gift annuity arrangement is a fixed amount paid at regular intervals. The exact amount is calculated to reflect the age of the beneficiary, which is determined at the time the contribution is made, and the annuity rate selected. As a matter of law, a charitable organization is free to offer whatever rate of return it wishes. Most charities utilize the rates periodically set by the American Council on Gift Annuities.

A charitable gift annuity is a contract between the donor and donee; all of the assets of the charitable organization are subject to liability for the ongoing payment of the annuities, unlike most other planned giving techniques. Some states require that charitable organizations establish a reserve for payment of gift annuities. For that reason many charitable organizations are reluctant to embark on a gift annuity program. Organizations that do embark on such a program attempt to reduce the risk surrounding ongoing payment of annuities by reinsuring them.

In general, an obligation to pay an annuity is a debt. The charitable organization involved would have acquisition indebtedness for purposes of the unrelated debt-financed income rules, but for a special rule. To come within this rule the value of the annuity must be less than 90 percent of the value of the property in the transaction, there can be no more than two income beneficiaries, there can be no guarantee as to a minimum amount of payments and no specification of a maximum amount of payments, and the annuity contract cannot provide for an adjustment of the amount of the annuity payments by reference to the income received from the transferred property or any other property.

13.12 What about gifts of life insurance?

Charitable contributions of life insurance policies are popular forms of giving. A gift of whole life insurance is an excellent way for an individual who has a relatively small amount of resources to make a major contribution to a charitable organization. If the life insurance policy is fully paid, the donor will receive a charitable deduction for the cash surrender value or the replacement value of the policy. If the premiums are still being paid, the donor receives a deduction for the premium payments made during the tax year. For the deduction to be available the donee charity must be both the beneficiary and the owner of the insurance policy.

13.13 Are there other ways to make deductible gifts of remainder interests?

Yes. Individuals may give a remainder interest in their personal residence or farm to charity. They then receive a charitable deduction without using a trust.

13.14 How does the federal government regulate fundraising for charitable purposes?

For the most part, federal regulation in this area is principally through the income tax laws. The chief subparts of the law in this area are IRS audits, the charitable gift substantiation requirements, the quid pro quo rules, the procedure for applying for recognition of tax exemption, the unrelated business rules, the annual information return requirements, the public charity rules, and the many intricacies of the law surrounding the income, gift, and estate tax charitable contribution deduction.

There is also some regulation at the hands of the U.S. Postal Service through its monitoring of use of the special bulk third-class mailing rates, and the Federal Trade Commission, as it regulates telemarketing, and the Federal Communications Commission, as it relates to television and radio broadcasting regulations.

13.15 How do state governments regulate fundraising for charitable purposes?

The attorneys general of the states have inherent authority to oversee charities. The states also have laws concerning the availability of tax exemptions, the deductibility of charitable gifts, the offering of securities, the sale of insurance programs, unfair trade practices, misleading advertising, and fraud—each of which can be applied in the realm of charitable fundraising.

All but three states have some form of statutory law governing the solicitation of charitable gifts. (The states that lack any such law are Delaware, Montana, and Wyoming.) Thirty-five states have formal, comprehensive charitable solicitation acts. To avoid unnecessary entanglement, most states exempt churches and perhaps other religious nonprofit organizations from most, if not all, charitable solicitation regulation because of First Amendment freedom of religion protections. Some states do, however, require an organization seeking such exemption to file an application form along with the payment of a nominal fee.

13.16 Are there exceptions to these state laws?

Usually. Some states exempt certain types of charities from the entirety of these regulations related to fundraising; others exempt them only from the registration and reporting requirements. As described above, the most common exception, for religious nonprofit organizations, rests primarily on constitutional law grounds.

13.17 Are these state laws constitutional?

In general, yes, although the tension in this field is intense. A state, for example, has the police power and can use this authority to protect its citizens against charitable fundraising fraud and other abuse. This type of regulation, however, needs to be more than *reasonable* in scope, as determined by the state. Fundraising for charitable purposes is one of the highest forms of free speech; thus governments can regulate it only by the narrowest of means.

Overall the charitable solicitation acts have been upheld, in the face of claims that they wrongfully hamper free speech or unduly burden interstate commerce. Some features of state and local charitable solicitation acts have been struck down as being unconstitutional violations of free speech rights. The most infamous of these legislated features are limitations on the fundraising costs of charitable entities or on the levels of compensation paid to professional solicitors.

The police power of the states (and local governments) directly clashes with the free speech rights of charities and their fundraisers. To date, this tension has been modulated by the courts, with the consensus being that the police power allows for the general application of the charitable solicitation laws, while constitutional law principles force governments to regulate in this area by the narrowest of means.

13.18 What IRS audit practices are applied to fundraising charitable organizations?

The IRS has specific concerns about charitable organizations that are engaged in charitable solicitation that are reflected in IRS audit guidelines promulgated for its examining agents. The IRS published audit guidelines for college and university audits. Although these guidelines technically apply only in the context of higher education and not to religious nonprofit organizations, they describe in considerable detail how the agent is to conduct the fundraising audit. There should be no doubt that an audit of any charitable organization, from the standpoint of its fundraising practices, would be conducted in a manner close to that summarized in these guidelines.

The IRS will want to identify each individual responsible for soliciting and accounting for charitable contributions. Copies of the appropriate job descriptions will be requested. The minutes of any committee involved in fundraising (such as a development, finance, or budget committee) will be reviewed; board minutes may be examined also, particularly if the board is involved in accepting gifts. Correspondence with donors will be reviewed, also, with gift agreements; the IRS will be searching for restrictions or conditions by which benefits may be provided to contributors. Any private benefit could affect the organization's tax exemption; certain benefits could affect the extent of deductibility of contributions. These guidelines do not expressly describe this practice, but the IRS will read correspondence and agreements, looking for anticipatory assignments of income (where the income can be taxed to the donor) and step transactions (where the capital gain element in a gift of property can be taxed to the donor).

13.19 How do the charitable giving rules apply?

The charitable giving rules apply in many ways, because they govern the deductibility of charitable gifts for federal tax purposes. The facets of this application include the definitions of the terms *charitable* and *gift,* the percentage limitations as to annual deductibility, the deduction reduction rules, the rules concerning gifts of partial interests, and a variety of rules pertaining to contributions of specific types of property. There are, however, three bodies of charitable giving law that have particular relevance in the realm of fundraising regulation: (1) the charitable gift substantiation requirements, (2) the quid pro quo contribution rules, and (3) the appraisal requirements.

13.20 What are the charitable gift *substantiation requirements*?

The essence of the *substantiation requirements* is that there is no federal income tax charitable contribution deduction for any charitable gift of $250 or more, unless the donor has contemporaneous written acknowledgment from the donee charitable organization. In cases where the charity has provided goods or services to the donor in exchange for the contribution, this contemporaneous written acknowledgment must include a good-faith estimate of the value of the goods or services. If no goods or services are provided, the substantiation document must state that fact. Some charitable organizations, not realizing this, are providing to their donors documents that technically are not in compliance with these rules—thus jeopardizing the charitable deductions. These rules are inapplicable to the provision of intangible religious benefits. If the contribution is of property, the acknowledgment must describe the property.

The donee charitable organization is not required to value the property for the donor and should not do so. Valuation of the donated property is the responsibility of the donor. The donee organization does have to place a value on the contributed property for purposes of its own financial records. Separate gifts to a charitable organization are regarded as independent contributions and are not aggregated for purposes of measuring the $250 threshold. Donations made through payroll deductions are considered separate payments from each paycheck. The IRS is authorized to establish (although it has not done so) anti-abuse rules to prevent avoidance of the substantiation requirements—for example, by writing separate smaller checks to the same charitable organization on the same date.

For substantiation to be *contemporaneous*, it must be obtained no later than the date the donor files a tax return for the year in which the contribution was made. If the return is filed after the due date or on an extended due date, the substantiation must have been obtained by the due date or extended due date. A charitable organization that knowingly provides false written substantiation to a donor may be subject to the penalties for aiding and abetting an understatement of tax liability. There are separate gift substantiation rules that apply in instances of contributions of automobiles, boats, airplanes, and the like.

13.21 What does the phrase *goods or services* mean?

On its face, the statutory requirement of a contemporaneous written acknowledgment containing a good faith estimate of the value of the *goods or services* would seem to mean consideration provided in exchange for the contribution, most likely tangible services or property. The courts, however, have expanded this clause to include expectations and understandings. For example, it was held that payments to a charitable organization were not deductible as charitable gifts, because the substantiation requirements were not met, in that there was an undisclosed return benefit in the form of the donors' *expectation* that the gift funds would be invested in a certain manner.

This conclusion was an error. Another provision of the Internal Revenue Code (outlawing charitable split-dollar insurance arrangements) uses the phrase *understanding or expectation*. If Congress had meant *goods or services* to embrace *expectations*, it would have so legislated. By reason of these holdings, charities must be cautious in preparing these substantiation documents, in that they must not only estimate and disclose any value of goods or services provided in exchange for a gift, but also hypothesize as to what donors *expect* to be provided—and value and disclose that.

13.22 Do these rules apply with respect to benefits provided to donors after the gifts were made, where there was no prior notification of the benefit, such as a recognition dinner?

Generally, no. These rules apply to payments made in consideration for some benefit provided by the donee charitable organization. These rules are applicable where a good or service is provided in *consideration* for a payment to the charity, meaning that the donor expects the good or service at the time the payment is made. Thus, a subsequent benefit generally does not need to be taken into account in determining the amount of the charitable deduction. If, however, the charitable organization always provides recognition dinners for certain donors, at some point, an "expectation" can be presumed, even when there is no express promise of it at the time of the gift.

13.23 **How do the substantiation rules apply to gifts made through charitable remainder trusts, charitable lead trusts, and pooled income funds?**

The rules do not apply to gifts made by means of charitable remainder trusts and charitable lead trusts. This is because donors to these trusts are not required to designate a specific charitable organization as the beneficiary at the time money or property is transferred to the trust. There may not be a charitable organization available to provide the requisite written acknowledgment. Also, even where a specific charitable beneficiary is designated, the designation is often revocable. By contrast, the law requires that one or more charitable organizations must maintain a pooled income fund, so contributions made by means of these funds must, to be deductible, be substantiated.

13.24 **What are the *quid pro quo contribution rules*?**

A *quid pro quo contribution* is a payment made partly as a contribution and partly for goods or services provided to the donor by the charitable organization. A charitable organization must provide a written disclosure statement to donors who make a quid pro quo contribution in excess of $75. The required written disclosure must inform the donor that the amount of the contribution that is deductible for federal income tax purposes is limited to the excess of any money, or the excess of the value of any property, the donor contributed over the value of the goods or services provided by the charity. The disclosure must provide the donor with a good faith estimate of the value of the goods or services the donor received. The charitable organization must furnish the statement in connection with either the solicitation or the receipt of the quid pro quo contribution. The disclosure must be in writing and presented in a manner that is reasonably likely to come to the attention of the donor. A disclosure in small print within a larger document may not satisfy the requirement.

A penalty is imposed on charitable organizations that do not meet these disclosure requirements. For failure to make the required disclosure in connection with a quid pro quo contribution of more than $75 there is a penalty of $10 per contribution, not to exceed $5,000 per fundraising event or mailing. An organization may be able to avoid this penalty if it can show that the failure to comply was due to reasonable cause.

13.25 **What is a *good faith estimate*?**

The statute does not define the phrase *good faith estimate.* The tax regulations state that a good faith estimate of the value of goods or services provided by a charitable organization is an estimate of the fair market value of the goods or services. These regulations add that an organization can use a reasonable methodology in making a good faith estimate, as long as it applies the methodology in good faith.

13.26 Are there any exceptions to the quid pro quo contribution rules?

There are seven exceptions. The first three apply where the only goods or services provided to a donor are those having an incidental value. The exceptions are:

1. Where the fair market value of all the benefits received is not more than 2 percent of the contribution or $50, whichever is less.
2. Where the contribution is $25 or more and the only benefits received by the donor in return during the calendar year have a cost, in the aggregate, of not more than a *low-cost article*. A low-cost article is one that does not cost more than $5 to the organization that distributes it or on whose behalf it is distributed.
3. Where, in connection with a request for a charitable contribution, the charity e-mails or otherwise distributes free, unordered items to patrons, and the cost of the items (in the aggregate) distributed to any single patron in a calendar year is not more than a low-cost article.
4. Where an *intangible religious benefit* is involved. For the exception to be available, the benefit must be provided by an organization exclusively for religious purposes and must be of a type that generally is not sold in a commercial transaction outside the donative context. (An example of a religious benefit is admission to a religious ceremony.) The intangible religious benefit exception does not apply to items such as payments for tuition for education leading to a recognized degree, travel services, or consumer goods.
5. Where no donative element is involved in the transaction with the charitable organization. (Illustrations of this are payments of tuition to a school, payments for health-care services to a hospital, and the purchase of an item from a museum gift shop.)
6. Annual membership benefits offered for no more than $75 per year that consist of rights or privileges that the individual can exercise frequently during the membership period. These benefits include free admission to the organization's events, free parking, and discounts on the purchase of goods.
7. Annual membership benefits offered for no more than $75 per year that consist of admission to events during the membership period that are open only to members of the charitable organization and for which the organization reasonably projects that the cost per person (excluding any overhead) for each event is within the limits established for low-cost articles.

13.27 How does a charitable organization value the involvement of a celebrity for purpose of the quid pro quo contribution rules?

If the celebrity performs at an event, using the talent for which he or she is celebrated (such as singing or standup comedy), the fair market value of the performance must be determined in calculating any benefit and thus any charitable deduction. If the celebrity does something else, however, his or her presence can be disregarded.

13.28 What are the *appraisal requirements*?

For most gifts of property (or collections of property) by an individual, partnership, or corporation to a charitable organization, where the value is in excess of $5,000, there are certain appraisal requirements. (Gifts of money and publicly traded securities are excepted from these appraisal rules.) Property to which the rules apply is termed *charitable property.*

The donor of charitable deduction property must obtain a *qualified appraisal* of the property and attach the *appraisal summary* (Form 8283) to the tax return on which the deduction is claimed. The law details the items of information that must be in a qualified appraisal and an appraisal summary. The appraisal must be conducted by a *qualified appraiser.*

If a claimed deduction is over $500,000, the individual, partnership, or corporation must obtain a qualified appraisal of the property and attach it to the appropriate income tax return. (These rules are inapplicable, however, with respect to gifts of money, publicly traded securities, inventory, and vehicles.)

13.29 What does the IRS look for with respect to new charitable organizations?

Nearly every organization that wants to be tax-exempt as a charitable entity, and be an organization eligible to receive tax-deductible gifts, must give notice to the IRS to that effect by filing an application for recognition of tax exemption. (The principal exceptions are those for churches and their integrated auxiliaries, and organizations that have gross receipts that normally are not in excess of $5,000.) The application requests certain information about the fundraising program of the organization. The organization must describe its actual and planned fundraising program, summarizing its actual use of, or plans to use, selective mailings, fundraising committees, professional fundraisers, and the like. Depending on the progress of its solicitation efforts, the organization can describe a very detailed fundraising program or it can state that it has yet to develop any specific processes for raising funds. If the organization has developed written material for the solicitation of contributions, it should attach copies. The application, which is publicly accessible, must contain a disclosure of the organization's fundraising costs. Depending on the length of time the organization has been in existence, this information will be reflected in the financial statement that is part of the application or in a proposed budget submitted with the application.

13.30 What reporting rules apply?

Nearly every charitable organization must file an annual information return with the IRS. The most notable exceptions are for churches and their integrated auxiliaries, and most organizations whose gross receipts normally are not in excess of

$25,000. The annual information return requires charitable (and other tax-exempt) organizations to use the *functional method of accounting* to report their expenses. This accounting method allocates expenses by function, including those for fundraising. Thus, swept into the fundraising category are not only direct fundraising costs, such as professional fundraisers' fees and telemarketing expenses, but outlays that are allocable only in part to fundraising, including joint-purpose mailings. The organization must maintain detailed records as to its fundraising and other expenses.

The IRS defines the term *fundraising expenses* to mean all expenses, including allocable overhead costs incurred in publicizing and conducting fundraising campaigns; soliciting bequests, grants from foundations or other organizations, and government grants; preparing and distributing fundraising manuals, instructions, and other materials; and conducting special fundraising events that generate contributions. The IRS does not differentiate, when referring to *professional fundraisers*, between fundraising counsel and solicitors. Organizations must report their receipts from and expenses of special fundraising events and activities, separating the information for each type of event.

Do the *unrelated business income* rules apply in the fundraising setting?

Yes. Several types of fundraising events or activities are technically *businesses* for federal income tax purposes. But for certain provisions in the federal law pertaining to unrelated businesses, some or all of the net income from these events would be taxable. Some of this revenue is sheltered from taxation on the rationale that the activity is not *regularly carried on*. This shelter protects activities that are conducted only once each year, such as the selling of holiday cards.

Some revenue-raising activities are considered related businesses. These include sales of various items in gifts shops and bookstores. Other sales in these shops and stores may be nontaxable by operation of the *convenience doctrine*.

Still other fundraising practices are protected against taxation by specific statutory exceptions. Some fundraising events that are run entirely by volunteers and businesses that are conducted substantially by individuals who are unpaid for their services are not taxed. It does not take much, however, for a court to conclude, for purposes of this exception, that someone is compensated.

Another exception is for businesses that sell items that were contributed to the organization. This rule was created for the benefit of thrift stores operated by nonprofit organizations, but it can also be applicable to frequent auctions.

Still another aspect of the law that can protect fundraising revenue from taxation is the exception for *royalties*. This exception can, for example, immunize income from an affinity card program and revenue from the rental of mailing lists from tax.

In these instances, the payments were for the use of the organization's name, logo, and mailing list.

13.32   Are there limitations on the use of the *royalty exception* in the fundraising setting?

Yes, but where these limitations are is a matter of some controversy. The IRS position is that for an item of revenue to be a tax-free royalty, it has to be passively derived—for example, investment income. This view of the law sees active participation by the tax-exempt organization in the revenue-raising process as meaning that some form of joint venture is occurring, thereby defeating the exclusion.

The opposite view is that a royalty is a royalty; that is, the factor of passivity is not required. This rationale, which rests on a careful reading of the legislative history of the unrelated business rules, defines a royalty as payment for the use of valuable intangible property rights.

This issue has been the subject of litigation over many years. The federal court of appeals that seems to have largely resolved the dispute split the difference with the parties. The current state of the law is that a tax-exempt organization can participate to some degree in the process of generating the royalty income (so that the income need not be entirely passive), but if that involvement in the process is substantial the royalty exception is defeated.

If the exempt organization's participation in the royalty-generation process appears to be substantial, there is still an opportunity to transform what is or may be a taxable unrelated activity into a nontaxable stream of income. Basically, this involves transferring the function to another party, giving that party the right to use the necessary intangible property rights previously held by the exempt organization, and crafting the appropriate royalty contract. If the transfer is done properly, the organization can enhance its revenue stream with a new source of revenue or with nontaxation of previously taxed revenue, or both.

13.33   Are there fundraising disclosure requirements for noncharitable organizations?

Yes, fundraising disclosure rules apply to exempt organizations other than charitable ones, unless the organization has annual gross receipts that are normally no more than $100,000.

Under these rules, each fundraising solicitation by or on behalf of an organization must contain an express statement, in a conspicuous and easily recognizable format, that gifts to it are not deductible as charitable contributions for federal income tax purposes. (There is exclusion for letters or telephone calls that are not part of a coordinated fundraising campaign soliciting more than ten persons during a calendar year.)

Failure to satisfy this disclosure requirement can result in a penalty of $1,000 per day (maximum of $10,000 per year), unless a reasonable cause justifies an exception. For an intentional disregard of these rules, the penalty for the day on which the offense occurred is the greater of $1,000 or 50 percent of the aggregate cost of the solicitations that took place on that day—and the $10,000 limitation does not apply. For penalty purposes, the IRS counts the days on which the solicitation was telecast, broadcast, mailed, telephoned, or otherwise distributed.

13.34 Are there any other federal law requirements as to fundraising?

There are several. Other applications of the federal income tax rules pertain to publicly supported charitable organizations that have that status by virtue of the facts-and-circumstances test. Among criteria for compliance with this test is that the charitable organization is attracting public support; the IRS wants to know whether the entity can demonstrate an active and ongoing fundraising program. An organization can satisfy this aspect of the test (where public support can be as low as 10 percent) if it maintains a continuous and bona fide solicitation effort, seeking contributions from the general public, the community, or the membership involved, or if it carries on activities designed to attract support from government agencies or publicly supported charitable organizations.

The U.S. Postal Service regulates some aspects of charitable fundraising by means of the postal laws. Qualified organizations (including charities) that have received specific authorization may mail eligible matter at reduced bulk third-class rates of postage. Cooperative mailings involving the mailing of any matter on behalf of or produced for an organization not authorized to mail at the special rates must be paid at the applicable regular rates.

Material that advertises, promotes, offers, or, for a fee or other consideration, recommends, describes, or announces the availability of any product or service cannot qualify for mailing at the reduced bulk third-class rates unless the sale of the product or the provision of the service is substantially related to the exercise or performance by the organization of one or more of the purposes constituting the basis for the organization's authorization to mail at those rates. The determination as to whether a product or service is substantially related to an organization's purpose is made in accordance with the analogous federal tax laws standards.

The Federal Trade Commission (FTC) has a role in the realm of fundraising for charitable purposes, primarily when the fundraising is in the form of telemarketing. The FTC has regulations on this subject, in amplification of the Telemarketing and Consumer Fraud and Abuse Prevention Act. These rules do not apply to telemarketing conducted for charitable organizations solely for the purpose of generating charitable gifts.

The FTC rules apply, however, to for-profit companies that raise funds or provide similar services to charitable and other tax-exempt organizations. These rules (1) define the term *telemarketing*, (2) require clear and conspicuous disclosures of specified material information, orally or in writing, before a customer pays for goods or services offered; (3) prohibit misrepresenting, directly or by implication, specified material information relating to the goods or services that are the subject of a sales offer, as well as any other material aspects of a telemarketing transaction;

(4) require express verifiable authorization before submitting for payment a check, draft, or other form of negotiable paper drawn on a person's account; (5) prohibit false or otherwise misleading statements to induce payment for goods or services; (6) prohibit any person from assisting and facilitating certain deceptive or abusive telemarketing acts or practices; (7) prohibit credit card laundering; (8) prohibit specified abusive acts or practices; (9) impose calling time restrictions; (10) require specified information to be disclosed truthfully, promptly, and in a clear and conspicuous manner, in an outbound telephone call; (11) require that specified records be kept; and (12) specify certain acts or practices that are exempt from the requirements. Although the rules on telemarketing practices do not always apply in the charitable fundraising setting, they serve as useful guidelines to proper telemarketing practices in that context.

13.35 What constitutes a *charitable gift*?

An uncontroversial, standard definition of a *gift* under the law is a "voluntary transfer of property to another made gratuitously and without consideration." A *charitable gift* may be described as one made for a charitable purpose, and made to a charitable organization. Charitable gifts made to qualified entities receive favorable tax treatment. The receiving entity does not pay tax on the receipt of the gift; the donor may deduct the gift from otherwise taxable income.

13.36 Can a family member be a designated beneficiary of a charitable gift?

Generally, contributions to specific individuals are not deductible, including gifts that are designated for use by a charitable organization for a specific individual. Therefore, designating a family member as a beneficiary would negate the deductibility of the charitable contribution. This premise holds true whenever the donor has specified by name the person to receive the gift, regardless of whether the person is needy or worthy. A possible exception is the support of an orphan or needy child, but the selection must have first been made by the organization rather than the donor, in accordance with its benevolence policies.

These restrictions are intended to prevent the use of a charity as a conduit for meeting the specific desires of donors where a direct gift would not be deductible. When the organization's board has determined beneficiaries in accordance with its policies, gifts ultimately supporting the ministry or charitable activities of specific employees whose identities are known in advance, for purposes such as missionary support, are tax-deductible contributions to an organization if they are not earmarked for personal use or individual control. The distinction is that the funds must remain under the control of the organization and be expended only as needed for reasonable compensation and business expenses of the recipient employee or related ministry costs.

13.37 What is the nature of an *unrestricted charitable gift*?

An *unrestricted charitable gift* is a gift to be applied toward a charitable purpose, regardless of the business form of the recipient. The donor has impliedly required that the gift be used for the charitable purpose of the receiving charity. The board of the charity is at liberty to apply an unrestricted gift to its charitable purposes according to its governance documents without restrictions, limitations, or conditions, in whatever manner the board deems to be most appropriate to achieve the organization's charitable purposes.

13.38 What are some examples of unrestricted charitable gifts?

Unrestricted charitable gifts include all types of gifts and funds given to a charity that are not subject to donor restrictions. Examples include unrestricted sponsorships, unrestricted charitable gifts from donors, and monies that are directed to be used for the general purposes of the charity or where there are no references to restrictions on the gift and government grants that are not restricted to a particular purpose or program. The board may vary the purposes for which those funds have been applied and use them in any other manner that the board determines to achieve the charitable purposes of the charity.

13.39 What is the nature of a *donor-restricted charitable gift*?

A donor-restricted charitable gift invokes restrictions for particular purposes. Restrictions are best avoided when possible because they limit options, may require administration and oversight, carry potential liability, and may be considerably less valuable to the recipient. *Donor restricted charitable gifts* are gifts for a charitable purpose subject to restrictions, limitations, conditions, terms, or directions imposed by the donor that would constrain or limit an organization's use of the gift. As a result, the board of an organization that receives a donor-restricted charitable gift must carefully identify the nature of the donor's restrictions and recognize the legal implications of the specific type of restriction imposed by the donor, as well as the results of failing to comply with them. If donors cannot be dissuaded from specific restrictions, casting the desired use as a nonbinding "suggestion" is preferable, and the entity should reiterate that, absent restrictions, gifts are for the general charitable purposes of the entity.

13.40 What is the nature of an *endowment fund*?

An *endowment fund* is the investment of funds to be held in a trust (or perhaps a corporation) established for the support of institutions such as churches, colleges, private schools, museums, hospitals, and foundations. The investment income may be used for the operation of the organization and for capital expenditures. The transfer of money or property donated to an institution is generally accompanied with the stipulation that it be invested and the principal remain intact. This allows for the donation to have a much greater impact over a long period of time than if it were spent all at once, due to the compounding of interest.

13.41 What is the nature of *donor-restricted use funds*?

As distinguished from endowment funds, *donor-restricted use funds* do not imply that the capital of a gift be held in trust and contemplate an expiration of the restriction. Restricted use funds assume a particular purpose with a finite end-point where the capital and any earned income will be expended immediately or over time, as contrasted with being held in perpetuity, and may be applied in accordance with certain specific charitable purpose restrictions. A building fund is a common example. Unlike endowment funds, where the restriction on the use of capital will continue indefinitely, donor-restricted use funds involve restrictions that eventually will be fulfilled, concluding the fund.

Restrictions often involve a combination of time, purpose, or a class of beneficiaries. Donors may establish purpose restrictions concerning the beneficiaries of the fund; the board should ensure that the restrictions are consistent with the overall purposes of the organization, do not unduly divert administrative attention to effect their fulfillment, and are not discriminatory or contrary to public or other policy.

13.42 How are donor-restricted use funds created?

From the inception of the restriction, as in the case of endowment funds, donor-restricted use funds can be established by the donor either through a currently made or testamentary gift that includes a time, purpose, or beneficiary restriction. Alternatively, a board may establish a restricted use fund by seeking donations from supporters or from the public for a specific purpose.

13.43 What is the nature of *restricted charitable trust property*?

Restricted charitable trust property is one of several terms that describe real property that is acquired, usually by gift, subject to certain terms of trust contained in the deed or conveying instrument for the property. Religious nonprofit organizations may receive or acquire property subject to specific terms of use that will continue in perpetuity, even if the land and buildings are sold. Categories of such religious use restrictions are: (1) restrictions pertaining to religious doctrine, such as requiring that the property be used only for individuals who avow and subscribe to a particular religious doctrine; (2) restrictions pertaining to use, such as use for a church, cemetery, or seminary; and (3) restrictions limiting the property to those who perform specified acts following a particular religious practice, such as the sacrament of communion only to be received by baptized members of a particular denomination. Absent the involvement of a court, such restrictions cannot be unilaterally removed or varied from.

13.44 How are restricted charitable trust properties created?

Restrictions affecting charitable trust properties are created at the inception of the transfer by the operation of specific clauses in a deed for land, occurring when a grantor donates property and by restriction requires the property to be used only for a particular purpose. The grantor may include a reversionary clause in the deed stipulating that the property is to revert to the grantor in the event that the terms of trust are not complied with. For example, in a hierarchical denominational context, a church's property deed may contain language stating that, should the property cease to be used for worship in accordance with the tenets of a particular denomination, the property shall revert to the grantor denomination. The organization should consider whether the specific wording in a deed creates a condition subsequent as different legal implications may flow from the distinction.

13.45 What happens when property subject to a restricted charitable trust is transferred?

The outcome in such a scenario may vary according to the law of the jurisdiction, but the general consideration is the preservation of the intention of the restriction, such that where land that is subject to a charitable trust is transferred, the proceeds of the sale will often remain subject to the terms of trust, or alternatively, if the property is being sold to a successor entity, the recipient will take the property subject to the same terms of trust as were set out in the original deed, even if the current deed makes no reference to those terms of trust.

13.46 What is the failure of a donor restriction?

It should be noted that a religious organization will seldom benefit from suggesting the inclusion of deed restrictions, conditions, reversions, and the like when the donation transfer could otherwise be made without them, especially if the donor may be unavailable or deceased to modify things later. The donor may also risk loss of a deduction by including them. Donor-restricted charitable gifts will fail sometimes, requiring the organization to undertake a complex series of steps, when either a restricted term becomes impossible or impractical, or a condition precedent or subsequent is unfulfilled, or a limited interest in a determinable gift comes to an end. Conditions placed on gifts that fail will affect the gift in different ways depending on the condition's relative position to the timing of the effectiveness of the gift. When a gift that is given to a charitable organization is subject to a condition precedent and the condition is unfulfilled, the gift fails to take effect. When a gift subject to a condition subsequent is given to that organization and the condition is unfulfilled, the gift may revert to the donor. The general rule, especially concerning written instruments, is that where a restriction on a gift to a charity would otherwise fail due to vagueness, impossibility, impracticality, or general uncertainty, a court may exercise jurisdiction to interpret the gifting instrument in a manner so as to preserve the intent and effectuate the gift, though conditional transfers tend to impede judicial options.

13.47   What is the failure of a restricted charitable trust?

As in the case of restrictions on donations, as either gifts or funds to the degree there is a distinction, a special-purpose charitable trust will fail where the donor's restriction is either impossible or impractical to comply with and where carrying forward the special-purpose charitable trust can no longer be accomplished. A charitable entity would seek the assistance of the courts in exercising its general scheme-making power through either a *cy-près* court application or the imposition of an administration of the property. This common-law doctrine provides that if property is given in trust to be applied to a particular charitable purpose, and it is or becomes impossible or impracticable or illegal to carry out the particular purpose, and if the transferor manifested a more general intention to devote the property to charitable purposes, the trust will not fail but the court will direct the application of the property to some alternative charitable purpose that falls within the general charitable intention of the grantor.

13.48   When have courts modified restricted charitable gifts to prevent the failure of the gift and give effect to the donor's intent?

Though jurisdictions vary, examples of initial and subsequent failures that can result in the application of the *cy-près* doctrine giving effect to general intention are insufficiency of subject matter, such as where the amount of the gift is too small to accomplish the intended purpose; where there is no suitable site available to carry out a designated building program; the gift is made to a nonexistent charity; the gift is made to an incorrectly described charity; the gift is made to a charity that has ceased to operate; the gift is made to a charity that has merged with another charity; the gift is made to a charity that has changed its charitable objects between the time that a will was made and the date of death; the trust property is unsuitable for the designated charitable purpose; the gift is surplus to the needs of the charitable purpose designated; the gift is refused by the charity; the charity is dissolved; and there is a surplus of capital or income remaining after the charitable purpose has been carried out.

13.49   What duties are associated with donor-restricted charitable gifts?

The primary duty of directors or trustees of a charitable organization is to carry out the purposes of the charity in accordance with the charitable objects set out in the governing documents in relation to unrestricted charitable property and in accordance with the applicable restrictions to special-purpose charitable trust funds. Deviations implying a breach of duty would include: a church that had received land in trust to further a particular doctrinal statement subsequently using the land for the benefit of individuals adhering to a different doctrinal statement; a church unilaterally attempting to alter the terms of a trust deed for church property without first obtaining court authorization; a charity diverting a fund intended for one charitable program for use in another charitable program; a charity withholding a fund from the purpose for which it was intended by the donor; the trustees of a charity concealing the existence of a fund by not communicating its existence to the persons or groups intended to benefit from it; a charity placing funds into an investment when all of the funds were intended by the donor to be expended in the short term in support of a particular operational program of the charity; a charity mixing its funds with another charity and then applying the combined funds for the purposes of the other charity; a charity using surplus funds from a specific fundraising effort for different charitable purposes from those communicated in the appeal without first obtaining court authorization; and a charity altering the terms of a donor's restriction without first obtaining court authorization.

13.50 What are the legal consequences of failing to comply with donor restrictions?

Obviously, the importance of the preceding questions raises awareness to the preservation and proper treatment of donor restrictions on gifts. While specific jurisdictions vary, each has placed significance on compliance through implementing consequences for deviation. Where a donor restriction is in the form of a special-purpose charitable trust and the charity fails to comply with its terms, then all of the directors or trustees of the charity would be in breach of trust and would be jointly and severally liable for the full amount of any loss suffered by the charity as a result of the failure to comply with the terms of the trust. In the event that the failure to comply with the donor restriction involves applying the gift for a purpose that is outside of the authorized corporate objects of a charitable corporation, the board members of the charity could be held personally liable on a joint and several basis for any resulting loss by virtue of having directly or indirectly approved an unauthorized activity of the charity outside of its corporate powers, and of course criminally liable if benefitting themselves or others from the diversion.

13.51 Are contributions by an individual directly to a foreign entity or organization not created or organized in the United States deductible?

No. Charitable contributions made directly to an organization not created in the United States, a state or territory, the District of Columbia, or a possession of the United States are not deductible. Also, contributions to a U.S. charity that transmits funds to a foreign charity are deductible only in limited circumstances.

For example, the charitable activity of "relief of the poor" of a U.S. organization is nonetheless charitable where the beneficiaries of the assistance are outside the United States.

13.52 Can contributions by an individual directly to a binational charitable foundation organized under the laws of both the U.S. and a foreign country qualify as a charitable contribution and be deducted for U.S. income tax purposes?

Regardless of where the foreign charity is located, a *gift* tax deduction will be available if the foreign charity has obtained a determination of tax-exempt status under Code Section 501(c)(3) from the IRS. Few foreign charities, however, go to the trouble of applying for IRS determination letters since U.S. individual donors are generally not entitled to U.S. income tax deductions even for gifts to foreign charities that have determination letters.

A U.S. gift tax deduction will be allowed for a direct contribution to a foreign charity under Code Section 2522(a) if (1) the donee is organized for Section 170(c) purposes (i.e., religious, charitable, scientific, literary, educational, etc.); (2) no part of its net earnings inures to the benefit of any individual; and (3) it does not violate prohibitions against self-dealing and involvement in lobbying and political campaigns.

13.53 Can deductible contributions to a U.S. charity be channeled abroad through a foreign branch office or subsidiary?

Donors can, under proper circumstances, deduct earmarked contributions to a domestic charity that will fund a subsidiary or foreign office of its domestic branch. Deductibility is not impaired when the domestic charity transfers funds to a division of its domestic office that is not separately organized, or an incorporated or otherwise formally organized foreign charity office separately existing from the domestic charity if the organized foreign charity office is controlled by the domestic charity. The foreign charity office is to be an administrative arm of the domestic charity, and the most definite and certain form of control exists when that charity is a corporate subsidiary of the domestic charity. As will be discussed below, this relationship is not the exclusive means by which there can be support of foreign charities by domestic charities, but otherwise stringent control measures are required that will be further described.

13.54 Can a U.S. public charity be formed exclusively to support a foreign charity or charities?

Whether some, most, or all of a domestic charity's resources remain in this country is not determinative of charitable status, but at the same time, a domestic charity cannot passively transfer earmarked contributions abroad as it is clearly impermissible for a U.S. charity to act as a mere conduit for the support of efforts abroad, even charitable ones. There are regulations governing "friends of" organizations that are established to support foreign charities. The rules are designed to ensure that the U.S. feeder organization is the true donee and not merely a conduit for sending funds abroad. The U.S. "intermediary" organization must review and approve each proposed foreign grant as being in furtherance of its own charitable purposes. Donations to the U.S. intermediary may not be earmarked by the donor for a specific foreign charity. Where all the contributions made domestically are inevitably turned over to efforts abroad, an organization has been determined to be merely a conduit and deductions were disallowed. A pattern of supporting foreign organizations that are not directly controlled by the domestic charity still will not preclude deductibility if the charity exercises requisite control over the decision to fund abroad. When the control is present, the IRS considers the proper and real recipient of the donations to be the domestic charity. Importantly, an organization cannot simply receive earmarked contributions for foreign efforts and thereby forward them on, merely because of the restrictions. However, donor restrictions can certainly be appropriate where a domestic organization has chosen a purpose abroad and announced and sought funds for it.

If a domestic charity does not operationally control the foreign charity, a deduction will still be allowed when the domestic charity has an independent presence in the country, has no obligation to support the foreign charity, the support is from undesignated funds and there is oversight exercised, and the support promotes the purposes of the domestic charity. If there is no independent presence by the domestic charity in the country, additional factors that have been considered by the IRS in determining that the requisite amount of domestic control resided in the domestic charity to support deductibility have been (1) the domestic board reviewed and approved of the foreign project and grant; (2) the establishment of project standards, review and oversight, and a special committee to assist in the management of contributions made to the domestic charity for the project; (3) the establishment of a separate bank account; (4) separate financial and administrative records of such contributions; (5) supervision of the expenditure of the funds in a manner consistent with the charter and policies of the domestic charity; (6) retention of absolute discretion to withdraw the special funds for use toward other exempt purposes of the domestic charity; and (7) advising potential contributors of this discretionary duty.

A supporting organization, however, is not considered to be operated in connection with a supported organization unless the organization refrains from operating in connection with any supported organization that is not organized in the United States.

13.55 What are the procedures that must be followed when U.S. charities make grants to foreign charities?

Whereas domestic charities may support each other's purposes and efforts without exercising control after the funding is transferred, grants to foreign charities carry the presumption, which will need to be rebutted through due diligence, that the receiving entity abroad will utilize the funds outside any form of control by the domestic entity.

Where the domestic charity is not in complete control of the recipient entity, the following steps should be considered as guidelines on the issue of grants to foreign charities: To the extent possible, all requests for funding for foreign charities or projects should be considered together with all other requests for funds with at least equal budgetary formality—prudent elements of the budgetary process should include at a minimum an adequate description of the charitable purposes to be served by the foreign charity or project; a determination by the board that such purposes are consistent with the charitable purposes of the funding organization and are deserving of funding; a budget submitted by the recipient charity showing proposed expenditures by sufficient description for the board to determine the economic efficiency of the project being funded; objectively stated standards by which progress toward the goals can be measured; an identification of the overseers within the recipient charity responsible for the funded projects; and a commitment by the recipient charity and its overseers to fully, faithfully, and timely comply with reporting and oversight requirements. The prospective grantor should seek in the reports submitted by foreign charities current financial statements reflecting actual charitable expenses compared with the projected charity budget previously submitted. All foreign charity funding requests should proceed with the understanding that the funding organization retains full control over all such funds, exercises absolute discretion as to their use, and retains the right to discontinue funding, including the return of funds already granted but not expended, if it is determined that the project goals or standards are not being met, or the budget is not being followed, or accountability standards are not complied with. The adopted guidelines should be made known to donors and acknowledged in writing by recipient organizations. Obviously, in addition to adopting and espousing adherence to guidelines, actual diligence must also be expended in oversight, and physical inspection with in-person meetings is often appropriate.

13.56 Are there any special restrictions that apply to corporate contributions?

U.S. corporations' grants for use abroad are subject to a special restriction applying to *corporate* contributions. Under IRC Section 170(c), corporate contributions intended for use outside of the United States are not deductible unless the donee is a U.S. *corporation.* For this reason, U.S. charities with international operations are generally organized in the form of corporations rather than as trusts or unincorporated associations. Although the distinction in form that has been drawn appears not to be supported by logic, a U.S. corporation may make a deductible donation for use abroad only if the donee "feeder" or "friends of" organization, community foundation, other U.S. public charity, or private foundation is organized in *corporate* form.

13.57 **What needs to be added to the bylaws of religious nonprofit organizations when they make grants to non-U.S. organizations?**

Religious nonprofit organizations making significant grants abroad in the role of intermediary or feeder organizations should consider adding to their bylaws an abbreviated version of the guidelines discussed herein, to the effect that the organization will (1) review the purposes of the foreign donee charity to determine that they are within the ambit of Code Section 170(c); (2) review and approve specific foreign projects and related solicitation programs; (3) enter into an acknowledgment or written agreement with the foreign donee specifying in detail the projects for which the grant will be used; (4) require accountings from the foreign donee each year until the grant has been fully expended so the U.S. feeder can account for the use of the funds; and (5) retain exclusive power to refuse any conditional or earmarked donations and avoid obligating itself to expend contributions for the use of foreign charities or projects.

13.58 **How has September 11, 2001 complicated the making of grants for charitable uses abroad?**

There are antiterrorism provisions contained in the Patriot Act directed to the prevention of the diversion of U.S. monies to those organizations that would use them for terrorist activities. These efforts include a victims' provision for monetary damages in the event of a terrorist act and prison sentences for diversion. Recordkeeping and the regular checking of the Specially Designated National List are the primary functions deserving of increased attention with respect to charitable grants abroad. This list is maintained by the Treasury's Office of Foreign Assets Control.

13.59 **Do treaty exceptions override the general statutory limitations on the deductions for contributions by U.S. citizens and residents to foreign charities?**

Generally, no. The policy of the United States is to address the deductibility of charitable contributions in the realm of domestic statutory law. With the *partial* exception of Canada, contributions directly made to foreign charities are ineligible for income tax deductibility primarily for the reason that financial abuses within foreign charities are deemed considerable while the practical oversight possible at the individual donor's level is negligible. Further, income tax deductibility for directly made foreign contributions, as opposed to reconveyed contributions to domestic charities, is viewed as a subsidy, and one that the U.S. is not prepared to undertake.

13.60 What are the *U.S.–Canada Tax Treaty*, the *U.S.–Mexico Tax Treaty*, and the *U.S.–Israel Tax Treaty*, and what are their effects?

These treaties relax direct contributions to foreign charities between the country parties, realize similarities between the parties in recognizing charitable status, provide that contributions cross-border may be deductible from at least *some* sources of taxable income, and alleviate the taxpayers' burden of determining the public charity status of the recipient and place the burden on the taxing authority. Certain income tax treaties contain more generous provisions regarding deductions for gifts by U.S. persons to foreign charities. Notably, the U.S. treaties with Canada, Israel, and Mexico allow U.S. donors to deduct donations to charities in the contracting state against their foreign-source income from that jurisdiction. Under certain circumstances, the U.S.–Canada treaty even more generously allows a U.S. donor to claim a deduction against U.S. income for gifts to Canadian charities. For example, a U.S. person may claim a deduction against U.S. income for a direct gift to a Canadian university that the donor or a member of the donor's family attended.

13.61 What is the future of U.S. treaty policy?

Treaties in the area of charitable contributions are thought to be exceptional and reserved for border neighbors with the United States, with Israel being an exception. Treaties *may* become more prevalent in the future as they are less visible and less publicly stirring than tax legislation, and because positive economic benefits may be perceived from the fact that treaties are reciprocal and interest foreign nationals in U.S. charity contribution.

CHAPTER 14

Combinations of Entities

14.1 What is *a subsidiary* in the nonprofit law context?

A *subsidiary*, in the nonprofit law context, is essentially the same as in the for-profit law context. It is a separate organization that has some special, formal *control* relationship with another organization; the other organization is the *parent* organization. For these purposes, the parent organization always is a tax-exempt organization. The subsidiary, however, may be a tax-exempt organization or a for-profit organization.

14.2 Why would a tax-exempt organization establish a subsidiary?

Part of the answer to this question depends on whether the subsidiary is a tax-exempt organization or a for-profit organization. In general, the principal reason a tax-exempt organization will establish a subsidiary is to house in another organization one or more activities that the parent organization either does not want, or cannot have, as part of its operations. Thus, a *bifurcation* occurs: What would otherwise be one entity is split into two entities. This type of bifurcation almost always is undertaken because of a requirement of law—often, the federal tax law.

14.3 How does a nonprofit organization control a subsidiary?

It depends on whether the subsidiary is a nonprofit or for-profit entity. If the subsidiary is a nonprofit, tax-exempt organization, the control is likely to be manifested by an *interlocking directorship* or, as it is more commonly called, *overlapping boards.* There are several models of this control mechanism. In one model, the board of directors of the parent organization selects at least a majority of the board of directors of the subsidiary. The *ex officio* approach is also common: The governing instrument of the subsidiary provides that certain individuals holding certain positions with the parent organization (such as its president or executive director) are, for that reason, the members of, or at least a majority of, the board of directors of the subsidiary. A third approach is a blend of the foregoing two methods. Whatever the method, it is important for the parent organization to have control of the subsidiary by being able to determine at least a majority of the subsidiary's board of directors. (Without that control element, there is no parent–subsidiary relationship.) It is not enough, for example, for the governing instruments of the "subsidiary" of a membership organization parent to state that the members of the subsidiary's board of directors must be members of the parent organization (unless the membership of the parent entity is exceedingly small).

Where the interlocking-directorship method is used, two other features are recommended. First, the articles of organization of the subsidiary should provide that its governing instruments cannot be amended, or that any such amendment may not become effective, without the prior approval of the board of the parent organization. The purpose of this provision is to prevent a board of the subsidiary from changing the documents to eliminate the interlocking directorate. Second, the governing instruments should make it clear, where directors of the subsidiary are appointed by the parent (rather than installed through use of the *ex officio* approach), that the board of the parent organization has the right to remove these directors as well.

A tax-exempt organization can also control another tax-exempt organization by utilizing the *membership feature*. The subsidiary entity is structured as a membership organization; the parent entity is thereafter made the sole member of the subsidiary organization. Prudence dictates that the governing instruments of the subsidiary state that the prior approval of the members is required to make amendments to those documents and that the members have the right to remove directors of the subsidiary. *Ex officio* positions can also be used in combination with the membership approach.

Where the subsidiary is a for-profit organization, it is almost certainly a corporation. The control mechanism will therefore be stock ownership. The *ex officio* feature can be used in conjunction with the stock approach. Other persons are allowed to hold stock as well, but the "parent" organization must own at least 51 percent of the subsidiary's stock.

14.4 What body can act as the incorporator to establish a subsidiary?

Almost always, the board of directors of a parent organization makes the decision to create and use a subsidiary. The board, usually assisted by legal counsel, also decides the form of the subsidiary and the nature of the control mechanism. The board might decide that the membership feature is to be used; if so, it would make the parent entity a member—most likely, the sole member. If the corporate form is used, along with some other control feature, the board of the parent would decide which individuals would serve as incorporators of the subsidiary.

14.5 Is there a minimum number of board members required for a subsidiary?

There is no rule of federal law on the point. State law is likely to dictate a minimum number of board members for the subsidiary, particularly if the subsidiary is a corporation. Most states require at least three board members for a corporation.

The number of board members of the subsidiary is far more likely to be determined by management or political factors. If the control mechanism is the membership feature, the number of board members is irrelevant (unless there is a state-law minimum). If the control mechanism is an interlocking directorate, the parent entity will want to be able to appoint or elect at least a majority of the members of the subsidiary's board. This factor would result in an odd-numbered board of directors of the subsidiary.

14.6 What legal requirements should be followed in maintaining the parent–subsidiary relationship?

The most basic requirement is that, at all times, the parent organization must be able to show that it "owns" (or, in many instances, controls) at least 51 percent of the subsidiary—whether by stock, membership, or board positions.

It is essential that all of the legal "niceties" of bona fide organizations be respected. The board of directors of the subsidiary—irrespective of the manner in which it is constituted—must have its own meetings (i.e., its meetings should not be a subset or a continuation of the meetings of the parent organization) and maintain minutes of those meetings, and the subsidiary should have its own bank account(s). The law will treat this aspect of bifurcation as a sham if each organization does not have the characteristics of a bona fide separate entity. If regarded as a sham, commonly referred to as "piercing the corporate veil," the arrangement is ignored and the two organizations are treated as one. When this happens, the purposes for creating the subsidiary are almost always nullified: The activities of the subsidiary are attributed to the parent.

14.7 What are the powers and oversight requirements of the parent organization?

The boards of directors of the two organizations—parent and subsidiary—have their own fiduciary or similar requirements. In general, the oversight function is accomplished through the control mechanism; whatever means is selected should afford the parent ample oversight opportunities. The law does not impose any particular standard in this context, other than the standard arising from the fact that the resources (income and assets) are indirectly resources of the parent, so that the parent should treat that bundle of resources as an asset and in accordance with the prudent person rule.

The power of the parent organization with respect to the subsidiary should be complete; the parent controls and sometimes owns the subsidiary. The subsidiary exists solely to do the bidding of the parent. The principal concern is that the power in the parent should not be exercised in such a way as to cause the arrangement to be perceived as a sham.

14.8 How is revenue from a for-profit subsidiary taxed?

In general, revenue that flows from a for-profit subsidiary to a tax-exempt parent is considered unrelated business income. The basic rule is that the parent entity must include the payment as an item of gross income derived from an unrelated business to the extent the payment reduces the net unrelated income, or increases any net unrelated loss, of the controlled entity. *Control* means ownership of more than 50 percent of the stock or other interest in the subsidiary, taking into account (if necessary) constructive ownership rules. These rules apply to the payment of any interest, annuity, royalty, or rent.

For example, if the subsidiary rents property from the parent, the rental income would almost certainly be unrelated income to the parent. Likewise, if the subsidiary borrows money from the parent organization, the interest paid to the parent is likely to be unrelated business income to the parent.

There are three exceptions to this general rule. One is that income in the form of dividends from a for-profit subsidiary to an exempt parent is not unrelated income.

 NOTE: This is the only type of income that is accorded this exempt treatment. Dividends are not taxable to the parent because the payment of them is not deductible by the subsidiary.

Another exception pertains to exempt functions in the subsidiary. The income resulting from exempt functions is not taxable. If the income flowing to the parent from the subsidiary is partially from an exempt function and partially from nonexempt activities, only the income from the latter source is regarded as unrelated business income.

The third exception consists of a temporary rule enacted in 2006, which applies with respect to payments to controlling organizations, in accordance with existing arrangements, received or accrued after December 31, 2005, and before January 1, 2008. Pursuant to this rule, the general law applies only to the portion of the payments received or accrued in a tax year that exceeds the amount of the payment that would have been paid or accrued if the payment had been determined under the federal tax law rules concerning the allocation of tax items among taxpayers. At this time, it is uncertain as to whether this rule will be extended.

14.9 What are the tax consequences of liquidation of a subsidiary into its parent organization?

The answer depends on a variety of factors. For example, have the assets in the subsidiary appreciated in value? If they have, there may be a capital gains tax when the assets of the subsidiary are transferred to the parent.

A federal tax law rule is directed at the tax consequences of liquidation of a subsidiary into a tax-exempt parent organization. Under this rule, where the assets in the subsidiary were used in an unrelated business, are transferred to the parent, and are used in a related business, the capital gains tax becomes applicable and remains applicable whenever the assets become employed in a related business, no matter how many years later. There is no tax, however, where the parent organization continues to use the assets in an unrelated business.

14.10 What are the federal tax reporting requirements with respect to subsidiaries?

If a subsidiary is a for-profit organization, it must file a tax return every year with the IRS. In this return, the corporation must indicate whether any entity owns, directly or indirectly, 50 percent or more of the corporation's voting stock or whether the corporation is a subsidiary in an affiliated group.

If the subsidiary is a tax-exempt organization, it (with some unlikely exceptions) must file an annual information return with the IRS.

NOTE: It is possible to have a subsidiary that is a nonprofit, but not tax-exempt, organization. This type of entity would file a tax return, the same as would a for-profit organization.

The existence of the parent–subsidiary relationship must be reflected on the tax-exempt subsidiary's annual information return. The subsidiary must identify the parent by name and state that it is a tax-exempt organization. If the tax-exempt subsidiary has unrelated business activity, it must file a tax return (Form 990-T) to report the income so derived.

The parent organization, being a tax-exempt entity, files an annual information return with the IRS. If the subsidiary is owned by the parent by means of stock, that holding would be reflected on the balance sheet of the annual information return, presumably as an asset. If a director, officer, or key employee of the parent, who is compensated by the parent, is also compensated by a subsidiary, that aggregate compensation may have to be reported on the annual information return. The existence of the parent–subsidiary relationship must be reflected on the parent's return. The parent must identify the subsidiary by name and state whether it is a tax-exempt or nonexempt organization.

If the subsidiary is a taxable corporation, the tax-exempt parent must complete a special part of the annual information return, stating the name, address, and employer identification number of the subsidiary, the percentage of ownership interest in the subsidiary, the nature of the business activities of the subsidiary, and the total income and end-of-year assets of the subsidiary.

If the parent organization is a tax-exempt charitable entity and the subsidiary is a tax-exempt entity other than a charitable one, the parent must prepare another special part of its annual information return, stating whether it, during the reporting year, transferred cash or other assets to the subsidiary, sold assets to or purchased them from the subsidiary, rented equipment or facilities to the subsidiary, reimbursed the subsidiary for expenses, loaned funds to the subsidiary or guaranteed a loan obligation of the subsidiary, performed any services for the subsidiary, or shared facilities, equipment, mailing lists, other assets, or paid employees with the subsidiary. The parent organization must identify the subsidiary by name, state the type of organization that the subsidiary is, and give a description of the relationship.

If the subsidiary organization is a tax-exempt charitable entity and the parent entity is a tax-exempt organization other than a charitable one, the subsidiary must prepare the special part of its annual information return as identified in the preceding paragraph.

Both organizations are subject to other federal tax reporting requirements, such as those relating to compensation of employees and to profit-sharing and pension plans.

14.11 What are the state law reporting requirements with respect to subsidiaries?

As a separate entity, each organization has its own state-law reporting responsibilities. For example, if each entity is a corporation, both are likely to have to file annual reports with the secretary of state. Trusts probably must file annually with the state attorney general. If either organization engages in fundraising, there must be compliance with the state's law concerning charitable solicitations, if necessary.

Each state's law should be reviewed to determine specific requirements.

14.12 Why would a tax-exempt organization establish a tax-exempt subsidiary?

The principal reason a tax-exempt organization establishes a tax-exempt subsidiary is because the parent entity wants to engage in an activity (or series of activities) that its tax status precludes but that is, under the law, an exempt function for another type of tax-exempt organization. Thus, the function that is nonexempt for the parent is housed in the subsidiary.

On occasion, an activity is placed in a tax-exempt subsidiary in an attempt to shield the parent organization from liability. This reason for creating a subsidiary is also warranted because of legal considerations.

Management or similar considerations, however, may warrant the conduct of a function in a tax-exempt subsidiary even though the function could be conducted by the exempt parent without jeopardizing its tax exemption.

14.13 **What are some of the common uses of tax-exempt subsidiaries?**

There are several of these uses, all built around the concept of bifurcation. The most common combination occasioned by the liability-shield reason for creating an exempt subsidiary is the use by a tax-exempt organization of a tax-exempt title-holding organization.

The most common combinations occasioned by the management reasons for creating an exempt subsidiary are the use by a tax-exempt, noncharitable organization of a charitable supporting organization and the use by a tax-exempt charitable organization of a separate charitable organization for fundraising purposes.

The most common combinations occasioned by the permissible-activity reason for creating an exempt subsidiary are:

1. A tax-exempt charitable organization with a tax-exempt social welfare organization subsidiary that engages in substantial lobbying activities
2. A tax-exempt charitable organization subsidiary of a charitable organization in another country, where the subsidiary is fundraising in the United States

NOTE: In general, only charitable gifts made to U.S. charities are deductible. Foreign charities seeking deductible contributions from U.S. donors need to establish a U.S.-based fundraising organization, and it cannot be merely a conduit of the funds.

3. A tax-exempt membership organization (such as a business association or labor organization) with a tax-exempt supporting organization
4. A tax-exempt organization with a subsidiary that is a political organization
5. A tax-exempt charitable organization with a tax-exempt business league subsidiary that engages in certification activities

NOTE: It is the view of the IRS that programs of certification of organizations' memberships are not charitable activities, because of the benefits flowing to the members. Since certification is an appropriate function for a business league, a separate organization of that nature is required.

14.14 Is it necessary for a tax-exempt subsidiary to obtain separate recognition of tax-exempt status?

It depends on the type of tax-exempt subsidiary. If the subsidiary is a charitable one, recognition of tax-exempt status must be obtained from the IRS (exceptions are unlikely). If the subsidiary is any other type of tax-exempt organization, recognition of exempt status may be acquired, but it is not mandatory.

However, even where recognition of tax exemption is not required, prudence dictates that the determination should be obtained. The subsidiary then has the comfort of knowing that the IRS agrees with its exempt status, and subsequent questions as to its tax status (assuming no changes in material facts) are precluded.

State laws should be reviewed to determine whether the subsidiary must or can obtain one or more tax exemptions (most likely, those with respect to income, sales, use, and/or property taxes).

14.15 Should the tax-exempt status of the subsidiary be as a charitable entity or as a supporting organization?

This question presumes that the subsidiary is to be a tax-exempt charitable (including religious, educational, and/or scientific) organization. The question also reflects common misunderstanding of the two tax statuses. If it is appropriate to cause the subsidiary to be a supporting organization—whether in relation to a public charity or another type of tax-exempt entity—the organization must have *both* tax classifications. This is because all supporting organizations are charitable ones.

The federal tax status of an organization as a charitable entity pertains to its tax-exempt status (and its ability to receive tax-deductible contributions). The tax status of an organization as a supporting organization pertains to its ability to avoid private foundation status.

14.16 What are the reporting requirements between the parent and subsidiary organization?

For the most part, the law does not impose any such requirements. This communication is left largely to the realm of suitable management. Some formal reporting requirements may be appropriate for certain supporting organizations.

If, however, the subsidiary is a supporting organization that is operated in connection with one or more supported organizations, the supporting organization must annually provide sufficient information to each supported organization to ensure that the organization is responsive to the needs or demands of the supported organization(s).

14.17 **If a tax-exempt subsidiary can raise money in its own name, what disclosure requirement should it observe with respect to the parent organization?**

This is largely a matter of state law. The state's charitable solicitation act—if any—will likely contain some disclosure requirement. It is common practice, however, for this type of subsidiary to reflect the existence of the parent on its stationery and fundraising literature.

As to the federal tax law, the charitable subsidiary must adhere to the charitable gift substantiation rules, the quid pro quo contribution rules, and the annual return reporting rules. If the subsidiary is a noncharitable, tax-exempt organization, there are disclosure requirements to which it must adhere concerning the nondeductibility of gifts and the availability of information or services from the federal government.

14.18 **What formal action is required to transfer funds between a tax-exempt parent and a tax-exempt subsidiary?**

Usually, a transfer of funds of this nature requires a formal action of the board of directors of the transferring organization—a board resolution, for example. This is particularly the case where the transfer is in the form of a contribution of capital or a loan from the parent to the subsidiary, or a rental arrangement or purchase of goods or services between the organizations. Other relationships, such as the sharing of employees, need not be the subject of formal board approval. Whatever the nature of the interorganization funding, it may have to be reported to the IRS.

14.19 **Can a tax-exempt subsidiary raise funds for an endowment and hold those funds separate from the parent?**

Yes. This type of subsidiary is likely to be a supporting organization; the maintenance of an endowment fund is a classic activity for this type of organization. It is possible for the endowment function to be in a publicly supported charitable organization—most likely, a donative publicly supported entity—but as the endowment grows, the extent of investment income may cause the organization to receive an inadequate amount of public support.

The supporting organization would be able to transfer income from the endowment fund to the supported organization (assuming that is the nature of the endowment structure). If the supported organization is not a charitable one, the funds transferred to the parent should be clearly restricted to charitable uses.

14.20 Why would a tax-exempt organization establish a for-profit subsidiary?

Usually, a tax-exempt organization establishes a for-profit subsidiary because of the existence, or planned existence, of an unrelated business, or set of unrelated businesses, that is too extensive to be conducted in the parent without jeopardizing the parent's tax-exempt status. Some exempt organizations incubate unrelated businesses within themselves and then transfer them (*spin them off*) to a for-profit subsidiary. Others create a subsidiary at the outset.

The approach to take may be a matter of management's judgment. If it is known at the beginning that the unrelated activity will be extensive, the for-profit subsidiary is basically dictated. If, however, the scope of the unrelated business is unknown at the outset and its prospects are dubious, the organization may want to commence with the business within itself and then spin it off when and if it becomes larger.

 NOTE: If the unrelated business is in the exempt organization, the only deductions that may be taken in calculating unrelated business taxable income are those that are directly related to the unrelated activity. (The IRS presently has a compliance check project by which it is examining the deduction calculation practices of a sample of the nation's colleges and universities, with subsequent implications for religious and other tax-exempt organizations.) When the unrelated business is in a for-profit subsidiary, all expenses are deductible as long as they are reasonable and necessary to the conduct of the business.

All things considered, a tax-exempt organization may wish to go slowly in establishing a tax-exempt subsidiary. If the subsidiary is created and, later, it turns out that it is not needed and the parent decides to liquidate it, there may be adverse tax consequences to the parent.

The decision as to whether to create a for-profit subsidiary can be a difficult one. At a minimum, it requires a determination as to whether the activity involved is related or unrelated. The subsidiary may also be needed if the activity (or activities) is to be conducted in a commercial manner.

14.21 What are some of the common uses of for-profit subsidiaries?

There is no limit in the law as to the type of business activity that can be operated out of a for-profit subsidiary; the tax-exempt organization can devise any type of business activity it wants as a means to generate revenue (which, however, is likely to be taxed). There is also no limit in the law as to the size of subsidiaries, either absolutely or in relation to the parent, or the number of for-profit subsidiaries a tax-exempt organization may have.

NOTE: To be tax-exempt, the parent entity must function primarily in furtherance of exempt functions. The use of one or more subsidiaries should not cause the organization to deviate from that standard.

Some tax-exempt organizations will place an unrelated business in a for-profit subsidiary even where the tax laws do not require it (i.e., where the business is relatively small). This is done for reasons of *politics* and *perception*, particularly where the business is competitive with commercial businesses in the community. As an illustration, a large national religious nonprofit ("ministry") began using its printing facilities, used primarily for its exempt functions, for occasional jobs for outside purchasers; as the business grew, some of the commercial printers in the community complained about the competition. To appease its critics, the ministry transferred its commercial printing operation to a for-profit subsidiary. The competition was still present, but the commercial printers were mollified when it came from a for-profit entity.

In this context, *competition* can be synonymous with controversy and sensitivity, particularly among small businesses. When a tax-exempt organization is in competition with a commercial business, the latter sees the competition as being *unfair*, in that the exempt organization does not have to pay taxes; with taxes not a cost of doing business, the exempt organization is (at least in theory) able to underprice the commercial business. Nonetheless, despite plaintiffs' attempts, the courts have been unwilling to hold that for-profit businesses have standing to merit ruling in favor of their competitors' challenge to their tax-exempt status.

The third use of a for-profit subsidiary by a tax-exempt organization is as a *partner in a partnership*, in lieu of the exempt organization's direct participation. The exempt parent may fear the potential of liability or participation in the partnership (usually, as a general partner) might adversely affect the parent's tax-exempt status.

NOTE: This is another area where it is critical that the bona fides and corporate formalities of the subsidiary be adhered to. This approach works only when the legal form of the subsidiary is respected. In one instance, the IRS ignored a tax-exempt organization's use of a for-profit subsidiary as the general partner in a partnership, and reviewed the facts as though the exempt organization was directly involved in the partnership.

If a for-profit organization that is a subsidiary of a tax-exempt organization is used in a partnership, *tax-exempt entity leasing rules* may come into play. These rules make the property involved depreciable over a longer recovery period, thereby reducing the annual depreciation deduction.

NOTE: These rules can be avoided where a corporate for-profit subsidiary is used as a partner in a partnership in lieu of a tax-exempt organization, if an election is made to treat any gain on disposition of the subsidiary (and certain other accrued amounts) as unrelated business income.

14.22 Are there limits on the use of tax-exempt assets to capitalize a for-profit subsidiary?

There are no specific limits. Basically, the rules are those that generally pertain to the requirement that the governing board of a tax-exempt organization act in conformity with basic fiduciary responsibilities.

IRS private letter rulings suggest that only very small percentages of an organization's resources ought to be transferred to subsidiaries, particularly where the parent entity is a public charity. The percentages approved by the IRS, however, are usually unduly low, and, in any event, probably pertain only to cash. In some instances, a specific asset may—indeed perhaps *must*—be best utilized in an unrelated activity, even though its value represents a meaningful portion of the organization's total resources.

14.23 Are there any rules concerning accumulations of income and other assets in a for-profit subsidiary?

No, the law is essentially silent on the point. Nonetheless, in a private determination issued in late 2004, the IRS wrote that tax-exempt organizations (particularly charitable ones) "bear a very heavy burden" to demonstrate, by "contemporaneous and clear evidence," that they have plans for the use of substantial assets in a subsidiary for exempt purposes. In this case, the charitable organization invested by means of a for-profit subsidiary, which grew rapidly. "This growth presents a continuing obligation," the IRS said, on the organization to "translate this valuable asset into funds, and use these funds for the expansion" of its exempt activities. The IRS suggested that some of the subsidiary's assets be sold or a portion of the subsidiary's stock be sold, with the proceeds used to fund programs of the exempt parent.

The IRS's lawyers said that the exempt organization "cannot be allowed to focus its energies on expanding its subsidiary's commercial business and assets, and neglect to translate that financial success into specific, definite, and feasible plans for the expansion of its charitable activities." The agency concluded that the "fact that the assets are being accumulated in a for-profit company under the formal legal control of a [tax-exempt organization] does not excuse [the tax-exempt organization] from using such assets for charitable purposes." The IRS concluded: "Excess accumulations, maintained in a subsidiary entity under legal control of the exempt organization, but under the de facto control of the founder, are deemed to be for the founder's personal purposes if no exempt purpose is documented or implemented."

The IRS did not cite any authority for these sweeping pronouncements. This is not surprising, inasmuch as there isn't any.

14.24 Can a supporting organization have a for-profit subsidiary?

Yes, a supporting organization can have a for-profit subsidiary. There was doubt about this for some time, inasmuch as this type of public charity is required to be operated *exclusively* to support or benefit one or more eligible public charities; in this context, *exclusively* means *solely*. There was concern, therefore, that the IRS would rule that a supporting organization cannot have a for-profit subsidiary because to do so would be a violation of the exclusivity requirement. The IRS did not so rule, but instead has held that, where the reason for organizing and utilizing a subsidiary is to assist the supporting organization in benefiting a supported organization, use of the subsidiary is allowable. IRS private letter rulings state that a supporting entity's use of a for-profit subsidiary will not jeopardize its tax-exempt status or its supporting organization status, as long as it does not actively participate in the day-to-day management of the subsidiary and both entities have a legitimate business purpose.

14.25 What is the legal definition of a *partnership*?

A *partnership* is a form of business enterprise recognized in the law as an *entity*, as are other enterprises, such as a corporation, limited liability company, or trust. It is usually evidenced by a document, which is a partnership agreement, executed between persons who are the partners. These persons may be individuals, corporations, and/or other partnerships. Each partner owns an interest in the partnership; these interests may or may not be equal.

In the federal tax law, the term *partnership* includes a "syndicate, group, pool, joint venture, or other unincorporated organization, through or by means of which any business, financial operation, or venture is carried on, and which is not . . . a trust or estate or a corporation." A partnership must have at least two members, who are its owners.

The concept of a partnership has long been given broad interpretation. In a classic example of this, a court defined a partnership as a relationship based on a "contract of two or more persons to place their money, efforts, labor, and skill, or some or all of them, in lawful commerce or business, and to divide the profit and bear the loss in definite proportions." Thus, co-owners of income-producing real estate who operate the property (either through an agent or one or more of them) for their joint profit are operating a partnership.

Partnerships are not taxed. They are *pass-through entities*; this means that the entity's income, deductions, and credits are passed along to the partners. An entity that does not qualify for tax purposes as a partnership will undoubtedly be regarded as an *association*, which means that it is taxed as a corporation. When that happens, certain tax attributes are lost.

There are two basic types of partnerships: the *general partnership* and the *limited partnership*.

14.26 What is a *general partnership*?

The difference between the two types of partnerships is delineated principally by the extent of the partners' liability for the acts of the partnership. Generally, liability for the consequences of a partnership's operations rests with the general partner or general partners. Moreover, a general partner is liable for satisfaction of the ongoing obligations of the partnership and can be called on to make additional contributions of capital to it. Every partnership must have at least one general partner. Sometimes where there is more than one general partner, one of them is designated as the managing general partner.

Many partnerships are comprised of only general partners, who contribute cash, property, and/or services. This type of partnership is a *general partnership*. The interests of the general partners may or may not be equal. In many respects, a general partnership is akin to a *joint venture*.

A general partnership is usually manifested by a partnership agreement.

14.27 What is a *limited partnership*?

A *limited partnership* is one that has limited partners as participants. A limited partner is a person whose exposure to liability for the functions of the partnership is confined to the amount of that person's contribution to (investment in) the partnership.

Some partnerships need or want to attract capital from sources other than the general partner or partners. This capital can be derived from investors, who are limited partners. Their interest in the partnership is, as noted, limited in the sense that their liability is limited. The limited partners are involved to obtain a return on their investment and perhaps to procure some tax advantages.

Thus, a partnership with both general and limited partners is a limited partnership.

A limited partnership is usually manifested by a partnership agreement.

14.28 Why is the partnership vehicle used?

As a general proposition, the partnership is used as a business enterprise because the parties bring unique resources to the relationship, and they want to blend these resources for the purpose of beginning and conducting a business. Another reason for the partnership form—particularly the limited partnership vehicle—is to attract financing for one or more projects. In some instances, the partnership vehicle is favored because of its tax status.

14.29 **What is the legal definition of a *joint venture*?**

A *joint venture* is a form of business enterprise recognized in the law as an *entity*, as are other enterprises, like a corporation or trust. Essentially, a general partnership and a joint venture are the same thing.

One court defined a *joint venture* as an association of two or more persons with intent to carry out a single business venture for joint profit, for which purpose they combine their efforts, property, money, skill, and knowledge, but they do so without creating a formal entity, namely, a partnership, trust, or corporation. Thus, two or more entities (including tax-exempt organizations) may operate a business enterprise as a joint venture.

The concept of a joint venture, however, is broader than that of a general partnership. One of the ways this fact can be manifested is evident when the law treats an arrangement as a joint venture for tax purposes, even though the parties involved insist that their partnership is something else (such as parties to a management agreement or a lease).

 NOTE: This issue can arise in the unrelated business income context, where a tax-exempt organization is asserting that certain income it is receiving is passive in nature (and thus not taxable) and the IRS is contending that the income (most frequently rent or royalty income) is being derived from active participation in a joint venture.

The federal tax law is inconsistent in stating the criteria for ascertaining whether a joint venture is to be found as a matter of law. According to the Supreme Court, "[w]hen the existence of an alleged partnership arrangement is challenged by outsiders, the question arises whether the partners really and truly intended to join together for the purpose of carrying on business and sharing in the profits or losses or both." The Court added that the parties' "intention is a question of fact, to be determined from testimony disclosed by their agreement considered as a whole, and by their conduct in execution of its provisions." In one instance, a court examined state law and concluded that the most important element in determining whether a landlord–tenant relationship or joint venture agreement exists is the intention of the parties. This court also held that the burden of proving the existence of a joint venture is on the party who claims that that type of relationship exists (such as the IRS).

Yet another court declared that "it is well settled that neither local law nor the expressed intent of the parties is conclusive as to the existence or nonexistence of a partnership or joint venture for federal tax purposes." The court wrote that this is the test to follow: "whether, considering all the facts—the agreement, the conduct of the parties in execution of its provisions, their statements, the testimony of disinterested persons, the relationship of the parties, their respective abilities and capital contributions, the actual control of income and the purposes for which it is used, and any other facts throwing light on their true intent—the parties in good faith and acting with a business purpose intended to join together in the present conduct of the enterprise."

This latter court wrote that the "realities of the taxpayer's economic interest rather than the niceties of the conveyancer's art should determine the power to tax." The court added: "Among the critical elements involved in the determination are the existence of controls over the venture and a risk of loss in the taxpayer." Finally, the court said that it is not bound by the "nomenclature used by the parties," so that a document titled, for example, a *lease* may in law be a partnership agreement.

14.30 Why is the joint venture vehicle used?

The joint venture vehicle is generally used when two or more persons share resources to advance a specific project or program. When the arrangement is formally established, it is often denominated a *general partnership*. As noted, however, parties to a transaction can find themselves treated as being in a joint venture as a matter of law.

Moreover, the term *joint venture* is often broadly used. The term appears in the formal definition of a *partnership*. It is often applied in other contexts, such as when the structure of a venture is based on use of a limited liability company.

14.31 How are joint ventures taxed?

Joint ventures are not taxed. They are *pass-through entities*; this means that the entity's income, deductions, and credits are passed along to the members. Thus, joint ventures are treated the same as partnerships for tax purposes.

There are basically two types of limited liability companies: the multimember limited liability company and the single-member limited liability company. In the case of a multimember limited liability company, the members may consist of one or more tax-exempt organizations and one or more for-profit entities, or the members may all be tax-exempt organizations. The single-member limited liability company is almost always disregarded for federal tax purposes; a tax-exempt organization can be the sole member of a limited liability company.

14.32 What is a *limited liability company*?

A *limited liability company* is a legal entity, recognized under state law. It is not a corporation, although it has the corporate attribute of limitation against personal liability. A limited liability company with at least two members generally is treated as a partnership for tax purposes.

Limited liability companies are not taxed. They are, when they elect to do so, treated the same as partnerships for tax purposes.

NOTE: Likewise, S corporations are treated as partnerships for tax purposes.

14.33 Can a tax-exempt organization be involved in a general partnership?

There is no question that a tax-exempt organization can be involved in a general partnership. The principal tax law issues become, however, whether involvement in the partnership jeopardizes the entity's exempt status and/or cause it unrelated business income. To date, with the exception of a few private letter rulings, all of the law on the point concerns public charities in general partnerships. Inasmuch as the law in this regard is the same as that pertaining to public charities in joint ventures, it will be discussed in that context.

14.34 Can a tax-exempt organization be involved in a limited partnership?

Again, the answer is a definite yes. And, again, the tax issues are whether tax exemption would be threatened and/or unrelated business income generated. Here, too, the law to date has focused only on public charities in limited partnerships as general partners.

Resolution of these issues depends on whether the exempt organization is in a limited partnership as a limited partner or a general partner.

14.35 Can a tax-exempt organization be involved in a limited partnership as a limited partner?

The answer is clearly yes, although there is little law on the point. When an exempt organization is a limited partner in a limited partnership, it is in the venture as an investor. The law then is likely to focus primarily on whether the investment is a prudent one for the organization and whether its board is adhering to the requisite principles of fiduciary responsibility.

14.36 Can a tax-exempt organization be involved in a limited partnership as a general partner?

Yes. This brings the discussion to one of the most critical aspects of this subject: the impact of involvement in a limited partnership by a public charity as a general partner on the charity's tax-exempt status. For years, the IRS has had great concerns on this point. Indeed, it was not until 1998 that the IRS formally stated that a charitable organization may form and participate in a partnership and be or remain tax-exempt.

NOTE: Nonetheless, the IRS has issued dozens of private letter rulings, technical advice memoranda, and general counsel memoranda stating that a public charity's involvement in a limited partnership will not endanger its exempt status. Indeed, on one occasion, the IRS ruled that the exempt status of a charitable organization should not be revoked because of its participation as a general partner in seven limited partnerships. Moreover, the IRS has *never* issued a published private determination that involvement in a limited partnership would cause loss or denial of a charity's exempt status.

NOTE: As to the last observation, there have been ruling requests in which the facts were altered to gain the favor of the IRS in this regard, and there have been ruling requests involving charities in limited partnerships that have been withdrawn in anticipation of an adverse ruling. Further, the IRS provided guidance indicating when an involvement in a joint venture by a charity could lead to loss of its exemption.

14.37 What are IRS concerns about public charities as general partners and limited partnerships?

Despite the fact that the debate, in and out of the IRS, over participation by public charities in limited partnerships as general partners has been openly raging for more than 25 years, the IRS and some courts are still not enamored with the idea. The primary concern the IRS has in this context is the potential for private inurement and/or private benefit accruing to the for-profit participants in the venture. More specifically, it is the view of the IRS that substantial benefits can be provided to the for-profit participants in a limited partnership (usually the limited partners) involving a tax-exempt organization as the general partner.

14.38 Why has the controversy lasted so long?

There are several reasons that this controversy about public charities in limited partnerships has spanned many years. One is the ongoing number, variation, and complexity of these arrangements. Another is the great prevalence of the use of limited partnerships in the health-care setting; as the law in that sphere has ballooned, so too has the general law concerning charities in partnerships. Still another reason is that the IRS adopted a very hard-line stance in this area at the beginning.

14.39 What was the original IRS hard-line position?

The original position of the IRS in this regard came to be known as the *per se rule*. Pursuant to this view, involvement by a charitable organization in a limited partnership as general partner meant *automatic* revocation or denial of tax exemption, irrespective of the structure or purpose of the partnership. The per se rule was grounded on the premise that substantial private economic benefit was being accorded to the limited partners.

Here is the IRS in 1978, in first articulating this per se rule, advising a public charity: "If you entered [into] the proposed partnership, you would be a direct participant in an arrangement for sharing the net profits of an income producing venture with private individuals and organizations of a non-charitable nature. By agreeing to serve as the general partner of the proposed . . . project, you would take on an obligation to further the private financial interests of the other partners. This would create a conflict of interest that is legally incompatible with you being operated exclusively for charitable purposes."

NOTE: This was the position the IRS staked out, even though the purpose of the partnership was to advance a charitable objective (the development and operation of a low-income housing project).

There were other instances of application of the per se rule in the late 1970s and into the 1980s. Some of these cases did not involve formal partnerships. For example, an IRS private letter ruling issued in 1979 concerned the issue of whether certain fees derived by tax-exempt lawyer referral services were items of unrelated business income. The IRS ruled that the fees paid by lawyers to the organizations, based on a percentage of the fees received by the lawyers for providing legal services to clients referred to them by these exempt organizations, constituted unrelated income. The reason: The subsequently established lawyer–client relationship was a commercial undertaking, and the ongoing fee arrangement with the percentage feature placed the organizations in the position of being in a joint venture in furtherance of those commercial objectives.

14.40 What became of the per se rule of the IRS?

The per se rule of the IRS was rejected by a court in a significant decision. The case concerned syndication of a play being staged at a tax-exempt theater.

NOTE: Before continuing with a description of this case, it should be noted that, as a matter of fundamental litigation practice, the party advocating the rule of law being asserted (here, the IRS) endeavors to select a situation involving facts that are the most compelling from the standpoint of its position. Inexplicably, the IRS advanced its cause in a blatant violation of standard litigation strategy. The theater group sponsoring the play was truly struggling financially, the play was being staged at the Kennedy Center in Washington, D.C., and the production was an engaging drama in the form of a sympathetic portrayal of the Supreme Court!

Needing financial assistance, the theater group underwrote its production costs with funds provided by private investors. The IRS sought to revoke the organization's tax-exempt status for attempting to sustain the arts in this fashion but lost, both at trial and on appeal. Again, the matter involved a limited partnership that was being used to further the exempt ends of the general partner. The courts in this case placed some emphasis on the facts that the partnership had no interest in the tax-exempt organization or its other activities, the limited partners had no control over the way in which the exempt organization operated or managed its affairs, and none of the limited partners nor any officer or director of a corporate limited partner was an officer or director of the charitable organization.

NOTE: Much later, the IRS pronounced this control element a "significant" factor in this type of analysis.

Shortly after this litigation, the IRS began to relax its stance in these regards. This new view was manifested in a 1983 general counsel memorandum, in which the lawyers for the IRS opined that it is possible for a charitable organization to participate as a general partner in a limited partnership without jeopardizing its tax exemption. The IRS lawyers advised that two aspects of this matter should be reviewed: whether (1) the participation may be in conflict with the goals and purposes of the charitable organization and (2) the terms of the partnership agreement contain provisions that insulate the charitable organization from certain of the obligations imposed on a general partner. In this instance, the limited partnership (a low-income housing venture) was found to further the organization's charitable purposes and several specific provisions of the partnership agreement were deemed to provide the requisite insulation for the charitable organization/general partner. Thus, the organization was permitted to serve as the partnership's general partner and simultaneously retain its tax exemption.

This development paved the way for the contemporary set of rules pertaining to public charities as general partners in limited partnerships.

NOTE: The official date marking the demise of the per se rule seems to be November 21, 1991, when the IRS office of general counsel wrote that the IRS "no longer contends that participation as a general partner in a partnership is *per se* inconsistent with [tax] exemption."

14.41 When can a tax-exempt organization be involved in a limited partnership as a general partner and still be tax exempt?

The current position of the IRS as to whether a charitable organization will have its tax-exempt status revoked (or recognition denied) if it functions as a general partner in a limited partnership is the subject of a three-part test.

Under this test, the IRS first looks to determine whether the charitable organization/general partner is serving a charitable purpose by means of participation in the partnership. If involvement in the partnership is serving a charitable purpose, the IRS applies the rest of the test. Should the partnership fail to adhere to the charitability standard, however, the charitable organization/general partner will be deprived of or be denied tax-exempt status.

The first element of this test is an aspect of the fundamental *operational test* that every exempt charity must meet. This test is an evaluation of the operations of the organization. In general, for tax purposes, the activities of a partnership are often considered to be the activities of the partners. This aggregate approach is applied for purposes of the operational test. Consequently, when a charitable organization is advancing charitable ends by means of a partnership, it continues to satisfy the operational test and thus be exempt.

The rest of this test is designed to ascertain whether the charity's role as general partner inhibits the advancement of its charitable purposes. Here the IRS looks to means by which the organization may, under the particular facts and circumstances, be insulated from the day-to-day responsibilities as a general partner and whether the limited partners are receiving an undue economic benefit from the partnership. It is the view of the IRS that there is an inherent tension between the ability of a charitable organization to function exclusively in furtherance of its exempt functions and the obligation of a general partner to operate the partnership for the benefit of the limited partners. This tension is the same perceived phenomenon that the IRS, when in deploying the per se rule, chose to characterize as a "conflict of interest."

An application of this test is reflected in a private letter ruling made public in 1985, which involved a charitable organization that became a general partner in a real estate limited partnership that leased all of the space in the property to the organization and a related charitable organization. The IRS applied the first part of the test and found that the partnership was serving charitable ends because both of the tenants of the partnership were charitable organizations.

NOTE: The IRS general counsel memorandum underlying this private letter ruling noted that if the lessee organization that was not the general partner had been an exempt organization other than a charitable one, the charity/general partner would have forfeited tax exemption.

On application of the rest of the test, the IRS found that the charitable organization/general partner was adequately insulated from the day-to-day management responsibilities of the partnership and that the limited partners' economic return was reasonable.

14.42 Are there any other aspects of this matter?

Yes. There seem to be other requirements that are added to the three-part test from time to time. For example, in one instance the IRS emphasized the facts that the charitable organization was "governed by an independent board of directors" composed of church and community leaders, and that it did not have any other relationship with any of the commercial companies involved in the project. The IRS added that there was not any information that indicated that the organization was controlled by or "otherwise unduly influenced" by the limited partners or any company involved in the development or management of the project.

One other point: It has never been clear as to why the IRS formulated the per se test in the first instance, inasmuch as it has always been understood that public charities can be general partners in limited partnerships—this is in the Internal Revenue Code, in two places. One provision speaks of a "partnership of which an [exempt] organization is a member." Another provision references a "partnership which has both a tax-exempt entity and a person who is not a tax-exempt entity as partners." These pronouncements from Congress would be wholly superfluous in the case of public charities if their mere participation as a general partner in a limited partnership would deprive them of their exempt status.

14.43 How do the unrelated business income rules apply in the partnership context?

Normally, the unrelated business income rules become applicable to a tax-exempt organization because of a business activity conducted directly by that organization. These rules, however, can also become activated when an unrelated business is conducted in a partnership of which an exempt organization is a member.

The rule applied in this context is a *look-through rule:* If a business regularly carried on by a partnership, of which a tax-exempt organization is a member, is an unrelated business with respect to the exempt organization, in computing its unrelated business taxable income the organization must include its share (whether or not actually distributed) of the gross income of the partnership from the unrelated business. This rule applies irrespective of whether the tax-exempt organization is a general or limited partner.

14.44 How does an exempt organization know what income and the like to report from a partnership?

A partnership generally must furnish to each partner a statement reflecting the information about the partnership required to be shown on the partner's tax return or information return. The statement must set forth the partner's distributive share of the partnership's income, gain, loss, deduction, or credit required to be shown on the partner's return, along with any additional information as provided by IRS forms or instructions that may be required to apply particular provisions of the federal tax law to the partner with respect to items related to the partnership.

The instructions accompanying the statement for partners (Schedule K-1, Form 1065) require the partnership to state whether the partner is a tax-exempt organization. Moreover, the partnership must attach a statement furnishing any other information needed by the partner to file its return that is not shown elsewhere on the schedule.

In the case of a partnership regularly carrying on a business, the partnership must furnish to the partners the information necessary to enable each tax-exempt partner to compute its distributive share of partnership income or gain from the business.

Partnerships of tax-exempt organizations, including those consisting wholly of exempt organizations, must annually file the federal information returns required of partnerships.

Also, a tax-exempt organization in a partnership runs the risk of being a party to a prohibited tax shelter transaction, which can give rise to entity-level and manager-level excise taxes. This body of law includes disclosure obligations. In 2007, the IRS proposed regulations that provide that a tax-exempt organization does not become a *party* to a prohibited tax shelter transaction solely because it invests in an entity that in turn becomes involved in this type of transaction.

14.45 Can a tax-exempt organization be involved in a joint venture?

There is no question that a tax-exempt organization can be involved in a joint venture. The principal tax law issues become—just as in the case of involvement in partnerships —whether involvement in the joint venture jeopardizes the entity's exempt status and/or causes it to receive unrelated business income. To date, nearly all of the law on the point concerns public charities in joint ventures.

There are two types of these involvements. One occurs where the public charity *intends* to be in a joint venture. The other occurs where the joint venture arrangement is imposed on the parties as a matter of law.

14.46 Why would a tax-exempt organization want to participate in a joint venture?

The basic reason that a public charity (or other type of tax-exempt organization) wants to participate in a joint venture is to carry out a single project or program, using the efforts, money, and/or expertise of one or more other parties. It is a resource-gathering, resource-sharing operation. Often the other party or parties are not exempt organizations.

14.47 What does a tax-exempt organization in a joint venture have to do to retain its tax-exempt status?

The basic rule is that a public charity (or other type of exempt organization) may enter into a joint venture with a for-profit organization (or other entity), without adversely affecting the charity's tax-exempt status, as long as doing so furthers exempt purposes and the joint venture agreement does not prevent it from acting exclusively to further those purposes. A joint venture does not present the private inurement or private benefit problems that are associated with participation by exempt organizations in limited partnerships, because there are no limited partners receiving economic benefits. In contrast, an involvement in a joint venture by a tax-exempt organization would lead to loss or denial of tax exemption if the primary purpose of the exempt organization is to participate in the venture and if the function of the venture is unrelated to the exempt purposes of the tax-exempt organization.

An example of an involvement in a joint venture that does not adversely affect a public charity's exempt status is a charitable organization participating in a venture with a for-profit entity to own and operate a freestanding alcoholism/substance abuse treatment center. Still another involves a charitable hospital that participates with a for-profit organization in a venture for the purpose of providing magnetic resonance imaging services in an underserved community.

A tax-exempt organization may enter into a joint venture with another tax-exempt organization, in furtherance of the exempt purposes of both of them.

As will be discussed, a joint venture of this nature may be structured by use of a limited liability company.

14.48   How can a tax-exempt organization be involved in a joint venture against its will?

The joint venture form is usually imposed on a relationship with one or more other parties involving a tax-exempt organization where the revenue received by the exempt organization from the relationship is to be taxed. This can happen because of the sweep of the definition of the term *joint venture.*

A classic example of this comes when a tax-exempt organization is endeavoring to characterize an item of income as a royalty, which is not taxable, while the IRS is asserting that the exempt organization and other parties are actively participating in a joint venture, so that the income is taxable.

On occasion, the IRS will invoke the joint venture rationale for the purpose of revoking or denying a tax exemption. The application of the private inurement doctrine is triggered by the inherent structure of the joint venture (private inurement per se), irrespective of the reasonableness of the compensation.

14.49   How do the unrelated business income rules apply in a joint venture context?

The unrelated business income rules apply in the joint venture context in the same way they do in the partnership setting. That is, the *look-through rule* applies, so if there is unrelated business income generated by the joint venture, the exempt organization's share of it must be taken into account by the exempt organization in ascertaining its taxable income for the year.

This is why, when the IRS sees an exempt organization characterizing income as excludable income (particularly as a royalty) and simultaneously actively participating in the undertaking that gives rise to the income, the IRS elects to impose a joint venture form on the arrangement, so as to cause the income to be taxable by application of the look-through rule.

CHAPTER **15**

Liability of Religious Organizations

15.1   What is *vicarious liability*?

Vicarious liability, in this context, is the idea that an employer can be held responsible for the negligent acts and omissions of its employees. When an employee of the organization is acting in the course of his or her employment, the organization is responsible for damages or injuries that the agent or employee negligently causes to any other person. The key here is that the employer must be in control of the employee when the negligent act or omission takes place. In other words, the employee must be acting in the course of his or her employment in order for the employer to be held liable for their actions. if "frolic" can be shown on the part of the employee, that is, the employee is acting on his or her own rather than on the behalf of the employer, then the employer cannot and will not be liable for those actions.

For religious nonprofit organizations, claims involving injuries from inadequate supervision of children, the operation of vehicles or equipment, and the mishandling of individuals with serious mental conditions appear to be the most frequent and numerous claims of vicarious liability.

15.2   Can an organization be liable for the acts of volunteers?

Yes. In the absence of some statutory protection from *vicarious liability*, a religious nonprofit organization may be held *indirectly* liable for the conduct of its volunteers, even though the volunteer himself would remain *directly* liable to the injured party. In practice, this vicarious liability means that the organization would have to pay for the damages of the injured party where the person who was directly liable is financially unable to pay or not legally obligated to pay.

Many organizations take false comfort in the enactment of federal legislation regarding volunteers to nonprofits. The legislation aims to protect volunteers from personal liability, not the organizations for which they volunteer. The Volunteer Protection Act (VPA) was signed into law in 1997. The Act was enacted in response to the withdrawal of volunteers from service to nonprofit organizations because of concerns about possible liability. By limiting lawsuits against such volunteers, it was thought that the number of volunteers would increase, thus promoting the ability of nonprofit organizations and governmental entities to provide services at a reasonable cost. The VPA preempts state laws "to the extent that such laws are inconsistent with the Act." The Act applies only to § 501(c)(3) organizations and governmental entities. In addition, the VPA does not prevent a nonprofit from bringing an action against a volunteer.

In summary, the VPA provides immunity for volunteers serving nonprofit organizations or governmental entities for harm caused by their acts or omissions if:

* The volunteer was acting within the scope of his or her responsibilities.
* If appropriate or required, the volunteer was properly licensed, certified, or authorized to act.
* The harm was not caused by willful, criminal, or reckless misconduct or gross negligence.
* The harm was not caused by the volunteer operating a motor vehicle, vessel, or aircraft.

Despite the VPA, many organizations remain *fully liable* for any harm caused through their volunteers, and all volunteers remain liable for some actions. Exceptions to the liability limitation include misconduct that is a crime of violence, hate crime, sexual offense, violation of federal or state civil rights law, and acts committed under the influence of alcohol or drugs.

15.3 Can an organization be directly liable for the negligent hiring of an individual?

Yes. *Negligent hiring* is a cause of action that asserts that an organization can be held liable for negligence if it put an individual in a position of authority or responsibility, and an injury results because of this placement. Negligent hiring allows a recovery to the injured party when the organization was aware, or should have been aware, of the propensity of an individual to commit the type of conduct that caused harm. Negligent hiring requires proof of actual negligence on the part of the employer before the injury occurred, at the time when the employee was originally hired. Negligent hiring can even be asserted in an attempt to impose liability on the employer for acts that are clearly outside the scope of the authority that the organization placed in the individual.

In its defense to a claim of negligent hiring, the organization should be able to show that it exercised reasonable care in the hiring of the individual. In so doing, the organization should generally be able to justify its decision to hire the individual by demonstrating that a diligent effort was undertaken in both the gathering and analyzing of information about the particular individual in question.

15.4 Does negligent hiring apply to volunteers?

Volunteers are not technically hired, but they are selected; therefore, the cause of action applicable as to volunteers is labeled *negligent selection*. Traditionally, a volunteer willing to donate his or her time, efforts, and energies was eagerly accepted with gratitude merely on presentation, but in today's society, unfortunately, cloaked motives and inexpensive technologies imply a much greater level of scrutiny than is required by an organization over the selection of every individual brought into its fold. An organization should be careful not to equate the absence of pay with lack of "risk" or lack of "importance" when selecting volunteers. Just as in negligent hiring, the organization should be able to demonstrate that it exercised reasonable care in the selection and appointment of its volunteers, especially where contact with children is involved.

15.5 Can an organization be liable for the negligent retention of an agent?

Yes. Just as in negligent hiring or selection, where the organization should be able to demonstrate that it exercised reasonable care in the decision-making process to use an individual for services, the organization can also be liable for retaining an agent who injures another after it has information that would indicate to a reasonably prudent organization that the individual should be dismissed. If the agent commits a tortious act that is consistent with the negative conduct the organization has become aware of, the organization can be liable for the damages suffered. In the case of negligent retention, the law follows a commonsense approach: An organization should not continue to retain an individual who has demonstrated a propensity to injure others, and the more egregious the agent's prior behavior appears to be, the greater the likelihood that the organization would be held responsible for not dismissing the individual in the event that any further consistent misconduct occurs.

15.6 Can an organization be liable for hazardous activities?

A typical religious nonprofit organization utilizes individuals on staff or volunteers to supervise others, give instructions, operate a physical plant, provide transportation, and organize and oversee all types of events, among innumerable other functions. Most church organizations also engage in onsite and offsite activities of a purely recreational nature. Such activities, like informal sporting events, often carry a significant degree of risk of harm to at least some of the participants and bystanders. Activities that would be considered hazardous if left unsupervised should be competently supervised by the organization, and activities that are considered inherently or unreasonably hazardous even when supervised, such as some extreme sports, should be pursued by interested individuals of their own volition as an activity apart from the organization. In making decisions about activities to avoid, consider such factors as whether there is an age limit to the activity elsewhere, whether safety gear is a common requirement, the suitability of the premises, the potential for disregard of the "rules," the risks that the least capable participants will bear, and the probable nature of the injuries in the event of their occurrence. The implication that any laws would be broken should disqualify the activity from consideration, such as unlicensed use or misuse of vehicles or equipment, activities involving firearms, discharging fireworks where prohibited, and the like.

15.7   Can an organization be liable based on inadequate or negligent supervision?

If an activity is normally safe under proper conditions, but would be considered particularly hazardous if left unsupervised, the organization must exercise the degree of supervision required to offset the foreseeable risks. Community standards will vary in this regard but a good general practice is to consider the likely approach of several of the more prudent of community organizations in addressing the same functions. Lack of supervision or inadequate supervision can result in liability. Choosing to provide no supervision at all because no competent supervision is available, but condoning the activity anyway, is inadvisable.

15.8   Should an organization implement a child abuse prevention policy?

Many states require mandatory reporting, under penalty of criminal prosecution, by any and all individuals who have reason to believe abuse or neglect of a child is occurring. Where reporting is not mandatory, it is still encouraged. In many states, the reporter is protected from civil liability so long as the report has been made in good faith. Organizations regularly undertaking the temporary care of children should be acquainted with the controlling laws and enforcement agencies in their jurisdiction and be cognizant that indications of child abuse are rarely volunteered, often denied, and sometimes very subtle. No organization can afford the assumption that abuse will not occur on its own premises. Authoritative publications are available providing comprehensive and systematic approaches to preventing child abuse. At a minimum, organizations should know the history of those who have contact with children, be aware that those who would harm children will seek out opportunities to interact with them, and be willing to remove caretakers on the basis of risk alone and not proof of misconduct or admission of wrongdoing.

15.9   Are *waiver of liability forms* useful?

Waiver of liability forms seek consent for an activity and procure important contact information. Such forms can be useful in shifting the awareness of the potential risks of an activity from the organization to the adults in charge of deciding whether participation is to be allowed. Forms that conspicuously release the organization from claims for negligence may be held enforceable when voluntarily entered into and properly and unambiguously drawn. It would be imprudent to over-rely on the legal enforcement of such forms inasmuch as courts generally have a bias against them. Regardless of the ultimate effectiveness of a release from liability, these forms can be useful in alerting the participant or the parent of the participant to a perceived objectionable activity, alerting the organization to the health conditions of the participant, and securing emergency contact details. Release forms are not a substitute for adequate supervision in those circumstances where that is appropriate.

15.10 What is *premises liability*?

Premises liability is the responsibility that one who controls property, the owner or lessee, bears for the particular conditions of that property that may cause harm to others. Religious organizations may be liable for injuries to others when they have not exercised reasonable care to maintain the premises in a safe condition, have not uncovered and remedied unsafe conditions through reasonable inspections, or have not warned injured parties about dangerous conditions that cannot be remedied.

Generally, premises liability for an injury arises when the owner or lessee of the premises had knowledge, or should have had knowledge, of some condition that posed an unreasonable risk of harm for which the owner or lessee did not exercise reasonable care to eliminate or reduce that caused injury to another. For example, legal responsibility is determined under the state law of *premises liability*. Under the premises liability law of most states, it is necessary to determine if the injured party was an invitee, a licensee, or a trespasser. The duty to the injured party can vary significantly depending on how the injured party is classified. The duties of a premises owner are typically not delegable to a third person or entity. In the definitions below, *premises* should be read broadly to include land, premises, or places of business operation, and *owner* should be read broadly to include anyone who has the legal right to control the property in question.

 NOTE: Some jurisdictions have modified these definitions..

An *invitee* is a person who is invited to enter or remain on the premises for a commercial benefit to the owner, or for a purpose directly or indirectly connected with business dealings with the owner. Typically, the premises owner owes the highest duty to use ordinary care to warn or otherwise protect an invitee from risks of harm.

A *licensee* is a person who is invited to enter or remain on the property for any purpose, other than a business or commercial one, with the express or implied permission of the owner or person in control of the premises. Typically, an owner is liable for physical harm caused to a licensee by a condition on the premises if, but only if, the injured party establishes that the premises owner knew or should have known of the condition and should have expected that the licensee would not discover or realize the danger.

A *trespasser* is a person who goes on the property of another without an express or implied invitation, for his or her own purposes, and not in the performance of any duty to the owner. Where premises owners are not aware of the presence of trespassers, they typically have no duty to warn a trespasser of any dangers or to make their premises safe for the benefit of a trespasser. If the premises owner is aware of the presence of trespassers, the premises owner may be obligated to exercise ordinary care in relation to the safety of a trespasser.

15.11 Does an organization have a duty to protect against attractive nuisances to children?

Yes. Religious nonprofit organizations may be subject to liability for physical harm to children who are trespassing on the organization's property when the trespass of the children is caused by an artificial condition on the property if:

1. The place where the condition exists is one on which the organization knows or has reason to know that children are likely to trespass; and
2. The condition is one of which the organization knows or has reason to know and that it realizes or should realize will involve an unreasonable risk of death or serious bodily injury to such children; and
3. The children because of their youth do not discover the condition or realize the risk involved in intermeddling with it or in coming within the area made dangerous by it; and
4. The utility to the organization of maintaining the condition and the burden of eliminating the danger are slight as compared with the risk to the children involved; and
5. The organization fails to exercise reasonable care to eliminate the danger or otherwise protect the children.

This doctrine is based on foreseeability of harm to the child, not attraction onto the property. The artificial or dangerous condition must pose an unreasonable risk of harm in light of the particular child's age. Conditions such as an unfenced pool or pond, unsecured toxins or dangerous dump sites, excavated areas, and the like can constitute attractive nuisances.

15.12 Does an organization have a duty to inspect its premises?

Religious organizations may be liable for injuries to others when they have not remedied unsafe conditions through reasonable inspections. The duty owed is to inspect the premises in the manner, timeframe, and with the level of diligence expected of a reasonably prudent person (organization) under similar circumstances. *Inspection* in this context includes the discernment to take action to eliminate dangerous conditions on the premises. The interval of regular inspections might vary depending on factors such as the volume of traffic in an area, susceptibility of an area to alteration, natural weather events, the inherent risks of an area, and the age and amount of existing wear in the area in question.

15.13 Can an organization be held liable for injuries sustained while their premises are being used by outside groups?

Religious organizations may be liable for injuries while their premises are used by outside groups. The question of liability ultimately turns on which party assumed the responsibility for and controlled the condition that caused the injury. Outside groups using a premises sometimes may be left unattended, but to minimize or avoid liability, the organization should be expressive in communicating the state of their property's condition before the time of use, reasonable in identifying and correcting any dangerous conditions before use, and insistent that the supervisors of the outside group familiarize themselves with the premises and present any questions to the organization before use.

15.14 What is the purpose of *charitable immunity statutes*?

Charitable immunity statutes are designed to restore a measure of charitable immunity for qualifying organizations in response to a perceived increase of civil liability since the time that states abrogated the doctrine. These acts protect from and limit liability where the entity has procured the specified insurance coverage, thus indicating a clear intention to spread risks, mitigate against the wholesale transfer of accumulated charitable resources, and to a lesser extent, help insure that relief could be obtained from smaller organizations that might otherwise have gone uninsured but for the benefits of the acts.

Although the immunity statutes are designed to provide broad protections for nonprofits, important exceptions remain. For example, in no case do charitable immunity laws provide protections in cases of gross negligence, intentional, or willful and wanton misconduct.

To avoid overreliance on such immunity statutes, a nonprofit manager should take these factors, as well as the group's own potential liability exposures, into account when assessing insurance needs.

15.15 What are the parameters for immunity from civil liability for the charitable organization?

Even where immunity is available, under most charitable immunity statutes acts or omissions are not covered that are proven to be intentional, willfully or wantonly negligent, or committed with conscious indifference or reckless indifference for the safety and rights of others. Immunity is intended to protect against claims of negligence—conduct that falls below the standard of care exercised by a reasonable person in similar circumstances. However, the aforementioned description of conduct excluded from protection of charitable immunity applies to those acts that fall just short of criminal liability and cannot be described as merely accidental or in terms of poor judgment. As discussed above regarding liability for hazardous acts, activities that involve any degree of a violation of law could also risk an allegation that the resulting injury is exempt from the protection of the charitable immunity.

15.16 What are the parameters for immunity from civil liability for employees?

Generally, under charitable immunity statutes, an employee, like a volunteer, of the organization that qualifies for charitable immunity also enjoys the protections afforded the organization so long as the claimed injury occurred in the course and scope of the employee's duties and functions in the organization. *Employees* exclude independent contractors but otherwise include any person paid for providing services to the charitable organization. Again, the immunity of the employee is generally conditioned on the organization procuring the specified insurance coverage, and is intended to protect against claims of negligence—conduct that falls below the standard of care exercised by a reasonable person in similar circumstances—but excludes from the protection of charitable immunity those acts that are proven to be intentional, willfully or wantonly negligent, or committed with conscious indifference or reckless indifference for the safety and rights of others.

15.17 What are the parameters for immunity from civil liability for volunteers?

Generally, a volunteer of the organization that qualifies for charitable immunity also enjoys the protections afforded the organization so long as the claimed injury occurred in the course and scope of the volunteer's duties and functions in the organization.

CHAPTER 16

Insurance Coverage Considerations

16.1   Should a religious nonprofit organization consider obtaining insurance coverage?

Yes. A religious nonprofit organization is well-advised to have insurance coverage in place that covers its activities. Before buying insurance, the organization should know why it is buying insurance and what risks it covers. Nonprofits often purchase insurance to shield corporate assets and protect the people who are devoting their energy, services, and talents to further the organization's mission and purpose.

16.2   What is *general liability insurance*?

Occurrence basis general liability insurance provides coverage under the policy in force at the time of the event, regardless of when the claim is reported or the suit is filed. Some insurance is provided on a *claims-made coverage basis* in which the claim must be reported during that policy period or any extended reporting period specified by the policy. The extended reporting period, commonly referred to as *tail coverage*, frequently is one year following the policy term. *Retroactive date coverage* is offered to include coverage for previous time periods in addition to the current policy term.

Casualty (general liability) coverage protects the insured from losses in which they are legally liable arising out of the ownership of property or activities on their premises. Coverage generally includes contractual liability, fire, legal liability, no-fault medical payments for bodily injuries, property damage of others, products liability, completed operations, damages to premises rented to you, personal and advertising injury, employee benefits liability, and business overhead expense; other types of claims are usually covered by this policy. Most general liability policies restrict coverage to the United States, its territories, and Canada.

16.3 What is *umbrella liability coverage?*

An umbrella (excess) liability policy provides excess limits over the primary general liability, auto liability, and the employers' liability section of workers' compensation policies. The policy offers a chosen aggregate limit and pays regardless of the number of claims during a one-year policy term.

16.4 What is *directors and officers* and *errors and omissions liability coverage?*

Directors and officers (D&O) and *errors and omissions* (E&O) liability coverage protects the officers, directors, and trustees of the nonprofit organization against damages from claims resulting from negligent or wrongful acts in the course of their duties, subject to the terms and conditions of the policy and circumstances involved. The policy may be extended to cover the nonprofit organization itself (entity coverage). The coverage is almost always a *claims-made policy* with defense cost inside the limits of protection. Excluded from coverage is third-party bodily injury or property damage, which would be covered under other policies.

16.5 What is *minister's professional and personal liability coverage?*

Minister's professional liability covers liability for counseling services. The church and all professional staff should be included in the definition of the named insured on the policy. *Personal liability* protects the minister and his or her family for both personal liability and damage to their personal property for events/activities when the homeowner's coverage is provided by the church.

16.6 What is *employee and volunteer dishonesty liability coverage?*

This coverage provides for losses of money, securities, and other property caused by theft or forgery by an employee or volunteer of the insured, acting alone or in collusion with others. It is often referred to as having employee "bonded" coverage.

16.7 What is *employment practices liability coverage?*

This coverage provides protection from issues relating to employment, benefits, hiring, termination, and sexual harassment.

16.8 What is *educator's legal liability coverage?*

This insurance provides for violation of intellectual property rights and many statutory obligations, and educational malpractice.

16.9 What is *sexual misconduct liability coverage?*

Most general liability policies *exclude* sexual abuse or molestation from coverage. Coverage for sexual misconduct can be added by endorsement or on a separate policy. An organization that provides programs for children is well-advised to consider this coverage.

16.10 What is *automobile liability coverage?*

Automobile liability insurance provides coverage with minimum legal limits to the insured for bodily injury and property damage claims arising out of the ownership, maintenance, use, and loading or unloading of owned vehicles. Physical damage, up to chosen limits, covers owned vehicles that are insured separately requiring a deductible. If an employee or volunteer uses his or her vehicle for church activities, the policy covering the vehicle is the primary insurer. The church's *non-owned liability coverage* may provide excess coverage if the vehicle owner's coverage is not adequate. *Hired vehicle coverage* is for the same coverage if a rental vehicle is used. *Uninsured motorist* covers physical damage and medical cost. *Underinsured coverage* offers protection above the other insured's policy limits. Medical coverage provides first-dollar coverage immediately without a deferred payment requiring proof of injury.

16.11 What is *travel accident insurance?*

Coverages available for travel accidents include accidental death and dismemberment, repatriation of remains, and medical evacuation domestically and internationally for individuals on the organizations business.

16.12 What is *foreign travel liability?*

Organizations sponsoring trips abroad may also consider foreign commercial liability, commercial foreign vehicle liability, and foreign workers' compensation and sickness insurance.

16.13 What is *property insurance?*

Property insurance covers buildings and personal property for damage or loss by certain perils or theft. The property insurance policy may be amended to include the following: replacement cost, property inflation, newly acquired property, property in transit, off-premises property, windows, valuable papers, computer equipment, media, sewer backup, boiler, and machinery. Flood and earthquake coverage, where appropriate, is a separate policy, and may be offered with state or federal assistance.

16.14 What is *builder's risk insurance*?

This insurance coverage protects the insured against damages to covered property from any covered cause of loss during construction.

16.15 What is a *bond*?

A bond guarantees performance of the terms of a contract, such as a financial (surety) or construction (performance) obligation.

16.16 What is *group medical insurance*?

Generally, there are five types of medical insurance policies: (1) the health maintenance organization (HMO), utilizing only co-pays with certain network physician and medical facilities; (2) the preferred provider organization (PPO), offering higher benefits with network providers and lower benefits with non-network providers; (3) the point of service (POS), which is generally a more restricted network of providers, but offers more benefits, such as x-ray and lab work included within the physician co-pay; (4) the fee for service (FFS) indemnity plans, which accept any physician or medical facility and are usually provided to out-of-state employees; and (5) the partially self-funded options, which allow the employer to set aside funds for self-insuring part of the potential risk. Coverage pays for eligible nonoccupational injury and illness with certain policy provisions, such as precertification review prior to treatment and any excludable conditions.

16.17 What is *disability and long-term care coverage*?

Short- and long-term disability coverage provides for qualified partial or full disability, a percentage of income up to certain limits following an elimination period to be paid on a physician-acknowledged onset of disability for a designated time frame until the insured is no longer disabled. Long-term care provides home health care, adult day care, assisted living, and nursing home coverage after an elected elimination period with chosen limits and time durations that are payable when one or more eligible activities of daily living (ADL) impairments have occurred.

16.18 What are optional provisions for the medical benefit plans?

Health savings accounts (HSAs), health reimbursement accounts (HRAs), and flexible spending accounts (FSAs) allow pre-tax savings to be applied toward eligible medical expenses up to certain limits when utilizing a qualified high-deductible health plan. Section 125 cafeteria plans or premium-only plans allow medical premiums and qualified expenses to be paid with pre-tax dollars.

16.19 What is *workers' compensation insurance*?

Two types of coverage are provided with workers' compensation and employer's liability policy. Workers' compensation provides, as a matter of right, for the payment of benefits to employees or beneficiaries for covered occupational injury, disease, or death. The amounts paid are set by state law. Employer's liability insures the employer for liability when employees or dependents are able to sue for such problems as employer negligence and unsafe working conditions. Some states have laws allowing employers to accept or reject the compensation system. This is commonly referred to as *opting out* of the system. In most states, employers who refuse the provisions of the workers' compensation law are denied the customary defenses to actions for injury by the injured employee.

16.20 What is *life insurance*?

There are several variations of two basic types of life insurance. The first is *term insurance*, providing the beneficiary a designated amount of protection generally for a limited time, due to death or life-threatening illness of an insured. The second type of policy commonly referred to as *whole life* or *universal life*, offers coverage through the insured's life, and develops tax-deferred interest-bearing cash accumulations.

Typical applications for religious nonprofit organizations are as follows:

1. Lender's required coverage on loans.
2. Executive bonus plans (sometimes referred to as Section 162 bonus plans) are a common way of providing nonqualified benefits to executives.
3. Deferred compensation allows an organization to provide select employees compensation at a future preselected date (retirement, severance, or disability) for services the employee renders on a current basis.
4. *Key person insurance* is a plan to compensate the organization for the loss or disability of its most valuable asset—the skill and experience of a key employee.

16.21 What is a *403(b) retirement savings plan*?

A *403(b) plan* is established for nonprofit organizations to allow pre-tax and tax-deferred elections and additions up to certain limits in an interest-bearing tax-sheltered annuity or/and a mutual fund managed by a custodial account for retirement benefits; 403(b) plans are discussed in further detail later on in this handbook.

CHAPTER 17

Real Property and the Religious Nonprofit

17.1 What is a *reversionary clause*?

A *reversionary clause* is a restrictive clause found in the document conveying property that requires, on the occurrence of a specific event or events, the property conveyed to revert to some other individual or group.

17.2 Where can reversionary clauses be found?

Reversionary clauses are most often a condition of the transfer of the property. Such clauses have been a tool employed by landowners for many years to retain control over the property they are conveying.

17.3 Can a religious nonprofit organization add reversionary clauses to property it is selling?

Yes. Denominations often use reversionary clauses to maintain control over local churches and the future use of the property and to retain denominational ties. For example, if a denomination sells property to an individual church, the denomination could require in the deed that, if the church is dissolved, the property must be transferred back to the denomination.

17.4 Are reversionary clauses enforceable against religious nonprofit organizations?

Yes. Reversionary clauses are valid and enforceable. So long as the reversionary clause is tied to an independent event or occurrence, a court is likely to enforce the clause because it can be done without the necessity of interpreting religious doctrine. As local churches increasingly look for autonomy from their denominational roots, reversionary clauses will be of increasing importance in determining which entity will retain control over property.

17.5   What is a *zoning law*?

A *zoning law* is a regulation promulgated by a local authority that controls the development of a city. A typical zoning ordinance will divide a city into different districts, including commercial and residential. Religious nonprofit organizations, including churches, are subject to zoning laws and must follow the regular methods established by local government to obtain any permission for variances that may be necessary. There may be certain exceptions to zoning laws through obtaining special-use permits or variances, but these are situations that are governed by the city and subject to their requirements, interpretation, and approval. A city is not permitted to discriminate against a religious nonprofit organization on the basis of religion in the application of its policies and procedures, but it is not a requirement that the city approve each and every special-use permit or application that it sees.

17.6   What are *building codes*?

Municipalities enact *building codes* to establish the minimum guidelines for construction in a city. They regulate sanitation, fire safety, building materials, and building design.

17.7   Where does a religious nonprofit organization find building codes that are applicable to it?

Building codes are found on the local level. In certain low-population or rural areas, building codes may be set on a statewide basis and establish the minimum requirements for the state.

17.8   Are building codes enforceable against religious nonprofit organizations?

Yes. Building codes are enforceable against religious nonprofit organizations because courts generally find that there is a compelling state interest in protecting the health, safety, and welfare of the public in enforcing those codes. There may be exceptions to certain building code requirements for areas that are designed specifically for religious worship. Otherwise, the enforcement of building codes is not generally seen as an infringement on the ability of people to worship or a requirement that they abandon their sincerely held religious beliefs.

17.9   Can a religious nonprofit organization or a church be excluded from a residential area?

It depends. Generally, churches may be constructed in residential areas. However, as churches increase in size, municipalities may create restrictions for churches being constructed in residential areas. While most churches will not be excluded from residential areas, they may be regulated through permit processes. Certain decisions to exclude churches from residential neighborhoods have been upheld based in part on the attempt to retain the integrity of the neighborhood. The same analysis applies to religious nonprofits.

17.10   Can activities of a religious nonprofit organization or a church located within a residential district be legally regulated?

Yes. Both are subject to regulation within a residential district. For example, the right to free exercise of religion does not create a right to ignore rules governing how a church is constructed, the number of parking spaces, and other issues related to the health and safety of the invitees of the church.

17.11   What is a *nuisance*?

A *nuisance* is something that creates a significant annoyance, inconvenience, or harm to others. It is, at its essence, an interference with the rights of others to enjoy their property.

17.12   Can the religious activities of a religious nonprofit organization or a church be deemed a nuisance?

Yes. For example, church nuisance issues in court often focus on the noise related to church services or the volume of traffic created by a church. Church activities may be deemed a nuisance even if there is a related free exercise of religion because churches are generally not above the law as it relates to the regulation of property use.

17.13   What types of activities are defined as a nuisance?

If, for example, a church holds services that run far into the night and that are so loud as to annoy its neighbors, that church may have in fact been a nuisance as defined by the law.

17.14   What is *eminent domain*?

Eminent domain is the government's power to take private land and use it for public purposes without the owner's consent. Eminent domain is often used, for example, by the government for the expansion of roads. While the government has the power to take the land, it must compensate the owner of the land for the value of the land that was taken.

17.15   Can government legally enforce eminent domain rights against a church?

The government can enforce its eminent domain rights against any private property holder, including a church. In the instance of a church, however, the First Amendment considerations of freedom of religion may prevail against the government's eminent domain proceedings. This is not usually applicable in the instance of a taking of a few feet of frontage for road expansion, but may be applicable if the government intends to take a substantial portion of church property.

17.16   Can a municipality prevent a religious nonprofit organization, including a church, from making changes to its property by enforcing *landmark laws*?

Yes. Many cities and municipalities have enacted zoning ordinances that permit them to designate certain buildings, including churches, as *landmarks* because of their historical importance. As a result of so-called *landmark laws*, structures deemed to be landmarks cannot, generally, be razed or renovated absent the prior approval of the local government. The Supreme Court has ruled that such landmark laws are presumptively valid and do not violate a religious nonprofit organization's First Amendment right to the free exercise of religion.

17.17   In a hierarchical church structure, who owns the church property and the right to make decisions about it when there is a dispute as to the property?

The Supreme Court has enunciated the *neutral principles* test to be applied when deciding church property issues. As such, most courts apply state law and the neutral principles test when resolving disputes over the ownership and right to control the property of hierarchical churches. In applying the neutral principles test, courts rely on state law as well as authoritative church documents (church deeds and the articles of governance of both the local and the hierarchical organization) that can be interpreted without considering religious doctrine, beliefs, or ecclesiastical principles.

17.18   In a congregational church structure, who owns the church property and the right to make decisions about it when there is a dispute as to the property?

In addition to applying the neutral principles test and state law, courts consider the majority vote of the congregation's membership when resolving disputes over the ownership and right to control the property of congregational churches.

NOTE: Almost all disputes involving title to church property are governed by state law. As such, an attorney familiar with the property laws of the church's state should be consulted and retained.

17.19 **Is church property public or private?**

Church property, irrespective of whether the church is *congregational* or *hierarchical*, is private property. The fact that a church invites the public to attend a worship service does not change the private character of the service nor the property on which it is held.

17.20 **Does the church have the right to remove a disruptive person from a service? What if the disruptive person is a member of the church?**

Yes. A church has the right to remove disruptive persons, whether members or not, from its services. In many states, a person commits a criminal offense if, with the intent to prevent or disrupt a private church meeting, procession, or gathering, he or she obstructs or interferes with a meeting, procession, or gathering by physical action or verbal utterance.

CHAPTER 18

Competition and Commerciality

18.1 **Just what is this matter of a nonprofit/for-profit competition all about?**

Like any civil society, the United States has three basic sectors: a for-profit, commercial, business sector; a nonprofit sector; and a governmental sector. A healthy democratic society requires the presence of these three sectors, and that each of them functions to the fullest extent within suitable bounds. Personal freedoms are enhanced and maintained to the extent of the vibrancy of these sectors.

By definition and necessity, this tripartite societal structure produces friction: the sectors clash. There is ongoing struggle over what the "suitable boundaries" of the sectors are. The resulting fights are over what functions belong in which sector. A most cursory glance at what is occurring with respect to the U.S. health-care delivery system illustrates the extent to which this battle can be waged.

For the most part, these are policy determinations to be resolved by lawmakers (those in all three branches of government). That is, there is very little in the way of formal legal constraints in this setting, other than those against transgressing the bounds of federal public policy, the dictates of constitutional law principles, or perhaps state law rules. Although this is the way the system is supposed to work, these struggles generate problems for nonprofit organizations.

It is a general precept that nonprofit organizations are supposed to remain "in their place." In many respects, the U.S. economic system is still based on principles of capitalism. This means that for-profit organizations are generally treated more favorably, as to this matter of clashes between the sectors, than nonprofit organizations. That is, it is generally thought to be inappropriate for nonprofit organizations to engage in activities that are engaged in by for-profit organizations. There is a preference here: If for-profits do it, nonprofits should not do it.

Conceptually, according to this mode of thinking, nonprofit organizations are not supposed to undertake activities that are being performed by for-profit organizations. Likewise, if for-profit organizations enter a field previously unoccupied by them but traditionally the province of nonprofit organizations, the nonprofits are expected to abandon the field. In general, then, nonprofit entities—and this is particularly the case with charitable organizations—are often expected to engage only in functions conceded to them by the for-profit (and perhaps government) sector.

18.2 What is the problem with nonprofit/for-profit competition?

It is basically one of economics. Almost always, the nonprofit organization is tax-exempt. This means that taxes are not a part of the entity's *costs of doing business.* Assuming all other expenses are the same as that of the for-profit counterpart, the tax-exempt nonprofit entity can engage in the competitive activity with a lower cost of operations. To acquire customers and increase market share, a nonprofit organization can pass the decreased cost of operation along to customers in the form of lower prices. What can result is a nonprofit organization and a for-profit organization performing the same activity for public consumption (sale of a good or performance of a service), with the nonprofit entity charging a lower price.

Usually the for-profit critics of competition involving nonprofit organizations charge *unfair* competition. When that word is used, the complainants are asserting that the pricing policies of nonprofit organizations are undercutting the sales of items by for-profit organizations. This use of exempt status to lower prices in competing with for-profits is at the heart of the complaints in this context about (unfair) competition.

A secondary complaint is based on the thought that a consumer, given the choice to purchase a good or service from a nonprofit entity or a for-profit entity, will select the former. This view holds that the consumer is more comfortable purchasing an item from a nonprofit organization; there seems to be a greater element of trust. This phenomenon—the grounds for assertions that nonprofit organizations ought not to be undertaking certain endeavors at all—is known as the *halo effect.*

18.3 How common is this form of competition?

It is rather common, and the practice is growing. There are essentially two manifestations of competition between nonprofit and for-profit entities.

One arises where the very essence of what the nonprofit organization does is competitive with for-profit organizations. A clear example of this is, as noted, found in the health-care field, where some hospitals and other forms of health-care providers are nonprofit and some are for-profit (proprietary entities). Predictably, this is generating much debate as to whether nonprofit hospitals should remain tax-exempt at all or be exempt to a much more limited

NOTE: An example of this issue is the tax-exempt credit union. There is an ongoing battle as to whether such entities should remain exempt, in view of the fact that many of their operations are competitive with for-profit financial institutions. These days, Congress is being lobbied hard on the subject with the National Credit Union Administration arguing for the exemption and the American Bankers Association contending for its repeal. This dispute was studied by the Congressional Research Service, which observed that "many believe that an economically neutral tax system requires that financial institutions engaged in similar activities should have the same tax treatment."

extent. Other areas in which there are counterparts in both sectors are schools, publishing entities, various types of consulting groups, providers of insurance, and financial institutions.

Most of the criticism in this area falls, however, in the realm of the other manifestation of competition. This is where the nonprofit organization is substantially engaging in tax-exempt (usually noncompetitive) activities, but is selectively engaging in one or more competitive functions. One of the most controversial contemporary illustrations of this point—which will be discussed in another setting—is the matter of travel tours. The travel industry is incensed because of the competitive tours being packaged and sold by exempt entities, such as religious organizations (including churches), universities, colleges, alumni associations, and similar organizations, as educational experiences. Other examples are discussed later.

18.4 Has Congress responded to these complaints about unfair competition?

Yes. The principal response has been formulation of the *unrelated business income rules*. Congress enacted these rules over 55 years ago. A major component of the Revenue Act of 1950, the rules were devised specifically to eliminate unfair competition between nonprofit and for-profit organizations.

This was done, or thought to be done, by placing the unrelated business activities of exempt organizations on the same tax basis as those conducted by for-profit organizations, where the two are in competition. The essence of this body of law is to separate the income of a tax-exempt organization into two categories: income from related business and income from unrelated business. The rationale is that, by taxing the income from unrelated business, the pricing differential that can lead to unfair competition is removed. This is known as *leveling the playing field*.

NOTE: One wag, sympathetic with the nonprofit sector in this regard, once said that the for-profits are not interested in seeing the playing field leveled. Rather, it was noted, the for-profits do not want the nonprofits to even be *on* the field.

The existence or nonexistence of competition is not, however, a statutory requirement for there to be unrelated business. Nonetheless, some courts place considerable emphasis on the factor of competition when assessing whether an undertaking is an unrelated business. This can also be the case when eligibility for tax-exempt status is under consideration.

NOTE: Some courts have rejected the thought that the unrelated business rules were enacted purely to eliminate this form of competition. Thus, one court wrote that "while the equalization of competition between taxable and tax-exempt entities was a major goal of the unrelated business income tax, it was by no means the statute's sole objective." Another court observed that "although Congress enacted the . . . unrelated business income rules to eliminate a perceived form of unfair competition, that aim existed as a corollary to the larger goals of producing revenue and achieving equity in the tax system."

There has also been some legislative activity in connection with commercial undertakings. The principal illustration of this approach was the decision by Congress in 1986 to eliminate the tax exemption for most prepaid healthcare plans, such as those offered by Blue Cross and Blue Shield organizations. Moreover, Congress allowed the tax-exempt status of prepaid group legal plans to expire in 1992.

18.5 What are some of the contemporary illustrations of issues in this area of competition?

There are many of them. Illustrations of this type of competitiveness are the operation of health clubs and fitness centers by nonprofits. Of course, there are commercial entities of this nature. Where the fees for use of these facilities are sufficiently high to restrict their use to limited segments of the community, the operations are nonexempt ones or unrelated businesses, as being competitive with commercial health clubs. In contrast, if a health club or similar facility provides communitywide benefits or advances education in a substantial manner, the activity is a related business.

NOTE: In an effort to attract and retain congregants, the creation and operation of fitness centers, bowling alleys, movie theaters, and the like is a trend among very large churches located in major metropolitan areas.

The religious nonprofit setting also provides further examples of competition between nonprofit and for-profit organizations. As an illustration, the commercial travel industry is, of course, a provider of tours. Yet, religious nonprofits also offer tours, ostensibly as a religious and educational experience. The IRS endeavors to differentiate between tours that are related activities and those that are unrelated (competitive) because they are primarily social, recreational, or other forms of vacation opportunities.

In 2000, the IRS issued regulations addressing this concern. These regulations contain examples that provide several factors to be considered in determining whether a travel tour is an exempt activity or an unrelated business activity resulting in taxable unrelated business income. Although the IRS examples are fairly black and white, the factors to be considered in determining whether the income is exempt from UBI tax are helpful. These factors are to be considered under a general facts-and-circumstances test.

The following are examples of questions a religious nonprofit should ask when considering a tour:

- Does the trip contribute significantly to the religious nonprofit's exempt purpose? (In other words, what is the organization trying to accomplish?)
- Will there be scheduled religious instruction or other religious activity that furthers the organization's exempt purpose?
- Will the tour guide be knowledgeable in the area of the activity?
- Will the promotional materials emphasize the educational or other exempt purpose of the trip?
- Will the instruction or other activity furthering the religious nonprofit organization's exempt purpose take up a significant amount of time in proportion to personal time?
- Will educational or other related materials be provided during the trip?
- Will the organization keep timely documentation of how the trip met its exempt purpose?

Other types of nonprofit organizations provide further illustrations of this point. For example, the sale of items to the public by a nonprofit museum from its gift shop is generally a related business on the grounds that the items sold generate interest in the museum's collection and promote visitation to it. However, that rationale can break down when items are sold nationally or even internationally by catalog or when the items that are sold are used in a utilitarian manner (such as furniture). These and other forms of sales activity by nonprofit organizations are often seen as enterprises that are competitive with for-profit organizations.

NOTE: In an effort to attract and retain congregants, the operation of coffee shops, cafes, religious bookstores, restaurants, and the like is a trend among very large churches located in major metropolitan areas.

18.6 What is the *convenience doctrine* and what is its effect on this area of competition?

For example, churches, universities, colleges, and schools can operate bookstores that sell many items that are also sold in commercial establishments. The same can be said for hospitals that maintain gift shops and foodservice operations. Some of the items are sold clearly in advancement of exempt purposes, such as the religious books and music recordings that a church sells to help further a congregant's religious study. A church bookstore or hospital gift shop, however, can sell clothing, sundry items, flowers, and the like without having those activities treated as unrelated businesses. Nonetheless, these activities are in competition with for-profit establishments, often small businesses.

Some of this sales activity is sheltered by the convenience doctrine. The *convenience doctrine* is a rule of law that states that a business conducted by a charitable or educational organization for the convenience of its congregants, patients, or students is not taxable as an unrelated business. This doctrine is thus of great utility to religious nonprofits, schools, colleges, universities, and hospitals.

Some of these activities, however, are considered exempt functions. Thus, for example, a college can sell sports clothing, coffee cups, and toilet paper, all bearing the institution's name and logo, and not pay any tax on the net proceeds because the sale of these items is an exempt function, in that it promotes interest in the college among the student body. Likewise, many of these same articles can be sold by a church. Additionally, a hospital can sell floral arrangements and other gift items without paying tax on the resulting net income because the sale of these items is an exempt function, in that the health of the patients is promoted by virtue of visits by friends and family bearing gifts. Yet the sale of each of these categories of goods is competitive with for-profit businesses.

 NOTE: The proprietor of a religious bookstore across the street from a church that is selling the same books and music as is contained in the church's bookstore is not comforted by these rationales.

A frequently overlooked aspect of this matter of competition between nonprofit and for-profit entities is the conduct of businesses that are regarded as nontaxable undertakings (sometimes even as related activities) because they are done in the name of fundraising. The simple application of the term *fundraising* to an activity, however, does not convert it from a taxable to a nontaxable activity.

Special-event fundraising involves many competitive functions: concerts, dances, dinners, auctions, bake sales, car washes, and more. Although these activities are by no means inherently charitable, they usually escape taxation on the ground that they are not regularly carried on.

NOTE: Often an organization is of the belief that a fundraising event is not regularly carried on because it is conducted over a few-days period. Yet the organization may spend months preparing for the event. Although the approach has been rejected in the courts to date, the IRS is of the view that *preparatory time* should be taken into account in determining regularity. When this is done, of course, a business that seemingly occupies only a short period of time can be transformed into one occupying a substantial portion of a year—and one that is taxable.

There are some statutory exceptions for fundraising events. Excluded from taxation are sales of items that were donated to the exempt organization (a special rule very helpful to nonprofit thrift shops and organizations that conduct auctions on a regular basis), businesses conducted substantially by volunteers, qualified sponsorship payments, use of premiums, qualifying entertainment activities, certain bingo games, and certain rentals of mailing lists. In some instances, revenue from fundraising activities can be protected from taxation by structuring it as royalty revenue.

Consequently, there are many opportunities under current law for nonprofit organizations to compete with for-profit ones, and not pay any income tax on the resulting revenue.

18.7 How does a religious nonprofit organization determine if an enterprise is an unrelated trade or business that is subject to taxation?

There are several considerations pertaining to whether a religious nonprofit organization's enterprise is an unrelated trade or business subject to tax on unrelated business income; the determination is dependent on the facts and circumstances.

NOTE: It is important to note that if the religious nonprofit organization receives income from an unrelated trade or business, such income is still taxable even though it is used exclusively for religious purposes.

The considerations include, but are not limited to, the following:

* Is the business conducted primarily for the convenience of its members or congregants? If so, then generally, the *convenience doctrine* states the income is not taxable as an unrelated business.
* Is all of the business's labor performed by unpaid volunteers? If so, it generally will not be considered to be an unrelated trade or business.

- Does the business sell merchandise substantially all of which has been received as gifts or contributions? If so, it generally will not be considered to be an unrelated trade or business.
- Is the business operated within the organization's building, or is it located in another facility?

By way of further example, if the business enterprise is a bookstore:

- Does it sell only religious merchandise (e.g., books and music) or does it also sell nonreligious items such as clothing, jewelry, computers, art, stationery supplies, and the like?
- Is the bookstore separately incorporated or does it operate under the religious nonprofit's corporate entity?
- If the bookstore sells nonreligious items, what is the percentage of its gross sales resulting from the sale of nonreligious items?
- Is the bookstore located on the religious nonprofit's property?
- What are the bookstore's hours of operation?
- Is the bookstore open to the public?
- Does the bookstore engage in advertising to the general public (on billboards, in the newspaper, or on radio, television, or web site)?
- What is the relative size of the bookstore's revenue in comparison with the religious nonprofit's revenues?

18.8 How does this matter of competition relate to commerciality?

To date, rather awkwardly. One of the greatest oddities in the law of tax-exempt organizations is that there is a two-track system of law operating in this area. There are the unrelated business income rules that, as noted, were fashioned largely in response to the thought that competition between nonprofit, tax-exempt and for-profit entities is unwarranted. There is also a growing body of law standing for the proposition that a nonprofit organization, particularly a charitable one, that operates in a commercial manner cannot qualify for tax-exempt status. This principle of law is known as the *commerciality doctrine.*

The subjects of competition and commerciality by no means fully overlap. The matter of competition is taken into account chiefly in ascertaining whether an activity is a related business or an unrelated business. This determination is based on statutory law. As noted, it involves a question as to whether a nonprofit entity and a for-profit entity are doing the same thing. These comparisons rarely lead to a decision as to a nonprofit organization's tax exemption.

In contrast, the commerciality doctrine goes to the heart of tax exemption issues. It bypasses the issues concerning unrelated income taxation. It is not based on statutory law but was conjured by the courts, initially almost inadvertently. The doctrine sometimes takes competition into account but, when it does, only as one of several factors. It tends to focus on the manner in which an organization is operating.

18.9 **What is the *commerciality doctrine*?**

The *commerciality doctrine* essentially is this: A nonprofit organization is engaged in a non-tax-exempt activity when that activity is engaged in a manner that is considered *commercial*. An activity is a commercial one if it is conducted in the same manner in the world of for-profit organizations.

When a court sees an activity being conducted by a for-profit business and the same activity conducted in the same fashion by a charitable organization, it is often affronted. The court is then stirred by some form of intuitive offense at the thought that a nonprofit organization is doing something that "ought to" be done only in the for-profit sector. Therefore, the court concludes that the nonprofit organization is conducting that activity in a commercial manner. This conclusion then results in a finding that the commercial activity is a nonexempt function, often leading to the decision that the nonprofit organization is not entitled to tax exemption.

 NOTE: The essence of the commerciality doctrine having been stated, it must also be said that, to date, it is being unevenly applied.

The doctrine grew out of some loose language in early court opinions. The Supreme Court started it all back in 1924. A case before the Court concerned a tax-exempt religious order that, although operated for religious purposes, also engaged in activities that the government alleged destroyed the order's exemption: investments in securities and real estate, and sales of items such as chocolate and wine. The Court ruled that the order should remain tax-exempt. Nonetheless, it found it necessary to state the government's argument in the case, which was that the order was "operated also for business and *commercial* purposes." The Court rejected this portrayal of the order, writing that there was no "competition" and that while the "transactions yield[ed] some profit [it was] in the circumstances a negligible factor."

This articulation of the government's argument by the Court is burdened with an unnecessary redundancy: Why the use of both words *business* and *commercial?* In any event, the Supreme Court did not enunciate a commerciality doctrine. By simply employing the word *commercial*, however, the Court gave birth to the doctrine.

The doctrine was formalized by the Court in 1945. On that occasion, it was reviewing a case concerning the tax exemption of a chapter of the Better Business Bureau, which was pursuing exempt status as an educational organization. The chapter was found to not qualify for exemption, inasmuch as it was engaging in the nonexempt function of promoting a profitable business community. The Court, in the closest it has come to expressly articulating the commerciality doctrine, wrote that the organization had a "commercial hue" and that its activities were "largely animated by this commercial purpose."

The 1960s saw the commerciality doctrine flourish. This came about because of a number of cases concerning nonprofit publishing organizations. One case, decided in 1961, pertained to a publisher of religious literature that, as the court put it, generated "very substantial" profits. Rejected was the IRS contention that profits alone precluded tax exemption. But then the court added these fateful words: "If, however, defendant (the IRS) means only to suggest that it (profits) is at least some evidence indicative of a *commercial* character we are inclined to agree." In finding the organization to not be tax-exempt, the court declined to apply the unrelated income tax rules. This court obviously thought that the organization's primary activities were unrelated, inasmuch as exemption was revoked, but, inexplicably, the word *commercial,* rather than *unrelated,* was used.

In a 1962 case, another nonprofit publishing organization failed to receive tax exemption because the "totality of [its] activities [was] indicative of a business, and . . . [the organization's] purpose [was] thus a commercial purpose and non-exempt." A 1964 case involving a religious organization that conducted training projects saw rejection of application of the commerciality doctrine, with the court observing that "we regard consistent nonprofitability as evidence of the absence of commercial purposes." In a 1968 case that was overruled, a lower court determined that a publisher of religious materials could not be tax-exempt because it "was clearly engaged primarily in a business activity, and it conducted its operations, although on a small scale, in the same way as any commercial publisher of religious books for profit would have done."

Several other commerciality doctrine cases followed. In 1980, a court said this: "Profits may be realized or other nonexempt purposes may be necessarily advanced incidental to the conduct of the commercial activity, but the existence of such nonexempt purposes does not require denial of exempt status so long as the organization's dominant purpose for conducting the activity is an exempt purpose, and so long as the nonexempt activity is merely incidental to the exempt purpose." In 1981, a publisher of religious materials lost its tax exemption because it became imbued with a "commercial hue" and evolved into a "highly efficient business venture." An appellate court, in 1984, even while overruling a lower court's decision that a religious publishing house was no longer exempt, found the opportunity to say that if an exempt organization's "management decisions replicate those of commercial enterprises, it is a fair inference that at least one purpose is commercial."

Recent cases in which commerciality was used as a basis for denial of tax exemption include one involving an organization selling religious tapes, one operating prisoner rehabilitation programs, and one operating a number of canteen-style lunch trucks.

There are several other commerciality doctrine cases depicting its evolution, but this is how the doctrine started and grew into its contemporary framework.

18.10 What factors are looked at in determining commerciality?

The commerciality doctrine is not so fully articulated as to enable a crisp response. The most expansive explanation of the commerciality doctrine was provided in an appellate court case decided in 1991. The organization involved was a nonprofit entity associated with a church that operated, in advancement of church doctrine, vegetarian restaurants and health food stores. The lower court wrote, in denying exemption as a charitable and/or religious organization, that the entity's "activity was conducted as a business and was in direct competition with other restaurants and health food stores." The court added (in what, by then, was an understatement): "Competition with commercial firms is strong evidence of a substantial nonexempt purpose."

This appellate court opinion stated the factors relied upon in its finding of commerciality. They were that (1) the organization sold goods and services to the public (thereby making the establishments "presumptively commercial"), (2) the organization was in "direct competition" with for-profit restaurants and food stores, (3) the prices set by the organization were based on pricing formulas common in the retail food business (with the "profit-making price structure looming large" in the court's analysis and the court criticizing the organization for not having "below-cost pricing"), (4) the organization utilized promotional materials and "commercial catch phrases" to enhance sales, (5) the organization advertised its services and food, (6) the organization's hours of operation were basically the same as those of for-profit enterprises, (7) the guidelines by which the organization operated required that its management have "business ability" and six months' training, (8) the organization did not utilize volunteers but paid salaries, and (9) the organization did not receive any charitable contributions.

These criteria should not be disregarded simply because they were articulated back in 1991. In 2003, a court ruled that an organization operating a conference center could not be tax-exempt as a charitable or educational entity because of a "distinctively commercial hue" associated with its operations. This court applied precisely the same criteria as was employed in the 1991 opinion.

What is to be made of the commerciality doctrine?

The doctrine of commerciality certainly is here to stay and is expected to grow in importance. Thus, the focus should be on the reach and the elements of the doctrine.

On the basis of the definition of the doctrine as articulated by a court in 1991, the doctrine is obviously too encompassing. For example, many tax-exempt organizations properly sell goods or services to the public; too much emphasis was placed by the court on that factor in the decision. Yet the court was correct in emphasizing competition, motive for engaging in the activity, and pricing. Probably the factor of advertising was appropriately included, although many nonprofit organizations advertise their exempt functions. Factors like hours of operation and payment of salaries seem nonsensical in the modern era.

In contrast, some of these factors are dismaying, if not old-fashioned and plainly silly. For example, what is to be made of the court's wish for "below-cost pricing"? How long can an entity function (in the absence of a large endowment) doing that?

NOTE: In considering the commerciality doctrine, one is reminded of the radio advertisement in which the owner of a business is excitedly announcing an upcoming spectacular sale, with prices slashed. Once he is finished, his very critical mother appears, admonishing him. She tells the public, in a heavy accent, "He's a nice boy but not too good with the math."

Equally discouraging is the reference to lack of contributions. This remains a bugaboo that should have been put to rest years ago. There is no requirement in the law that, to be charitable, an organization must be funded, primarily or at all, by gifts. Indeed, the law is clear that an organization funded entirely by exempt-function income or investment income can be charitable. The absence of contributions should not be an element in evaluating the presence of commerciality. Another factor that is foolish, if not completely unrealistic today, is reliance on the lack of volunteer assistance in concluding that an organization is commercial.

One of these elements that is particularly galling is the fact that the nonprofit organization's employees have some expertise and training. This country is long overdue in improving the quality of nonprofit organization operations in the realm of, for example, management, law, and fundraising. Much impressive progress in this regard is being made. Today there are more college programs, seminars, books, and the like in the field than ever. In the midst of all of this, along comes a court, finding knowledgeable employees of a nonprofit entity evidence that it is operating commercially!

So, while the commerciality doctrine is playing an increasing role in determining eligibility for tax-exempt status, the law is still awaiting a comprehensive and realistic definition of the doctrine.

18.12   Are there other factors that are taken into account in determining commerciality?

Yes, usually by the media. These critiques are often based on a fundamental misunderstanding of what is meant by a nonprofit, tax-exempt organization. Two examples will suffice.

The *Kansas City Star*, piqued at the decision of the National Collegiate Athletic Association (NCAA) to leave that city and move to Indianapolis, published six days in a row a series of articles about the organization. The opening article proclaimed that "for a lesson in commercialism, you can't beat" the NCAA. According to the article, over the past 23 years, the NCAA's revenues increased 8,000 percent. It has a $1.7 billion television contract, a staff of 250 individuals, a real estate subsidiary, a marketing division, and it licenses its name and logo for use on clothing. It owns a Learjet. It is a "powerful sports cartel that is addicted to making money."

The *New York Times*, enervated by the celebration of the 50th anniversary of the Educational Testing Service (ETS), published an article about the organization. It seems that the ETS has "quietly grown into a multinational operation complete with for-profit subsidiaries, a reserve fund of $91 million, and revenue last year of $411 million." This article portrayed ETS as an entity transformed into a "highly competitive business operation that is as much multinational monopoly as nonprofit institution, one capable of charging hefty fees, laying off workers and using sharp elbows in competing against rivals."

These and other inflammatory analyses are likely to have a lot to do with the evolution and enlargement of the commerciality doctrine. Being, unfortunately, all too typical, these articles missed the point of what is meant by being a nonprofit organization. Check off the list: There is nothing in the federal tax law prohibiting an exempt organization from operating in more than one country, having one or more for-profit subsidiaries, having a reserve fund, charging fees, and entering into licensing and other contracts. The articles focus on factors that are reflective of a yearning for an earlier, simpler era when nonprofit organizations were mostly struggling charities, eking out a year-by-year existence with barely enough in the way of contributions and held together by a dedicated cadre of volunteers. Thus, commerciality is seen in the size of the organization, the fact it has a paid staff, and ownership of an airplane.

 NOTE: This view is even stretched to find commerciality in the fact that a nonprofit organization lays off workers and uses "sharp elbows" against rivals. Terminating an individual's employment can be no more than sound management practice. And anyone worried about sharp elbows in this context has not been paying any attention to hospitals, colleges, and universities lately.

These and like reports, of course, include legitimate factors to take into account in determining commerciality. These are the reasons for (but not necessarily the extent of) expansion, increase in and use of revenues, the charging of "hefty fees," and maybe even being a monopoly.

The *New York Times* article stated, "Competition with for-profit rivals is a trend that bedevils nonprofit institutions across the country." As noted at the outset, there is much truth to this statement. What is also "bedeviling" nonprofit organizations these days is the confusion about them that is fostered by muddled analyses such as these.

18.13 What is the future of the commerciality doctrine?

For the short term, the doctrine will continue to be developed in the courts. At some point in time, Congress will be motivated to either write an expansive definition of the term or augment the existing rules that presently are confined to insurance.

The nonprofit community can expect many more reports in the media such as those noted earlier, as the debate over this type of competition intensifies. Nonprofit organizations are likely to lose this battle on one or more fronts, perhaps including restrictive federal and/or state statutory law changes. If this happens, the process will have been hastened and inflamed by misleading reports such as these, which reflect great ignorance of what it means to be a nonprofit organization and what such organizations are allowed to do as a matter of law.

18.14 What should tax-exempt organizations be doing in this regard in the interim?

A tax-exempt, nonprofit organization should examine its operations in light of the elements of the commerciality doctrine enumerated earlier. The organization should evaluate each program activity the way the IRS or a court might do, by asking these questions: (1) Is the program competitive with an activity in the for-profit sector? (2) Why is the program being carried on? (3) If fees are charged for the provision of a good or service, how are the prices set? (4) Are prices calculated to return income in excess of related expenses (i.e., generate a profit)? (5) Are exempt functions subsidized by contributions and/or grants (fundraising) or by an endowment fund? (6) Does the organization advertise or otherwise promote its operations? and (7) Are the salaries paid to employees and fees paid to vendors and other independent contractors reasonable? The organization should formulate the best possible answers to these questions from its standpoint (as always, staying within the bounds of veracity). It should be prepared to defend itself against charges of commerciality.

Once these rationales are devised, they should be reflected in all written materials developed by the organization. This is particularly important in respect to language in the articles of organization, annual information returns, annual reports, footnotes in financial statements, promotional literature, newsletters, and minutes of the board of directors. In many instances, as part of assembling a case that an organization is operating in a commercial manner, an IRS examiner or judge will select quotations from an organization's materials, using them against the organization.

CHAPTER 19

Intellectual Property

19.1 What is *intellectual property*?

Intellectual property refers to ownership of nonphysical property rights in creative thought or works that have basically been recorded or reduced to written form. Common examples for the religious nonprofit organization are creative works that constitute copyrights and trademarks.

19.2 Do religious nonprofit organizations own intellectual property?

Creative works that are created at a religious nonprofit organization could include sermons, scriptural studies, books, pamphlets, original music, graphics, and educational or teaching materials. Who owns these rights, the organization or the person who created them, is subject to the *works-made-for-hire* analysis.

19.3 What is the *works-made-for-hire doctrine*?

While the general principle is that creative works are owned by the individual who authored the work, the work may actually be considered the property of the employer (religious nonprofit organization) if the author prepared the work either (1) as an employee within the scope of his or her employment or (2) as a specially ordered or commissioned work if the parties have agreed in writing that the *work is made for hire*.

19.4 **If I report my taxes as a self-employed contractor for a religious nonprofit organization, can I still be considered as an "employee" for purposes of the works-made-for-hire doctrine?**

Yes; while the same tests to determine if one is an employee or is self-employed for federal income tax reporting purposes are used in this context, the courts are liberal in finding that an author was an employee at the time a creative work was created.

19.5 **When is a creative work made in the *scope of an employee's employment*?**

While there is not a definitive test or determination, it is generally a question of the facts and circumstances under which the work was created. If the religious nonprofit organization's resources were used, such as creating the work during regular business hours, on the organization's property, using the organization's staff and equipment or materials such as a computer, copy machine, library, or secretarial support, the greater the likelihood that the work will be viewed as a work for hire.

19.6 **How can a religious nonprofit organization eliminate any disagreement about whether a creative work was made as a work for hire?**

The religious nonprofit organization can set out an agreement one way or the other as part of a written employment contract or as a separate written agreement. Most religious nonprofit organizations should have no objection to the minister or leader owning the rights to his or her works. However, the IRS does ask about this issue in some of its inquiries.

19.7 **What is a *copyright*?**

A *copyright* is the exclusive property right to control the use of a particular work that has been reduced to a tangible format or medium. The medium does not have to be permanent, but must be capable of being perceived, reproduced, or otherwise communicated for more than a temporary amount of time.

A copyright is created as soon as it is reduced to a tangible medium. This could mean writing it on paper or putting it on a video or audio recording. However, to protect it from being stolen or used without permission, the author will need to register the copyright.

The kinds of works that can be copyrighted include literary works, which could include books, periodicals, manuscripts, phonorecords, computer programs, film, tapes, discs, cards, and other writings. It could also be musical works, dramatic works, pantomimes and choreographic works, pictorial graphs and sculptural works, motion picture and audiovisual works, sound recordings, architectural works, compilations and derivative works.

For works created now, the minimum registration period is 95 years. If the author is a natural person (individual), the registration lasts for the lifetime of the author plus 70 years.

19.8 Why would a religious nonprofit organization want to register its copyrights?

The registration process is the best way to be certain that no one uses the works without the religious nonprofit organization's permission and helps the organization seek royalties from that use. Wrongful use of a copyright work is called *infringement*. A copyright claim for infringement cannot be made unless the copyright in question has been registered with the U.S. Copyright Office. In addition, having received the Copyright Office's Certificate of Registration creates a presumption before the court that the work belongs to the author and not another person. Also, by registering the copyright, the court is authorized to award extra money and attorneys' fees to the author on a showing of an infringement.

19.9 What is the *fair use exception* to the copyright law?

The law permits fair use of copyrighted works for purposes such as criticism, comment, news reporting, and teaching. In determining if there has been a *fair use*, the court would consider (1) the purpose and character of the use, including whether such use is of a commercial nature or is for nonprofit educational purposes; (2) the nature of the copyrighted work; (3) the amount and substantiality of the portion used in relation to the copyrighted work as a whole; and (4) the effect of the use on the potential market for, and value of, the copyrighted work.

19.10 What is the *religious services exception* to the copyright law?

Performance of a nondramatic musical work or of a dramatic-musical work of a religious nature or display of a work, in the course of services at a place of worship or other religious assembly, does not constitute copyright infringement. The requirement that the performance be "in the course of services" excludes activities at a place of worship that are for social, educational, fundraising, or entertainment purposes.

19.11 What is the *nonprofit performance exception* to the copyright law?

A public performance of a nondramatic literary or musical work is excused from the copyright law restrictions if (1) the performance does not have a profit motive, (2) no fee or compensation is paid to the performers, promoters, or organizers for the performance, and (3) there must be either no direct or indirect admissions charge, or alternatively, if an admission charge is assessed, then any amounts left after deducting the reasonable costs of producing the performance must be used solely for educational, religious, or charitable purposes.

19.12 What damages are available if someone is found to be responsible for infringing on a copyright?

The range of damages for wrongfully using someone else's copyright include injunction to stop further misuse, impoundment and destruction of infringing products, payment of actual monetary damages suffered by the owner, payment of any profits made by the infringing party to the owner, penalties set by law that can range from as low as $200.00 to as high as $100,000.00 depending on the circumstances, and costs of court and attorneys' fees. There are also criminal offenses that can be made against an infringer that, on conviction, can result in fines and prison, or both.

19.13 What is a *trademark*?

A *trademark* includes any word, name, symbol, or device, or any combination thereof, used to identify and distinguish a person's goods from those manufactured or sold by others and to indicate the source of the goods.

19.14 What is a *service mark*?

Basically, it is the same thing as a trademark except it involves identification and distinguishing of services, rather than goods.

19.15 How does someone obtain protection of a trademark or service mark?

Trademarks and service marks are registered with the United States Patent and Trademark Office. There is a review process where the government verifies that no one else has the same trademark or one that is so similar as to cause confusion, mistake, or deception. The application is also published in a public format and anyone claiming to have a similar mark can file an objection. Once the process has been completed, and any objections have been resolved, the Trademark Office will register the mark.

19.16 What duties do I have to protect my trademarks and service marks?

When someone knowingly uses a trademark without permission it is called *infringement.* When someone uses a product or service in such a way that it is similar to your trademark or service mark, either intentionally or unknowingly, that is also called infringement. It is a trademark and service mark owner's job to protect marks from infringement, or risk losing them. The standard for deciding if another mark is infringing is if there is a "likelihood of confusion" between them.

19.17 Is there a fair use exception to the trademark restrictions?

There is a *fair use* defense to claims of trademark infringement. It is different from the copyright "fair use" exception. You can make use of a particular term or device if it is being used in its common or primary sense and not as part of a competing trademark. More specifically, it is a *fair use* if the word is being used to describe your goods or services.

19.18 What is a *patent*?

A *patent* protects a new and useful idea, which includes a process or machine. It is granted by the federal government, providing an inventor with exclusive rights to make, use, and sell a patented invention. Patents have a fixed term, usually 17 to 20 years.

19.19 What is a *trade secret*?

A *trade secret* may consist of any formula, pattern, device, or compilation of information that is used in one's business and that gives one an opportunity to obtain an advantage over competitors who do not know or use it. To be labeled a trade secret, there must be a substantial element of secrecy. A trade secret is not registered or filed anywhere and may be of unlimited duration.

19.20 What is the *face-to-face teaching activities exception* to copyright law?

Performance or display of a work by instructors or pupils in the course of face-to-face teaching activities of a nonprofit educational institution, in a classroom or similar place devoted to instruction, is not a violation of copyright law.

19.21 Can a church make and distribute recordings of worship services in which copyrighted music is performed?

While the performance of copyrighted materials is probably protected under the Public Performance or Religious Activities exception, the recording of the performance is not. Therefore, the religious nonprofit organization would presumably need to do one of the following: (1) Obtain advance permission from the copyright owner to make and distribute recordings; (2) avoid the use of copyrighted materials in the services; (3) turn off the recording device while the copyrighted songs are being performed and consider replacing them with recordings of songs as to which the organization has legal rights; (4) obtain a compulsory license that allows the organization to use the songs for much broader purposes; (5) obtain a blanket license from the copyright owners to make use of all of their songs; and (6) do nothing and hope for the best (never a good idea).

CHAPTER 20

Lobbying and Political Activities

20.1 What is *lobbying*?

The word *lobbying* derives from the caricature of someone hanging around in a lobby, waiting for the opportunity to whisper in the ear of a government official in an effort to influence the official's decision or vote. In its broadest sense, lobbying is an attempt to influence the public policy and issue-resolving functions of a regulatory, administrative, or legislative body. The term is generally used, however, to describe efforts to influence the voting of one or more members of a legislative body on one or more items of legislation. The legislative body may be a federal, state, or local one. Although lobbying is often regarded as an unsavory practice, it has a constitutional law basis: It is a form of free speech as a petitioning of a government for a redress of grievances. The U.S. Supreme Court observed that the "very idea of a government republican in form implies the right on the part of its citizens to meet peaceably for consultation in respect to public affairs to petition for redress of grievances."

The Federal Regulation of Lobbying Act defines the term to mean an attempt by a person, who receives compensation or other consideration for the effort, to influence the passage or defeat of legislation. The federal income tax law, concerning lobbying by public charities that are under the expenditure test, defines the phrase *influencing legislation* as meaning "(1) any attempt to influence any legislation through an attempt to affect the opinions of the general public or any segment thereof, and (2) any attempt to influence any legislation through communications with any member or employee of a legislative body, or with any government official or employee who may participate in the formulation of the legislation." Essentially the same definition is used in the tax regulations pertaining to lobbying by public charities that are under the substantial part test and in the federal tax rules concerning the business expense deduction.

With respect to the business expense deduction rules, however, the term *lobbying* also includes efforts to influence the President of the United States, the

Vice President, Cabinet members, and top White House staff. The federal law proscriptions on lobbying, however, generally do not pertain to lobbying of members of an executive branch or of independent regulatory agencies.

20.2   **What is** *legislation*?

In general, the word *legislation* means a bill or resolution that has been introduced in a legislative body; it may or may not be considered by that body. The term is defined in the federal tax law, for purposes of the expenditure test, as "action with respect to acts, bills, resolutions, or similar items by the Congress, any state legislature, any local council or similar governing body, or the public in a referendum, initiative, constitutional amendment or similar procedure." For purposes of the substantial part test, the term is similarly defined in the federal tax regulations.

20.3   **Is lobbying a necessary or appropriate activity for a nonprofit organization?**

For many nonprofit organizations, lobbying not only is a necessary activity, it is a critical one. It is a matter of policy as to whether it is appropriate for them to engage in that activity, particularly when they are tax-exempt. There is nothing inherently illegal about lobbying by nonprofit organizations. Indeed, these organizations have the constitutional right to petition the government. The U.S. Supreme Court, however, held that it is not unconstitutional for the law to deprive charitable organizations of tax-exempt status if they engage in substantial lobbying.

There is a belief among many policymakers that it is inappropriate for charitable organizations to engage in lobbying. This view is largely based on the precept that a person should not be able to receive an income tax deduction for a gift to a charity that is used to advance that person's views on legislation; this is seen as a subsidy of one person's viewpoint by others. Consequently, public charities are constrained as to how much lobbying they can engage in without loss of tax exemption.

20.4   **What are the most current federal tax rules concerning lobbying that are unique to tax-exempt organizations?**

The principal rule is that public charities may engage in lobbying activities only to the extent they are not substantial. A public charity that engages in substantial attempts to influence legislation is considered an *action organization* and is likely to have its tax exemption denied or revoked. Some tax-exempt organizations can have lobbying as their principal or even their sole function; these include social welfare organizations and trade and business associations. Members of an association, however, are likely to have their dues deductions reduced to the extent the organization lobbies.

20.5 How do charitable organizations measure substantiality?

In general, there is no precise formula for measuring whether lobbying activities are substantial. It is common practice, however, to evaluate the extent of lobbying in terms of a percentage of total funds expended in a period of time or total time expended over a particular period. These are merely informal guidelines, however; the IRS will not commit to any specific percentages. On occasion, substantiality is found as a consequence of an organization's impact on a legislative process, irrespective of outlays of funds or time. The case law makes it clear that this is a case-by-case determination. The decision that an organization has engaged in a substantial amount of lobbying is usually made in hindsight, after the particular legislative process has concluded.

20.6 Is there more than one form of lobbying?

Generally, the law regards lobbying as being *direct* or *grassroots*. Direct lobbying occurs when the lobbying organization communicates, for purposes of influencing legislation, with a member of a legislative body, an individual who is on the staff of such a member, or an individual who is on the staff of a committee of a legislative body. For purposes of the expenditure test, there is a direct lobbying communication only where the communication refers to specific legislation. In the setting of the business expense deduction, direct lobbying includes communications with certain members of the federal executive branch. When the results of research are used in lobbying, the research activities themselves are automatically considered lobbying. Whether research activities in other settings constitute lobbying is a matter determined on a facts-and-circumstances basis.

Grassroots lobbying takes place when the lobbying organization communicates, for purposes of influencing legislation, with the public, or a segment of it, in an effort to induce the persons contacted to communicate with a legislative body for the purpose of influencing legislation. Under the expenditure test, a grassroots lobbying communication takes place only where the communication refers to specific legislation, reflects a view on the legislation, and encourages the recipient of the communication to take action with respect to the legislation. This latter element is known as a *call to action*.

20.7 What are the various ways by which lobbying can be accomplished?

Lobbying is communication. It can be accomplished using any means of communication between human beings. Forms of direct lobbying include personal contact, correspondence, telephone calls, facsimiles, telegrams, position papers and other publications, contact via the Internet (e-mail), and formal testimony. Grassroots lobbying includes these forms, along with television, radio, web site, and print media advertisements.

20.8 Are there laws concerning lobbying by nonprofit organizations other than the federal tax rules?

Yes. The principal law outside the federal tax context is the Federal Regulation of Lobbying Act. Those who lobby for compensation as a principal portion of their activities must register with and report to the Clerk of the House of Representatives and the Secretary of the Senate. The Byrd Amendment prohibits the use of federal funds received as grants, contracts, loans, or cooperative agreements for attempts to influence an officer or employee of a governmental agency in connection with the awarding, obtaining, or making of any federal contract, grant, loan, or cooperative agreement. Regulations published by the Office of Management and Budget provide that costs associated with most forms of lobbying activities do not qualify for reimbursement by the federal government. Most states have laws regulating lobbying by nonprofit and other organizations.

20.9 What are *political activities*?

Political activities are of two categories, one subsuming the other. The broader of the two categories refers to any activity that is undertaken with a political purpose, that is, to affect the structure or other affairs of government. The narrower definition refers to an activity that is engaged in to assist or prevent an individual's election; this latter type of political activity is a *political campaign activity*. The narrower range of activities requires participation or intervention in a political campaign.

For example, the presentation of testimony before the Senate Committee on the Judiciary regarding a nominee of the President to the Supreme Court is a political activity. This is not a political campaign activity, however, because there is no *campaign* for a public office. By contrast, a contribution to the campaign organization of an individual to assist him or her in attempting to win election to the U.S. Senate, the U.S. House of Representatives, or a state legislature is a political campaign activity.

20.10 What are the rules, for tax-exempt organizations, concerning political activities?

There are several rules, but two are particularly important. One is that a charitable organization is not allowed to participate in or intervene in any political campaign on behalf of or in opposition to any candidate for a public office. This constraint pertains to political campaign activities; if violated, the organization becomes classified as an *action organization* and must pay a tax and/or suffer revocation of its tax-exempt status.

The other rule concerns organizations that are political organizations, that is, have political activities as their exempt function. These organizations frequently engage in political campaign activities; they also undertake political activities that are not political campaign activities.

The business expense deduction is not available for an expenditure for political campaign purposes. If a tax-exempt organization, such as a trade or business association or a labor union, were to make such an expenditure, the extent of deductibility of the organization's dues might be affected. Because of the federal campaign laws, organizations of this nature should not engage in political campaign activities directly but can do so by means of political action committees.

20.11 What do *participation* and *intervention* mean?

Essentially, the words *participation* and *intervention* mean the same thing: an involvement in some way, by an individual or an organization, in a political campaign. These types of activities include the solicitation or making of political campaign contributions, the use of resources of an organization to benefit or thwart the candidacy of an individual in a political campaign, the volunteering of services for or against a candidate for a public office, and the publication or distribution of literature in support of or in opposition to a candidate for public office.

Traditionally, the IRS broadly defines these terms—sometimes finding violation of the political campaign activity constraint when some elements of the prohibited activity are not present. For example, a charitable organization was denied tax exemption because its purpose was to implement an orderly change of administration of the office of a governor in the most efficient and economical fashion possible by assisting the governor-elect during the period between his election and inauguration. In this instance, while there was to be participation and/or intervention in a government's affairs, there was no *candidate* or *campaign*. The IRS ruled, however, that the organization's "predominant purpose is to effectuate changes in the government's policies and personnel which will make them correspond with the partisan political interests of both the Governor-elect and the political party he represents."

In another illustration of these rules, one that is more in conformity with the language of the prohibition, the IRS ruled that charitable organizations may not evaluate the qualifications of potential candidates in a school board election and support particular slates in a campaign. Today, however, that organization would likely qualify for tax exemption as a charitable entity if its activities were confined to the evaluative function.

In this context, the IRS has historically taken a hard-line position with respect to advocacy organizations that become entangled with political issues; where the objectives of these organizations can be achieved only though political change, they cannot—in the government's view—be charitable. In support of this position, a court held that an organization established with the dominant aim of bringing about world government as rapidly as possible could not qualify as a tax-exempt charitable organization. This approach is difficult to rationalize under the contemporary law, however, because of the absence of any involvement in a *campaign* for or against a *candidate* for *public office*.

20.12 Can a charitable organization educate the public about candidates and issues in the setting of a political campaign?

Yes. The IRS, however, has been rather grudging in allowing this type of activity. In fact, there can be a fine line between participating in a political campaign and engaging in public education about that campaign. Organizations like the League of Women Voters and the Commission on Presidential Debates, which utilize the resources of organizations such as universities, have moved the law to a point where there is, today, a fuller recognition of *voter education* activities.

The contemporary view is that a charitable organization, as a part of an education process, can disseminate the views, voting records, and similar information about candidates in the context of a political campaign where neutrality is, or substantially is, observed. The key factor is that the organization may not indicate partisanship on the issues. Popular practices include the compilation and dissemination of the voting records, or responses to questionnaires elicited by the organization, of members of a legislature on a variety of topics. Also in vogue is the issuance of "report cards"—a listing of votes on selected issues in which a legislator receives a "+" if his or her vote coincided with the organization's position and a "–" if it did not.

Factors the IRS takes into account are: Is there comment on an individual's overall qualifications for public office? Are there statements expressly or impliedly endorsing or rejecting an incumbent as a candidate? Has the organization observed that voters should consider matters other than voting, such as services on committees and constituent services? Is the material distributed to the organization's constituency or the public? Is the dissemination of publications timed to coincide with an election campaign, particularly during its closing days? In one instance, the IRS position was stated this way: "[I]n the absence of any expressions of endorsement for or in opposition to candidates for public office, an organization may publish a newsletter containing voting records and its opinions on issues of interest to it provided that the voting records are not widely distributed to the general public during an election campaign or aimed, in view of all the facts and circumstances, towards affecting any particular elections."

The expansionist view as to what is participation or intervention in a political campaign is derived from a federal court of appeals opinion authored over 35 years ago. There, a religious ministry organization was denied tax-exempt status, in part because of ostensible interventions in political campaigns. The organization, by means of publications and broadcasts, attacked candidates and incumbents (the President and members of Congress) who were considered too liberal, and endorsed conservative officeholders. The court summarized the offense: "These attempts to elect or defeat certain political leaders reflected . . . the organization's objective to change the composition of the federal government." Open criticism of an elected public official, including one who is eligible for reelection, however, was held violative of this proscription, even where not done in the context of a political campaign. It is unlikely that this aspect of the opinion would be reiterated by the court today.

There is, therefore, great confusion in the federal tax law as to the reach of prohibition on political campaign activities by public charities. That is, there is far less guidance in this area than there is in the realm of lobbying activities by public charities, where considerable detail is given in regulations, rulings, and court opinions.

The federal and state political campaign regulation rules apply to charitable organizations, and this can operate as an additional set of limitations on their ability to participate in political campaigns. For example, the prohibition on the making of campaign contributions is applicable to charitable entities.

20.13 Does the law differentiate between the political positions of organizations and those of individuals associated with them?

Yes. An individual does not lose his or her rights to engage in political activity solely by reason of being an employee or other representative of a public charity. The IRS, however, expects that an individual in this position will make it clear in the appropriate context that the political views expressed are his or hers, and not those of the organization. For example, in its tax guide for churches and ministers, the IRS stated that "[m]inisters and others who commonly speak or write on behalf of religious organizations should clearly indicate, at the time they do so, that public comments made by them in connection with political campaigns are strictly personal and are not intended to represent their organization." As a practical matter, this distinction is often difficult to credibly maintain.

20.14 When is an individual a *candidate*?

For the proscription on political campaign activity to be applicable, the public charity must be a participant in the campaign of an individual who is a *candidate* for *public office*. The federal tax regulations define the phrase *candidate for public office* to mean an "individual who offers himself, or is proposed by others, as a contestant for an elective public office, whether such office be national, state, or local." An individual becomes a candidate for a public office on the date he or she announces his or her candidacy for that office. But the fact that an individual is a prominent political figure does not automatically make him or her a candidate. This is the case notwithstanding speculation in the media and elsewhere as to the individual's plans or where an individual is publicly teasing about running for office. The label *candidate* is often applied with the benefit of hindsight.

20.15 When does a *campaign* begin?

The federal tax law lacks any definition of the term *campaign*. For the proscription on political campaign activity to be applicable, the public charity must be a participant in the *campaign* of an individual seeking a public office. This body of law is silent as to when there is a commencement of a political campaign; again, it is the practice of the IRS to apply a facts-and-circumstances test. The IRS has been known to assert the launching of a campaign far in advance of a formal announcement of candidacy.

20.16 **What is a *public office*?**

For the proscription on political campaign activity to be applicable, the public charity must be a participant in the campaign of an individual seeking a *public office*. This term is specifically defined in two sets of federal tax regulations to mean a policymaking position in the executive, legislative, or judicial branch of a government; it means more than mere public employment. (These regulations relate to the definition of the phraseology in the rules concerning disqualified persons with respect to private foundations and in defining exempt functions of political organizations.)

On occasion, the IRS will openly decline to follow that definition. For example, an intra-party position, such as a precinct delegate, clearly is not a public office, yet the IRS pursued the revocation of the tax-exempt status of a public charity that influenced the selection of individuals to such delegate positions, on the ground that they are types of "public offices."

20.17 **Is there a substantiality test for charitable organizations concerning political activities?**

For the most part, no. The position of the IRS on this point is that the proscription on political activities by charitable organizations is an absolute one. The statute stating this proscription does not contain a substantiality test, as it does with respect to legislative activities.

The judiciary, however, is reluctant to foreclose the possibility of a de minimis test in any setting. One court observed that "courts recognize that a nonexempt purpose, even 'somewhat beyond a de minimis level,' may be permitted without loss of exemption." Thus, for example, it is unlikely that the inadvertent application of $1.00 of the funds of a public charity to a political campaign activity would be treated as a violation of the language of the statute.

20.18 **What happens when a public charity engages in a political campaign activity?**

Actual practice is often different from what the applicable statutes mandate. A public charity's participation in a political campaign is a ground for revocation of tax-exempt status, assuming the participation is greater than a very insignificant involvement. Also, it is the basis for assessment of an initial 10 percent excise tax on the organization and a 2.5 percent tax on each of the organization's managers, and additional taxes of 100 percent on the organization and 50 percent on its managers. To date, however, few instances have been made public where the IRS has assessed that tax. Moreover, there have been situations where the organization negotiated a closing agreement with the IRS by admitting the violation, promising to not repeat it, and making the agreement public; in these circumstances, the IRS has refrained from revoking the exemption.

- It can trigger accelerated tax assessment rules when it finds that the political campaign activities constraint on public charities is being violated. Under these procedures, the IRS need not wait until the close of the organization's tax year to commence an audit; it can prematurely terminate the entity's year and promptly begin the audit process.
- It has special authority to request a court injunction to stop political campaign activity by a public charity in certain circumstances.

20.19 Do these rules apply to churches and other religious organizations?

As a matter of statutory law, yes. An institution of religious worship—such as a church, synagogue, or mosque—or any other type of religious organization is barred from political campaign activity. These entities are charitable ones for tax purposes and the federal tax law prohibits charitable organizations from participating or intervening in political campaigns. Moreover, churches and the like are public charities, where these rules are focused.

20.20 Are these rules enforced against religious organizations?

Not very often. When it is done, the enforcement tends to be selective. There are a few court cases where these rules have been applied to religious organizations other than churches and the like. There have been, and continue to be, however, many instances where churches are directly involved in political campaigns. Candidates have campaigned in churches as part of the religious services and members of the ministry have routinely engaged in campaigns for presidents, members of Congress, governors, mayors, and individuals seeking those and other positions. Even when these practices are reported in the public media or complaints are filed with the IRS, the traditional posture of the agency rarely acts.

Nonetheless, the IRS, in 2004, decided to step up its enforcement and guidance efforts in this area, with focus on churches and other charitable organizations. It launched a compliance check project in that year and another with respect to the political campaign in 2006. The IRS published extensive reports on its findings as a result of these efforts, which led to the publication of extensive guidance for churches and other entities as to what constitutes political campaign involvement. In 2007, the IRS published *Revenue Ruling 2007-41*, which outlines how churches, and all § 501(c)(3) organizations, can stay within the law regarding the ban on political activity. This ruling sets out twenty-one factual situations involving § 501(c)(3) organizations and activities that may be prohibited campaign intervention. In each situation, the ruling applies tax law and regulations and concludes that prohibited political activity has or has not occurred.

20.21 Is the prohibition against political campaigning by religious organizations constitutional?

Yes. As long as churches and other religious organizations are treated in this regard no differently from other public charities, there is no unwarranted entanglement of church and state or impingement on the practice of religious beliefs.

The converse argument is that government should not be able to dictate what churches or similar institutions say in the context of propagation of their religious beliefs. This argument is more compelling where the church is speaking out on social issues and, only in that setting, is supporting or criticizing political candidates. It is less attractive when the church involvement is purely political, such as where a member of the ministry endorses a particular candidate from the pulpit during a church service.

In one case a church had its tax-exempt status revoked for participation in the 1992 presidential campaign; it had paid for newspaper advertisements attacking candidate Bill Clinton's positions on social issues. The courts (trial and appellate) held that the IRS had the authority to revoke exempt status. Both courts also concluded that the revocation of the tax exemption of this church was not contrary to the First and Fifth Amendments of the U.S. Constitution.

CHAPTER 21

Employee Compensation

21.1 What is the definition of *compensation*?

Compensation means all items of compensation provided by a tax-exempt organization in exchange for the performance of services. These items include (1) all forms of cash and noncash compensation, such as salary, fees, bonuses, and severance payments; (2) all forms of deferred compensation that is earned and vested, whether or not funded, and whether or not paid under a deferred compensation plan that is a qualified plan, but if deferred compensation for services performed in multiple prior years vests in a later year, that compensation is attributed to the years in which the services were performed; (3) the amount of premiums paid for liability or other insurance coverage, as well as any payment or reimbursement by the organization of charges, expenses, fees, or taxes not ultimately covered by the insurance coverage; (4) all other benefits, whether or not included in income for tax purposes, including payments to welfare benefit plans on behalf of the persons being compensated, such as plans providing medical, dental, life insurance, severance pay, and disability benefits, and both taxable and nontaxable fringe benefits (other than certain working condition fringe benefits and de minimis fringe benefits), including expense allowances or reimbursements or forgone interest on loans that the recipient must report as income; and (5) any economic benefit provided by a tax-exempt organization, whether provided directly or through another entity owned, controlled by, or affiliated with the organization, whether the other entity is taxable or tax-exempt.

21.2 How does *executive* compensation differ from *regular or non-executive* employee compensation?

All compensation paid to all employees, be they executive or non-executive, non-profit or for-profit, is required to be *reasonable*. *Non-executive compensation* is usually easier to measure because it most often consists only of W-2 wages and retirement benefits. *Executive compensation* usually contains these same elements, as well as other components; it also can be more difficult to measure or calculate, with some components often being left out of the calculation simply because they were not thought of at the time.

21.3   What are the other components unique to religious nonprofit organizations that would be included in calculating executive compensation?

Generally, executive compensation will contain components that other non-executive employee compensation simply does not have. In a religious nonprofit organization setting, such components might include bonuses, birthday collections, and "Love Offerings" (typically paid to a minister as a show of appreciation), but nonetheless considered compensation; housing allowances and parsonage provisions; pension and other retirement benefits; provision or use of an automobile; country club memberships; church credit card usage with a grace period for repayment (this can equate to an impermissible interest-free loan); and use of church assets for personal benefit.

The tax law standards used in determining the reasonableness of compensation are described in detail in the next chapter.

21.4   What is the income exclusion available for *ministers of the gospel* by use of a parsonage or housing allowance?

Section 107 allows a *minister of the gospel* to exclude from income the rental value—including utilities—of a home the church furnishes as part of his or her compensation (a parsonage) or the rental allowance it pays under the same circumstances to the extent the minister uses the allowance to rent or provide a home. The home or rental allowance the church provides must be as payment for services that ordinarily are the duties of a minister of the gospel. The services ministers perform are sacerdotal functions, such as the conducting of religious worship and the control, conduct, and maintenance of religious organizations (including religious boards, societies, and other integral agencies of such organizations), under the authority of a religious body.

On May 20, 2002, Congress passed the Clergy Housing Allowance Clarification Act of 2002, and President George W. Bush signed it into law. One of the purported purposes of the new law was to support the constitutionality of the parsonage allowance. The parsonage allowance is now limited to the fair rental value of a minister's home.

Some churches and religious nonprofit organizations provide a parsonage for the minister's use. The value of the use of an employer-provided home is generally taxable to the recipient. However, because the home is part of the minister's compensation for services provided in the exercise of ministry, the value is excluded for income tax purposes (but not for self-employment tax). In addition, the organization may designate a portion of the minister's cash compensation as a nontaxable housing allowance for furnishing, utilities, and other maintenance items.

NOTE: The value of the parsonage and housing allowance is part of the minister's compensation package. It must, therefore, be considered when determining whether the minister's total compensation is reasonable.

NOTE: Ministers of the Gospel receive a double benefit—the value of a housing allowance is exclusive under Section 107 and mortage interest and real estate taxes are deducitble under Section 256(a)(6).

21.5 What is *deferred compensation*?

Deferred compensation is an arrangement in which some portion of an employee's income is paid to him or her at a date after which that income is actually earned. Typical examples of deferred compensation may include pensions, retirement plans, and stock options. The primary benefit for the use of most deferred compensation plans is the deferral of tax to the date at which the employee actually receives the income. Internal Revenue Code Section 409A imposes detailed requirements on the timing of deferral elections and of distributions with the penalty of imposing additional tax on the taxpayer prior to actual receipt of the deferred income if these requirements are not complied with.

21.6 What is a *qualified retirement plan*?

A *qualified retirement plan* is a plan that meets the requirements of Internal Revenue Code Section 401(a) and the Employee Retirement Income Security Act of 1974 (ERISA) and is thus eligible for favorable tax treatment. These plans offer several tax benefits: They allow employers to deduct annual allowable contributions for each participant; contributions and earnings on those contributions are tax-deferred until withdrawn for each participant; and some of the taxes can be deferred even further through a transfer into a different type of IRA.

21.7 What is a *403(b) plan*?

A *403(b) plan* is a retirement plan similar to a 401(k) plan, but one which is offered by nonprofit organizations, such as churches, ministries, universities, and some charitable organizations. There are several advantages to 403(b) plans: Contributions to the plan lower taxable income; larger contributions can be made to the account; earnings can grow tax-deferred; and some plans allow loans. Contributions can grow tax-deferred until withdrawal, at which time the money is taxed as ordinary income (which is sometimes a disadvantage).

21.8 What is a *nonqualified retirement plan*?

A *nonqualified retirement plan* is a retirement plan that does not meet the IRS (or ERISA) requirements for favorable tax treatment. Nonqualified retirement plans are usually funded by employers and considered more flexible than, but do not have the tax benefits of, qualified retirement plans. Under a nonqualified retirement plan, benefits are paid at the retirement age in the form of annuities, which are taxed as ordinary income the same as wages, or in lump-sum payments, which may be transferred into an Individual Retirement Account to defer taxes.

21.9 What is a *Rabbi trust?*

A *Rabbi trust* is a type of trust used in nonqualified deferred-compensation plans in the United States where a portion of the current income of an employee is deferred and not taxable to the employee. The employer sets aside the assets in a separate trust for the employee's future. Ordinarily, this would cause current inclusion into gross income even though the employer has not reduced the money placed into the trust to income because of the economic benefit doctrine. The IRS ruled that the trust would not result in income according to Section 83(a) of the Internal Revenue Code if the assets of the trust were made available to the reach or attachment of the employer's general creditors. This is because until the employee is vested (eligible to actually receive the trust money), he or she is under a substantial risk of forfeiture of the money under Section 83(a) and, as such, it is not subject to current inclusion into gross income.

All nonqualified deferred-compensation plans must involve substantial risk of forfeiture or other methods of avoiding constructive receipt, such as conditioning payment upon performance of future conditions or service. The unique feature of the Rabbi trust is that the money placed in it is protected from changes of heart of the employer. Once placed in the trust, the money cannot be taken back or removed by decisions of the employer. So as long as the employer's financial position is good and its creditors are not attempting to seize assets, the Rabbi trust money is protected.

The first of these trusts was created for the benefit of a Jewish Rabbi, thus resulting in the name. The IRS has further clarified the acceptable rules for Rabbi trusts along with a model trust document and the required features to avoid violations of constructive receipt of income by the employee.

21.10 What is *excessive compensation?*

Excessive compensation occurs when the total compensation paid to an executive or other employee, inclusive of all forms of compensation, exceeds the bounds of reasonableness as promulgated by the IRS. There is no bright-line test to go by to determine either reasonableness or when compensation becomes excessive. The IRS has set forth factors to be taken into consideration when testing if compensation is excessive or reasonable. These factors are discussed further in later chapters.

21.11 How does the IRS measure whether compensation is excessive?

The criteria that have been fashioned in determining the reasonableness of compensation are:

- Compensation levels paid by similarly situated organizations, both tax-exempt and taxable, for functionally comparable positions
- The location of the organization, including the availability of similar specialties in the geographical area
- Written offers from similar institutions competing for the services of the individual involved
- The background (including experience and education) of the individual involved
- The need of the organization for the services of a particular individual
- The amount of time an individual devotes to the position

An additional criterion that intermediate sanctions have brought to this area of the law is whether the compensation was approved by an independent board.

NOTE: The intermediate sanctions regulations merely extend this guidance: "Compensation for the performance of services is reasonable if it is only such amount as would ordinarily be paid for like services by like enterprises under like circumstances." Given the immense focus on compensation in relation to the excess benefit transaction standard, this meager offering in the regulations is not particularly helpful.

The regulations offer some interesting rules as to what *circumstances* are to be taken into account, particularly in terms of moments in time. The general rule is that the circumstances to be taken into consideration are those existing at the date when the contract for services was made. Where reasonableness of compensation cannot be determined under those circumstances, however, the determination is to be made based on all facts and circumstances, up to and including circumstances as of the date of payment. Here is the best rule of all in this regard: In no event shall circumstances existing at the date when the contract is questioned be considered in making a determination of the reasonableness of compensation.

NOTE: Court opinions hold that reasonableness can be ascertained taking into account developments that occurred after the transaction was consummated. A court found that an event that occurred two years after the transaction in question could be taken into account in determining reasonableness.

NOTE: The need of the organization for the individual's services is a critical factor. Recently, the IRS issued a Technical Advice Memorandum recognizing that there are instances in which an individual may be considered the "locomotive" of the organization (e.g., what would the Billy Graham Evangelistic Association be without Reverend Billy Graham?). This is not an isolated consideration. It is also a new concept as it regards IRS recognition. It should only be looked at along with the totality of the other considerations enumerated herein.

21.12 Who determines *reasonableness*?

Ultimately, only a trier of fact (a judge or jury) could determine absolute reasonableness of compensation. Prior to that, reasonableness might be determined by the IRS on inquiry and audit of a religious nonprofit. If the religious nonprofit has set compensation using independent data, and an independent board or committee has documented the process, the compensation is presumed to be reasonable, and the IRS must then undertake to prove it is unreasonable. If the organization did not use any one of the above (independent data, independent board, and documentation of the process), the IRS may deem the compensation as unreasonable, and the burden is then on the organization to prove reasonableness.

21.13 What is the rebuttable presumption of reasonableness as it relates to compensation?

The rebuttable presumption arises where the compensation was approved by a board of directors or trustees (or a committee of the board) that was composed entirely of individuals who (1) do not have a conflict of interest with respect to the compensation arrangement, (2) obtained and relied on appropriate data as to comparability prior to making its determination, and (3) adequately documented the basis for its determination.

NOTE: This committee may be composed of any individuals permitted under state law to so serve and may act on behalf of the board to the extent permitted by state law. As will be noted, however, committee members who are not board members are likely to be organization managers.

As to the first of these criteria, which essentially requires an *independent* board (as opposed to a *captive* board), a reciprocal approval arrangement does not satisfy the independence requirement. This arrangement occurs where an individual approves compensation of a disqualified person and the disqualified person in turn approves the individual's compensation.

As to the second of these criteria, appropriate data includes compensation levels paid by similarly situated organizations, both tax-exempt and taxable, for functionally comparable positions; the location of the organization, including the availability of similar specialties in the geographical area; independent compensation surveys by nationally recognized independent firms; and written offers from similar institutions competing for the services of the disqualified person.

As to the third of these criteria, adequate documentation includes an evaluation of the individual whose compensation was being established, and the basis for determining that the individual's compensation was reasonable in light of that

NOTE: There is a safe harbor for organizations with annual gross receipts of less than $1 million when reviewing compensation arrangements. This requires data on compensation paid by three comparable organizations in the same or similar communities for similar services. A rolling average based on the three prior tax years may be used to calculate annual gross receipts.

evaluation and data. The organization's written or electronic records must note the terms of the transaction that was approved, the date of approval, the members of the governing body (or committee) who were present during debate on the transaction or arrangement that was approved and those who voted on it, the comparability data obtained and relied on by the governing body (or committee) and how the data was obtained, and the actions taken with respect to consideration of the transaction by anyone who is otherwise a member of the governing body (or committee) but who had a conflict of interest with respect to the transaction or arrangement.

If these three criteria are satisfied, penalty excise taxes can be imposed only if the IRS develops sufficient contrary evidence to rebut the probative value of the evidence put forth by the parties to the transaction. For example, the IRS could establish that the compensation data relied on by the parties was not for functionally comparable positions or that the disqualified person in fact did not substantially perform the responsibilities of the position.

A similar rebuttable presumption arises with respect to the reasonableness of the valuation of property sold or otherwise transferred (or purchased) by an organization to (or from) a disqualified person if the sale or transfer (or purchase) is approved by an independent board that uses appropriate comparability data and adequately documents its determination.

21.14 Can a bonus system be utilized?

Yes, a bonus system may be utilized in compensating an executive of a religious nonprofit. Such a system is scrutinized under the same rules as regular compensation. In other words, it must be reasonable when viewed as a part of total compensation. The topic of bonuses is further discussed in the next chapter.

21.15 How should a bonus compensation program for employees be defined?

There need not be any formally defined plan. That is, the management of the organization could simply decide that the merits of an individual's work warrant additional compensation.

If a bonus compensation program is defined, the management of the organization could be allowed, by the board of directors, to make additional payments of certain amounts at a specified time, such as at year-end. The board may want to set parameters for these bonuses, stated as ranges of absolute amounts or percentages of overall compensation.

If bonuses are stated as percentages, additional care should be exercised, particularly where the compensation is a function of an element other than the individual's preexisting compensation. For example, the compensation of a fundraiser could be, in whole or part, a percentage of the amount of contributions raised during a particular period. Percentages of this nature can trigger special scrutiny because the compensation arrangement may be a distribution of net earnings, which is prohibited by the doctrine of private inurement. These compensatory programs are often more like commissions than bonuses.

 NOTE: If a form of percentage compensation is deemed appropriate, one feature to consider to avoid private inurement is a ceiling on the amount to be paid. This ceiling is a safeguard against a windfall. Use of this type of ceiling makes it easier to justify the compensation as being reasonable.

21.16   What role should the board of directors play in the annual review and approval of bonus awards to employees?

The federal tax law is evolving to the point where it is being expected that the board of directors of a nonprofit organization, particularly a charitable one, will fix the parameters of all compensation programs, not just those pertaining to bonuses. Thus, as part of the exercise of its fiduciary responsibility, the board should set policy for each component of the organization's compensation plan.

In instances of private inurement, it is becoming a more common practice for the IRS and the attorneys general to fault the board for its lack of involvement and to force the board to develop policies for the ongoing review of the organization's compensation practices.

21.17   How is a bonus compensation program reported to the IRS and disclosed to the public if the filing of an annual information return is required?

There is no express requirement that a bonus compensation program or similar program be specifically reported to the IRS or disclosed to the public. The compensation of the five highest-paid employees of a public charity must, however, be identified on the organization's annual information return filed with the IRS. Information on this return is accessible to the public. A bonus or similar amount paid to one of these employees should be reported as part of his or her total compensation.

21.18 Can a portion of compensation be based on performance of the nonprofit entity or results achieved?

Basing compensation on performance of the entity and/or results achieved is perfectly allowable. As a practical matter, it makes the most sense. The danger, however, is when results are not achieved or the entity encounters a year of lower gross revenue, and the compensation is not adjusted downward in accordance with the shortfall on results or revenue. In that case, the IRS may take the position that the compensation is unreasonable on its face due to the organization's failure to follow its own rules or parameters governing compensation.

21.19 What happens if performance exceeds even the bonus goals?

If an executive outperforms the goals set for him or her in a given year, additional compensation may be warranted; however, the use of a professional in measuring this additional compensation is advised. Additionally, a year in which performance exceeds stated goals may be taken into consideration in future years as "past undercompensation."

21.20 What happens if the executive or the religious nonprofit organization underperforms as it relates to bonus goals?

Underperforming in relation to bonus goals can be a tricky area for a religious nonprofit. Obviously, if there is any part of compensation tied to goal achievement, it should be reviewed in light of nonperformance and its treatment should be well-documented by the organization. If not paid, the organization should document the decision and basis for not paying. If paid in light of underperformance, the organization must document a justifiable reason for the payment in light of its parameters regarding compensation.

21.21 What if board members include the executive or disqualified persons?

In that case, the executive or disqualified persons should excuse themselves from the meeting in which compensation is discussed or set. The absence of the executive or disqualified person should be duly noted in the meeting minutes and reflected as well in any resolution resulting from the meeting.

21.22 What is an *independent compensation committee*?

An *independent compensation committee* is a committee appointed by the board of directors to conduct fact-finding of comparability data regarding the compensation of disqualified persons. The committee reports its findings back to the board and makes recommendations thereon. An independent compensation committee may not be necessary if the organization has a truly independent board. This type of a committee is a useful tool when comprised of qualified individuals who are fully disinterested, especially in the case of a captive board or mixed board consisting of other disqualified persons (i.e., family members, officers, and/or other control parties).

21.23 Why have an independent compensation committee?

Independent compensation committees are most useful when the board of directors of a religious nonprofit organization contains disqualified persons and their family. For example, it is not uncommon for a church or ministry board to contain the senior minister, his or her spouse, and other family members. In these cases, the appointment of an independent compensation committee containing truly independent members may be the most effective and useful way of avoiding the potential for improper influence in the setting or discussion of executive compensation.

21.24 What is a *compensation study*?

A *compensation study* is a report secured by the board of directors on an organization's compensation of certain individuals, usually those at the executive level. Properly done, the compensation study should last the organization at least a few years, barring significant changes in the organization or its compensation structure. The process for determining the reasonableness of compensation is much like that of valuing an item of property. The concept is akin to conducting an appraisal—an evaluation of factors that have a bearing on value. A compensation expert gathers data including all sources of compensation for the individual and compares it both within the organization and to comparable outside organizations. It is allowable for comparability data to contain comparables from similar organizations in both the nonprofit and for-profit world. This is so because executives for a religious nonprofit may well be hired from the for-profit world or a nonprofit's executive may be susceptible to being hired away into the for-profit world.

21.25 Who performs them?

There are many professionals who perform compensation studies. Most often they are human resource companies, accountants, or consultants who specialize in the field. The key when using this type of a professional is to find one who has completed compensation studies for the particular type of organization involved and is familiar with other similar types of religious nonprofits. These types of professionals will usually have access to the type of comparability data that should be used in a good compensation study.

21.26 Why use a professional?

The use of a professional for undertaking a compensation study is advisable because the process can often be difficult, costly, and time-consuming. Gathering comparable data alone often proves to be difficult. For example, most churches do not publish or report their salaries paid, and they are not required to file a Form 990 return that is available to the public. If a non-church religious non-profit organization files an IRS Form 990 return, that data can be public, but it is still often hard to research for comparability purposes. The use of a professional can streamline the process and ensure that the correct data was utilized. Also, as a practical matter, using a professional may also give the organization the added covering of a malpractice insurance policy if the data or report are successfully contested by the IRS.

Remember the importance of *independence* when performing a compensation study. It is advisable to not have an agent of the organization, a board member, an employee, or a church member as a part of the compensation study, no matter how qualified the person. It is crucial to keep the expert at arm's-length and independent.

21.27 How should the religious nonprofit organization go about selecting a compensation study expert?

There are a lot of self-proclaimed "experts" when it comes to performing compensation studies. Religious nonprofit organizations should ask several questions when researching whom to hire. A few of the questions would be: How many compensation studies have you or your organization conducted? What types of compensation studies have you or your organization done? What resources do you use to make comparisons? What degrees, licenses, or other qualifications do you hold that sets you or your organization apart in the field of compensation studies?

21.28 Can compensation studies be performed from within the religious nonprofit organization, perhaps by the CFO or bookkeeper?

Yes. A compensation study can be performed from within the religious nonprofit organization, so long as the person(s) undertaking the study use independent data, the compensation is set by an independent board or committee, and the use of the data is well-documented. Although costly, the time and effort needed to compile truly independent and relevant data may prove to be overwhelming. The use of a qualified expert is recommended as it cuts down on time and is a good way to ensure that independent and relevant data is used. Moreover, it shifts the burden from the religious nonprofit organization to the compensation expert to defend the study's results and methodology.

21.29 What data should be used for a compensation study?

All sources of compensation for the individual should first be reviewed and taken into account. This will include base salary, bonuses, incentive compensation, pension plans, fringe benefits, and housing allowance. The study will then take that information and compare it within the organization to other compensated positions, then to like organizations, as that data is available. Additionally, the study may compare the information on the individual to the for-profit world. The IRS, as mandated by the courts, must allow for comparison of nonprofit employees to those in the for-profit world. However, a study with only for-profit comparisons will not likely pass IRS scrutiny should there be an inquiry or audit.

21.30 Which employees or executives of religious nonprofit organizations should have a compensation study performed for their compensation?

Those within the organization who would be considered "highly compensated" should have a study performed to justify their compensation if ever inquired of by the IRS. In a church, this typically will include the senior minister and sometimes the executive minister. In a non-church religious nonprofit organization, pursuant to the rules of the IRS, the chief executive officer should have a compensation study; sometimes the compensation of the chief operating officer and the chief financial officer should be studied as well. Additionally, other disqualified individuals or insiders such as family members of the senior minister that are on the payroll should have a compensation study. Of course, if the compensation of any of these individuals is unusually low, then a study may not be warranted. Finally, if any of the executives or insiders are owners of a for-profit business with 35 percent or more of the stock in that entity and the entity transacts business with the religious nonprofit organization, those individuals should have a compensation study performed with the compensation of the for-profit business being taken into consideration as it will certainly be taken into consideration if ever inquired of by the IRS.

21.31 What time period should compensation studies cover?

Obviously, at the minimum, a compensation study should cover the coming year for which compensation of an individual is being set. Most often, the religious nonprofit organization will want a study that covers at least two years, and maybe three years, depending on predictable trends of the organization.

Sometimes, it is necessary to perform a compensation study for past years. This may be so because of an inquiry into previous years by the IRS and no study having been performed by the religious nonprofit. This is called a "defensive compensation study." This type of study is performed when it is anticipated that the IRS may seek to challenge the compensation of an executive as unreasonable.

21.32 What does *past undercompensation* mean?

Past undercompensation means an employee's compensation, usually an organization executive, is being reviewed, and the board or independent compensation committee is determining whether compensation for that person was too low in previous years. Past undercompensation usually occurs when a senior executive, such as the senior minister, has led the church or ministry into large growth and rapidly increasing donations over a few years without having had his or her compensation adjusted accordingly. If a religious nonprofit wants to look at past undercompensation for an executive, the use of a professional and a qualified study is highly recommended because gathering the necessary information often proves difficult and the results of the study will likely receive a high degree of scrutiny.

21.33 Why is the IRS so concerned about executive compensation in the nonprofit world and what are their "hot button" issues in this regard?

Recently, the IRS began a compliance check project focusing on compensation paid by charitable organizations. The purpose is to identify and police abuses by nonprofits of compensation practices. This project is ongoing, although the IRS has issued a preliminary report. A separate compliance check project pertaining to compensation has been started, with the concern solely the compensation practices of tax-exempt hospitals. The results of these two projects are likely to be of considerable relevance and importance to exempt religious organizations.

The stated goal of this initiative is to determine how exempt organizations manage the organization, maintain controls over compensation, report compensation on the Form 990, and address questionable compensation issues and individuals who are questionably compensated while increasing awareness of compensation issues among nonprofit organizations. As it relates to religious nonprofit organizations, the compensation of disqualified persons generally is being examined. This topic is discussed more fully in later chapters.

21.34 What is the IRS looking for?

The IRS is interested in how compensation is established—that is, what are the policies and procedures, what are the duties and responsibilities of the individual in question, did the board approve the compensation, was a compensation committee used, was the process documented, and is compensation in line with the 1099s and W-2s of the organization?

The IRS has said "the mere act of sending out the letters [inquiries to nonprofit organization] has heightened everyone's sensitivity about how compensation is set and how it is reported . . . . This is a good thing. Expect to see more of this approach in the future."

21.35   **What is *private inurement*?**

Private inurement is a term used to describe a variety of ways of transferring some or all of an organization's resources (income and/or assets) to persons in their private capacity. Private inurement is supposed to occur with for-profit organizations; in these organizations, profit (net earnings) is intended to be shifted from the entity to the private persons (usually the owners of the organization). By contrast, nonprofit organizations may not engage in forms of private inurement; that is the essence of the term *nonprofit*. Thus, the doctrine of private inurement is the fundamental dividing line between nonprofit and for-profit organizations. It is a particularly critical factor for charitable organizations in acquiring and maintaining tax-exempt status.

In the nonprofit setting, the private inurement standard references transfers of *net earnings*. On its face, this phraseology suggests that private inurement transactions are akin to the payment of dividends. That is not the case, however; the law has evolved to the point where many types of transactions are considered forms of private inurement even though there is no transmission of "net earnings" in a formal accounting sense.

 **NOTE:**   The IRS provided its view of the term's contemporary meaning: Private inurement "is likely to arise where the beneficial benefit represents a transfer of the organization's financial resources to an individual solely by virtue of the individual's relationship with the organization, and without regard to accomplishing exempt purposes." On another occasion, the IRS was more blunt: The prohibition on inurement means that an individual "cannot pocket the organization's funds."

As the first of these quotes indicates, one of the ways the law determines the presence of private inurement is to look to the ultimate purpose of the organization. If the organization is benefiting individuals in their private capacity and not doing so in the performance of exempt functions, private inurement likely is present. If so, the organization may not qualify as a tax-exempt organization or, for that matter, a nonprofit organization.

The private inurement law does not prohibit transactions with insiders. (These transactions may well be accorded greater scrutiny by the IRS or a court, however.) Thus, a nonprofit organization, including those devoted to religious purpose, can pay an insider compensation, rent, interest on loans, and the like. At the same time, the amount paid must be reasonable—that is, it must be comparable to similar payments in the commercial setting.

Private inurement focuses on types of transactions. It also requires the involvement of one or more *insiders* of the organization. Although it is the view of the IRS that the private inurement rule is absolute, some courts have suggested that there is some form of a de minimis floor underlying it. (However, any such de minimis threshold is not likely to be as generous as the insubstantiality test underlying the private benefit doctrine.)

21.36 **When is a person an insider?**

A person is an *insider* with respect to a nonprofit organization when he, she, or it has a special relationship with the organization. (The federal tax law borrowed the term from the federal securities law, which prohibits, among other practices, "insider trading.") Usually the special relationship arises out of a governance arrangement; that is, an organization's insiders include its directors, trustees, and officers. Key employees can be embraced by the term if their duties and responsibilities are akin to those of an officer.

The rules concerning private inurement are quite similar to those involving self-dealing in the private foundation setting. In that setting, insiders are termed *disqualified persons.* In the foundation context, the equivalent term for insiders described above is *foundation managers.*

A person can be an insider because of some other relationship with the nonprofit organization. A founder of the entity, a substantial contributor, or a vendor of services could be an insider, particularly where, because of that relationship, he or she has a significant voice in the policymaking or operations of the organization.

There are attribution rules in this area. Controlled businesses and family members may also be treated as insiders.

21.37 **What types of tax-exempt organizations are expressly subject to the private inurement rule?**

Under the federal income tax law, the types of tax-exempt organizations that are bound by the private inurement rule are charitable (including religious, educational, and scientific) organizations, social welfare organizations, business leagues (including trade, business, and professional associations), social clubs (including country clubs and golf and tennis clubs), and veterans' organizations.

21.38 **What is *private benefit*?**

The term *private benefit,* unlike *private inurement,* is not part of the definition of a nonprofit organization. Rather, private benefit is a term used in the context of tax-exempt organizations, principally charitable entities. It is a part of the operational test, which looks to determine whether a tax-exempt charitable organization is being operated primarily for exempt purposes. The essence of the private benefit requirement is that the entity is not supposed to be operated for private ends, other than insubstantially.

21.39 **What is the difference between private inurement and private benefit?**

There are two principal differences between private inurement and private benefit:

1. A private inurement transaction must be with an insider. A private benefit transaction can involve anyone. Thus, the private benefit doctrine has a much broader sweep than does the private inurement doctrine. Any transaction or arrangement that may constitute private inurement also is a form of private benefit.

2. In the view of the IRS, the private inurement doctrine is absolute; that is, there is no de minimis threshold. (The courts have suggested that there is some threshold in this setting, albeit a rather small one.) By contrast, insubstantial private benefit does not cause any violation of the private benefit limitation.

21.40 What happens when a nonprofit organization engages in either practice?

If a form of private inurement is engaged in by a charitable organization or other tax-exempt organization to which the doctrine applies, the organization may forfeit its ability to be categorized as tax-exempt under the federal income tax law. More fundamentally, the organization would violate the state law definition of a nonprofit organization and may lose its nonprofit designation under state law.

The intermediate sanctions rules also need to be taken into account in this context. The IRS is developing regulations that will stipulate the criteria the agency will use, in an instance of an act of private inurement, in applying the sanctions rather than revoke exempt status. Thus, it is now possible for a church or other charitable organization to be involved in a private inurement transaction or other arrangement and lose exempt status.

If a substantial amount (or more than an insubstantial amount) of private benefit is caused by a charitable organization, the organization loses its ability to be tax-exempt as a charity.

21.41 What are the principal types of transactions that constitute private inurement?

Among the many and varied types of private inurement that the IRS and the courts have identified over the years, the most predominant are unreasonable (excessive) compensation, unreasonable borrowing arrangements, unreasonable rental arrangements, and unreasonable asset sales transactions. In this context, the emphasis once again is on transactions that are reasonable.

21.42 When is *compensation* private inurement?

This is one of the most-often-asked questions. The answer as a matter of law is easy to articulate. An item or package of compensation is private inurement when it is paid to an insider and it is unreasonable and excessive. The process by which reasonableness is determined and the factors that must be taken into account are, however, vague. The determination depends on the material facts and circumstances.

The court cases in this area focus on egregious violations, and, because they are fact specific, they offer little guidance. The IRS has offered no particular assistance in illuminating this topic. The administration of the intermediate sanctions rules, however, is clarifying the matter of the factors and to some extent is addressing the matter of the process.

There are seven general factors that can be used to ascertain whether an item or package of compensation is reasonable. Before enumerating them, however, a preliminary aspect of this matter must be stated. The compensation of an individual by a nonprofit organization must take into account the complete compensation package, not just the salary component. In addition to the base salary, these elements include any bonuses or commissions, incentive compensation, fringe benefits, consulting fees, and retirement, pension plans, and housing allowances.

The determining factors are:

- The amount and type of compensation received by others in similar positions
- The compensation levels paid in the particular geographical community
- The amount of time the individual is spending in the position
- The expertise and other pertinent background of the individual
- The size and complexity of the organization involved
- The need of the organization for the services of the particular individual
- Whether the compensation package was approved by an independent board

The first two factors are based on commonality: What are others in similar positions in similar locales being paid? The geographical factor is relatively easy to isolate; the other aspects may not be. If the comparison is of association executives or foundation trustees, the exercise may be relatively mechanical, because of annually published salary surveys. In other instances, the basis of comparison may not be so clear. For example, in ascertaining the reasonableness of the compensation of a televangelist, should the comparison be with a local member of the ministry or a television personality?

The third factor—the amount of time devoted to the position—is very important. A compensation arrangement may be quite reasonable where the individual is working full-time, but excessive where he or she is working for the organization less than full-time. Thus, the analysis must take into account whether the individual is receiving compensation from other sources and, if so, the amount of time devoted to them.

NOTE: The annual information return (Form 990) filed by most tax-exempt organizations requires that the details of compensation received by a director, officer, or key employee of the filing organization be disclosed when (1) more than $100,000 was paid by the organization and one or more related organizations, and (2) more than $10,000 of the compensation was provided by a related organization.

The sixth factor relates to a topic the IRS is currently addressing to a considerable extent. The IRS is generally approving, albeit reluctantly, of incentive compensation programs. There has been a crackdown on tax-exempt hospitals that are providing inducements to physicians to attract them away from their private practice and to the hospitals' medical staffs. The principles being laid down in this setting are spilling over into aspects of the compensation practices of other nonprofit organizations.

The seventh factor is notable for a variety of reasons. This element is giving the IRS an opportunity to have a greater say in determining who is to sit on the board of directors of a nonprofit organization. Where an independent board is in place, the founders or other principals of the organization lack control. Thus, this element strongly advances the thought that ostensibly "high" compensation, when derived from a controlled board, is presumptively unreasonable.

NOTE: As discussed in a previous chapter, there may be some other avenues to travel with respect to this last factor. One approach is to create an independent compensation committee of the board, which would make recommendations in this area to the board. The other is to seek the opinion of a qualified firm that has expertise in ascertaining the reasonableness of individuals' compensation.

21.43 Are the seven factors mentioned above the only elements to take into account in determining the reasonableness of compensation?

No. The seven factors referenced above are the ones basically used in nearly every compensation analysis case. Other factors may, however, be taken into account. These include whether there is a percentage factor in the calculation of compensation. The data gleaned from national compensation surveys may be important. The location of the organization is a factor, as is (in the compensation context) the existence of written offers from similar organizations competing for the services of an individual.

21.44 How do the *intermediate sanctions rules* interrelate?

The intermediate sanctions system is an alternative to the sanction of revocation of the tax exemption of an organization that participates in a private inurement transaction.

The *intermediate sanctions rules* impose excise taxes, rather than loss (in most instances) of exempt status, on the participants in a private inurement transaction. These rules impose penalty excise taxes as an intermediate—or alternative—sanction in cases where an organization exempt from tax as a charitable organization(other than a private foundation) or a social welfare organization has engaged in an *excess benefit transaction.* In this case, intermediate sanctions can be imposed on disqualified persons who improperly benefited from the transaction and on managers of the organization who participated in the transaction knowing that it was improper.

An excess benefit transaction includes any transaction in which an economic benefit is provided to, or for the use of, any disqualified person if the value of the economic benefit exceeds the value of consideration (including the performance of services) received by the organization for providing the benefit.

A rebuttable presumption can arise to the effect that a transaction was not an excess benefit one if the exempt organization's board had (1) delegated authority to make decisions with respect to the transaction to those board members who did not have a conflict of interest; (2) considered specific information relevant to the decision, including as much information on comparable transactions as could be collected through reasonable efforts; (3) documented the basis for its decision; and (4) approved the transaction, including a limit on the total amount that could be transferred to the controlling person in advance of its occurrence.

A disqualified person who benefited from an excess benefit transaction is subject to a first-tier penalty tax equal to 25 percent of the amount of the excess benefit (in an instance of unreasonable compensation, the amount of the compensation that is excessive). Organization managers who participated in an excess benefit transaction knowing that it was improper are subject to a first-tier penalty tax of 10 percent of the amount of the excess benefit (subject to a maximum tax of $20,000).

Additional, second-tier taxes can be imposed on a disqualified person if there was no correction of the excess benefit transaction within a specified time period. In this case, the disqualified person can be subject to a penalty tax equal to 200 percent of the amount of the excess benefit. For this purpose, the term *correction* means undoing the excess benefit to the extent possible, establishing safeguards to prevent future excess benefit, and, where a full undoing of the excess benefit is not possible, taking such additional corrective actions as are prescribed by federal tax regulations.

The intermediate sanction for excess benefit transactions can be imposed by the IRS in lieu of or in addition to revocation of the tax-exempt status of the errant organization. If more than one disqualified person or manager is liable for a penalty excise tax, then all such persons are jointly and severally liable for the tax. The IRS has the authority to abate the excise tax penalty if it is established that the violation was due to reasonable cause and not to willful neglect, and that the transaction at issue was corrected within the allowed correction period.

Needless to say, this would be a substantial hardship where the individual acted in good faith and has already spent the salary. Unable to satisfy the disgorgement and tax requirement (and related legal fees), bankruptcy (to shed nontax debt) may be the only resort. Meanwhile, one or more board members could also be taxed and the organization could have its tax exemption revoked.

NOTE: This intermediate sanctions scheme is not as benign as it may appear; one entangled in it can face heavy taxes and disgorgement obligations. Suppose an individual was compensated by a public charity in the annual amount of $200,000 and the IRS determined that $50,000 of the compensation was an excess benefit. First, the individual would be assessed a tax of $12,500 (25 percent of $50,000). Second, the individual would be required to timely correct the transaction, which is to say return the excess compensation ($50,000) to the exempt organization before the first-tier tax is assessed or a deficiency notice mailed. How is an individual making $200,000 annually going to come up with $62,500 in this relatively short time period? Third, if the transaction is not timely corrected, there would be a second-tier tax of $100,000 (200 percent of $50,000). Now the individual owes the exempt organization and the government $162,500, plus interest. Further, suppose that, as is often the case, the audit is for a three-year period. The tab then becomes nearly $500,000 ($487,500, to be precise) plus interest.

21.45 When is a *loan* private inurement?

A loan to an insider, by a nonprofit organization that is subject to the private inurement doctrine, can be private inurement. That would be the case where the terms of the loan are unreasonable.

The factors to be taken into account in assessing the reasonableness of a loan include the amount of the loan in relation to the organization's resources, whether the terms of the loan are reduced to writing (such as a note), the amount of any security, the rate of interest, the term of the note, and how the transaction is reflected on the books and records of the lender and borrower. The latter factor is significant in determining the intent of the parties, especially whether it was really expected that the loan would be repaid. (If not, the "loan" would be regarded as additional compensation.) Thus, another factor would be the zealousness of the organization in securing payments or levying against the security, should the borrower cease making timely payments.

NOTE: While all of these factors are important, the interest rate is particularly significant. If the rate is not reasonable (such as a point or two over the prime rate), the transaction may well be questioned. A no-interest loan to an insider would—absent the most extenuating of circumstances—be private inurement.

As with compensation, the test usually is one of commonalities: What would the elements of a similar loan be if made in the commercial setting?

21.46 When is a *rental arrangement* private inurement?

The rental of property from an insider, by a nonprofit organization that is subject to the private inurement doctrine, can be private inurement. That would be the case where the terms of the rental are unreasonable.

The factors to be taken into account in assessing the reasonableness of a rental arrangement include the amount of the rent, whether the terms of the transaction are reduced to writing (such as a lease), the term of the rental, and the need of the organization for the particular property. Regarding the latter element, the ability of the nonprofit organization to rent similar property from an unrelated party may be a factor in the analysis.

There can also be private inurement where a nonprofit organization rents property to an insider. The first of the above three factors is also relevant in this setting. Another factor to be applied would be the extent to which the organization pursued rent collection where the tenant (an insider) fell behind in rent payments.

 NOTE: While all of these factors are important, the amount of the rent is particularly significant. If the rental rate is not reasonable, the transaction may well be questioned. An excessive amount of rent paid to an insider would be a classic form of private inurement.

As with compensation, the test usually is one of commonalities: What would be the elements of a similar rental transaction if made in the commercial setting?

21.47 Are there other forms of private inurement?

Yes. One form of private benefit is the provision of services to insiders. Here it is essential to separate exempt functions from the possibility of private inurement. For example, an organizational rendering of housing assistance for low-income families qualifies as a charitable undertaking; private inurement may be taking place where housing is provided to some of the charitable organization's key employees.

The participation by a nonprofit organization, particularly a charitable one, in a partnership or joint venture may raise issues of private inurement. The IRS is especially concerned about a situation where a public charity is considered to be running a business (such as a partnership) for the benefit of private interests. The scrutiny in this area is most intense where the charitable organization is the (or a) general partner in a limited partnership and some or all of the limited partners are insiders with respect to the organization.

The position of the IRS as to public charities in limited partnerships as general partners is this: To avoid loss of tax-exempt status, the organization must be in the partnership for the purpose of advancing its charitable purposes, it must be protected against the day-to-day duties of administering the partnership, and the payments to the limited partners cannot be excessive.

The IRS is more relaxed as to the involvement of charities as limited partners in partnerships and joint ventures. There the test largely is whether the organization is furthering exempt ends. If it is, tax-exempt status is not likely to be disturbed.

21.48   What is the tax treatment of communal groups?

The IRS has invoked the private inurement doctrine in the context of the tax treatment of communal groups. The IRS's original position was that, generally, where individuals reside in a communal setting in the context of professing religious beliefs, with room, board, and other costs provided by the organization, the result is unwarranted private benefit to the individuals, which precludes tax exemption. This position has been upheld by the courts. These and similar cases could have enormous implications.

The IRS's present position is that communal groups can qualify as religious organizations where the facilities and benefits provided by the organization to its membership "do not exceed those strictly necessary to exist in a communal religious organization. . . ." References such as "primitive," "stark," and "deprivation in material terms of life" are used in the memorandum.

21.49   How is *private benefit* determined in actual practice?

The law on this point is particularly vague. The range of transactions embraced by the private benefit doctrine is not as precise as that captured by the private inurement doctrine. However, every instance of private inurement is also a form of private benefit.

Because there is no requirement of the presence of an insider to bring the private benefit doctrine into play, the doctrine can become applicable with respect to any type of circumstance and any type of person. It is a fallback, catchall concept that is used to prevent the resources of a charitable organization from being misapplied—that is, applied for noncharitable ends.

There is some authority for the proposition that two types of private benefit exist: primary private benefit and secondary private benefit.

21.50   What is *primary* private benefit?

The concepts of primary and secondary private benefit were illustrated by a case involving a nonprofit school. The purpose of the school was to train individuals to be political campaign managers and consultants. The court was troubled by the fact that the graduates of the school ended up working for candidates of the same political party. Although the school's programs did not constitute political campaign activities, nor violate any other then-existing rule barring tax exemption, the court nonetheless wanted to deny tax-exempt status to the school.

The court achieved this objective by conjuring up the idea of these two levels of private benefit. The first level of private beneficiaries—those enjoying *primary private benefit*—were the students of the school. This type of private benefit, however, could not be employed to deny tax-exempt status because it was also an exempt educational function. To prevent the school from acquiring tax exemption, the court turned to secondary private benefit.

21.51 What is *secondary* private benefit?

Secondary private benefit is private benefit that flows to one or more persons as the consequence of the provision of private benefit to the primary beneficiaries. It is not clear whether secondary private benefit is taken into account if primary private benefit is of a nature that would cause denial or revocation of exemption.

The court in the above-described case ruled that, although the primary private benefit did not prevent tax exemption, the secondary private benefit did. The secondary private beneficiaries were the political candidates who received the services of the school's graduates. This type of private benefit was held to be more than incidental.

NOTE: The concept of secondary private benefit has not been applied before or since this opinion was issued. It is a troublesome rule of law because of its reach. Taken literally, every school has secondary private beneficiaries: those who employ its graduates and thus acquire the benefits of the knowledge and skills the school taught. For example, the partners of a law firm who utilize the training of newly graduated associates are secondary private beneficiaries to a far greater economic and other extent than the political candidates who hire trained campaign managers and consultants.

21.52 What is the current status of the private benefit doctrine?

The courts and the IRS are applying the private benefit doctrine in ways that range far beyond situations involving inappropriate benefits accorded to individuals. The private benefit doctrine can also be invoked in circumstances where benefit is impermissibly provided to for-profit corporations. This is the case, for example, in instances involving whole-entity joint ventures and ancillary joint ventures. Indeed, it now appears (if the IRS is correct) that private benefit can be extended by charitable organizations to other tax-exempt organizations.

Also, the IRS has become rather selective in its application of the private benefit doctrine. Recent rulings involve situations where there is private benefit that is more than incidental, yet the IRS rationalizes the arrangement as being unavoidable in connection with the achievement of exempt purposes and thus permissible. Yet, when the IRS is on a crusade to eradicate the tax exemption of a subset of charitable organizations, such as credit counseling and down payment assistance organizations, it applies the private benefit doctrine ruthlessly.

21.53 Is it possible for a donor, when making a gift to a religious nonprofit organization, to realize a private benefit from the gift?

No. No private benefit is inherent in this type of a transaction, even where the donor is an insider. The benefits that flow from forms of donor recognition are not private benefit that would adversely affect tax-exempt status. For example, a gift transaction where a building or a scholarship fund is named after the contributor does not involve an extent of private benefit that would threaten the donee's tax exemption. It either is not considered this type of private benefit at all or is regarded as so incidental and tenuous as to be ignored for tax purposes.

It is quite possible, however, for a donor to receive a private benefit in exchange for a contribution, in the form of a good or service. For example, an individual could give to a charity a contribution to be used in constructing a building that would house the charity's offices. If the contributor was provided free office space in the building in exchange for the gift, that would be private benefit. The private benefit, if more than incidental, could cause the charity to lose its tax exemption. (The donor usually must reduce the charitable contribution deduction by the value of the good or service received.)

21.54 How is incidental private benefit measured?

There is no precise, mechanical test for assessing private benefit. A facts-and-circumstances test must be applied in each case. The private benefit doctrine is a subjective legal concept. It enables the IRS or a court to assert private benefit in nearly every instance in which misdirection of the resources of a charitable, and perhaps other nonprofit, organization is occurring.

CHAPTER 22

Intermediate Sanctions

22.1 What does the term *intermediate sanctions* mean?

Before the intermediate sanctions rules were enacted, the IRS had only two formal options when it found a substantial violation of the law of tax-exempt organizations by a public charity or a social welfare organization: Do nothing or revoke the organization's tax exemption. These rules, however, provide the IRS with a third alternative—one that is certainly more potent than doing nothing (including, perhaps, issuing some informal warning) and less draconian than revocation of tax exemption. It is, thus, an *intermediate* sanction.

In the instance of a transaction covered by these rules, tax sanctions are to be imposed on the disqualified persons who improperly benefited from the transaction and perhaps on organization managers who participated in the transaction knowing that it was improper.

22.2 What is the effective date of the intermediate sanctions rules?

The effective date of these rules generally is September 14, 1995. The sanctions do not apply, however, to any benefits arising from a transaction pursuant to a written contract that was binding on that date and continued in force through the time of the transaction, and the terms of which have not materially changed.

22.3 When were these rules enacted?

The intermediate sanctions law came into being on enactment of the Taxpayer Bill of Rights 2 (Act). This legislation was signed into law on July 30, 1996.

22.4 What is the legislative history of this legislation?

On July 11, 1996, the Senate adopted the legislation as passed by the House of Representatives, on April 16, 1996, without change. The House vote was 425–0; the Senate voted by unanimous consent. There is no report of the Senate Finance Committee and no conference report. Thus, the report of the House Committee on Ways and Means, dated March 28, 1996 (House Report), constitutes the totality of the legislative history of the intermediate sanctions rules.

22.5 Have the Treasury Department and the IRS issued guidance as to these rules?

Yes. Final regulations to accompany the intermediate sanctions rules were issued on January 21, 2002—five and a half years after the underlying statute was signed into law.

NOTE: These regulations are not nearly as helpful as the nonprofit professional community had hoped. For the most part, they merely restate what is in the statute and the legislative history or can be found in the comparable rules in the private foundations context. Most of the interesting subtleties are embedded in the examples. Some areas of this body of law where guidance would be appropriate are completely unaddressed by the regulations, such as the criteria for determining whether sales, lending, and rental transactions are reasonable. Guidance as to whether compensation is reasonable is skimpy. Indeed, in one instance, the regulations are in conflict with the legislative history.

22.6 What types of tax-exempt organizations are involved in these rules?

These sanctions apply with respect to public charities and tax-exempt social welfare organizations. These entities are termed, for this purpose, *applicable tax-exempt organizations*. These entities include any organization described in either of these two categories of exempt organizations at any time during the five-year period ending on the date of the transaction.

NOTE: Just because an organization is not an *applicable tax-exempt organization* does not mean that it is not caught up in these rules. This is because an exempt organization can be a disqualified person.

22.7 Are there any exceptions to these rules?

No. That is, all public charities and social welfare organizations are applicable tax-exempt organizations.

22.8 To what types of transactions do these rules apply?

This tax scheme has as its heart the *excess benefit transaction*. The definition of an *excess benefit transaction* is based on the contract law concept of *consideration*. It generally is any transaction in which an economic benefit is provided by an applicable tax-exempt organization directly or indirectly to or for the use of any disqualified person, if the value of the economic benefit provided by the exempt organization exceeds the value of the consideration (including the performance of services) received for providing the benefit. This type of benefit is known as an *excess benefit*.

22.9 How is *value* measured?

The standard is that of *fair market value*. The fair market value of property, including the right to use property, is the price at which property or the right to use it would change hands between a willing buyer and a willing seller, neither being under any compulsion to buy, sell, or transfer property or the right to use it, and both having reasonable knowledge of relevant facts.

22.10 Can an economic benefit be treated as part of the recipient's compensation?

Yes, but with some qualifications. An economic benefit may not be treated as consideration for the performance of services unless the organization clearly intended at the onset and made the payments as compensation for services. Items of this nature include the payment of personal expenses, transfers to or for the benefit of disqualified persons, and non-fair-market-value transactions benefiting these persons.

In determining whether payments or transactions of this nature are in fact forms of compensation, the relevant factors include whether (1) the appropriate decision-making body approved the transfer as compensation in accordance with established procedures (such as an approved written employment contract executed on or before the date of the transfer) and (2) the organization and the recipient reported the transfer (other than in the case of nontaxable fringe benefits) as compensation on relevant returns or other forms. These returns or forms include the organization's annual information return filed with the IRS, the information return provided by the organization to the recipient (Form W-2 or Form 1099), and the individual's income tax return (Form 1040).

With the exception of nontaxable fringe benefits and certain other types of nontaxable transfers (such as employer-provided health benefits and contributions to qualified pension plans), an organization is not permitted to demonstrate at the time of an IRS audit that it intended to treat economic benefits provided to a disqualified person as compensation for services merely by claiming that the benefits may be viewed as part of the disqualified person's total compensation package. Rather, the organization is required to provide substantiation that is contemporaneous with the transfer of the economic benefits at issue.

22.11   What happens if an economic benefit cannot be regarded as part of the recipient's compensation?

If this happens, there basically is no other way to justify the provision of the benefit as something other than an excess benefit transaction—even if the amount involved is reasonable. This outcome is termed an *automatic excess benefit transaction*. This is a huge trap for disqualified persons of applicable tax-exempt organizations. The parties involved should be certain that these benefits are either covered by an exception or properly treated as compensation. Otherwise, the excise tax and correction requirement will be applicable.

Recent enforcement activities by the IRS reflect the fact that this is a high-enforcement area for the agency. Recent rulings involving churches and other public charities reflect the IRS's application of the automatic excess benefit transaction concept in cases concerning the use of cell phones, laptops, automobiles, credit cards, real property, and the like. The value of these uses is treated as additional compensation. Another aspect of this trap is spousal travel, where a director or other insider can find that exempt organization–paid travel and similar expenses for the benefit of the insider's spouse is additional compensation, subject to both income tax and one or more intermediate sanctions excise taxes.

22.12   What does the phrase *directly or indirectly* mean?

The phrase *directly or indirectly* means the provision of an economic benefit directly by the organization or indirectly by means of a controlled entity. Thus, an applicable tax-exempt organization cannot avoid involvement in an excess benefit transaction by causing a controlled entity to engage in the transaction.

22.13   What does the phrase *for the use of* mean?

A benefit can be provided *for the use of* a disqualified person even though the transaction involving an applicable tax-exempt organization is with a nondisqualified person. A benefit of this nature might be enhancement of reputation, augmentation of goodwill, or some form of marketing advantage.

22.14   Is there any other definition of the term *excess benefit transaction*?

Yes. The term *excess benefit transaction* includes any transaction in which the amount of any economic benefit provided to or for the use of a disqualified person is determined in whole or in part by the revenues of one or more activities of the organization, but only if the transaction results in impermissible private inurement. In this context, the excess benefit is the amount of impermissible private inurement. This category of arrangement is known as a *revenue-sharing arrangement*.

A revenue-sharing arrangement may constitute an excess benefit transaction regardless of whether the economic benefit provided to the disqualified person exceeds the fair market value of the consideration provided in return if, at any point, it permits a disqualified person to receive additional compensation without providing proportional benefits that contribute to the organization's accomplishment of its exempt purpose. If the economic benefit is provided as compensation for services, relevant facts and circumstances include the relationship between the size of the benefit provided and the quality and quantity of the services provided, as well as the ability of the party receiving the compensation to control the activities generating the revenues on which the compensation is based.

NOTE: Under preexisting law, certain revenue-sharing arrangements were determined by the IRS to not constitute private inurement. It continues to be the case that not all revenue-sharing arrangements constitute improper private inurement. The Department of the Treasury and the IRS are not bound, however, by any particular prior rulings in this area.

22.15 Are any economic benefits disregarded for these purposes?

Yes. One set of disregarded benefits is the payment of reasonable expenses for members of the governing body of an applicable tax-exempt organization to attend meetings of the governing body of the organization. This exclusion does not encompass luxury travel or spousal travel.

An economic benefit provided to a disqualified person that the disqualified person receives solely as a member of a charitable class that the applicable tax-exempt organization intends to benefit as part of the accomplishment of the organization's exempt purposes is generally disregarded for these purposes.

22.16 In the context of compensation, how does one determine whether it is *excessive*?

Existing tax law standards (including those standards established under the law concerning ordinary and necessary business expenses) apply in determining reasonableness of compensation and fair market value. This concept is essentially the same as that in the private inurement context, as discussed in the previous chapter.

NOTE: In this regard, an individual need not necessarily accept reduced compensation merely because he or she renders services to a tax-exempt, as opposed to a taxable, organization.

Compensation that is excessive is a form of excess benefit transaction; the portion that is considered excessive is an excess benefit.

22.17   What are the tax law standards used in determining the reasonableness of compensation?

The criteria that have been fashioned in determining the reasonableness of compensation are:

* Compensation levels paid by similarly situated organizations, both tax-exempt and taxable, for functionally comparable positions
* The location of the organization, including the availability of similar specialties in the geographical area
* Written offers from similar institutions competing for the services of the individual involved
* The background (including experience and education) of the individual involved
* The need of the organization for the services of a particular individual
* The amount of time an individual devotes to the position

An additional criterion that intermediate sanctions have brought to this area of the law is whether the compensation was approved by an independent board.

NOTE: The intermediate sanctions regulations merely extend this guidance: "Compensation for the performance of services is reasonable if it is only such amount as would ordinarily be paid for like services by like enterprises under like circumstances." Given the immense focus on compensation in relation to the excess benefit transaction standard, this meager offering in the regulations is of little help.

The regulations offer some interesting rules as to what *circumstances* are to be taken into account, particularly in terms of moments in time. The general rule is that the circumstances to be taken into consideration are those existing at the date when the contract for services was made. Where reasonableness of compensation cannot be determined under those circumstances, however, the determination is to be made based on all facts and circumstances, up to and including circumstances as of the date of payment. Here is the best rule of all in this regard: In no event shall circumstances existing at the date when the contract is questioned be considered in making a determination of the reasonableness of compensation.

NOTE: There are court opinions holding that reasonableness can be ascertained taking into account developments that occurred after the transaction was consummated. A court found that an event that occurred two years after the transaction in question could be taken into account in determining reasonableness.

22.18 What items are included in determining the value of compensation?

Compensation for these purposes means all items of compensation provided by an applicable tax-exempt organization in exchange for the performance of services. These items include (1) all forms of cash and noncash compensation, such as salary, fees, bonuses, parsonage and housing allowance, and severance payments; (2) all forms of deferred compensation that is earned and vested, whether or not funded, and whether or not paid under a deferred compensation plan that is a qualified plan, but if deferred compensation for services performed in multiple prior years vests in a later year, that compensation is attributed to the years in which the services were performed; (3) the amount of premiums paid for liability or other insurance coverage, as well as any payment or reimbursement by the organization of charges, expenses, fees, or taxes not ultimately covered by the insurance coverage; (4) all other benefits, whether or not included in income for tax purposes, including payments to welfare benefit plans on behalf of the persons being compensated, such as plans providing medical, dental, life insurance, severance pay, and disability benefits, and both taxable and nontaxable fringe benefits (other than certain working condition fringe benefits and de minimis fringe benefits), including expense allowances or reimbursements or forgone interest on loans that the recipient must report as income; and (5) any economic benefit provided by an applicable tax-exempt organization, whether provided directly or through another entity owned, controlled by, or affiliated with the organization, whether the other entity is taxable or tax-exempt.

22.19 Do these rules apply to rental transactions?

Where an applicable tax-exempt organization rents property to a disqualified person, it is crucial that the amount of the rent, and the other terms and conditions of the transaction, be reasonable. There should be a lease, a reasonable term, probably a security deposit, and other terms and conditions that are customary with respect to the type of rental arrangement involved.

NOTE: The regulations are silent on this point, other than to define the term *value* in the context of the right to use property.

22.20 Do these rules apply to lending transactions?

Where an applicable tax-exempt organization lends money to a disqualified person, it is crucial that the amount lent, and the other terms and conditions of the transaction, be reasonable. There should be a note, a reasonable term, a reasonable rate of interest, probably some form of security, and other terms and conditions that are customary with respect to the type of lending arrangement involved.

Terms and conditions must also be reasonable where an applicable tax-exempt organization is borrowing money from a disqualified person.

NOTE: The regulations are silent on this point.

22.21 Do these rules apply to sales transactions?

Where an applicable tax-exempt organization sells property to a disqualified person, it is crucial that the amount received, and the other terms and conditions of the transaction, be reasonable. The consideration received by the organization need not be only money; it is permissible for property to be exchanged and for the consideration to be represented by one or more notes.

NOTE: The regulations are silent on this point, other than to define the term *fair market value.*

22.22 Who has the burden of proof in a dispute with the IRS as to whether a transaction involves an excess benefit?

In an administrative proceeding with the IRS, generally the burden of proof is on the disqualified person who participated in the transaction. There is, however, a rebuttable presumption of reasonableness, with respect to a compensation arrangement with a disqualified person.

NOTE: This rebuttable presumption is not a matter of statute (that is, it is not in the Act); it is provided in the House Report. Also, it is reflected in the regulations.

This presumption arises where the arrangement was approved by a board of directors or trustees (or a committee of the board) that

1. Was composed entirely of individuals who do not have a conflict of interest with respect to the arrangement

NOTE: This committee may be composed of any individuals permitted under state law to so serve and may act on behalf of the board to the extent permitted by state law. As will be noted, however, committee members who are not board members are likely to be organization managers.

2. Obtained and relied on appropriate data as to comparability prior to making its determination
3. Adequately documented the basis for its determination

As to the first of these criteria, which essentially requires an *independent* board (as opposed to a *captive* board), a reciprocal approval arrangement does not satisfy the independence requirement. This arrangement occurs where an individual approves compensation of a disqualified person and the disqualified person in turn approves the individual's compensation.

As to the second of these criteria, *appropriate data* includes compensation levels paid by similarly situated organizations, both tax-exempt and taxable, for functionally comparable positions; the location of the organization, including the availability of similar specialties in the geographical area; independent compensation surveys by nationally recognized independent firms; and written offers from similar institutions competing for the services of the disqualified person.

NOTE: A safe harbor is available for organizations with annual gross receipts of less than $1 million when reviewing compensation arrangements. This requires data on compensation paid by three comparable organizations in the same or similar communities for similar services. A rolling average based on the three prior tax years may be used to calculate annual gross receipts.

As to the third of these criteria, *adequate documentation* includes an evaluation of the individual whose compensation was being established, and the basis for determining that the individual's compensation was reasonable in light of that evaluation and data. The organization's written or electronic records must note the terms of the transaction that was approved, the date of approval, the members of the governing body (or committee) who were present during debate on the transaction or arrangement that was approved and those who voted on it, the comparability data obtained and relied on by the governing body (or committee) and how the data was obtained, and the actions taken with respect to consideration of the transaction by anyone who is otherwise a member of the governing body (or committee) but who had a conflict of interest with respect to the transaction or arrangement.

If these three criteria are satisfied, penalty excise taxes can be imposed only if the IRS develops sufficient contrary evidence to rebut the probative value of the evidence put forth by the parties to the transaction. For example, the IRS could establish that the compensation data relied on by the parties was not for functionally comparable positions or that the disqualified person in fact did not substantially perform the responsibilities of the position.

A similar rebuttable presumption arises with respect to the reasonableness of the valuation of property sold or otherwise transferred (or purchased) by an organization to (or from) a disqualified person if the sale or transfer (or purchase) is approved by an independent board that uses appropriate comparability data and adequately documents its determination.

22.23 What does the phrase *conflict of interest* mean?

The regulations define the term by defining what is *not* a conflict of interest. Thus, a member of a governing body (or a committee of it) does not have a conflict of interest with respect to a compensation arrangement or transaction if the member:

- Is not the disqualified person and is not related to any disqualified person participating in or economically benefiting from the compensation arrangement or transaction;
- Is not in an employment relationship subject to the direction or control of any disqualified person participating in or economically benefiting from the compensation arrangement or transaction;
- Is not receiving compensation or other payments subject to approval by any disqualified person participating in or economically benefiting from the compensation arrangement or transaction;
- Has no material financial interest affected by the compensation arrangement or transaction; and
- Does not approve a transaction providing economic benefits to any disqualified person participating in the compensation arrangement or transaction who in turn has approved or will approve a transaction providing economic benefits to the member.

22.24 What does the term *disqualified person* mean?

The term *disqualified person,* in this context, means

- Any person who was, at any time during the five-year period ending on the date of the excess benefit transaction involved, in a position to exercise substantial influence over the affairs of the applicable tax-exempt organization involved (whether by virtue of being an organization manager or otherwise)
- A member of the family of an individual described in the preceding category
- An entity in which individuals described in the preceding two categories own more than 35 percent of an interest

22.25 What is the scope of the *substantial influence rule*?

An individual is in a position to exercise substantial influence over the affairs of an organization if he or she, individually or with others, serves as the president, chief executive officer, or chief operating officer of the organization. An individual serves in one of these capacities, regardless of title, if he or she has or shares ultimate responsibility for implementing the decisions of the governing body or supervising the management, administration, or operation of the organization.

An individual also is in this position if he or she, independently or with others, serves as treasurer or chief financial officer of the organization. An individual serves in one of these capacities, regardless of title, if he or she has or shares ultimate responsibility for managing the organization's financial assets and has or shares authority to sign drafts or direct the signing of drafts or authorize electronic transfer of funds from the organization's bank account(s).

A person can be in a position to exercise substantial influence over a tax-exempt organization despite the fact that the person is not an employee of (and does not receive any compensation directly from) a tax-exempt organization but is formally an employee of (and is directly compensated by) a subsidiary—including a taxable subsidiary—controlled by the parent tax-exempt organization.

NOTE: There is a conflict between the legislative history of these rules and the regulations. The legislative history states that an individual having the title of *trustee, director,* or *officer* does not automatically have status as a disqualified person. The regulations, however, provide that persons having substantial influence include any individual serving on the governing body of the organization who is entitled to vote on matters over which the governing body has authority.

There are some categories of persons who are deemed to not be in a position to exercise substantial influence. One is any other public charity. Another is an employee of an applicable tax-exempt organization who receives economic benefits of less than the amount of compensation referenced for a highly compensated employee, is not a member of the family of a disqualified person, is not an individual referenced above as considered to have this influence, and is not a substantial contributor to the organization.

A person who has managerial control over a discrete segment of an organization may be in a position to exercise substantial influence over the affairs of the entire organization.

Facts and circumstances that tend to show the requisite substantial influence include the fact that the person founded the organization; is a substantial contributor to the organization; receives compensation based on revenues derived from activities of the organization that the person controls; has authority to control or determine a significant portion of the organization's capital expenditures, operating budget, or compensation for employees; has managerial authority or serves as a key advisor to a person with managerial authority; or owns a controlling interest in a corporation, partnership, or trust that is a disqualified person.

Facts and circumstances that tend to show an absence of substantial influence are where the person has taken a bona fide vow of poverty as an employee, agent, or on behalf of a religious organization; the person is an independent contractor (such as a lawyer, accountant, or investment manager or advisor), acting in that capacity, unless the person is acting in that capacity with respect to a transaction from which the person might economically benefit either directly or indirectly (aside from fees received for the professional services rendered); and any preferential treatment a person receives based on the size of that person's contribution is also offered to any other contributor making a comparable contribution as part of a solicitation intended to attract a substantial number of contributions.

22.26 What does the term *organization manager* mean?

An *organization manager* is a trustee, director, or officer of an applicable tax-exempt organization, as well as an individual having powers or responsibilities similar to those of trustees, directors, or officers of the organization, regardless of title.

An individual is considered an *officer* of an organization if he or she (1) is specifically so designated under the articles of incorporation, bylaws, or other organizing documents of the organization or (2) regularly exercises general authority to make administrative or policy decisions on behalf of the organization. An individual who has authority merely to recommend particular administrative or policy decisions, but not to implement them without approval of a superior, is not an officer.

 NOTE: Independent contractors, acting in a capacity as lawyers, accountants, and investment managers and advisors, are not officers.

An individual who is not a trustee, director, or officer and yet serves on a committee of the governing body of an applicable tax-exempt organization that is invoking the rebuttable presumption of reasonableness based on the committee's actions is an organization manager for these purposes.

22.27 What does the term *member of the family* mean?

The term *member of the family* is defined as constituting:

* Spouses, ancestors, children, grandchildren, great-grandchildren, and the spouses of children, grandchildren, and great-grandchildren—namely, those individuals so classified under the private foundation rules
* The brothers and sisters (whether by the whole or half blood) of the individual and their spouses

22.28 What is the definition of a *controlled entity*?

The entities that are disqualified persons because one or more disqualified persons own more than a 35 percent interest in them are termed *35 percent controlled entities*. They are:

- Corporations in which one or more disqualified persons own more than 35 percent of the total *combined voting power*
- Partnerships in which one or more disqualified persons own more than 35 percent of the profits interest
- Trusts or estates in which one or more disqualified persons own more than 35 percent of the beneficial interest

NOTE: The term *combined voting power* includes voting power represented by holdings of voting stock, actual or constructive, but does not include voting rights held only as a director or trustee.

In general, constructive ownership rules apply for purposes of determining what are 35 percent controlled entities.

22.29 What are the sanctions?

The intermediate sanctions themselves are in the form of tax penalties. A disqualified person who benefited from an excess benefit transaction is subject to and must pay an initial excise tax equal to 25 percent of the amount of the excess benefit. Again, the excess benefit is the amount by which a transaction differs from fair market value, the amount of compensation exceeding reasonable compensation, or (pursuant to tax regulations) the amount of impermissible private inurement resulting from a transaction based on the organization's gross or net income.

NOTE: In addition, the matter must be rectified—corrected—by a return of the excess benefit, plus additional compensation, to the applicable tax-exempt organization.

An organization manager who participated in an excess benefit transaction, knowing that it was this type of a transaction, is subject to and must pay an initial excise tax of 10 percent of the excess benefit (subject to a maximum amount of tax of $20,000), where an initial tax is imposed on a disqualified person. The initial tax is not imposed where the participation in the transaction was not willful and was due to reasonable cause.

An additional excise tax may be imposed on a disqualified person where the initial tax was imposed and if there was no correction of the excess benefit transaction within a specified time period. This time period is the *taxable period,* which means—with respect to an excess benefit transaction—the period beginning with the date on which the transaction occurred and ending on the earlier of

1. The date of mailing of a notice of deficiency with respect to the initial tax, or
2. The date on which the initial tax is assessed.

In this situation, the disqualified person would be subject to and must pay a tax equal to 200 percent of the excess benefit involved.

22.30 **What does the term *correction* mean?**

The term *correction* means undoing the excess benefit to the extent possible and taking any additional measures necessary to place the organization in a financial position not worse than that in which it would be if the disqualified person had been dealing under the highest fiduciary standards.

Correction of the excess benefit occurs if the disqualified person repays the applicable tax-exempt organization an amount of money equal to the excess benefit, plus any additional amount needed to compensate the organization for the loss of the use of the money or other property during the period commencing on the date of the excess benefit transaction and ending on the date the excess benefit is corrected. Correction may also be accomplished, in certain circumstances, by returning property to the organization and taking any additional steps necessary to make the organization whole.

NOTE: The regulations do not state what these "certain circumstances" might be nor do they reveal what the "additional steps" might entail.

22.31 **What does the term *participation* mean?**

The term *participation* includes silence or inaction on the part of an organization manager where he or she is under a duty to speak or act, as well as any affirmative action by the manager. An organization manager, however, will not be considered to have participated in an excess benefit transaction where the manager has opposed the transaction in a manner consistent with the fulfillment of the manager's responsibilities to the applicable tax-exempt organization.

22.32 **What does the term *knowing* mean?**

A person participates in a transaction, *knowing* that it is an excess benefit transaction, only if the person (1) has actual knowledge of sufficient facts so that, based solely on those facts, the transaction would be an excess benefit transaction, (2) is aware that the act under these circumstances may violate the excess benefit transactions rules, and (3) negligently fails to make reasonable attempts to ascertain whether the transaction is an excess benefit transaction, or the person is in fact aware that it is an excess benefit transaction.

Knowing does not mean having reason to know. Evidence tending to show, however, that a person has reason to know of a particular fact or particular rule is relevant in determining whether the person had actual knowledge of the fact or rule. For example, evidence tending to show that a person has reason to know of sufficient facts so that, based solely on those facts, a transaction would be an excess benefit transaction is relevant in determining whether the person has actual knowledge of the facts.

22.33 What does the term *willful* mean?

Participation in a transaction by an organization manager is *willful* if it is voluntary, conscious, and intentional. No motive to avoid the restrictions of the law or the incurrence of any tax is necessary to make the participation willful. Participation by an organization manager, however, is not willful if the manager does not know that the transaction in which the manager is participating is an excess benefit transaction.

22.34 What does the term *reasonable cause* mean?

An organization manager's participation is due to *reasonable cause* if the manager has exercised his or her responsibility on behalf of the organization with ordinary business care and prudence.

NOTE: If a person, after full disclosure of the factual situation to a lawyer (including in-house counsel), relies on the advice of the lawyer—expressed in a reasoned written legal opinion—that a transaction is not an excess benefit transaction, the person's participation in the transaction will ordinarily not be considered knowing or willful and will ordinarily be considered due to reasonable cause, even if the transaction is subsequently held to be an excess benefit transaction. The absence of advice of legal counsel with respect to an act does not, by itself, give rise to an inference that a person participated in the act knowingly, willfully, or without reasonable cause.

NOTE: A written legal opinion is *reasoned* so long as it addresses the facts and applicable law. An opinion is not reasoned if it does nothing more than recite the facts and state a conclusion.

22.35 Can there be joint liability for these taxes?

Yes. If more than one organization manager or other disqualified person is liable for an excise tax, then all of these persons are jointly and severally liable for the tax.

22.36 If the executive of a religious nonprofit organization is receiving compensation that he or she believes to be unreasonable, should the executive voluntarily reduce the compensation or wait to see whether the IRS raises the issue?

An executive in this position should not rely on his or her "gut feelings" about the reasonableness of the compensation. The first step an individual in this position should take is to determine whether the compensation arrangement is even subject to these rules. If the compensation is set by a pre-1995 binding unaltered contract, the excess benefit transaction rules do not apply with respect to it.

NOTE: The payment of excessive compensation in these circumstances could still amount to private inurement.

If these rules do apply, the second step is to have the organization procure an independent opinion on the subject. It may turn out that the executive was wrong in his or her judgment. If it develops that the compensation is in fact excessive, however, the executive should work with the organization's board of directors in causing the salary to be lowered to the highest appropriate amount, so as to avoid future excess benefit transactions.

It is not a good idea to wait to see what the IRS may do. This is a self-reporting system. A delay will involve interest and perhaps penalties should the IRS become aware of the matter. Thus, the prudent approach, having reduced the compensation, is to pay the tax and correct the past transgression(s) by correcting the situation. This would be done by returning the excess benefit, plus a suitable amount of interest, for the year(s) involved to the employer organization.

NOTE: If the board is notified of this situation by the executive and does nothing, the board members could be personally liable for taxes.

22.37 If the IRS raises questions about an executive compensation, should the executive voluntarily reduce his or her compensation in order to minimize the risk of imposition of the sanctions?

That usually would be a bad idea. Assuming the compensation is subject to these rules, a reduction in compensation in the face of an IRS inquiry would be an admission that the compensation has been too high. The better approach is to work with the board of directors of the employer organization to obtain outside advice and then proceed from there.

If all else fails and the compensation is found to be excessive, the IRS may be approached to see whether there is any basis for abatement on the ground of reasonable cause.

22.38 **If the board of directors approves an employment contract with an executive and later determines that the compensation provided in the contract is excessive, what steps, if any, should the board take prior to expiration of the contract?**

There is a lot here for the board to do and consider. First step: See whether the contract is sheltered by the effective date rules. If it is, that is the end of the matter (although it could still amount to private inurement). If it is not, then the board should seek an outside evaluation of the compensation level and determine the portion of it (if any) that is considered excessive.

A contract that is covered by the intermediate sanctions rules and embodies unreasonable compensation is nonetheless a binding contract. Thus, unless there is a provision in the agreement that allows it—an excellent idea, by the way—the board cannot unilaterally adjust the compensation level. (That would be a breach of contract.) Rather, the board should work with the individual—who, after all, will bear the brunt of the penalties—and proceed as discussed earlier.

 NOTE: If the excess benefit transaction consists of the payment of compensation for services under a contract that has not been completed, termination of the employment or independent contractor relationship between the organization and the disqualified person is *not* required in order to correct.

22.39 **Is there any relief from this tax? Is there any basis for being excused from these penalties?**

Yes, there are some forms of relief. One of the more fascinating aspects of the intermediate sanctions rules is the *initial contract exception*. Pursuant to this element of the law—a huge exception in relation to the general rule—the intermediate sanctions regime does not apply to a fixed payment made by an applicable tax-exempt organization to a disqualified person pursuant to an initial contract. An *initial contract* is a binding written contract between the tax-exempt organization and a person who was not a disqualified person immediately prior to entering into the contract. A *fixed payment* is an amount of money or other property specified in the contract involved, or determined by a fixed formula specified in the contract, which is to be paid or transferred in exchange for the provision of specified services or property. If the parties make a material change to an initial contract, the contract is treated as a new contract—so that the exception is no longer available—as of the date the material change is effective. Otherwise, the initial contract exception can continue, as a matter of law, without limit.

Also, the IRS has the authority to abate the intermediate sanctions excise tax in certain circumstances, principally where a taxable event was due to reasonable cause and not to willful neglect, and the transaction at issue was corrected within the specified taxable period.

22.40 How are these taxes reported and paid?

Under the law in existence prior to the enactment of intermediate sanctions, charitable organizations and other persons liable for certain excise taxes must file returns by which the taxes due are calculated and reported. These taxes are those imposed on public charities for excessive lobbying and for political campaign activities, and on private foundations and/or other persons for a wide range of impermissible activities. These returns are on Form 4720.

In general, returns on Form 4720 for a disqualified person or organization manager liable for an excess benefit transaction tax must be filed on or before the fifteenth day of the fifth month following the close of that person's tax year.

22.41 Can an organization reimburse a disqualified person for these taxes?

Yes. Any reimbursements by an applicable tax-exempt organization of excise tax liability are, however, treated as an excess benefit unless they are included in the disqualified person's compensation during the year in which the reimbursement is made. (This rule is consistent with that noted earlier, which is that payments of personal expenses and other benefits to or for the benefit of disqualified persons are treated as compensation only if it is clear that the organization intended and made the payments as compensation for services.) The total compensation package, including the amount of any reimbursement, is subject to the requirement of reasonableness.

22.42 Can an organization purchase insurance for a disqualified person to provide coverage for these taxes?

Yes. But again, the payment by an applicable tax-exempt organization of premiums for an insurance policy providing liability insurance to a disqualified person for excess benefit taxes is an excess benefit transaction unless the premiums are treated as part of the compensation paid to the disqualified person and the total compensation (including premiums) is reasonable.

22.43 Does the payment of an intermediate sanctions tax have any direct impact on a tax-exempt organization?

Yes. There are three ways in which the payment of an intermediate sanctions tax can have an impact on a tax-exempt organization. One would occur when the payment of the tax triggers a reimbursement by the organization pursuant to an indemnification or coverage under an insurance policy that it has purchased.

The second way an impact can occur arises from the fact that applicable tax-exempt organizations are required to disclose on their annual information returns the amount of the excise tax penalties paid with respect to excess benefit transactions, the nature of the activity, and the parties involved. This disclosure may have an adverse impact on the organization's reputation, with negative implications for membership development and fundraising.

The third of these impacts is that the payment of an intermediate sanctions tax by a disqualified person may be indicative of an act of private inurement that, if sufficiently substantial, may endanger the organization's tax-exempt status.

22.44 Is there a limitations period after which these taxes cannot be imposed?

Yes. A three-year statute of limitations applies, except in the case of fraud.

22.45 Do intermediate sanctions take precedence over other sanctions used by the IRS?

Basically, yes. Intermediate sanctions may be imposed by the IRS in lieu of or in addition to revocation of an organization's tax-exempt status. In general, these intermediate sanctions are to be the sole sanction imposed in those cases in which the excess benefit does not rise to a level where it calls into question whether, on the whole, the organization functions as a charitable or social welfare organization.

In practice, the revocation of tax-exempt status, with or without the imposition of these excise taxes, is to occur only when the organization no longer operates as a charitable or social welfare organization, as the case may be. Existing law principles apply in determining whether an organization no longer operates as an exempt organization. For example, in the case of a charitable organization, that would occur in a year, or as of a year, the entity was involved in a transaction constituting a substantial amount of private inurement.

As noted, the IRS is developing criteria by which it will determine when to apply the intermediate sanctions penalties, when to apply the private inurement doctrine to revoke exempt status—and when to do both.

22.46 Does the private inurement doctrine have an impact on definitions of excess benefit transactions?

Absolutely. The concepts of private inurement and excess benefit transaction are much the same. Thus, a great amount of existing law as to what constitutes private inurement is applied in determining what amounts to excess benefit transactions. Although this is the case particularly with respect to compensation issues, it is also true in the realms of lending, borrowing, sales arrangements, and the like. Indeed, some of this law is specifically said by the legislative history to be predicated on the private inurement doctrine, such as the rules pertaining to revenue-sharing transactions.

22.47 Won't private foundation rules as to self-dealing have a similar impact?

There is no question about it. Much of what the law terms *self-dealing* in the foundation context is used in ascertaining what are excess benefit transactions. The definition of self-dealing, although more specific, has generated a large amount of law (including private letter rulings and the like) that is shaping the contours of the concept of the excess benefit transaction. Moreover, the law underlying many of the private foundation terms—such as the definition of *disqualified person,* transactions for the benefit of disqualified persons, meaning of *organization manager,* meaning of *member of the family,* and the process of correction—is being followed in the development of the law of intermediate sanctions.

22.48 Won't determinations as to what is an excess benefit shape the law of private inurement and self-dealing?

Very much so; just as those two terms are influencing the meaning of excess benefit transaction, as the coming months and years bring findings of what is an excess benefit transaction, these determinations will in turn shape the meaning of private inurement and self-dealing. Thus, each of these three terms will be constantly influencing the reach and content of the other two. To an extent, the private benefit doctrine will also be affected by this ongoing confluence of these various bodies of law.

CHAPTER 23

Unrelated Business Activities

23.1 **A religious nonprofit organization often needs more money than it can generate. Management of the organization is thinking about raising money by charging fees for certain activities, products, or services, but is concerned about taxation. Where does it begin?**

Basically, the management of the religious nonprofit organization should not lose sight of the fundamental fact that the organization is a nonprofit, tax-exempt entity. Thus, the organization needs to be operated *primarily* for its exempt purposes. If there is to be any taxable income, it will be income that is derived from business activities that are *unrelated* to the organization's tax-exempt purpose. As long as operations are primarily for exempt purposes, the organization need not fear loss of its tax-exempt status. The income derived from the other, nonexempt activities, however, may well be subject to the federal income tax.

23.2 **How does an organization measure what is primary?**

That often is not easy to do; there is no mechanical formula for measuring what is *primary*. The measurement is done on the basis of what the law likes to term the *facts and circumstances*. The IRS heartily rejects the thought of applying any particular percentage in measuring primary activities, and invokes this principle of law on a case-by-case basis. In this stance, the IRS is uniformly supported by the courts.

NOTE: Percentages are used in this and comparable contexts all the time, if only as a guide. The term *primary* has been assigned percentages in other settings; for unrelated business income purposes, it can mean at least 65 percent. By comparison, *substantial* is sometimes defined as at least 85 percent; *substantially* all is sometimes set at 90 percent. *Incidental* is sometimes defined as up to 15 percent.

If these percentages have any validity—and to a limited extent, they do for evaluation purposes—an organization could have as much as one-third of its activities or income be unrelated. There are IRS private letter rulings upholding unrelated income in excess of 40 percent; however, in these cases, the amount of *time* actually devoted to the unrelated business was considerably less. It seems unlikely that any organization receiving over one-half of its income from unrelated business would be tax-exempt.

A prudent assessment or review would cause a tax-exempt organization to seriously evaluate its situation, if its unrelated income annually exceeds 20 or 25 percent of total revenue. The remedies may include establishing a for-profit subsidiary.

The statement that there is no mechanical formula for measuring what is *primary* is not precisely accurate. In the case of tax-exempt title-holding companies, the maximum amount of unrelated business income that they can have in a year without endangering tax exemption is 10 percent. This rule does not, however, apply with respect to any other type of tax-exempt organization. For most tax-exempt organizations, 10 percent is too narrow a limitation on permissible unrelated activity.

23.3 How does a religious nonprofit organization know whether an activity is a related one or an unrelated one?

This is both one of the easiest and hardest questions in the law of tax-exempt organizations.

The easy answer is that an unrelated activity is one that does not substantially advance the exempt purposes of the organization. That is, it is an activity that the organization engages in for the purpose of earning money, rather than furthering one or more programs. The fact that the money earned is used for exempt purposes does not alone make the activity itself related.

The more complex answer is that the activity must be evaluated against as many as five levels of analysis. These are:

1. Is the activity a *trade or business*?
2. Is it regularly carried on?
3. Is the conduct of the activity *substantially related* to the conduct of exempt functions?

4. Is the activity exempted from taxation by one or more statutory exceptions?

5. Is the income from the activity exempted from taxation by one or more statutory exceptions?

23.4 What is the rationale underlying the *unrelated income rules*?

The basic structure of these rules was enacted in 1950. The essence of this body of law is to separate the income of a tax-exempt organization into two categories: (1) income from related business and (2) income from unrelated business. The income from unrelated business is taxed as if it were earned by a for-profit, taxable company.

The primary objective of these rules was to eliminate a source of *unfair competition* with the for-profit sector by placing the unrelated business activities of exempt organizations on the same tax basis as those conducted by nonexempt organizations, where the two are in competition. Some courts place considerable emphasis on the factor of competition when assessing whether an undertaking is an unrelated business. The existence or nonexistence of competition, however, is not a statutory requirement for there to be unrelated business.

In actuality, the enactment of these rules has not quelled the cries of "unfair competition" from the business sector, particularly small business owners. Nearly six decades later, the issue is not so much that unrelated business by nonprofits is competitive; rather, the competition is usually derived from *related* businesses. In part, this is the result of (1) shifts in the definition of related and unrelated activities and (2) the entry of for-profits into fields of endeavor previously confined to nonprofit entities. Some small business advocates want competitive practices prohibited, as a way of "leveling the playing field." These individuals are of the view that unrelated income taxation is not enough; they fret about the fact that some consumers are attracted to, and thus bring their business to, nonprofits just because they are nonprofit—a situation informally known as the *halo effect*.

Thus, the purpose of the unrelated income tax itself is to equalize the economics of a transaction, irrespective of whether the vendor of a good or service is tax-exempt or taxable. If an organization can sell a product and not pay income tax on the sales proceeds, that organization can charge a lower price for that product and have more "profit" remaining than an organization selling the same product and having to pay taxes as a cost of doing business. This ability, and occasional practices of price undercutting, is the foundation for the claim of "unfair competition."

23.5 Are these claims of unfair competition leading to anything, such as law changes?

It does not look like it. Years ago, when the small business lobbying on this subject was at its peak, some thought that Congress would toughen the rules. There was a series of hearings before the Subcommittee on Oversight, of the House Committee on Ways and Means, in 1986–1987. The chairman of the subcommittee pushed hard for legislation but could not build a consensus for change. The nonprofit community lobbied very effectively against various proposals, the small business lobby did a particularly poor job of sustaining its efforts, and the movement for revising these laws atrophied. The individual who was the subcommittee chairman is no longer in Congress, and there is no interest, in either chamber, in law change in this area. Still, efforts to make it more difficult for nonprofits to compete are unfolding in several states.

23.6   What is the *trade or business* requirement?

A statutory definition of *trade or business* is specifically applicable in the unrelated business setting. The phrase means any activity that is carried on for the production of income from the sale of goods or the performance of services. That definition is, of course, quite broad and encompasses nearly everything that a tax-exempt organization does.

In fact, the law regards a tax-exempt organization as a bundle of activities. They may be related or unrelated, but they are still *businesses*.

23.7   Does this mean that the law considers the programs of exempt organizations as businesses?

Yes. Each of the organization's programs is considered a separate business. In fact, a program may embody several businesses. For example, the bookstore operated by a college is a combination of businesses. These generally include sales of books, cosmetics, computers, appliances, and clothing. The same is true with respect to hospital and museum gift shops and associations' sales of items to their members. In the case of charitable organizations, many of their fundraising activities are businesses.

It is difficult to convince the IRS that a particular activity is not a business. The most likely instances where an exempt organization can prevail on this point are with respect to its investment activities and infrequent sales of assets. Occasionally a court will be more lenient, as illustrated by an opinion finding that an association's monitoring activities with respect to insurance programs for its membership, where the insurance and claims processing functions were elsewhere, did not rise to the level of a trade or business.

Moreover, an activity does not lose its identity as a trade or business if it is carried on within a larger aggregate of similar activities or within a larger complex of other endeavors that may or may not be related to the exempt purposes of the organization. This means that an activity cannot be hidden from scrutiny, as to whether it is a business, by tucking it in with other activities. The IRS has the authority to review each business of an exempt organization in isolation, in search of unrelated activity. That is, it can—figuratively speaking—fragment an organization into as many businesses as it can define. In the jargon of the field, this is known as the *fragmentation rule*.

23.8 **When the federal tax law regards an exempt organization as a composite of businesses, isn't that different from how nonprofit organizations see themselves?**

There is no question about that. Unfortunately, the matter gets murkier. Actually, the statutory definition of *business* states that the term *trade or business* "includes" that definition of it. That word has opened the door for the courts and the IRS to add requirements and possibilities that may cause an activity to be a business. Some courts use other criteria, such as competitive activity or commerciality, and then jump all the way to the conclusion that the activity is an unrelated business.

For example, in a completely different area of the tax law, dealing with whether a gambler gambling only for personal ends is engaged in a business for expense deduction purposes, the Supreme Court held that, for an activity to be considered a trade or business, it must be carried on with a profit motive. The Court specifically wrote that this definition of trade or business was not to be used in other tax settings. However, some lower courts ignored that admonition and grafted that rule onto the definition of exempt organizations' unrelated business income.

23.9 **Why would a tax-exempt organization object to the additional element of the definition concerning profit motive? Wouldn't that rule always favor exempt organizations, causing some activities to not be businesses in the first instance?**

Actually, it does not always work that way. In some instances, an exempt organization *wants* an activity to be considered an unrelated business. This is because income from unrelated activity and losses from other unrelated activity can be aggregated to produce a single, bottom-line item of net income or net loss.

For example, suppose an exempt organization has two unrelated activities. One produces $100,000 of net income, the other generates $70,000 of net losses. On the unrelated business income tax return, the income and losses from the two businesses are blended, and the organization pays the unrelated income tax on only $30,000. This works, however, only when both activities are in fact *businesses*.

Suppose the second of these activities consistently, year-in and year-out, yields losses. The IRS will usually take the position that, because the activity always results in an annual loss, it is not being conducted with the requisite profit motive. If that position is sustained, the activity is not considered a *business*, in which case the $70,000 of loss could not be offset against the $100,000 of gain. Then the organization would have to pay the unrelated income tax on the full $100,000.

All of this is happening even though the tax regulations state that the fact that a trade or business does not produce a net profit is not sufficient to exclude it from the definition of a trade business.

23.10 What are some of the other elements being grafted onto this definition?

Sometimes a business is found when an exempt organization is in competition with for-profit enterprises. The existence of profits may lead a court to the conclusion that an undertaking is a business (usually an unrelated business). The IRS may assert the presence of unrelated business just because a fee is charged for the product or service. Moreover—and this is becoming a growing practice—courts will jump to the conclusion that an unrelated business exists where the activity is undertaken in a *commercial* manner.

23.11 What is a *commercial activity*?

The commerciality doctrine has been conceived by the courts, although it is not fully articulated. There is, with one relatively minor exception, no mention of *commerciality* in the Internal Revenue Code. The same is the case with respect to the tax regulations.

The doctrine essentially means that a tax-exempt organization is engaged in a nonexempt activity when that activity is conducted in a manner that is considered *commercial*. An activity is a commercial one if it is undertaken in the same manner as it would be if it were being conducted by a for-profit (commercial) business. The most contemporary explication of the commerciality doctrine sets forth these criteria: (1) the tax-exempt organization sells goods or services to the public; (2) the exempt organization is in direct competition with one or more for-profit businesses; (3) the prices set by the organization are based on pricing formulas common in the comparable commercial business setting; (4) the organization utilizes advertising and other promotional materials and techniques to enhance sales; (5) the organization's hours of operation are basically the same as those of for-profit enterprises; (6) the management of the organization is trained in business operations; (7) the organization uses employees rather than volunteers; and (8) there is an absence of charitable giving to the organization.

23.12 What are these statutory and regulatory references to the commerciality doctrine?

In 1986, Congress added to the federal tax law a rule stating that an organization cannot qualify as a tax-exempt charitable entity or a social welfare entity if a substantial part of its activities consists of the provision of commercial-type insurance. While that term is not statutorily defined, it generally means any insurance of a type provided by commercial insurance companies. The reach of this aspect of commerciality is being accorded broad interpretation in the courts.

As far as the regulations are concerned, there is a brief mention of commerciality in the rules pertaining to whether an activity is regularly carried on. There it is stated that business activities of an exempt organization will ordinarily be deemed to be regularly carried on "if they manifest a frequency and continuity, and are pursued in a manner generally similar to comparable commercial activities of nonexempt organizations."

23.13 What are the rules as to whether a business activity is regularly carried on?

This test was derived because of the purpose of the unrelated business rules: An activity cannot be competitive with for-profit business if it is not regularly carried on.

Thus, income from an unrelated business cannot be taxed where that business is merely sporadically or infrequently conducted. The frequency and continuity of the activity, the manner in which the activity is pursued, and the continuing purpose of deriving income from the activity largely determine whether the activity is regularly carried on.

23.14 How is *regularity* measured?

There is no precise means of measurement. An activity that consists of a single, one-time-only transaction or event is certainly irregular. For this reason, a sole sale of an item of property often is not taxable. Most fundraising events, such as annual dances and theater outings, are usually not taxed because of this rule.

Beyond that, it is a judgment call. A business occupying only a few days in a year would not be regularly carried on. For example, the tax regulations offer a quaint illustration of the operation of a sandwich stand by a hospital auxiliary for two weeks at a state fair. That business is said to not be regularly carried on. But it cannot be said with any certainty when too many days of activity cause the line to be crossed. The regulations add that the operation of a commercial parking lot for 1 day in each week of the year is a regularly carried on business. Operation on 52 days out of 365, or operation on 1 day each week, obviously reflects an operation that is regularly carried on.

23.15 Are there any other aspects of this level of analysis?

Yes, there are three other aspects of regularity.

One is that, where a business activity is, in the commercial sector, carried on only during a particular season, the duration of this season, rather than a full year, is the measuring period for an exempt organization. For example, an organization selling Christmas trees or Christmas cards would measure regularity against the length of the Christmas season.

23.16 What are the other two aspects of regularity?

One is that the IRS has adopted the view that there is more to the measurement of regularity than just the time expended for the event itself. The IRS takes into consideration the amount of time the organization spends in preparing for the event—*preparatory time*—and the time expended afterward in connection with the event—*winding-down time.* If an exempt organization were to sell a product commercially for a few days each year, in assessing regularity, it is—according to the IRS view—supposed to include the preparatory time of lining up the product, creating advertising, soliciting purchasers, and the like, as well as the winding-down time spent assessing the operation and arranging for the return of unsold items.

23.17   Do some operations get converted into regular ones by using that approach?

That can be the case. But there's more. The law in general recognizes the concept of a *principal* and an *agent. A principal* is a person who hires another person to act in his, her, or its stead, for the principal's benefit; the second person is an *agent.* Generally, the law considers the acts of an agent to be those of the principal. This means that the acts of an agent are attributed to the principal.

In the unrelated business setting, it is common for an exempt organization to contract with a company to perform a service. If the company is considered an agent of the organization and the company's function is in connection with an unrelated business, the IRS will take the position that the time spent by the company is attributed to the exempt organization in determining whether the unrelated activity was regularly carried on.

For example, in one case, a university contracted with a publisher to produce programs for its home football games. The contract reserved advertising space in the programs for the university, any income generated by sales of that space was retained by the university, and the university hired an advertising agency to sell its space. The IRS determined that the revenues from the sale of the advertisements constituted unrelated business income inasmuch as the advertising agency was an agent of the university. Because of the agency relationship, the agency's activities were attributable to the university for purposes of determining whether the university regularly carried on the business of selling program advertising. A court, however, rejected this approach to the determination of regularity. At the same time, the IRS disagrees with this holding and is adhering to its position in issuing rulings.

23.18   What about the third level of analysis concerning the substantially related requirement?

This is where the issue usually is: whether the business that is regularly carried on is *related* or *unrelated.* The general rule is that the income from a regularly conducted trade or business is subject to tax unless the income-producing activity is substantially related to the accomplishment of the organization's tax-exempt purpose.

To determine whether an activity is related, an examination is made of the relationship between the business activity and the accomplishment of the organization's exempt purpose. The fact that the income from the business is used for exempt programs does not make the activity a related one.

A trade or business is *related* to tax-exempt purposes only where the conduct of the business has what the tax law terms a *causal relationship* to the achievement of an exempt purpose. The business is *substantially* related only if the causal relationship is recognizably large or material. Thus, for the conduct of a trade or business from which a particular amount of gross income is derived to be substantially related to an exempt purpose, the production or distribution of the goods or the performance of the services from which the gross income is derived must contribute importantly to the accomplishment of these purposes. Where the production or distribution of goods or the performance of services does not contribute importantly to the accomplishment of the organization's exempt purposes, the income from the sale of the goods or services does not derive from the conduct of a related business.

23.19 How is *relatedness* determined?

There is no formula in this setting. Judgments as to whether there is a causal relationship and whether there is substantiality are made in the context of the facts and circumstances involved. Unfortunately, however, there is not much "straightforwardness." This aspect of the tax law is complex and murky.

23.20 What are some examples of these judgments?

There are dozens of IRS rulings and court opinions in this area.

In one instance, a local bar association sold standard legal forms to its member lawyers for their use in the practice of law. These forms were purchased from a state bar association. The IRS ruled that the sale of the forms was an unrelated business because it did not contribute importantly to the accomplishment of the association's exempt functions. (There is a court opinion to the contrary, however.) Another court held that the sale of preprinted lease forms and landlords' manuals by an exempt association of apartment owners and managers was a related business.

This IRS ruling illustrates that, just because an association's membership uses a product in their own businesses, the sale of the product does not become a related business for the association. When an association of credit unions published and sold a consumer-oriented magazine to its members, the IRS held that to be an unrelated business because the magazine was distributed to the depositors of the members as a promotional device.

Other instances of unrelated businesses of associations include the sale of equipment to members, the operation of an employment service, the conduct of other registry programs, the selling of endorsements (including the right to use the association's name and logo), and the charging of dues to certain categories of purported associate members.

23.21 **Are there any other aspects of the substantially related test?**

There are four other aspects of this test. One of them is the *size and extent test*.

In determining whether an activity contributes importantly to the accomplishment of an exempt purpose, the *size and extent* of the activity must be considered in relation to the size and extent of the exempt function it purports to serve. Thus, where income is realized by a tax-exempt organization from an activity that is in part related to the performance of its exempt functions, but that is conducted on a scale larger than is reasonably necessary for performance of the functions, the gross income attributable to that portion of the activities in excess of the needs of exempt functions constitutes gross income from the conduct of an unrelated business.

Another of these aspects is the *same state test*. As a general rule, the sale of a product that results from the performance of tax-exempt functions does not constitute an unrelated business where the product is sold in substantially the same state it is in on completion of the exempt functions. This rule is significant for organizations that sell articles made by handicapped individuals as part of their rehabilitation training. By contrast, where a product resulting from an exempt function is exploited in business endeavors beyond what is reasonably appropriate or necessary for disposition in the state it is in on completion of tax-exempt functions, the activity becomes transformed into an unrelated business. For example, an exempt organization maintaining a dairy herd for scientific purposes may sell milk and cream produced in the ordinary course of operation of the project without unrelated income taxation. If, however, the organization were to utilize the milk and cream in the further manufacture of food items, such as ice cream and pastries, the sale of these products would likely be the conduct of an unrelated business.

Another of these subtests of substantiality is the *dual use test*. This concerns an asset or facility that is necessary to the conduct of exempt functions but is also employed in an unrelated endeavor. Each source of the income must be tested to see whether the activities contribute importantly to the accomplishment of exempt purposes. For example, a museum may have a theater for the purpose of showing educational films in connection with its program of public education in the arts and sciences; use of that theater for public entertainment in the evenings would be an unrelated business. Likewise, a school may have a ski facility that is used in its physical education program; operation of the facility for the public would be an unrelated business.

The fourth of these subtests is the *exploitation test*. In certain instances, activities carried on by an exempt organization in the performance of exempt functions generate goodwill or other intangibles that are capable of being exploited in unrelated endeavors. When this is done, the mere fact that the income depended in part on an exempt function of the organization does not make it income from a related business. This type of income will be taxed as unrelated business income unless the underlying activities themselves contribute importantly to the accomplishment of an exempt purpose. For example, income from advertising in a publication with exempt function content generally is taxable income resulting from an exploitation of an exempt resource.

23.22 How is the unrelated business income tax calculated?

In general, the tax is determined in the same manner as with for-profit entities. The unrelated income tax rates payable by most tax-exempt organizations are the corporate rates. Some organizations, such as trusts, are subject to the individual income tax rates. There is a specific deduction of $1,000.

This tax falls on *net* unrelated business income. An exempt organization is allowed to subtract its business expenses from gross unrelated income in arriving at taxable net unrelated income. The law generally states that a deductible expense must be *directly connected* with the carrying on of the business; an item of deduction must have a proximate and primary relationship to the carrying on of the business. This standard is more rigorous than the one applied to for-profit and individual taxpayers, where the law allows the deductibility of expenses that are reasonably connected with the taxable endeavor. In practice, however, exempt organizations often follow the standard of reasonableness, particularly when allocating expenses. Because of the looseness of the tax regulations, this approach has been upheld in the courts.

The IRS has recently evidenced renewed interest in this area. It is in the process, by means of a compliance check project, of examining the expense-allocation practices of tax-exempt colleges and universities in the unrelated business context. The outcome of this project is likely to have implications for churches, other exempt religious organizations, and exempt organizations in general.

There is one exception to the directly connected test. This exception is for the charitable contribution deduction allowed in computing taxable unrelated income. In general, this deduction cannot exceed 10 percent of the unrelated business taxable income otherwise computed.

These taxes are paid by means of an unrelated business income tax return. Tax-exempt organizations must make quarterly estimated payments of this tax.

23.23 What types of activities are exempt from unrelated income taxation?

An interesting feature of the federal tax laws is the series of *modifications* that are available in calculating (or avoiding) taxable unrelated business income. Although these modifications largely exclude certain types of income from taxation, they also exclude three types of research activities from the tax. This tripartite set of exclusions is somewhat of an oddity, in that research activities generally are exempt functions.

One exclusion is for research for the federal government, or any of its agencies or instrumentalities, or any state or political subdivision of a state. Another exclusion is for research performed for any person; however, the research institution must be a college, university, or hospital. The third exclusion is as broad as the second: The organization must be operated primarily for the purpose of carrying on fundamental research, and the results of the research must be freely available to the general public.

The modifications also eliminate from taxation revenue derived from the lending of securities by exempt organizations to brokers.

Other statutory exceptions shelter types of activities from unrelated income taxation. One is for a business in which substantially all of the work in carrying on the business is performed for the tax-exempt organization without compensation. Any unrelated business can be protected from taxation by this exception, including the business of advertising. This exception can be useful in shielding fundraising functions (special events) from taxation.

NOTE: The concept of compensation is broadly applied. In one instance, the revenue from gambling events was held taxable because the workers, all of whom were volunteers, were frequently tipped by the patrons.

Another exception is for a business that is conducted by a tax-exempt charitable organization, or a state college or university, primarily for the convenience of its members, students, patients, officers, or employees. This broad exception—known as the *convenience doctrine*—is relied on heavily by churches, colleges, universities, and hospitals. Much of the income from sales of items in exempt organization bookstores and gift shops is rendered nontaxable because of this rule.

Another exception is for a business that sells merchandise, substantially all of which was contributed to the exempt organization. This exception is generally utilized by thrift shops that sell donated clothing, books, and the like to the general public.

Still other exceptions are for certain businesses of associations of employees conducted for the convenience of their members, the conduct of entertainment at fairs and expositions by a wide range of exempt organizations, the conduct of trade shows by most exempt organizations, the performance by hospitals of certain services for smaller hospitals, the conduct of certain bingo games by most tax-exempt organizations, qualified pole rentals by exempt mutual or cooperative telephone or electric companies, the distribution of low-cost articles incidental to the solicitation of charitable contributions, and the exchanging or renting of membership or donor mailing lists between tax-exempt charitable organizations.

23.24   What types of income are exempt from unrelated income taxation?

The *modifications* described above shield a wide variety of forms of income from unrelated income taxation. These forms of income generally are annuities, capital gains, dividends, interest, rents, and royalties. For the most part, there is little controversy in this area as to the definition of these income items, inasmuch as the terms are amply defined elsewhere in the federal tax law.

There is, nonetheless, an underlying festering controversy. It is the view of the IRS that the exclusion is available only where the income is investment income or is otherwise passively received. This approach to these modifications rests on the rationale for the unrelated income rules, which is to bring parity to the economics of competitive activities involving nonprofit and for-profit organizations. Passive income, by definition, is not derived from competitive activity and thus should not be taxed. But the IRS wishes to tax net income from the active conduct of commercial business activities.

This dichotomy presents itself in connection with the exclusion for rental income. Where a tax-exempt organization carries on rental activities in the nature of a commercial landlord, the exclusion is not available. The exclusion, however, is not normally voided simply because the exempt organization provides normal maintenance services. In practice, this opportunity for taxation is obviated by the use of an independent building management and leasing company.

There can be disputes as to whether an income flow is truly rent or is a share of the profits from a joint venture; revenue in the latter form is generally taxable. A contemporary illustration of this distinction is the litigation surrounding crop-share leasing. The IRS has lost all of the cases brought to date; the courts have held that the funds received by the exempt organization were in the form of excludable rent and not from a partnership or joint venture.

The contemporary battles in this context are being waged over the scope of the exclusion for royalties. In part, this is because exempt organizations have more latitude than with any other type of income in structuring transactions to shape the resulting income. In this instance, the objective is to make the income fit the form of a royalty or at least dress it up like a royalty. For the most part, the dilemma is presented because the statute does not define the term *royalty*.

The courts and the IRS, however, have developed a definition of the term *royalty*, which is that it is a payment for the use of a valuable intangible right, such as a trademark, trade name, service mark, logo, or copyright.

23.25   How can the royalty exclusion be effectively utilized?

The key to effective utilization of the royalty exception in this context is to minimize the tax-exempt organization's involvement in the efforts that give rise to payment of the royalty. It is tempting for an organization to do just the opposite; for example, if an organization has an affinity card program, it will be inclined to engage in various practices (such as mailings, inserts in publications, and activities at the annual conference) to stimulate its members' use of the cards. While activity of this nature is permissible if it is insubstantial, the more active the organization is in this regard, the greater the likelihood that the royalty exception will not be available.

An alternative approach is to bifurcate the arrangement: Execute two contracts, one reflecting passive income/royalty payments and the other, payments for services rendered. The income paid pursuant to the second contract would likely be taxable. The organization would endeavor to allocate to the royalty contract as much of the income as reasonably possible. The difficulty with this approach is the form-over-substance rule: Two contracts of this nature are easily collapsed and treated as one for tax purposes.

23.26 Are there any exceptions to the rule stating these exclusions?

Yes, there are three exceptions. One pertains to the payment of otherwise-excludable income from a controlled organization. The general rule is that payments of annuities, interest, rent, and/or royalties by a controlled corporation to a tax-exempt controlling organization are taxable as unrelated income. This is the case even though these forms of income are otherwise passive in nature. For this purpose, an organization controls another where the parent entity owns at least 50 percent of the voting power of all classes of stock entitled to vote and at least 50 percent of all other stock of the corporate subsidiary. This control element can also be manifested by an interlocking of directors, trustees, or other representatives of the two organizations.

The second exception consists of a temporary rule enacted in 2006, which applies with respect to payments to controlling organizations, in accordance with existing arrangements, received or accrued after December 31, 2005, and before January 1, 2008. Pursuant to this rule, the general law applies only to the portion of the payments received or accrued in a tax year that exceeds the amount of the payment that would have been paid or accrued if the payment had been determined under the federal tax law rules concerning the allocation of tax items among taxpayers. At this time, it is uncertain as to whether this rule will be extended.

The third exception is found in the rules concerning unrelated debt-financed property. Where income is debt-financed income, the various exclusions referred to above are unavailable.

23.27 Are there any exceptions to these exceptions?

Yes. The rule concerning the taxation of income from a controlled subsidiary does not apply where the funds are dividends, because dividends are not deductible by the payor corporation. Thus, where other types of income are deductible by the controlled entity that provides the income, the exempt organization that receives the income must regard it as unrelated business income.

23.28 What are the contemporary unrelated business issues for religious nonprofit organizations?

Activities conducted by volunteers: An activity is not considered an unrelated business activity if substantially all of the work is completed by volunteers. This rule removes from the unrelated business arena common fundraising events by religious nonprofits such as the seasonal sales of wreaths, menorahs, or Christmas cards by youth groups or the sales of candy by school groups.

This exception also applies to items made through rehabilitation activities if items are sold without additional processing by non-volunteers. For example, a religious nonprofit organization operates a craft shop to provide training skills to the homeless. The participants are not paid for their work in the craft shop. The organization sells the crafts. The sale of these crafts is not an unrelated business activity because (1) the producers of the crafts are not paid and (2) no modifications are made by paid individuals after the participants have completed their work and before the sale of the products.

Activities for the convenience of members: An activity conducted for the convenience of a tax-exempt organization's congregants, members, students, officers, or employees is generally excepted from the definition of income that is unrelated, and therefore subject to unrelated business income (UBI) tax. Common examples are a religious nonprofit organization operating a bookstore that sells foodstuffs and clothing, coffee shops, or a cafeteria for its member or employees.

Mailing lists: Section 513(h) of the Internal Revenue Code provides that the rental of a tax-exempt organization's mailing list of donors is not an unrelated business activity if it is rented to another tax-exempt organization. As to the rental of tax-exempt organizations' mailing lists to for-profit organizations, the IRS and courts are divided over whether it is an unrelated business activity or a royalty arrangement. The IRS strongly believes rental of a mailing list is an unrelated business activity because:

- Section 513(h) of the Internal Revenue Code excludes only rentals to other tax-exempt organizations from unrelated business activities. Thus, the IRS argues Congress intended rentals to for-profit organizations to be a trade or business.
- Substantial services are provided (e.g., maintenance of mailing lists) and this raises the activity to the level of a trade or business.

The courts have generally looked to both the amount of revenue generated from, and the services provided to, the for-profit entity by the tax-exempt organization. In one case, the court found the tax-exempt organization's activities were so substantial that the organization was carrying on a business. In other cases, the courts found the activities related to the rental were so minor that the activities were a royalty arrangement.

The IRS consistently takes the position that maintenance of a mailing list is a substantial activity, which makes the mailing list rental a trade or business. The courts, on the other hand, have found that the tax-exempt organization maintains the lists for its own tax-exempt purposes, such as providing magazines and newsletters to members and donors. Therefore, no services are provided in connection with the rental of the list.

The courts' answer to the IRS's second argument that Internal Revenue Code Section 513(h) infers that mailing list rentals to for-profit entities result in UBI is that when the section was enacted, the Chairman of the Ways and Means Committee stated that the enactment of Section 513(h) of the Internal Revenue Code "carries no inference whatever that mailing list revenues beyond its scope or prior to its effective date should be considered taxable to an exempt organization."

The courts have interpreted this comment to mean the rental of mailing lists to for-profit entities by itself does not make it an unrelated business. Instead, the courts have ruled that what determines whether the rental of a mailing list is a royalty or an unrelated trade or business depends on the scope of services the tax-exempt organization provides.

Affinity cards: In looking for new ways to increase revenues, tax-exempt organizations are entering agreements regarding "affinity cards." These are credit or debit cards issued by for-profit entities designed for, and marketed to, members of a group or organization. In many cases, the tax-exempt organization provides its mailing list and minimal services in return for a fee for each card issued and a fee for each transaction.

The tax-exempt organization generally treats income from these arrangements as royalties. However, the IRS has aggressively attacked this position in several cases. The IRS classifies these arrangements as unrelated business activities. The courts have also addressed this issue on several occasions. As with mailing list rentals, the courts have looked to the level of involvement by the tax-exempt organization in the activity. In at least four cases, the courts found the tax-exempt organization performed minimal services and ruled the arrangement was a royalty.

NOTE: Although several courts have decided in favor of tax-exempt organizations treating income from the rental of mailing lists, logos, and the like as royalties, the IRS continues to pursue this issue.

If a tax-exempt organization is considering renting mailing lists or other intangible assets, such as logos, the organization faces two hurdles. First, the level of services required of the tax-exempt organization must be analyzed to determine if they will be classified as minimal. Second, the organization has to decide if it is willing to litigate the issue if audited by the IRS.

Because of the complexity of this issue and the strong stance of the IRS, it is strongly recommended that any tax-exempt organization involved in, or considering, such an arrangement consult nonprofit counsel.

Income from travel tours: Religious nonprofits frequently offer travel tours, ostensibly as a religious and educational experience. The IRS endeavors to differentiate between tours that are related activities and those that are unrelated (competitive) because they are primarily social, recreational, or other forms of vacation opportunities.

In 2000, the IRS issued regulations addressing this concern. These regulations contain examples that provide several factors to be considered in determining whether a travel tour is an exempt activity or an unrelated business activity resulting in taxable unrelated business income. Although the IRS examples are fairly black and white, the factors to be considered in determining whether the income is exempt from UBI tax are helpful. These factors are to be considered under a general "facts-and-circumstances" test.

The following are examples of questions a religious nonprofit should ask when considering a tour:

* Does the trip contribute significantly to the religious nonprofit's exempt purpose? (In other words, what is the organization trying to accomplish?)
* Will there be scheduled instruction or other religious activity that furthers the organization's exempt purpose?
* Will the tour guide be knowledgeable in the area of the activity?
* Will the promotional materials emphasize the educational or other exempt purpose of the trip?
* Will the instruction or other activity furthering the religious nonprofit's exempt purpose take up a significant amount of time in proportion to personal time?
* Will educational or other related materials be provided during the trip?
* Will the organization keep timely documentation of how the trip met its exempt purpose?

NOTE: Keep in mind that the IRS does not give any factor more weight than any other but will look at all aspects in deciding whether the trip qualifies as an exempt activity.

Corporate sponsorships: Prior to the Taxpayer Relief Act of 1997, the IRS took the position that corporate sponsorship of a tax-exempt organization's activities was an unrelated business activity. The 1997 act provided a safe harbor for certain sponsorship payments. Thus, payments from a person engaged in a trade or business are not considered UBI if they are *qualified sponsorship payments.*

Qualified sponsorship payments are defined as payments made by an entity in return for the sole benefit of the use or acknowledgment of its name, logo, or product lines in connection with the tax-exempt organization's activities. They do not include payments entitling the entity to the use of its name, logo, or product lines in periodicals of the tax-exempt organization or payments made in connection with conventions or tradeshows. Additionally, they do not include payments contingent on the attendance level at the event or other degree of public exposure.

Qualified sponsorship payments generally do include those received for distributing or displaying the entity's products at a sponsored event. However, regulations state that if the sponsor receives a substantial benefit in return for the payment, the portion of the payment allocable to the substantial benefit is considered unrelated business income, not a qualified sponsorship payment. If the amount allocable to the qualified sponsorship payment cannot be determined, the entire amount is unrelated business income. Pursuant to the regulations, a benefit is substantial if it exceeds 2 percent of the sponsorship payment.

Qualified sponsorship payments also include payments received for using the entity's name or logo in acknowledging the entity's support for a tax-exempt organization's fundraising or educational event. Advertising is not considered a qualified sponsorship payment.

 NOTE: It is possible to structure a transaction so that part of the payment is attributed to advertising and part to a qualified payment. For example, a religious nonprofit provides a program for each concert during a tour. A for-profit organization is recognized in the program for its support in exchange for a cash payment. The promotion in the program contains the phrase "Visit our web site for the finest selection of music CDs and cassettes." A poster is also displayed in the lobby of the organization during each concert. The poster states only that the concert is sponsored by the for-profit entity and lists its address and telephone number. The amount of the payment allocable to the benefit of the program would be considered advertising and as such would be unrelated business income, while the portion of the payment allocable to the poster would be a qualified sponsorship payment. The problem in this case would be determining the allocation between the two benefits. If such an allocation cannot be made, the entire payment must be classified as advertising.

Low-cost articles: The distribution of low-cost articles in association with the solicitation of contributions is not an unrelated business activity. This exception applies only if the cost of all articles distributed to a single donor in one year does not exceed $8.90 for 2007 (adjusted for inflation). These items must be unsolicited, and the recipient must have the right to keep the article even if he or she does not make a donation. This exception allows exempt organizations to provide premiums when soliciting donations under the safe harbor rule for contributions and other receipts.

Sales of donated merchandise: Sales of merchandise, substantially all of which has been received as contributions, is not an unrelated business activity. Accordingly, if a church or ministry wishes to open a thrift store that sells donated clothes, it would not pay UBI tax on the income from the store.

23.29 How do the unrelated business rules apply in the context of charitable fundraising?

There are instances when an activity is deemed a fundraising event, although technically it is an unrelated business. There are, however, a host of exceptions that shield the resulting income from taxation. The principal exceptions are for activities that are not regularly carried on, the volunteer exception, and the exception for donated goods.

Another area of unrelated income taxation that entails charitable fundraising is the rental and exchange of mailing lists (those of donors and/or members). Where the parties to the transaction are eligible to receive tax-deductible contributions (chiefly, charitable and veterans' organizations), the resulting revenue is not taxed. Otherwise, the net funds from the transaction are taxable, unless the monies can be cast as royalties. Even in instances where lists are simply exchanged (that is, there is no transfer of money), it is the view of the IRS that a taxable transaction occurs (unless the exception applies), with the amount "received" being the fair market value of the list received; usually there are no offsetting deductible amounts.

23.30 How is the unrelated income tax reported?

The unrelated business income tax is calculated and reported on the unrelated business income tax return (Form 990-T). This is a public document that must be made available by the tax-exempt organization to anyone who properly requests a copy of the return.

CHAPTER 24

IRS Audits of Religious Nonprofit Organizations

24.1 Should a religious nonprofit organization be concerned about accumulating a large amount of net assets or large fund balance?

Yes, they should be somewhat concerned. There is no law that places a restriction on the amount of money or property that an exempt organization can accumulate. At the same time, a large and growing accumulation of assets can be a signal that inadequate or infrequent exempt functions are taking place.

Occasionally, the IRS supplies what is known as the *commensurate test*. The agency compares an organization's program activities with the extent of its financial resources to see if it is doing enough in the way of exempt functions. A large fund balance accumulation is an element that the IRS would take into consideration in applying this test.

A factor to take into account in this context is the reason for the accumulation. The organization may denominate some or all of these assets as an endowment fund, a building fund, or some other reserve. This can go a long way in dispelling concerns about what may otherwise appear to be an unreasonable accumulation.

24.2 Are there special rules pertaining to the IRS's audits of religious nonprofit organizations?

Generally, there are no special rules pertaining to the IRS's audits of religious nonprofit organizations; the normal audit rules apply. As it pertains to churches, however, Congress has imposed special limitations on how and when the IRS may conduct *church tax inquiries* and *church tax examinations* of churches. For these purposes, a church includes any organization claiming to be a church or a convention or association of churches, but the term does not include church-supported schools or other organizations that are incorporated separately from the church.

24.3   How is the IRS organized from the standpoint of its audit function?

The IRS, an agency of the Department of the Treasury, is administered at the national level by its office in Washington, DC. This office is headed by a Commissioner of Internal Revenue, who generally superintends the assessment and collection of all taxes imposed by any law providing for federal (internal) revenue. An Oversight Board is responsible for overseeing the IRS in its administration, conduct, direction, and supervision of the execution and application of the internal revenue laws.

The fundamental organization of the IRS involves four operating divisions, one of which is the Tax Exempt and Government Entities (TE/GE) Division. Within this arrangement is the Exempt Organizations Division, which develops policy and administers the law of tax-exempt organizations. The Director of this division, who reports to the Tax Exempt Entities/Government Entities Commissioner, is responsible for planning, managing, and executing nationwide IRS activities in the realm of exempt organizations. The Director also supervises and is responsible for the programs of the offices of Customer Education and Outreach, Rulings and Agreements, Examinations, and Exempt Organizations Electronic Initiatives.

Another component of the IRS at the national level is the Office of the IRS Chief Counsel, which is part of the Legal Division of the Treasury Department. The Chief Counsel is the principal legal advisor on federal tax matters to the Commissioner. Among the Associate Chief Counsels is the Associate Chief Counsel (Employee Benefits and Exempt Organizations). One of the functions of this Associate Chief Counsel's office, which includes an Assistant Chief Counsel with direct responsibility in the exempt organizations area, is to develop legal policy and strategy in the field of tax-exempt organizations.

The Examinations office, based in Dallas, Texas, focuses on exempt organizations examinations programs and review projects. Its support functions include Examination Planning and Programs, Classification, Mandatory Review, Special Review, and Examinations Special Support. The TE/GE strategic plan calls for improvement of the presence of the IRS in the exempt organizations community to promote greater overall law compliance and fairness in the sector. The IRS is working to balance its workforce resources between the examination and determination functions, and to develop more effective methods of allocating and utilizing Examinations resources.

One of the agency's initiatives in this area is establishment of an Exempt Organizations Compliance Unit, to address exempt organizations customer compliance using correspondence and telephone contacts. Another new component of this office is the Data Analysis Unit, which is using various databases and other information to investigate emerging compliance trends to improve the identification and selection of source work in the exempt organizations area.

24.4 What is the IRS Whistleblower Office?

The IRS Whistleblower Office, which was established by the Tax Relief and Health Care Act of 2006, acts to process tips received from individuals who spot tax problems in their workplace (including religious nonprofit organizations) while conducting day-to-day personal business or anywhere else they may be encountered. To encourage individuals to step forward as whistleblowers, the office offers rewards worth between 5 percent and 30 percent of the total proceeds that the IRS collects if the IRS moves ahead based on the information provided.

On February 2, 2007, the Internal Revenue Service named a director of its new Whistleblower Office. The director is responsible for administering the program designed to receive information that helps uncover tax cheating and to provide appropriate rewards to whistleblowers.

24.5 From where does the IRS derive its audit authority?

The IRS is empowered by statute to audit the activities and records of all persons in the United States, including tax-exempt organizations. This examination activity is designed to ensure that exempt organizations and other persons are in compliance with all pertinent requirements of the federal tax law.

24.6 What issues are addressed in a religious nonexempt organizations audit?

An IRS audit of this type of organization may address matters such as continuation of tax-exempt status, private inurement and/or private benefit, ongoing non-private foundation status, legislative and/or political campaign activities, susceptibility to the tax on unrelated business income, deferred compensation and retirement programs, tax-exempt bond financing, and employment tax issues.

24.7 Why is an IRS audit initiated?

Although the IRS, from time to time, initiates audits of particular types of tax-exempt organizations (such as churches, religious organizations, health-care organizations, associations, colleges and universities, and private foundations) as a matter of national policy, audits are typically commenced based on the size of the entity and the length of time that has elapsed since any prior audit. Often an audit is commenced as the result of an examination of an information or tax return; one of the functions of the IRS is to ascertain the correctness of returns. Other reasons for the development of an audit include complaints filed by disgruntled (often former) employees, media or third-party reports of alleged wrongdoing by a taxpayer, selection based on a person's claim for a refund of taxes, or selection as part of an IRS program to focus on a particular problem area (often termed an *industry* by the IRS).

NOTE: Examples of audits of the latter category that are taking place at this time are of entities that are suspected of paying excessive amounts of compensation to their executive personnel, public charities (including religious organizations) that may be engaged in political campaign activity, charitable organizations that are not properly reporting fundraising results and excess benefit transactions, and exempt organizations directly involved in or accommodating abusive tax shelters.

24.8 How is an IRS audit initiated?

An IRS audit is usually initiated in the field, under the auspices of the appropriate district office. The examiners involved are specialists in tax-exempt organization matters and function under the direction of a supervisor in the district office.

NOTE: The IRS prepared material to guide national headquarters and field personnel who have responsibilities for the examination of tax-exempt organizations. This material, which is publicly available, is known as the *Exempt Organizations Examination Guidelines Handbook*.

The Exempt Organizations Division at the National Office of the IRS has the responsibility for establishing the procedures and policy for the conduct of exempt organization audit programs.

24.9 What items of a tax-exempt organization will the IRS review on audit?

The IRS is authorized to examine any books, papers, records, or other data that may be relevant or material to an inquiry. The records that must be produced during an audit of a tax-exempt organization will likely include all organizational documents (such as articles of organization, bylaws, resolutions, and minutes of meetings), documents relating to tax status (such as any application for recognition of tax exemption and IRS determinations as to exempt and private status), financial statements (including underlying books and records), recent annual information returns, and newsletters, journals, and other publications. Other items that may be requested will depend on the type of audit being conducted; the audit may or may not encompass payroll records, pension and retirement plans, returns of affiliated organizations, and the like. In some instances, an organization may find it appropriate to produce information only on the presentation of a summons.

24.10 Are there different types of IRS audits?

Yes. Some examinations are *office examinations,* where contact between the IRS and a taxpayer is by IRS office interview. A *correspondence audit* involves an IRS request for additional information from a taxpayer by letter, fax, or e-mail correspondence. Other examinations are *field examinations,* in which one or more IRS agents review the books and records of the taxpayer on the taxpayer's premises. IRS audits of tax-exempt organizations of any consequence are field examinations.

One of the problems with IRS audit practices in the past was that a typical audit focused on a single organization, ignoring subsidiaries and other affiliates and joint ventures. This deficiency (from the government's viewpoint) was remedied with the development of the *coordinated examination program* (CEP), where complex issues were addressed and managed using a team audit approach. The objectives of the CEP were to (1) perform effectively planned and managed coordinated examinations, (2) secure support for district assistance where appropriate, and (3) accumulate and disseminate novel examination techniques, issues unique to specific organizations, tax avoidance and evasion schemes, and other useful examination information.

The coordinated examination program has been phased out; its replacement is the *team examination program* (TEP). The TEP audit is utilized in connection with a wider array of exempt organizations than was the case with the coordinated examination program. The IRS identifies, then examines, TEP entities entailing significant potential noncompliance. Field examinations of large, complex organizations, which require coordination among IRS functions (and perhaps other government agencies), will be conducted using team audit procedures.

NOTE: Early experience indicates that the TEP approach may utilize fewer personnel and not last as long. With the CEP audit, agents often established offices within the exempt organization; that does not seem to be happening with TEP audits.

Another relatively contemporary IRS examination technique is the *package audit.* This type of audit arises out of the review of one or more annual information returns and/or unrelated business income tax returns. It entails ascertaining whether the exempt organization is filing or has filed all other required federal tax returns, such as the employment tax returns, other information returns, employee benefit plan returns, and the returns of related entities.

24.11 **How does an exempt organization cope with IRS personnel during an audit?**

Carefully and courteously. The techniques for coping with IRS personnel on the occasion of an audit are easily summarized, but their deployment and success are likely to depend heavily on the personalities involved. The key staff personnel, accountants, and legal counsel of the audited organization should be involved in the process from the beginning, and it is advisable to select one individual who will serve as liaison with the IRS during the audit. The projected duration of the audit and the procedures that are to be followed by the parties involved should be ascertained at the outset, and records should be carefully maintained as information and documents are examined or copied by the revenue agents. All interviews of those associated with the audited organization should be monitored by the liaison individual, with appropriate records made of each interview. At least some of the questioning should occur only in the presence of legal counsel.

Where issues arise, one or both sides may decide to pursue the technical advice procedure.

24.12 **What does the IRS do after the audit has been completed?**

If the organization is required to file an annual information return (Form 990), on completion of an audit the IRS will take one of three actions:

1. If the IRS determines that there are no inaccuracies with the taxpayer's return, the taxpayer will be issued a *no-change letter,* which indicates that no change is being made to the taxpayer's tax liability as reported.
2. If the IRS determines that the taxpayer has overpaid tax, the IRS will issue an over-adjustment entitling the taxpayer to a tax refund.
3. If the IRS determines that there is a deficiency in the amount of tax paid or reported by the taxpayer, or some other taxpayer error (such as a failure to file a required tax form), the IRS agent will present the taxpayer with findings that assert a deficiency in tax. If the taxpayer agrees with the alleged deficiency, a form can be executed and the taxpayer is sent a statement for the additional tax owed. If the taxpayer disagrees with the IRS on the point, the collections process will commence.

If the organization is a church or convention or association of churches and, as such, not required to file an annual information return, then special rules apply.

24.13 **What is the likelihood that a tax-exempt organization will be audited by the IRS?**

Overall, the likelihood that an exempt organization will be audited by the IRS is remote. The IRS has limited audit resources, and the number of tax-exempt organizations is increasing. The IRS simply does not have the personnel to audit all exempt organizations on a regular basis. Nonetheless, the IRS is increasing its general examination and compliance check project efforts, with more audit activity today than has been seen in several years. Consequently, the IRS audit focus is confined to the larger organizations or those within a targeted industry or field.

24.14 Can the IRS prevent abuse by tax-exempt organizations by means other than examination and revocation of exempt status?

Yes, but this remedy is limited. The IRS now has the authority (as of late 2003) to *suspend* the tax-exempt status of an organization that has been designated as supporting or engaging in terrorist activity or supporting terrorism. Contributions made to an organization during the period of suspension of exemption are not deductible for federal tax purposes.

Specifically, federal income tax exemption and the eligibility of an organization to apply for recognition of exemption must be suspended for a particular period if it is a terrorist organization. Contributions to such an organization are not deductible during the period, for income, estate, and gift tax purposes.

An organization is a *terrorist organization* if it is designated or otherwise individually identified (1) under provisions of the Immigration and Nationality Act as a terrorist organization or foreign terrorist organization, (2) in or pursuant to an executive order that is related to terrorism and issued under the authority of the International Emergency Economic Powers Act or the United Nations Participation Act for the purpose of imposing on such organization an economic or other sanction, or (3) in or pursuant to an executive order issued under the authority of any federal law, if the organization is designated or otherwise individually identified in or pursuant to the executive order as supporting or engaging in terrorist activity or supporting terrorism, and the executive order refers to this federal law.

The period of suspension of tax exemption begins on the date of the first publication by the IRS of a designation or identification with respect to the organization and ends on the first date that all designations and identifications with respect to the organization are rescinded pursuant to the applicable statutory law or executive order.

A person may not challenge a suspension of tax exemption, a designation or identification of an entity as a terrorist organization, the period of a suspension, or a denial of a charitable deduction in this context in an administrative or judicial proceeding. This law provides for a refund or credit of income tax (if necessary) in the case of an erroneous designation or identification of an entity as a terrorist organization.

24.15 Are there special rules pertaining to the IRS's audit of a church?

Yes. Congress has imposed special limitations on how and when the IRS may conduct *church tax inquiries* and *church tax examinations* of churches. For these purposes, a church includes any organization claiming to be a church or a convention or association of churches, but the term does not include church-supported schools or other organizations that are incorporated separately from the church.

24.16 What are the restrictions on church tax inquiries and examinations?

The restrictions on church tax inquiries and examinations are found in IRC Section 7611 (§ 7611). As a result of § 7611, the IRS has scaled back authorities with respect to a church and may only initiate a church tax inquiry if the Director, Exempt Organizations, Examinations, reasonably believes, based on a written statement of the facts and circumstances, that the organization (1) may not qualify for exemption or (2) may not be paying tax on an unrelated or other taxable activity.

Restrictions on church tax inquiries and church tax examinations found in § 7611 do not apply to all church inquiries by the IRS. The most common exception relates to routine requests for information. For example, the IRS requests information from churches about filing of returns, compliance with income or Social Security and Medicare tax withholding requirements, supplemental information needed to process returns or applications, and other similar inquiries.

Restrictions on church tax inquiries and church tax examinations do not apply to criminal investigations or to investigations of the tax liability of any person connected with the church (e.g., a contributor or minister).

24.17 What is a *church tax inquiry*?

A church tax inquiry—an inquiry of a church's tax liabilities—commences when the IRS requests information or materials from a church of a type contained in church records, other than routine requests for information or inquiries regarding matters that do not primarily concern the tax status or liability of the church.

Prior to commencement of an investigation, the IRS is required to provide written notice to the church, containing a general explanation of the federal statutory tax law provisions authorizing the investigation or that may otherwise be involved in the inquiry, a general explanation of the church's administrative and constitutional rights in connection with the audit (including the right to a conference with the IRS before any examination of church records), and an explanation of the concerns that gave rise to the investigation and the general subject matter of the inquiry.

Despite these requirements, however, the IRS is displaying a remarkable—and dismaying—propensity to ignore one or more of these rules and launch a church tax inquiry in much the same manner as the agency would commence an audit of any other type of tax-exempt organization. The church is allowed a reasonable period in which to respond by furnishing a written explanation to alleviate IRS concerns. If the church fails to respond within the required time, or if its response is not sufficient to alleviate IRS concerns, the IRS may, generally within 90 days, issue a second notice informing the church of the need to examine its books and records.

24.18 What is a *church tax examination*?

A church tax examination—an examination of church records or religious activities—may commence only if, at least 15 days prior to the examination, the IRS provides written notice to the church, and to the appropriate IRS regional counsel, of the proposed examination. This notice is in addition to the notice of commencement of a church tax inquiry previously provided to the church.

The notice of examination must contain a copy of the notice of church tax inquiry previously provided to the church; a description of the church records and activities that the IRS seeks to examine; and a copy of all documents collected or prepared by the agency for use in the examination and that are subject to disclosure under the Freedom of Information Act.

24.19 What is the *conference of right* and what is its purpose?

The IRS is required, as part of the notice of examination, to offer the church an opportunity to meet with an IRS official to discuss, and attempt to resolve, the concerns that gave rise to the examination and the general subject matter of the inquiry. The organization may request this meeting at any time prior to the examination. If the church requests a meeting, the IRS is required to schedule the meeting within a reasonable time and may proceed to examine church records only following a meeting. This meeting is commonly referred to as the *conference of right*.

The purpose of the meeting between the church and the IRS is to discuss the relevant issues that may arise as part of the inquiry, in an effort to resolve the issues of tax exemption or liability without the necessity of an examination of church records. The church and the IRS are expected to make a reasonable effort to resolve outstanding issues at the meeting, and the IRS is expected to remind the church at the meeting, in general terms, of the stages of the church audit procedures and the church's right under such procedures.

24.20 What *church records* may be examined by the IRS during an audit?

The IRS may examine *church records* only to the extent necessary to determine the liability for, and the amount of, any federal tax. This may include examinations to determine the initial or continuing qualification of the organization as a tax-exempt entity, to determine whether the organization qualifies to receive tax-deductible contributions, or to determine the amount of tax, if any, to be imposed on the organization.

All regularly kept church corporate and financial records, including corporate minute books, contributor lists, membership lists, and private correspondence between the church and its members in the possession of the church constitute *church records*.

For examinations regarding revocation of tax-exempt status, where no return is filed, the IRS is limited initially to an examination of church records that are relevant to a determination of tax status or liability for the three most recent taxable years preceding the date on which the notice of examination (the second notice) is sent to the church. If the church is proven to not be exempt for any of these years, the IRS may examine relevant records and assess tax (or proceed without assessment), as part of the same audit, for a total of six years preceding the notice of examination date.

24.21 Can the IRS examine the religious content and activities of a church during its tax inquiry and/or audit?

For § 7611 purposes, a church includes any organization claiming to be a church. As such, only in the rare instance that an IRS examining office possesses information establishing that an organization's claim to church status is frivolous may religious content and activities be examined, and then, only to the extent necessary to determine whether the organization claiming church status is, in point of fact, a church.

The First Amendment prohibits the government from restricting the free exercise of religion. The courts have interpreted the First Amendment as providing for an absolute freedom of religious belief. Thus, IRS personnel engaged in church tax inquiries or examinations may not question or evaluate the content of a religious belief. However, actions undertaken as a result of religious beliefs are subject to government regulation, including taxation, when such actions implicate a compelling government interest. The government regulation of religiously motivated conduct, however, is restricted to the extent necessary to enforce that interest. Religiously motivated conduct that violates federal, state, or local law may be restricted or prohibited entirely. Although churches and religious organizations are generally exempt from income tax, certain activities of a church may be subject to tax, such as income from an unrelated business. A church may lose its tax-exempt status by engaging in conduct that violates the restrictions of the Internal Revenue Code.

24.22 What is the deadline for completing any church tax inquiry or examination?

In accordance with § 7611, the IRS is required to complete any church tax inquiry or examination, and make a final determination with respect to the examination or inquiry, not later than two years after the date on which the notice of examination is supplied to the church.

The running of this two-year period is suspended for any period during which (1) a judicial proceeding brought by the church against the IRS with respect to the church tax inquiry or examination is pending or being appealed, (2) a judicial proceeding brought by the IRS against the church or any official of the church to compel compliance with any reasonable IRS request for examination of church records or religious activities is pending or being appealed, or (3) the IRS is unable to take actions with respect to the church tax inquiry or examination by reason of an order issued in a suit involving access to third-party records. The two-year period is also suspended for any period in excess of 20 days, but not in excess of 6 months, in which the church fails to comply with any reasonable IRS request for church records or other information.

This two-year period can be extended by mutual agreement of the church and the IRS.

24.23 What is the remedy should the IRS violate any of the church audit provisions?

The exclusive remedy for any IRS violation of the § 7611 church audit procedures is as follows: Failure of the agency to substantially comply with (1) the requirement that two notices be sent to the church, (2) the requirement that the appropriate IRS representative approve the commencement of a church tax inquiry, or (3) the requirement that offer of an IRS conference with the church be made (and a conference held if requested), will result in a stay of proceedings in a summons proceeding to gain access to church records (but not in dismissal of the proceeding) until a court determines that these requirements have been satisfied. The two-year limitation on the duration of a church audit is not suspended during these stays of summons proceedings; however, the IRS may correct the violations without regard to the otherwise applicable time limits prescribed under the § 7611 procedures.

Otherwise, there is no judicial remedy for IRS violation of the church examination procedures contained in § 7611. The failure of the IRS to comply with these rules may not be raised as a defense or as an affirmative ground for relief in a judicial proceeding.

PART IV

The Constitution, Religious Freedom, and Interaction with the Government

CHAPTER 25

Protection of Religious Liberties

25.1 **What is the source of constitutional protection of religious liberties?**

The *religion clause* in the First Amendment of the Constitution is the source of protection for religious liberties. The *Free Exercise Clause of the First Amendment* taken with the *Establishment Clause of the First Amendment* makes up the religion clause.

The clause reads in full: "Congress shall make no law respecting an *establishment* of religion, or prohibiting the *free exercise* thereof."

The Constitution, along with the Bill of Rights, introduced a new relationship between government and religion through the adoption of the First Amendment's religion clause. Prior to 1789, when the First Amendment was first proposed, and 1791, when it was actually ratified, almost every European country maintained a close relationship between church and state. James Madison, one of the drafters of the First Amendment, believed that all religions would flourish when the government did not promote some religious beliefs to the exclusion of others.

The Free Exercise Clause has often been interpreted to include two freedoms: (1) the freedom to believe, and (2) the freedom to act. The former liberty is said to be absolute, while the latter often faces governmental restriction.

The Establishment Clause has been interpreted as the prohibition of (1) the establishment of a national religion by Congress and (2) the preference of one religion over another or of religion over nonreligious philosophies, in general.

25.2 **What is the primary test(s) that all law or government action must pass so as not to violate the Establishment Clause?**

Since 1971, the federal courts have utilized the three-pronged *Lemon test* (see *Lemon v. Kurtzman*, 403 U.S. 602 (1971)), to ensure the separation of the government and religion.

Under the Lemon test, a court must ask:

1. Whether the government's action has a secular or a religious purpose;
2. Whether the primary effect of the government's action is to advance or endorse religion; and
3. Whether the government's policy or practice fosters an excessive entanglement between government and religion.

If any of these three prongs is violated, the government's action is deemed unconstitutional under the Establishment Clause of the First Amendment to the United States Constitution. In recent years, the Supreme Court has also asked whether the governmental action in question constitutes a prohibited endorsement of religion, thus violating the Establishment Clause. According to the *endorsement test*, a government action is invalid if it creates a perception in the mind of a reasonable person that the government is either endorsing or disapproving of religion.

25.3 What is the test(s) applied by the Supreme Court toward an individual's right to freely exercise religious beliefs?

Constitutional questions regarding the right to freely exercise one's religion generally arise when a civic obligation to comply with a law conflicts with a citizen's religious practices or beliefs. If a law specifically targets a particular religion or particular religious practice, under the current state of the Supreme Court's rulings, it would violate the First Amendment. Debate arises when a law is generally applicable and religiously neutral but, nevertheless, has the effect of "accidentally" or "unintentionally" interfering with a particular religious practice or belief.

The Supreme Court has been closely divided on interpretation of the rights conveyed by the free exercise clause. In 1990, in a controversial opinion, the Court greatly narrowed a 35-year-old constitutional doctrine that had required a government entity to prove that it had a *compelling interest* whenever a generally applicable law was found to infringe on a claimant's religious beliefs or practices. According to current constitutional law principles, a government burden on a religious belief or practice requires little justification as long as the law in question is determined to be *generally applicable* and *neutral,* meaning it does not target a specific religion or religious practice. Moreover, the Court has ruled that it would no longer give *heightened scrutiny* to the government's refusal to grant exemptions to generally applicable laws that unintentionally burden religious beliefs or practices.

The Court's decision to narrow the compelling interest test resulted in Congress's passage of the Religious Freedom Restoration Act (RFRA). The Act, which was signed by President Clinton on November 17, 1993, restored the over-three-decades-old compelling-interest test that government must meet when a generally applicable law unintentionally burdened a claimant's religious practices and beliefs and ensured its application in all cases where religious exercise is substantially burdened.

25.4 What rights did Congress intend to confer on individuals in passing the *Religious Freedom Restoration Act* (RFRA)?

The legislation contained in the RFRA was widely supported by the public and sought to restore the compelling interest test that government must meet when a generally applicable law unintentionally burdened a claimant's religious practices and beliefs and ensured its application in all cases where religious exercise is substantially burdened. The RFRA was short-lived, however. In 1997, the Supreme Court struck down the provisions of the Act, holding that it forced state and local governments to provide more protections than required by the First Amendment. The RFRA still remains applicable to federal statutes, which must meet the compelling interest standard in free-exercise cases. Several states have, however, passed their own version of RFRA, all of which reinstate the compelling interest test to varying degrees.

25.5 Our country's Constitution prohibits the government from establishing *it* and, at the same time, protects the rights of its citizenry to engage in *its* free exercise; federal, state, and local laws protect against discrimination based on *it*, while giving organizations that promote *it* preferential tax treatment. *Religion*, what is its definition?

It is difficult to define what religion is, and what it is not. Local, state, and federal laws use the term *religion* as does the Internal Revenue Code, the Civil Rights Act of 1964, and countless court cases. The federal income tax law provides for tax exemption for religious organizations, yet, there is no statutory or regulatory definition of the terms *religious* or *religion* for this purpose. Indeed, because of the religion clauses of the First Amendment, it would be unconstitutional for the federal government to adopt and apply a strict definition of the term. Nonetheless, government officials, judges, and justices have, from time to time, grappled with the meaning of the term *religion.*

This definitional challenge is not limited to the courts, Congress, or the Internal Revenue Service; and academia wrestles with defining religion as well.

The *Encyclopedia of Religion* defines religion this way:

> In summary, it may be said that almost every known culture involves the religious in the above sense of a depth dimension in cultural experiences at all levels—a push, whether ill-defined or conscious, toward some sort of ultimacy and transcendence that will provide norms and power for the rest of life. When more or less distinct patterns of behavior are built around this depth dimension in a culture, this structure constitutes religion in its historically recognizable form. Religion is the organization of life around the depth dimensions of experience—varied in form, completeness, and clarity in accordance with the environing culture. [*Religion* (First Edition). Winston King. *Encyclopedia of Religion*, ed. Lindsay Jones, vol. 11, 2nd ed. Detroit: Macmillan Reference USA, 2005, pp. 7692–7701.]

25.6   To qualify as a religious organization, must the organization propagate a belief in God or the existence a Supreme Being?

No. The United States Supreme Court interprets the term *religion* broadly and does not include as a requirement the belief in the existence of God or a Supreme Being or that religions need be based on a belief in the existence of God. In 1961, the Court stated that "neither [the federal nor state government] can constitutionally pass laws or impose requirements which aid all religions as against nonbelievers, and neither can aid those religions based on a belief in the existence of God as against those religions founded on different beliefs." The Court noted that "among religions in this country which do not teach what would generally be considered as a belief in the existence of God are Buddhism, Taoism, Ethical Culture, Secular Humanism and others."

25.7   Is the display of the Ten Commandments and other religious symbols on public property constitutional?

The placement of religious symbols on public property has been heavily litigated as implicating of the Establishment Clause, the Free Exercise Clause, and the Free Speech Clause of the Constitution. The most frequently used test for analysis of religious display cases is the *Lemon test*. Under the Lemon test, a court must ask (1) whether the government's action has a secular or a religious purpose; (2) whether the primary effect of the government's action is to advance or endorse religion; and (3) whether the government's policy or practice fosters an excessive entanglement between government and religion. If any of these three prongs is violated, the government's action is deemed unconstitutional under the Establishment Clause of the First Amendment to the United States Constitution.

In 1989, the Court held that religious display cases must be analyzed on a case-by-case basis, taking into account the history and circumstances surrounding the religious display to determine whether it violated the First Amendment. The case-by-case approach was affirmed in 2005 by the Court when it decided two cases regarding the display of the Ten Commandments. In one case from Texas, the Court found the display was constitutional and in a case from Kentucky the Court found the display to be unconstitutional. It is fair to say that the state of the law in the area of displays of religious symbols on public property is uncertain, unsettled, and certain to receive additional attention by the Court.

25.8   Is it constitutional for the government to place the words "In God We Trust" on its currency and on public buildings, and "under God" in the classrooms of public schools via the pledge of allegiance?

The legend, "In God We Trust," became a part of the design of United States currency in 1957 and has appeared on all currency since 1963. President Dwight D. Eisenhower signed the act that added the phrase "under God" in the Pledge of Allegiance; he also announced "(f)rom this day forward, the millions of our school children will daily proclaim in every city and town, every village and rural schoolhouse, the dedication of our Nation and our people to the Almighty."

Today, the governmental use of the word "God" is a source of debate and contention. Opponents of the phrases "In God We Trust" and "under God" argue that the religion clauses of the First Amendment require that the mottos be removed from all public use, on coins and paper money, and the Pledge. Opponents of the usage argue that religious freedom includes the right not to believe in the existence of deities and that the gratuitous use of the word *God* infringes on the religious rights of the unreligious and that an endorsement of any deity by the government is unconstitutional.

On June 14, 2004, Chief Justice William Rehnquist wrote a majority opinion that asserts the phrase "under God" does not endorse or establish religion. Instead, the opinion asserts that the phrase merely acknowledges the nation's religious heritage, in particular the role of religion for the Founding Fathers of the United States. Thus, inclusion of the words "under God" in the Pledge (and by logical extension, its placement on public buildings or government currency) is a secular act rather than an act of indoctrination in religion or expression of religious devotion.

25.9 Can the government display a nativity scene or Chanukah menorah during the holiday season without violating the Establishment Clause?

Yes. The display of nativity scenes on public property takes one of two forms: publicly sponsored and privately sponsored, both of which can be displayed on public property. A privately sponsored nativity scene is one that is erected and maintained by private citizens. Courts have held that both are constitutional, and both can be displayed on public property. The main difference is that a publicly sponsored nativity scene should have some form of secular display in the same context, while a privately sponsored nativity scene need not have any secular symbols, but should have a disclaimer indicating that the display is privately sponsored.

25.10 Can the government refuse to rent or prohibit the use of public facilities to religious nonprofit organizations solely because the meetings conducted by the organization promote a particular religious tenet or belief?

No. Numerous federal and state courts have held that if public facilities are made available to nonreligious groups, they must also be made available to religious groups without limitation.

25.11 Is prayer in public schools constitutional?

No. The Supreme Court's decisions over the past 40 years set forth principles that distinguish impermissible governmental religious speech from the constitutionally protected private religious speech of students.

For example, teachers and other public school officials may not lead their classes in prayer, devotional readings from the Bible, or other religious activities. Nor may school officials attempt to persuade or compel students to participate in prayer or other religious activities. Such conduct is, according to the Court, "attributable to the State" and thus violates the Establishment Clause.

Although the Constitution forbids public school officials from directing or favoring prayer, students do not "shed their constitutional rights to freedom of speech or expression at the schoolhouse gate." In addition, the Supreme Court has made clear that "private religious speech, far from being a First Amendment orphan, is as fully protected under the Free Speech Clause as secular private expression." Moreover, not all religious speech that takes place in the public schools or at school-sponsored events is governmental speech. For example, according to the Supreme Court, "nothing in the Constitution . . . prohibits any public school student from voluntarily praying at any time before, during, or after the school day," and students may pray with fellow students during the school day on the same terms and conditions that they may engage in other conversation or speech (for example, "Meet-You-at-the-Pole" prayer events held at the flagpoles of public schools).

25.12   Is prayer at public school sporting events, such as football games, constitutional?

No. In 2000, the Supreme Court ruled that a policy permitting student-led, student-initiated prayer at football games violates the Establishment Clause of the First Amendment. The Court held the policy unconstitutional by a six-to-three decision. School prayer remains a controversial topic in American jurisprudence.

25.13   Is prayer at public schools' graduation ceremonies constitutional?

No. In 1992, the Supreme Court ruled that employees of a public school district may not induce, endorse, assist, or promote prayer at their graduation ceremonies. This would forbid prayers presented by a school principal, a teacher, or a minister from the community. Judge Anthony Kennedy prepared the majority opinion. In that case, he wrote that the "Constitution forbids the State to exact religious conformity from a student as the price of attending her own high school graduation."

The school principal in this case had decided to include an invocation and benediction during the ceremony. He chose a minister from the community to give these prayers and provided him with a copy of a publication entitled *Guidelines for Civic Occasions.* It contained suggestions for the delivery of non-sectarian prayers.

CHAPTER 26

Guidance on Partnering with the Federal Government

26.1 **Are religious nonprofit organizations permitted to apply for and receive funds from the government to provide charitable services to the public?**

Yes. Every year the federal government spends billions of dollars for charitable services to the public. As it pertains to religious nonprofit organizations, because of constitutional concerns regarding the separation of church and state, the government has been reluctant—and sometimes made it impossible—for religious-based groups to provide federally funded services. Bureaucratic and administrative technicalities abound. Moreover, government officials are often unfamiliar with the work that faith-based and community groups do. In August 2001, the White House Office of Faith-Based and Community Initiatives (FBCI) released a report, *Unlevel Playing Field*, that identified many of the barriers that religious nonprofit organizations face in accessing federal funds.

The guiding principle behind FBCI is that religious nonprofit organizations should be able to compete on an equal footing for public dollars to provide public services. Underpinning the FBCI is the belief that the federal government, within the framework of Constitutional church–state guidelines, should encourage religious nonprofit organizations to reach out to help even more people in need.

Religious nonprofit organizations, with the assistance of government funds, serve communities in important ways. For example, more than two-thirds of federally supported residences for the elderly are operated by religious nonprofit organizations. And about one in every six child-care centers in the United States is housed in a religious facility. Moreover, the nation's largest "chains" of child-care services are operated by the Roman Catholic Church and the Southern Baptist Convention. The number of centers in religious facilities is growing faster than the total number of centers. According to government reports, religiously affiliated hospitals received more than $45 billion in 1998 from Medicare, Medicaid, and other governmental funding programs. These statistics demonstrate that the use of government funds by religious nonprofit organizations is not new.

26.2   What kinds of grants are available from the federal government?

The federal government uses two kinds of grants:

1. *Discretionary grants* are grants handed out by an agency of the federal government—for instance, a homeless assistance grant given out by the Department of Health and Human Services to a homeless shelter.
2. *Formula or block grants* are grants that put federal money in the hands of states, cities, or counties for them to distribute to charities and other social service providers, usually under their own rules and regulations.

Religious nonprofit organizations can apply directly to the federal government, or they can apply for funds to a third-party entity that distributes money it receives from the federal government.

 NOTE: More money is available from programs administered by states and localities than from the federal government directly. For example, in 2001, the Department of Health and Human Services awarded $25 billion directly to grant applicants, but it gave $160 billion to states and localities, which in turn made much of this money available to nongovernmental organizations.

26.3   How can a religious nonprofit organization find out about federal grants?

The White House Office of FBCI has prepared a list of general information about more than a hundred programs operated by the Departments of Justice, Agriculture, Labor, Health and Human Services, Housing and Urban Development, Education, and the Agency for International Development. The list—which is available in the brochure *Federal Funding Opportunities for Organizations that Help Those in Need* and at www.fbci.gov—includes programs from these agencies that are of interest to small, grassroots groups. Religious nonprofit organizations can use this list as a starting point to find about opportunities that may interest them.

Once the organization finds a program that interests it, the organization can get more information about when and how to apply for funds from the agency contact in the listing. A religious nonprofit organization can also use the Catalog of Federal Domestic Assistance (CFDA) as a resource. To use the CFDA, locate the CFDA number from the information provided in the list in *Federal Funding Opportunities for Organizations that Help Those in Need.* Enter that number into the "program number" box on the CFDA's web site at http://www.cfda.gov/public/faprs.htm.

26.4 How does a religious nonprofit organization go about applying for a federal grant?

All federal grants must be announced to the public. These announcements (sometimes called a "Program Announcement," "Request for Proposal," "Notice of Funding Availability," or "Solicitation for Grant Applications") are the federal government's attempt at looking for charities and other groups to provide a federally funded service. Each grant announcement contains instructions on how to apply, including where to get an application packet, information necessary for the application, the date the application is due, and agency contact information.

Grant announcements are issued throughout the year. There is no single document that contains every federal grant announcement and no uniform format for these announcements. Currently, most grant announcements are listed in the Federal Register, a daily publication that can be accessed on the Internet (http://www.gpo.gov/su_docs!aces/acesl40.litnml) and at major public libraries. The Catalog of Federal Domestic Assistance (www.cfda.gov) also contains information about grant announcements. In addition, agency web sites contain information on funding opportunities.

Religious nonprofit organizations interested in government funds should check for information on the web site for the White House Office of FBCI (www.fbci.gov), as well as on the web sites for the agency centers.

Many states and cities also have liaisons that can help religious nonprofit organizations identify grant opportunities.

26.5 What if a religious nonprofit organization is a small one and can't afford to hire a grant writer to help it seek a federal grant. Is there any help available for the organization?

Yes. Most federal agencies have staffers who are available to help organizations apply for and manage their grants. Applicants may call the official identified in the grant announcement or contact an agency's regional office. These agency staff are supposed to be available to answer questions over the phone. They may also refer applicants to local or nearby technical assistance workshops or to organizations that are under contract with the federal government to provide this kind of assistance.

Assistance is supposed to be made available from one of the more than thirty organizations funded by the Department of Health and Human Services' Compassion Capital Fund. These organizations are designed to help small religious nonprofit organizations learn about the grant process. They are also supposed to help small groups with other challenges, such as training volunteers and staff or expanding the reach of the services they provide. They do this at no cost to the organization. More information about the Compassion Capital Fund and the organizations it funds is available at www.hhs.gov/fbci.

In addition, many state governments and cities provide grant-writing workshops, as do a number of nonprofit organizations and foundations.

26.6 What are *Charitable Choice* laws?

Charitable Choice is the general name for several laws that President Clinton signed into law during the period of 1996–2000. These laws were designed to give people in need choices among the charities offering them services. The Charitable Choice laws apply to four federal programs: Temporary Assistance to Needy Families (TANF) and the Community Services Block Grant (CSBG) programs (both overseen by the Administration for Children and Families at the United States Department of Health and Human Services (HHS)); programs for substance abuse and mental health (overseen by the Substance Abuse and Mental Health Services Administration (SAMHSA) at HHS); and the Welfare-to Work program (overseen by the Department of Labor).

These laws are designed to clarify both the rights and the responsibilities of religious nonprofit organizations that receive federal funds. They specify that religious nonprofit organizations cannot be excluded from the competition for federal funds simply because they are religious. These laws also provide that religious nonprofit organizations that receive federal funds may continue to carry out their missions consistent with their beliefs. For example, they may maintain a religious environment in their facilities, and they may consider their religious beliefs in hiring and firing employees.

Conversely, the Charitable Choice laws also impose certain restrictions on religious nonprofit organizations. They spell out specific do's and don'ts for religious nonprofit groups receiving federal money. The laws specify that religious organizations that receive federal funds must serve all eligible participants, regardless of those persons' religious beliefs. They also prohibit religious organizations from using federal funds to support any inherently religious activities (such as worship, religious instruction, or proselytization). In addition, recipients of services provided under the SAMHSA and TANF Charitable Choice laws have a right to be provided with services from an alternative provider to whom they have no religious objection.

The Community Service Block Grant and SAMHSA versions of the Charitable Choice laws also require religious organizations to maintain separate accounts for the federal funds they receive.

26.7 Do the Charitable Choice laws mean that religious nonprofit organizations can apply for funds only from these four federal programs?

No. The Charitable Choice laws merely set out guidelines for government funding of religious nonprofit organizations in these four programs. However, all federal programs that permit nonprofit organizations to apply for funds are also open to religious organizations.

26.8 Do the Charitable Choice laws mean that religious nonprofit organizations get "special treatment" by the government?

No. These laws do not set aside government funds for religious nonprofit organizations. Organizations that receive federal funding are held to the same standards as all other providers of services. For example, they must comply with the accounting requirements that apply to other organizations, and they must demonstrate that their organization serves the purposes of the program. These laws merely recognize that religious nonprofit organizations can have a legitimate and vital role to play in the provision of federally funded social services, and attempt to clarify how these programs should be operated.

26.9 What if a religious nonprofit applies for a federal grant, but its request is denied?

It depends. There is no guarantee that an organization will receive a grant if it applies. However, if it does not receive a grant, the organization can try to find out why it did not receive funding and how it could improve a future application. The organization should follow up with the program officer identified in the announcement. This individual should either be able to provide it with information about its application, or point it to the right person to contact. In addition, the organization may request to obtain written comments on its proposal, which could be helpful in making future grant requests. Because many organizations compete for federal funds, many groups apply several times before a reward is received. Getting feedback on its application can help an organization improve its chances of receiving funds.

26.10 What happens if the organization is successful in applying for a grant?

The religious nonprofit organization will receive a grant award notification stating the duration of the award, the dollar amount, and a program contact. It may also receive a set of attachments that outline basic requirements that it must follow as a condition of compliance with the federal or state agency making the grant.

26.11 What can an organization do to ensure it correctly follows the federal and state regulations that apply to the grant?

A religious nonprofit organization should be sure that it uses grant funds only for the intended purposes of the grant program. Being a diligent steward of federal funds will help ensure its projects remain in good standing with the awarding federal or state agency. In addition, the organization should be sure to familiarize itself with the guidance documents, regulations, and requirements specifically associated with the program under which it was awarded a grant.

26.12 Which guidance documents and regulations apply to a grant project?

Program regulations: Program regulations typically will be identified in the Federal Register notice announcing the grant competition or in the larger grant application package. Each program has a set of regulations that govern how grant projects are to be implemented by grantees. Some programs may have very detailed guidance concerning allowable and unallowable costs, spending caps on specific budget categories, and staffing requirements. For example, a program might require a project director to work full-time on the project. Other programs may have few program-specific regulations.

Agency guidance documents: Most federal agencies have issued guidance documents that apply to both their discretionary and formula grant programs. These documents may not be very useful to a religious nonprofit organization while it is researching funding opportunities or applying for a grant program. However, they are extremely helpful for grantees seeking daily administrative guidance. If an award is granted, the awarding agency will provide the organization either with a hard copy of this document or with electronic access to the document.

OMB circulars: The Office of Management and Budget issues documents that are called *circulars.* These circulars are essentially letters of instruction that allow the federal government to address public questions or concerns that apply to all federal agencies. Of greatest interest to grantees are the OMB circulars that apply to cost principles. These circulars provide guidance on specific allowable and unallowable expenditures for a grantee, based on the type of organizational entity it is. The circular that applies to all nonprofits, including religious organizations, is OMB Circular A-122. If, after reviewing the program regulations and the agency guidance documents, a grantee still has a question about whether a given expenditure is allowable, it should refer to OMB Circular A-122.

Although nonprofits should follow the rules in OMB Circular A-122, they may sometimes administer a grant in partnership with organizations that are not nonprofits. The rules that apply to other types of organizations are reflected in the following documents: State and Local Governments and Federally Recognized Tribal Governments OMB Circular A-87, Colleges and Universities (also called *institutions of higher education* or *IHEs*) OMB Circular A-21, Hospitals 45 Code of Federal Regulations (CFR) 74, and For-Profits 48 CFR 31.

26.13 What are some of the legal obligations that accompany a federal grant?

Financial reporting requirements: To make sure that grant funds are used properly, organizations that receive federal funds must file regular financial status reports. These forms should not take long to fill out, but they are important. The basic financial report form is a one-page document called Standard Form 269. Many agencies have adapted this form to suit their own programs.

Cost-sharing, matching: These are two terms that often are used interchangeably with one another. Certain programs have a requirement that grant applicants pledge that they will contribute a certain level of financial support to the project once they are awarded grants and become grantees. The amount of financial support varies from program to program, and not all grant programs have cost-sharing or matching requirements. Whether cost-sharing or matching requirements apply to a particular program will be noted in the Federal Register notice that announces a grant competition for that program. Depending on the particular program, a grantee's cost-share or match may be made in cash, in an in-kind contribution (such as facilities, equipment, and supplies), or in staff time. For example, a program may require a 50 percent match from its grantees. That means that, if a grantee receives a $100,000 award, it will have to bring to the project an additional $50,000 in either cash or some type of in-kind contribution.

Recordkeeping: A religious nonprofit organization will be required to maintain financial and programmatic records for its project for up to three years following the project's conclusion. For example, if it received a grant for a three-year project period that began on October 1, 2006 and ended on September 30, 2009, it would be required to maintain all of the records regarding that grant until September 30, 2012.

Performance reporting: Typically, all grantees will be required to submit to the awarding agency both periodic (usually annual) and final performance reports that detail the project's accomplishments as well as any shortcomings. The awarding agency provides instructions as to the format and the degree of detail that needs to be included in these reports. For grant projects funded for only one year, only a single report may be required. Along with performance reports, some programs require grantees to participate in national evaluation surveys. Such surveys provide information on the national need for and the impact of this particular grant program.

Audit: All religious nonprofit organizations that receive federal funds are subject to basic audit requirements. These audits are intended only to examine the federally funded parts of an organization's operations and are not designed to identify unrelated problems. The audits are necessary to make sure that federal dollars have been spent properly on legitimate costs. It is therefore extremely important for grant recipients to keep accurate records of all transactions conducted with federal funds.

Most organizations are not audited by the government itself, although the federal government has the right to audit any program that receives public money at any time. For example, organizations that spend less than $300,000 a year in federal funds are generally asked only to perform a "self-audit." For organizations that spend a total of $300,000 or more in federal funds (calculated based on awards from all federal programs), an audit by a private, independent outside legal or accounting firm is required.

26.14 What are some of the common problems found by auditors?

Typically, the problems (or "audit exceptions") that auditors identify are a result of a grantee's poor recordkeeping or of the grantee's failure to understand the types of activities or items that may be purchased using grant funds. Although it is very important for the grantee to spend grant funds only on permissible grant expenses, it is equally important that the grantee document the way in which it has spent federal funds. Poor documentation can result in an otherwise successful grantee being unable to demonstrate the effectiveness of its project.

NOTE:

- Tips for maintaining good records include: Document the time and effort of staff working on the grant.
- Maintain an up-to-date inventory that lists all office equipment, supplies, and furniture. Each phone, computer, copier, fax machine, printer, desk, cabinet, and chair purchased by the project or provided by the grantee as in-kind contribution should be placed on such a list.
- Avoid the term miscellaneous. The larger the dollar amount associated with the line item "miscellaneous," the more closely auditors are likely to scrutinize the budget category. If there must be a "miscellaneous" line item in the budget, be sure and provide specific examples of items that are grouped together in this category.
- Justify travel expenses. Travel may be an allowable expense and may even be a mandatory activity under certain grant programs. The organization must ensure that the travel is necessary for the project's success, that grant funds are used to pay only for the travel of essential staff, and that expenses are accurately documented. Be sure and review the travel guidelines in the applicable OMB circulars.

26.15 After a grant project has ended, may an organization keep items it purchased with grant funds?

This depends on the nature of the program and the type and cost of the items in question. In many cases, grantees are allowed to keep the items they purchase after the grant is over so that they may continue running the project without federal funds and because it simply would not be cost effective for the government to remove the items from one grantee and give them to others. There are instances, however, when the government will take title to items, such as research equipment, from a former grantee and provide the items to a new grantee that will be completing the grant project. Grantees should check the specific terms and conditions of their grant and if they have any questions, they should check with the federal program contact person.

26.16 What are *indirect costs*?

Indirect costs, which are sometimes called "administrative costs" or "overhead," are costs that are not easily assignable to a particular project or unit within an organization. They benefit the organization as a whole, but do not benefit any project in particular.

The government recognizes indirect costs as a legitimate expenditure and has established a budget category for organizations to list their overhead costs. In order for an organization to request funds to cover its indirect costs, however, it would need to establish an "indirect cost rate" with a federal agency. By establishing an indirect cost rate, the organization is able to pay a certain percentage of its indirect costs with federal funds. Certain grant programs place a cap on the amount of indirect costs an organization may receive.

Although having an indirect cost rate is something that may benefit an organization long-term, especially if it will be administering multiple grant projects, it is not something that an organization must have in order to receive a federal grant. If the organization is a small organization or it only has one grant project, it should be fairly easy to calculate the direct costs that are associated with its projects. Applicants should remember that unless they have an established indirect cost rate agreement with a federal agency, they are not eligible to request indirect costs for their grant proposals, unless the terms of the grant explicitly state that recovery is allowed.

26.17 What are the rules on funding religious activity with federal money?

The United States Supreme Court has said that religious nonprofit organizations may not use direct government funding to support "inherently religious" activities—a phrase that has been used by the courts in church–state cases. Basically, it means a religious nonprofit cannot use any part of a direct federal grant to fund religious worship, instruction, or proselytization. Instead, organizations may use government money only to support nonreligious social services that they provide. Therefore, religious nonprofit organizations that receive direct governmental funds should take steps to separate, in time or location, their inherently religious activities from the government-funded services that they offer. Such organizations must also carefully account for their use of all government money.

This does not mean your organization can't have religious activities. It means it cannot use taxpayer dollars to fund them. Some religious organizations set up separate charitable organizations to keep programs that receive government money separate from those that engage in inherently religious activities.

 NOTE: This rule of thumb is different if your organization receives federal money that comes in the form of vouchers or other indirect aid. In simple terms, an indirect aid program is one that gives funds or certificates to individuals in need, which can be used to obtain services from a number of qualified organizations. An example of indirect aid is a child-care certificate that a parent can use for daycare at a participating child-care center. School vouchers are another example of indirect aid. The United States Supreme Court upheld a school voucher program in Cleveland where the vouchers were used for education at religious schools. However, the vast majority of programs involve direct aid to organizations (i.e., money that goes directly to the organizations themselves), not vouchers or indirect aid.

26.18   How does the religious nonprofit organization separate its religious activities from the federally funded social service program?

Very carefully. A religious nonprofit organization should take steps to ensure that its inherently religious activities, such as religious worship, instruction, or proselytization, are separate—in time or location—from the government-funded services that it offers. If, for example, a church receives federal money to help unemployed people improve their job skills, it may conduct this program in a room in the church and still have a Bible study taking place in another room in the same church (but no federal money can he used to conduct the Bible study). A faith-based social service provider may conduct its programs in the same room that it uses to conduct religious activities, so long as its government-funded services and its religious activities are held at different times. If an organization has any questions or doubts, it should check with the official who administers its federal funds.

26.19   Can people who receive federally funded services from the organization also participate in its religious activities?

Yes, provided that important rules are followed. It may be that some people have chosen to receive services from the organization because it is faith-based. But religious nonprofit organizations that receive direct federal aid may not require program participants to attend or take part in any religious activities. Although the organization may invite participants to join in its religious services or events, it should be very careful to reassure them that they can receive government-funded help even if they do not participate in these activities, and their decision will have no bearing on the services they receive. In short, any participation by recipients of taxpayer-funded services in such religious activities must be completely voluntary. For example, a church that receives direct government aid to provide shelter to homeless individuals may not require those individuals to attend a Bible study or participate in a prayer preceding a meal as part of the government-funded services they provide.

26.20   What about religious activities that a religious nonprofit organization has with its staff and volunteers in the presence of those whom it is helping?

According to governmental guidelines, a religious nonprofit organization may gather volunteers and employees together to engage in religious activities, such as prayer. An example might be a soup kitchen where volunteers say a prayer together before the meal is served. It is important for religious groups to make sure that a prayer in these circumstances is voluntary, and understood to be voluntary, for program participants.

26.21 Can federal funds be used to purchase religious materials or materials that are faith-filled?

No. Religious nonprofit organizations may not use federal funds to purchase religious materials—such as the Bible, Torah, Talmud, Koran, or other religious or scriptural materials. If there are any questions about the appropriateness of the materials, the organization may want to consult an attorney or ask the government official who is administering the program for guidance.

26.22 Can federal funds be used to pay the salary of a member of a religious nonprofit organization's staff?

Yes, provided that this staff person is delivering the federally funded service and is not engaged in religious worship, instruction, or proselytization. The staff member may be a rabbi, priest, imam, or minister, so long as he or she does not engage in these activities while being paid with public dollars. For example, a minister may teach an anger management seminar to ex-offenders as part of a federal grant. But the minister must keep his or her teaching on the subject of anger management separate from his pastoral duties and ministerial responsibilities.

26.23 What if the staff member working for the government-sponsored program works only part-time?

It is fine for a faith-based organization to employ someone on its staff to perform religious duties while also having that person administer part of a federally funded program. There are, however, rules that must be followed carefully. The part-time worker must not engage in inherently religious activities while working on the federally funded portion of his or her job. And that part-time worker must also document that he met his time commitment to the government-sponsored program by keeping careful time records of his activities. This will make sure that government funds are spent only on program activities.

26.24 Will the way in which the religious nonprofit organization hires employees change if it receives federal funding?

In most circumstances, no; there is no general federal law that prohibits religious organizations that receive federal funds from hiring on a religious basis. Nor does the Civil Rights Act of 1964, which applies regardless of whether an organization receives federal funds, prohibit religious nonprofit organizations from hiring on a religious basis. Please see Chapter 10 for more information on this topic.

26.25   If a religious nonprofit organization receives federal funds, can it choose not to provide services to some people?

No. If a religious nonprofit organization takes federal money, it may not discriminate against a person seeking help who is eligible for the service. For example, if a religious organization receives public money to run an emergency food distribution program, it may not serve only persons of its particular faith and turn away others. In addition, and as discussed above, the organization may not require those people it serves to profess a certain faith or participate in religious activities in order to receive the service it provides for the federal government.

26.26   What will happen if the religious nonprofit organization violates any of these rules?

If an organization violates the requirements specified in its grant or otherwise improperly uses the funds it receives, the organization may be subject to legal action. Among other things, it may lose its grant funds, be required to repay the funds received, and pay any damages that might be awarded through court action. If an organization uses its funds fraudulently, it could be subject to civil penalties and criminal prosecution.

26.27   Does a religious organization have to form a special nonprofit organization in order to receive federal funding?

Generally, no; there is no general federal requirement that an organization incorporate or operate as a nonprofit or obtain tax-exempt status under Section 501(c)(3) of the Internal Revenue Code in order to receive federal funds. However, some federal, state, or local programs may impose such a requirement. Although it will take some time and cost some money, a religious organization may wish to establish a separate nonprofit organization to use the government funds it receives. Taking this step can make it easier for a religious organization to best account for the public funds that it receives and spends. It will also be easier for the government to monitor the group's use of grant funds without intruding on the group's internal affairs in the event that an audit is conducted.

26.28   Can a religious nonprofit organization use facility space on its church property to provide a federal service, and if so, does it have to take down any religious symbols inside?

Religious organizations may use space in their churches, synagogues, mosques, or other places of worship to provide federally funded services. In addition, there is no requirement that it remove religious symbols from these rooms. For example, a religious organization may operate a federally funded daycare center in a church basement, or provide computer training in a classroom adjacent to a synagogue.

There is no need to remove the Star of David or the cross in the building in order to deliver a federally funded service there. The organization may also keep its organization's name even if it includes religious words, and it may include religious references in the organization's mission statements.

26.29 **If a religious nonprofit organization has a religious name and its chartering documents contain religious references, is it still eligible to receive federal funding?**

Yes. A religious organization does not need to change its identity—including its name or government documents—in order to qualify for a federal grant. Nor does it need it to remove religious art, icons, scripture, or other religious symbols from its property or its publications—although all of these must have been purchased with private funds.

26.30 **If a religious nonprofit organization has a requirement that the members of its governing board be members of its faith, is it still eligible to receive federal funding?**

Generally, yes. A religious organization does not need to change the way it selects members for its governing board in order to qualify for a federal grant. However, there may be some grant programs that depart from this general rule. For example, the law requires Community Action Agencies (organizations that are eligible to receive Community Service Block Grant funds) to have boards that are composed of elected public officials, low-income neighborhood residents, and representatives of other organizations. A religious group that is interested in organizing or participating in a Community Action must comply with this requirement.

Index

Accounting period, change of, Q 12.1
Age Discrimination in Employment Act of 1967, Q 11.8
Alternative dispute resolution, Q 11.22, Q 11.23
American National Red Cross Governance Modernization Act of 2007, Q 2.14
Americans with Disabilities Act of 1990, Q 11.9–Q 11.11
Annual information return:
  amendment of, Q 9.13
  copies of, Q 9.14
  defined, Q 9.1, Q 9.8
  disclosure, lack of, Q 9.16, Q 9.17
  due date, Q 9.10, Q 9.11
  exceptions from filing, Q 9.3
  filing of, Q 9.2, Q 9.4, Q 9.12
  final, Q 9.15
  and governance principles, Q 2.2
  gross receipts, defined, Q 9.5, Q 9.7
  normally, defined, Q 9.6
  penalties, Q 9.18, Q 9.19
  short version, Q 9.9
Apostolic organizations, Q 3.12, Q 9.8
Application for recognition of exemption, Q 8.8, Q 8.10, Q 8.12, Q 8.13, Q 8.25, Q 8.26, Q 8.33–Q 8.35, Q 8.37–Q 8.43
Appraisal of gift property requirements, Q 13.28
Arbitration, Q 11.25, Q 11.26
Articles of incorporation, defined, Q 2.16
Articles of organization, Q 1.8, Q 2.16
Association of churches, defined, Q 3.7
At-will employment relationship, Q 10.31
Audits, IRS:
  abuse prevention by IRS, Q 24.14
  authority for, Q 24.5
  church audit rules, Q 24.15–Q 24.23
  church records, Q 24.20
  church tax examination, defined, Q 24.18
  church tax inquiry, defined, Q 24.17
  conference of right, Q 24.19
  coping with, Q 24.11
  and fund balances, Q 24.1
  and IRS organization, Q 24.3
  initiation of, Q 24.7, Q 24.8

  issues for religious organizations, Q 24.6, Q 24.9
  likelihood of, Q 24.13
  and net assets, Q 24.1
  post-audit IRS functions, Q 24.12
  of religious organizations, Q 24.2
  types of, Q 24.10
  Whistleblower Office, IRS, Q 24.4

Board members:
  management responsibilities, Q 2.8
  personal liability, Q 2.12
Boards of directors:
  borrowing by, Q 7.5
  composition of, Q 5.5, Q 5.7
  construction of, lawful, Q 5.6
  functions of, Q 5.2
  importance of, Q 5.1
  indemnification of, Q 5.19
  initial, Q 5.4
  minutes of meetings of, Q 5.15
  mistakes by, Q 5.16
  and officers, Q 5.9, Q 5.10
  origin of, Q 5.1
  personal liability of, Q 5.17, Q 5.18
  regular, Q 5.4
  related members, Q 5.8
  rental of property, Q 7.6
  sale of property, Q 7.6
  voting by, Q 5.13, Q 5.14
Business, qualification to do, Q 1.11
Bylaws, defined, Q 1.8, Q 2.18

Charitable choice laws, Q 26.6–Q 26.8
Charitable gift annuity, defined, Q 13.11
Charitable giving rules:
  charitable donees, Q 13.1
  charitable gift, defined, Q 13.35, Q 13.36
  contributions of money, Q 13.2
  contributions of property, Q 13.3
  corporations, gifts by, Q 13.56
  donor-restricted use funds, Q 13.41, Q 13.42
  endowment funds, Q 13.40
  foreign charities, gifts to, Q 13.51–Q 13.55, Q 13.57, Q 13.58
  planned giving, see Planned Giving
  restricted charitable trust property, Q 13.43–Q 13.45

  restricted gifts, Q 13.39, Q 13.46–Q 13.50
  treaty rules, Q 13.59–Q 13.61
  unrestricted gifts, Q 13.37, Q 13.38
Charitable immunity statutes, Q 15.14–Q 15.17
Charitable lead trust, defined, Q 13.10
Charitable remainder trust, defined, Q 13.8
Child abuse:
  definition of, Q 10.27
  reporting of, Q 10.11, Q 10.28, Q 10.29
  prevention policy, Q 15.8
Church:
  defined, Q 3.4
  IRS audits of, Q 3.13, also see Audits, IRS
Civil Rights Act of 1964, Q 11.1–Q 11.7, Q 26.24
Clergy:
  authority of, Q 10.5, Q 10.6
  and child abuse, Q 10.10, Q 10.11, Q 10.27–Q 10.29
  clergy-penitent privilege, Q 10.12–Q 10.21
  commissioned, Q 10.5
  confidentiality, duty of, Q 10.9–Q 10.11
  defamation, Q 10.24, Q 10.25
  disputes involving, Q 10.2
  employee classification, Q 10.3
  employee benefits, Q 10.4, Q 10.7
  exemptions, Q 10.8
  independent contractor classification, Q 10.3
  legal liability, Q 10.23, Q 10.26
  licensed, Q 10.5
  ordained, Q 10.5
  penal institutions, visiting privileges, Q 10.22
  privileged communications, Q 10.14–Q 10.17
  retirement plans for, Q 10.7
  selection of, Q 10.1
Clergy Housing Allowance Clarification Act of 2002, Q 21.4
Clergy-penitent privilege, Q 10.12–Q 10.21
Commerciality, Q 18.8–Q 18.14
Commission, of clergy, Q 10.5
Compensation:
  board members, Q 21.21

Compensation: (continued)
  bonuses, Q 21.14–Q 21.17
  and communal groups, Q 21.48
  compensation committee, Q 21.22,
    Q 21.23
  compensation study, Q 21.24–Q 21.31
  deferred compensation, defined,
    Q 21.5
  definition of, Q 21.1
  excessive compensation, defined,
    Q 21.10–Q 21.13
  executive compensation, Q 21.2–Q 21.3
  403(b) plan, defined, Q 21.7
  housing allowance, Q 21.4
  insiders, Q 21.36
  and intermediate sanctions rules,
    Q 21.44
  IRS concerns, Q 21.33, Q 21.34
  nonqualified retirement plan, Q 21.8
  parsonage allowance, Q 21.4
  past undercompensation, defined,
    Q 21.32
  performance-based, Q 21.18–Q 21.20
  private benefit, defined, Q 21.38
  private benefit doctrine, Q 21.39,
    Q 21.40, Q 21.49–Q 21.54
  private inurement, defined, Q 21.35
  private inurement doctrine, Q 21.37,
    Q 21.39, Q 21.40–Q 21.47
  qualified retirement plan, defined,
    Q 21.6
  Rabbi trust, defined, Q 21.9
  reasonableness, Q 21.12, Q 21.13
Competition, with for-profits,
    Q 18.1–Q 18.5
Confidentiality, duty of, Q 10.9, Q 10.10
Conflict of interest:
  and charitable contributions, Q 6.9
  defined, Q 6.2, Q 6.5
  and intermediate sanctions, Q 22.23
  and negotiation for discounted
    prices, Q 6.10
  disclosure of, Q 6.6, Q 6.7
Conflict of interest policy:
  legal efficacy of, Q 6.4
  provisions of, Q 6.3
Congregational church, administration of:
  definition of, 10.1
  disputes with members, Q 4.11
  members, classes of, Q 4.5
  members, discipline of, Q 4.10
  members' legal authority, Q 4.7
  members' personal liability, Q 4.8
  members' rights, Q 4.1, Q 4.2, Q 4.3
  membership meetings, Q 4.9
  membership qualification, Q 4.6
  proxy voting, Q 4.4
  voting, by members, Q 4.2, Q 4.3, Q 4.4
Congregational church organization,
    defined, Q 3.10
Constitution, defined, Q 2.17
Convenience doctrine, Q 18.6
Convention of churches, defined, Q 3.7
Corporate governance principles:
  church, for, Q 2.3
  definition of, Q 2.1
  emerging, Q 2.2
  and federal tax law, Q 2.14

  and personal liability, Q 2.12
  and watchdog agencies, Q 2.13
Corporate records:
  inspection of, by members, Q 12.10
  inspection of, by public, Q 12.11
  maintenance of, Q 12.5
  retention of, Q 12.6
Corporate sponsorship rules, Q 23.28
Corporations, Q 1.8, Q 1.17

Deacons, Q 5.3
Defamation, Q 10.24, Q 10.25
Determination letter, IRS, defined, Q 8.24
Discrimination:
  age, Q 11.1, Q 11.8
  color, Q 11.1
  compensation, Q 11.7
  disability, Q 11.9–Q 11.11
  military personnel, Q 11.2
  national origin, Q 11.1
  pregnancy, Q 11.6
  race, Q 11.1
  religion, Q 11.1
  sex, Q 11.1
Dissolution clause, defined, Q 2.21
Distribution rules, Q 8.15
Duty of care, defined, Q 2.9
Duty of loyalty, defined, Q 2.10
Duty of obedience, defined, Q 2.11

Elders, Q 5.3
Employee compensation, Q 7.2
Employee rights:
  alternative dispute resolution,
    Q 11.22–Q 11.26
  background checks, Q 10.33
  bona fide occupational qualification,
    defined, Q 11.5
  disabilities, Q 11.9–Q 11.11
  discrimination, Q 11.1, Q 11.6–Q 11.9
  employee manuals, Q 10.37
  employment contracts, Q 10.36
  and liability, Q 10.35
  military, services to, Q 11.12
  new hires, Q 10.32
  and religious organizations, Q 10.30
  sexual harassment, Q 11.13–Q 11.17
  termination of service, Q 11.18–Q 11.21
  Title VII, Q 11.2–Q 11.11.4
Endowment funds, Q 13.40, Q 14.19
Equal Pay Act of 1963, Q 11.7
Establishment Clause, Q 3.2, Q 25.1, Q 25.2
Expenditures in general, Q 7.7

Faith-Based and Community Initiatives,
    White House Office of, Q 26.1, Q 26.3
Federal government grants, Q 26.2–Q 26.5,
    Q 26.9–Q 26.16
Federal Regulation of Lobbying Act, Q 20.1
Fiduciary, defined, Q 2.5, Q 2.6, Q 2.15
Fiduciary responsibility, Q 2.5, Q 2.8, Q 7.4
Forms, IRS:
  990, Q 9.1–Q 9.9, Q 12.1
  990-EZ, Q 9.8, Q 9.9
  990-N, Q 8.71
  990-T, Q 8.15, Q 9.2, Q 9.9, Q 23.30
  1023, Q 8.23, Q 8.38, Q 8.50, q 8.51,
    Q 8.53–Q 8.64

  1024, Q 8.23
  1028, Q 8.23
  1040, Q 22.10
  1065, Q 9.8, Q 14.44
  1099, Q 22.10
  1128, Q 12.1
  2758, Q 9.11
  2848, Q 8.35
  4506-A, Q 9.14
  4720, Q 22.40
  8283, Q 13.28
  I-9, Q 10.32
  W-2, Q 21.2, Q 22.10
  W-4, Q 10.32
Free Exercise Clause, Q 3.2, Q 25.1, Q 25.3
Fundraising regulation:
  appraisal requirements, Q 13.28
  and charitable giving rules, Q 13.19
  constitutionality of, Q 13.17
  disclosure requirements, Q 13.33
  federal, Q 13.14, Q 13.29, Q 13.34
  gift substantiation requirements,
    Q 13.20–Q 13.23
  and IRS audits, Q 13.18
  of noncharitable organizations, Q 13.33
  police power, Q 13.17
  reporting rules, Q 13.30
  royalty exception, Q 13.32
  state, Q 13.15–Q 13.17
  quid pro quo contribution rules,
    Q 13.24–Q 13.27
  and unrelated business rules,
    Q 13.31, Q 23.29

Gift substantiation requirements,
    Q 13.20–Q 13.23
Governance principles, Q 2.1, Q 2.2
Government funding, Q 26.1,
    Q 26.17–Q 26.21
Group exemption:
  advantages of, Q 8.67
  disadvantages of, Q 8.68
  establishment of, Q 8.66, Q 8.69
  maintenance of, Q 8.70
  reporting requirements, Q 8.71, Q 8.72
  subordinate organizations, Q 8.72, Q 8.73
  termination of, Q 8.74

Harassment campaign, defined, Q 8.22
Hierarchical church organization,
    defined, Q 3.9, Q 10.1

Immunity, Q 5.18
Incorporation, Q 5.18
Incorporators, Q 1.12
Indemnification, Q 5.18
Insurance, religious organizations and:
  automobile liability coverage, defined,
    Q 16.10
  bond, defined, Q 16.15
  builder's risk insurance, defined, Q 16.14
  coverage in general, Q 16.1
  directors and officers insurance,
    Q 5.18, Q 16.4
  disability and long-term care coverage,
    defined, Q 16.17
  educator's legal liability coverage,
    defined, Q 16.8

employee and volunteer dishonesty
  liability coverage, defined, Q 16.6
employment practices liability coverage,
  defined, Q 16.7
errors and omissions liability coverage,
  defined, Q 16.4
foreign travel liability, defined, Q 16.12
403(b) retirement savings plan,
  defined, Q 16.21
general liability insurance, defined,
  Q 16.2
group medical insurance, defined,
  Q 16.16
life insurance, defined, Q 16.20
medical benefit plans, Q 16.18
minister's professional and personal
  liability coverage, defined, Q 16.5
property insurance, defined, Q 16.13
sexual misconduct liability coverage,
  defined, Q 16.9
travel accident insurance, defined,
  Q 16.11
umbrella liability coverage, defined,
  Q 16.3
workers' compensation insurance,
  defined, Q 16.19
Integrated auxiliaries of churches, Q 3.8
Intellectual property:
  copyright, infringement of, Q 19.12
  copyrights, Q 19.7–Q 19.12
  definition of, Q 19.1
  employment, work made in scope of,
    Q 19.5, Q 19.6
  face-to-face teaching activities exception,
    Q 19.20
  fair use, Q 19.9
  nonprofit performance exception,
    Q 19.11
  ownership of, Q 19.2
  patent, defined, Q 19.18
  religious services exception, Q 19.10
  service marks, Q 19.14–Q 19.16
  trade secret, defined, Q 19.11
  trademarks, Q 1.9, Q 19.13–Q 19.17
  works-made-for-hire doctrine,
    Q 19.3, Q 19.4
  worship services, distribution of
    recordings, Q 19.21
Intermediate sanctions:
  abatement, Q 22.39
  burden of proof, Q 22.22
  and compensation, Q 22.10, Q 22.11,
    Q 22.16–Q 22.18, Q 22.36–Q 22.38
  conflicts of interest, Q 22.23
  controlled entity, defined, Q 22.28
  correction, defined, Q 22.30
  definition of, Q 22.1
  directly or indirectly, defined, Q 22.12
  disqualified person, defined, Q 22.24
  effective date, Q 22.2
  enactment of, Q 22.3
  exceptions, Q 22.7
  excess benefit transactions, Q 22.14,
    Q 22.15
  for the use of, defined, Q 22.13
  and indemnification, Q 22.41
  and insurance, Q 22.42
  IRS guidance, Q 22.5

knowing, defined, Q 22,32
legislative history of, Q 22.4
lending transactions, Q 22.20
member of the family, defined, Q 22.27
organization manager, defined, Q 22.26
organizations involved, Q 22.6
participation, defined, Q 22.31
and private inurement doctrine, Q 22.46,
  Q 22.48
reasonable cause, defined, Q 22.34
rental transactions, Q 22.19
sales transactions, Q 22.21
sanctions, Q 22.29, Q 22.35,
  Q 22.40–Q 22.42, Q 22.45
and self-dealing rules, Q 22.47, Q 22.48
statute of limitations, Q 22.44
substantial influence rule, Q 22.25
tax-exempt organization, impact on,
  Q 22.43
transactions involved, Q 22.8
value, measurement of, Q 22.9
willful, defined, Q 22.33

Joint ventures:
  definition of, Q 14.29
  taxation of, 14.31
  tax-exempt organizations in,
    Q 14.45–Q 14.48
  unrelated business rules, Q 14.49
  use of, Q 14.30
Judicial abstention doctrine, Q 10.1, Q 10.9

Lawyer for religious organization:
  compensation of, Q 1.7
  role of, Q 1.5, Q 1.6
Legislative activities:
  appropriateness of, Q 20.3
  forms of, Q 20.6, Q 20.7
  legislation, defined, Q 20.2
  lobbying, defined, Q 20.1
  and non-tax law rules, Q 20.8
  and tax law rules, Q 20.4, Q 20.5
Liability of, religious organizations:
  and agents, Q 15.5
  attractive nuisances, Q 15.11
  charitable immunity statutes,
    Q 15.14–Q 15.17
  child abuse policies, Q 15.8
  hazardous activities, Q 15.6
  negligence, Q 15.3, Q 15.7
  premises, injury on, Q 15.13
  premises, inspection of, Q 15.12
  premises liability, defined, Q 15.10
  vicarious liability, Q 15.1
  and volunteers, Q 15.2, Q 15.4
  waiver forms, Q 15.9
Licensing, of clergy, Q 10.5
Life insurance, gifts of, Q 13.12
Limited liability companies, Q 1.8,
  Q 1.17, Q 14.32
Loans, Q 21.45
Lobbying, see Legislative Activities

Mediation, Q 11.24, Q 11.26
Military Selective Service Act, Q 10.5,
  Q 10.8
Ministers, see Clergy
Minutes, Q 12.7, Q 12.8

Name, of nonprofit organization,
  Q 1.19
Non-church religious organization,
  defined, Q 3.6
Nonprofit organization:
  actions by, Q 3.5
  control of, Q 1.14
  defined, Q 1.1, Q 1.2
  form of, Q 1.18
  incorporation of, Q 1.9, Q 1.10
  legal standards for operation of, Q 2.4
  name of, protection, Q 1.19
  owners of, Q 1.13
  qualification to do business, Q 1.11
  religious, Q 3.3
  starting, Q 1.8
  types of, Q 1.17
Not-for-profit, defined, Q 1.2

Officers:
  functions of, Q 5.11
  indemnification of, Q 5.19
  positions, Q 5.12
Operational test, defined, Q 2.22, Q 9.16
Ordination, of clergy, Q 10.5
Organizational test, defined, Q 2.22

Partnerships:
  definition of, Q 14.25
  general partnership, Q 14.26
  IRS concerns with, Q 14.37–Q 14.40
  limited partnership, Q 14.27
  tax-exempt organizations in,
    Q 14.33–Q 14.36, Q 14.41, Q 14.42
  unrelated business rules, Q 14.43,
    Q 14.44
  use of, Q 14.28
Pastors, see Clergy
Personal board meeting book, Q 12.9
Planned giving:
  charitable gift annuity, Q 13.11
  charitable lead trusts, Q 13.10
  charitable remainder trusts, Q 13.8
  defined, Q 13.4
  income interests, Q 13.5, Q 13.6
  life insurance, gift of, Q13.12
  pooled income funds, Q 13.9
  remainder interest, gift of, Q 13.7
  remainder interests, Q 13.5, Q 13.6,
    Q 13.13
Political activities:
  campaign, commencement of, Q 20.15
  candidate, defined, Q 20.14
  constitutionality of rules concerning,
    Q 20.21
  education, contrasted with, Q 20.12
  individuals, by, Q 20.13
  political activities, defined, Q 20.9
  public office, defined, Q 20.16
  and religious organizations,
    Q 20.19–Q 20.21
  tax law rules, Q 20.10–Q 20.13,
    Q 20.16–Q 20.20
Pooled income fund, defined, Q 13.9
Prayer, constitutionality of,
  Q 25.11–Q 25.13
Pregnancy Discrimination Act, Q 11.6
Primary purpose test, defined, Q 2.22

Index

Private benefit doctrine, Q 7.2, Q 21.38, Q 21.39, Q 21.50–Q 21.54
Private inurement doctrine, Q.1.1, Q 7.2, Q 21.35–Q 21.37, Q 21.39
Program expenditures, Q 7.1, Q 7.3
Prudent person rule, Q 2.5
Public policy doctrine, Q 8.6

Quid pro quo contribution rules, Q 13.24–Q 13.27

Real property, religious organizations and:
    activities, regulation of, Q 17.10
    building codes, Q 17.6–Q 17.8
    disruptive person, removal of, Q 17.20
    eminent domain, Q 17.14, Q 17.15
    landmark laws, enforcement of, Q 17.16
    nuisances, Q 17.11–Q 17.13
    property, public or private, Q 17.19
    property, ownership of (hierarchical structure), Q 17.17
    property, ownership of (congregational structure), Q 17.18
    residential area, exclusion from, Q 17.9
    reversionary clauses, Q 17.1–Q 17.4
    zoning law, defined, Q 17.5
Reasonable, defined, Q 2.7
Recognition of exemption, defined, Q 8.9
Registered agent, defined, Q 1.15, Q 1.16
Religion:
    advancement of, Q 8.5
    defined, Q 3.1, Q 25.5
Religion Clauses, Q 3.2, Q 25.1–Q 25.3
Religious Freedom Restoration Act, Q 25.3, Q 25.4
Religious liberties:
    constitutional protection, Q 25.1–Q 25.3
    prayer, constitutionality of, Q 25.11–Q 25.13
    public facilities, use of, Q 25.10
    Religious Freedom Restoration Act, Q 25.4
    religious symbols, display of, Q 25.7–Q 25.9
Religious nonprofit organizations:
    discrimination, Q 11.1–Q 11.11
    as employers, Q 10.30–Q 10.37
    qualification as, Q 25.6
Religious order, defined, Q 3.11
Rental arrangements, Q 21.46
Retirement plans, Q 10.7
Ruling, IRS, defined, Q 8.24

Self-dealing, defined, Q 6.1
Subsidiaries:
    accumulations in, Q 14.23
    board members of, Q 14.5
    capitalization of, Q 14.22
    control of, Q 14.3
    definition of, Q 14.1
    disclosure requirements, Q 14.17
    endowment funds, Q 14.19
    establishment of, Q 14.2, Q 14.4, Q 14.12
    funds transfers, Q 14.18
    liquidation of, Q 14.9
    reporting requirements, Q 14.10, Q 14.11, Q 14.16
    revenue from subsidiary, taxation of, Q 14.8
    parent-subsidiary relationship, Q 14.6, Q 14.7
    reasons for, Q 14.20
    of supporting organizations, Q 14.24
    uses of, Q 14.13, Q 14.21
    tax exemption for, Q 14.14, Q 14.15
Supporting organizations, Q 14.15, Q 14.24
Statement of faith, defined, Q 2.20
Statement of purpose, defined, Q 2.19
Substantially completed applications, defined, Q 8.36
Supreme Being, belief in, Q 25.6

Tax-exempt organizations, Q 8.1, Q 8.2, Q 8.4
Tax exemption:
    acquisition of, Q 8.7
    application for recognition of, Q 8.8, Q 8.10, Q 8.12, Q 8.13, Q 8.25, Q 8.26, Q 8.33–Q 8.35, Q 8.37–Q 8.43
    categories of, Q 8.4
    changes affecting, Q 8.29, Q 8.30, Q 8.31
    and churches, Q 8.50, Q 8.51
    disclosure of, Q 8.14, Q 8.15, Q 8.16, Q 8.17, Q 8.18
    distribution requirement, exceptions, Q 8.20
    expedited processing of application, Q 8.27
    forfeiture of, Q 8.52
    Form 1023, Q 8.53–Q 8.64
    group, Q 8.66–Q 8.74
    inspection requirement, exceptions, Q 8.19
    meaning of, Q 8.3
    reacquisition of, Q 8.48

    recognition of, Q 8.9, Q 8.11, Q 8.23
    religion, advancement of, Q 8.5
    revocation of, Q 8.47
    ruling, effectiveness of, Q 8.28, Q 8.44, Q 8.46
    rulings as to, IRS, Q 8.32, Q 8.45, Q 8.65
    scope of, Q 8.49
    state, Q 12.2–12.4
Taxpayer Bill of Rights 2, Q 22.3
Ten Commandments, Q 25.7
Trademarks, Q 1.19, Q 19.13–Q 19.17
Trustees, Q 5.3
Trusts, Q 1.8, Q 1.17

Ultra vires act, defined, Q 1.20
Uniformed Services Employment and Reemployment Rights Act, Q 11.12
Unincorporated associations, Q 1.3, Q 1.4, Q 1.8, Q 1.17
Unrelated business rules:
    activities, exempted, Q 23.23
    business, unrelated, Q 18.7, Q 23.1, Q 23.3, Q 23.7, Q 23.8, Q 23.10
    commercial activity, Q 23.11, Q 23.12
    convenience doctrine, Q 18.6
    corporate sponsorship, Q 23.28
    exceptions, Q 23.26
    exceptions to exceptions, Q 23.27
    and fundraising, Q 13.31, Q 13.32, Q 23.29
    income, exempted, Q 23.24
    and joint ventures, Q 14.49
    modifications, Q 23.23, Q 23.24
    and partnerships, Q 14.43, Q 14.44
    primary activities, Q 23.2
    profit motive, Q 23.9
    rationale for, Q 23.4
    regularly carried on test, Q 23.13–Q 23.17
    relatedness, Q 23.18–Q 23.21
    and religious organizations, Q 23.28
    royalty exclusion, Q 23.25
    subsidiaries, revenue from, Q 14.8
    tax calculation, Q 23.22
    tax reporting, Q 23.30
    trade or business requirement, Q 23.6
    and unfair competition, Q 23.5

Vicarious liability, defined, Q 15.1
Volunteer Protection Act, Q 15.2

Waiver of liability forms, Q 15.9
Widely available, defined, Q 8.21

CPSIA information can be obtained at www.ICGtesting.com
Printed in the USA
LVOW070606161112

307571LV00002B/3/P